D0506288

Churchill
goes to war

CHURCHILL'S PRINCIPAL TRAVELS

Place	Codename	Conference Date	Present	Transport
Placentia Bay + Iceland	Riviera	9–12 Aug 1941	Churchill, Roosevelt	*Prince of Wales*
Washington I + Bermuda	Arcadia	22 Dec 1941 – 13 Jan 1942	Churchill, Roosevelt	Out *Duke of York*, Return Clipper *Berwick*
Washington II	Argonaut	18 June 1942	Churchill, Roosevelt	Clipper *Bristol*
Moscow + Gibraltar, Cairo, Tehran		12 Aug 1942	Churchill, Stalin	Liberator *Commando*
Casablanca + Cairo, Adana, Cyprus, Tripoli, Algiers	Symbol	30–1 Jan 1943	Churchill, Roosevelt	Liberator *Commando*
Washington III + Algiers, Gibraltar and Tunis	Trident	12–15 May 1943	Churchill, Roosevelt	Out *Queen Mary* Return Clipper *Bristol* Avro York
Quebec + New York	Quadrant	13–23 Aug 1943	Churchill, Roosevelt	Out *Queen Mary* Return *Renown*
Cairo + Gibraltar, Algiers and Malta	Sextant	23–6 Nov 1943	Churchill, Roosevelt	York *Ascalon*
Tehran + Cairo, Tunis and Marrakech	Eureka	28 Nov – 6 Dec 1943	Churchill, Roosevelt, Stalin	Return *King George V*
Quebec + New York	Octagon	12–14 Sept 1944	Churchill, Roosevelt	*Queen Mary*
Moscow + Naples and Cairo	Tolstoy	9–19 Oct 1944	Churchill, Stalin Return York *Ascalon*	Out York *Ascalon* and MW100
Athens		24/5–29 Dec 1944	Churchill with Greek leaders	Skymaster
Yalta + Malta and Cairo	Argonaut	4–11 Feb 1945	Churchill, Roosevelt, Stalin Return Skymaster	Out Skymaster EW999
Potsdam	Terminal	17 July – 2 Aug 1945	Churchill, Roosevelt, Stalin	Skymaster

Churchill
goes to war

WINSTON'S WARTIME JOURNEYS

Brian Lavery

CONWAY

A Conway book

© Brian Lavery, 2007

First published in Great Britain
in 2007 by Conway,
an imprint of Anova Books,
The Old West London Magistrates Court,
10 Southcombe Street,
London W14 0RA
www.anovabooks.com
www.conwaymaritime.com

British Library Cataloguing in Publication Data:
A catalogue record for this book is available from the British Library

ISBN: 978144860555

Editing, design and map illustrations by DAG Publications Ltd

Printed by Cromwell Press Ltd, Wiltshire

Contents

Acknowledgements

This book originated with a newspaper enquiry about the dangers of Churchill's voyages, and developed from a short lecture I delivered in 2001. I was relatively familiar with the maritime sources involved, and this was helped by a stay on board the *Queen Mary* in Long Beach in 2002, and by searches among the plans collection of the National Maritime Museum, helped particularly by Jeremy Michell. I must also thank other former colleagues at the National Maritime Museum, including Roger Knight, Nigel Rigby and Simon Stephens. Over the years I have benefited from discussions with many maritime historians, including Eric Grove and Jock Gardiner, not to mention the late, lamented David Lyon and David Syrett.

Although I have worked as a maritime historian for the last thirty years or so, I had an early interest in aviation which I have drawn on for this book. Retrospectively I must thank the officers of the Air Training Corps and the pages of *Flight* magazine for a long-term background in the subject. It has been fascinating to re-discover this world, aided particularly by the staff of the British Airways Archive at Heathrow. Most of the sources come from the National Archives and Churchill College Cambridge, and thanks are due to the staffs of both organisations, as well as the London Library. The Imperial War Museum was particularly helpful in finding illustrations. John Lee of Anova Books and David Gibbons and Anthony A. Evans of DAG Publications edited the text and corrected some of my elementary mistakes.

Introduction

Winston Churchill's voyages to meet Roosevelt, Stalin and other leaders were carried out at the height of the Second World War in circumstances of great discomfort and danger. No life was more valuable than his, as he represented his country's will to resist the Nazis. Long-distance air travel had only just become practicable, but there were risks in take-off and landing and in flying too high, as well as being shot down by the enemy. Sea travel also had its dangers, as U-boats infested the Atlantic and bombers attacked shipping in the Mediterranean. Like most of the British effort in the Second World War, Churchill's voyages were under-prepared and improvised, and used a good deal of American technology. Their story begins with a relatively simple trip to meet Roosevelt in a battleship in 1941, through hazardous flights across enemy-occupied North Africa, to the highly organised and fateful conferences at Yalta and Potsdam in 1945.[1]

This book tells the story of Churchill's long-distance voyages, outside Western Europe. They are seen through many different eyes – of Churchill himself, his ministers and the senior army, navy and air force officers who went with him: his secretaries and typists, the officers and crews of the ships who transported him, the pilots, navigators and engineers of his aircraft, and the women coders who handled his signals. It tells of the interaction between Churchill and his staff, and describes the development of a community amongst his regular travelling companions – like all communities it changed from time to time, and had many differences and divisions within it. It also emphasises the increasing acceptance of women as part of the travelling party, in ever-greater danger and in positions of responsibility.

Churchill also made many shorter voyages, within the United Kingdom and Europe, which form a separate story. Apart from his trips in an unsuccessful attempt to bolster up the French will to fight in the spring of 1940, they were usually to observe the situation on the ground and maintain the morale of troops and workers, rather than achieve diplomatic objectives. Even within the United Kingdom they were not without their risks, and no one was entirely safe from bombing during the war. His European trips were much more dangerous, perhaps even more so than those to more distant destinations. He flew to France several times when that country was on the verge of collapse, and much of its airspace was dominated by the enemy; and he visited the troops in Normandy soon after D-day, and came close to the front line as the armies advanced into Germany.

For Churchill always craved excitement and danger. He was always proud of having come under fire on his 21st birthday. He wrote frankly to his mother: 'Bullets are not worth considering. Besides I am so conceited that I do not think the Gods would create so potent a being for so prosaic an ending.'[i] His military career was short and not particularly successful, but part of him always remained a soldier, ready to bear hardship and danger if needs must, and contemptuous of the staff and politicians who stayed well away from the front line. As his physician said of him during the Second World War, 'It is not his idea to see it through in the security of Whitehall; he wants to see for himself what is happening at the Front. It is not unreasonable, he will pout, to want to go into things there.'[2]

One might take a Freudian view that Churchill's neglect by both his parents, their habit of travelling without him and leaving him behind with his nurse or sending him to boarding school, gave him an early desire for travel – he later wrote approvingly that 'famous men are usually the product of an unhappy childhood'. But in the early stages he craved affection far more than travel, and he resented, for example, being sent away to learn French at the age of 16. He campaigned against going –'How frightfully dull it would be' – and he hated the journey – 'Fatigue, the passage, the strange food, the cold, home sickness, the thoughts of what was behind & what was before ...'[3]

His father's early death perhaps made him aware that life was short and had to be lived to the full. He developed a low boredom threshold and loved taking risks but the Victorian army did little to satisfy these needs. He soon found that military life was 99 per cent routine with only the occasional thrill of action. He decided that politics would be closer to his talents, but in the meantime he furthered a career as a war correspondent, always moving towards the scene of action but still in control of his destiny. Even so, his first sea trip across the Atlantic was not a success. 'I do not ever contemplate taking a sea voyage for pleasure', he wrote to his mother, 'and I shall always look upon journeys by sea as necessary evils which have to be undergone in the carrying out of any definite plan.'[4] But the arrival in the United States and seeing action in Cuba compensated for all that, and soon he would find ways to make the actual travelling more useful and even enjoyable. It was in voyages to Cuba, Egypt and South Africa that he developed his love of travel, his ways of making himself comfortable in a ship or a train and getting the best out of the experience. After that travel became a passion, perhaps an addiction. To Stalin he was 'that desperate fellow' who was prepared to travel anywhere in wartime at great personal risk. His doctor Lord Moran thought that he used travel as an escape from the pressures of office.

On one level the mature Churchill had less need to travel than most politicians, for he had extraordinary skills at long-distance communication. His books were well written and sold well. His radio broadcasts were legendary and still raise a tingle in the spine. More privately, his letters and telegrams were persuasive or inspirational as the occasion demanded. But he convinced himself that personal contact was the best way to get things done. As he said in Quebec in 1944, 'What an ineffectual method of conveying human thought correspondence is ... telegraphed with all its rapidity, all the facilities of ... modern intercommunication. They are simply dead, blank walls compared to personal ... contacts.'[5] He continued to believe this in the 1950s and coined the term 'summit meeting'. He hoped that the American, British and Soviet leaders would be able to resolve the Cold War by face-to-face contact.

Churchill had the advantage of living in an age of transport revolutions. The first and perhaps the greatest, the building of the railways, was virtually over by his birth in 1874 and the great lines and networks of Europe, India and North America were largely complete. Apart from that, nothing on land moved faster than a horse. At sea, the steamship had been around for decades but it was still a specialised vessel. It was only in 1885 that steam tonnage overtook sail, which was soon pushed to the fringes. For passenger transport, the steam turbine was developed late in the century and applied to fast Channel ferries and Atlantic liners like the *Aquitania* early in the next. Both these types would play crucial parts in Churchill's travels. The motor car was developed in the 1880s and 1890s and its use expanded stage by stage over the next half century, though it was not until the 1950s that it became popular, and it took several decades for British roads to catch up with the demand.

The greatest advance was in the air. In 1874 there were only gliders, balloons and primitive airships. The Wright brothers first flew 29 years later, and Churchill was well aware of the possibilities of flying for war purposes by 1912. Transport aircraft were first used for passenger and courier services during the Versailles peace conference in 1919, and had become much more widespread by the late 1930s. Transatlantic passenger air transport was already taking place, and its development plays a key part in Churchill's own story. When he retired in 1955 the jet airliner was already in service, and the revolution was almost complete. By this time he had come to regret it; 'I wish flying had never been invented,' he is reported as saying in 1954. 'The world has shrunk since the Wrights got into the air; it was an evil hour for poor

England.'[6] Finally, Marconi invented radio and made his first transatlantic transmission in 1901. It developed during the next 40 years, helped by Churchill during his term at the Admiralty in 1911–15. It allowed a travelling statesman to maintain some contact with his affairs, at the risk of giving away secrets or exposing his position.

Churchill was always aware of these developments. He had no particular technical training but he loved technology – he played a major part in the invention of the tank in World War I and believed he had invented the Mulberry harbours which were set up off Normandy in 1944. He loved to be photographed beside the latest war machines. Of course most people were aware of the developments in transport, but Churchill was the first world statesman to have the temperament and the need to use them to the full.

Churchill's wartime desire for travel coincided with his country's needs, if not always world needs. The declining power of the Empire was reflected in the fact that he was always the one who travelled, and usually to ask favours or state his position – he constantly had to persuade Roosevelt and his advisers to send more resources to Europe, and to apologise to Stalin for delays in launching the second front in northern Europe. Churchill longed for a conference in London, 'the greatest city in the world, the capital of the nation which first entered the war against Germany and very heavily battered during the conflict', but it never happened, partly because Stalin hated travel and Roosevelt was less than enthusiastic, but also because of Britain's weakness by the later stages of the war.

Some historians have concluded that Churchill's meetings with world leaders had less effect than he thought, though there is no doubt that they had considerable influence on the strategy of the world war, though perhaps less on the post-war settlement. His voyages also provide a story of risk-taking, initiative and improvisation, community and endurance.

I

A Lavish Lunch
and a Good Train

The Prime Minister was late for his lunch on 24 July 1941, as the War
Cabinet meeting in his room in the House of Commons dragged on. His
guests gathered in the Spartan conditions of the Downing Street Annexe,
actually a block away in a basement in Great George Street. They included the
Solicitor General and his wife, Lord Strabolgi, an eminent banker and adviser
to the government of India, Charles Eade, the editor of the *Sunday Dispatch*,
Churchill's secretary John Colville, and three cousins of the family. They had
all travelled through the bombed streets of wartime London. All were well
connected in one way or another, but none could avoid the hardships of war
– a meagre ration of uninspiring food, long hours on war work or in air-raid
shelters, severely rationed clothing and restrictions on travel. They sat on hard
'utility' chairs among the beige-painted brick walls in the claustrophobic,
windowless room and were entertained by Churchill's wife Clementine as the
meal began.[1]

The familiar rotund, dynamic figure of Winston Churchill burst in before
the end of the first course and he launched into the conversation. There was
no sign of the arrogance and grumpiness which his wife had warned him
about a year ago during Britain's greatest crisis. The Prime Minister did not
try to dominate, and no one waited for him to begin a new topic. In fact, Mrs
Churchill was more prominent, talking in a loud voice and laughing a good
deal, but in a charming manner that was enough to win over Charles Eade. She
ribbed her husband, pointing out that he was eating rabbit, which he claimed
not to like. It was 'a well-dressed up dish', its identity not immediately obvious,
but Churchill defended its taste. He 'liked bunny'. Bunny was very good,
though he didn't want to eat it all the time. He produced a few of his classic
aphorisms – 'Anger is a waste of energy. Steam which is used to blow off a
safety valve would be better used to drive an engine.' And 'Opinions differ.
That is why we have check waistcoats.' Over the hubbub of conversation
Charles Eade thought he heard the Prime Minister refer to Geoffrey Dawson,
ex-editor of *The Times*, as a Quisling, after the man who had betrayed Norway
the previous year. It was the worst possible insult in the circumstances, and
Eade asked Churchill to confirm it. Churchill grinned roguishly and said, 'I

have not made any comment about the editor of *The Times*', amid laughter from those close to him. His cousin Lady Wimborne suggested that after the war was won the Germans should be eliminated by killing off their babies. Churchill joked, 'Need we wait as long as that?' but he quickly brought matters back to reality. If a group of civilised people could talk on these terms even in jest, what might the Nazis be capable of doing if they won? Churchill could not inform his guests, but over the past week he had begun to receive decoded signals from the German armies in Russia with increasingly disturbing news. They reported massacres of 'Jews', 'Jewish plunderers' and 'Jewish Bolshevists', sometimes several thousand at a time.

The ladies withdrew in traditional fashion to give the men a chance to get out pipes, cigarettes and cigars and talk about politics and war. Strabolgi had inside knowledge of the fuel situation in Germany and predicted they would lose the war if they did not beat Russia within three months. Churchill described how the former French Prime Minister Reynaud had told him in 1940 that Britain's neck would be wrung like a chicken – a remark he would use to great effect later. The party broke up and Churchill went off for his usual afternoon nap, in preparation for another meeting of the War Cabinet.

Despite his immense responsibilities and problems, Churchill had much to be cheerful about. Even in the darkest hours of 1940, when the British army was defeated in France and brought back exhausted and largely unarmed from the beaches and harbour of Dunkirk, he relished the role of war leader and believed that destiny had fitted him for it. Since then he had overseen the Battle of Britain in which the German attack on the Royal Air Force had petered out. The enemy had impatiently switched to the day bombing of London, then the night bombing of British cities during the long dark winter of 1940–1. That had failed to break British morale, the army was reorganised, the navy was still intact and German invasion became increasingly unlikely. There were disasters overseas when Greece and Crete were invaded, but now the front in North Africa was stable and an offensive was planned.

By the spring of 1941 the biggest remaining danger was the U-boat, which threatened to cut Britain off from supplies of food, raw materials and weapons. There was progress even there, for codebreakers at Bletchley Park near London were now able to read enemy signals to and from U-boats at sea. Escort ships were still woefully inadequate, but convoys could be routed away from the worst concentrations of submarines, and merchant ship losses were down from 108 in June to 28 in July.

Most important of all, Britain was no longer alone. In June Hitler had turned his attention to his real enemy, the Soviet Union. Ignoring a non-aggression pact of less than two years' standing, he took the bulk of his forces away from Western Europe and the Mediterranean, to launch a surprise attack across the Soviet borders. Churchill had been a fanatical anti-Communist in the past but he gave wholehearted support to the Soviet war effort. Stalin's armies retreated at first, but now they were fighting far better than anticipated, and for the moment the Nazis had their hands full.

Yet if he was nowhere near defeat, Churchill was equally far from victory. He had never believed that the British could win the war alone and his main hope, as expressed to his son while shaving in May 1940, was that he could somehow induce the United States to come in as she had done in 1917–18. So on that summer evening he was attentive when Harry Hopkins, President Roosevelt's special envoy, called at Downing Street after a meeting with members of the British War Cabinet. Hopkins was a former social worker and administrator of Roosevelt's New Deal policy in the 1930s. Arriving in London at the height of the Blitz, his unkempt appearance caused some shock in British government circles at first – he was described as 'looking as though he had spent the previous night sleeping in a hay loft'. (He was in fact suffering from stomach cancer, which played havoc with his digestive system.) Convinced that the Prime Minister and the President should somehow meet, he soon impressed Churchill with his intellect and forthright manner. It was he who coined the phrase 'Arsenal of Democracy', which the President used to describe America's role in supporting Britain at war.

Churchill sat with the lean, almost emaciated Hopkins in the sunlit garden behind the famous house, and was told that President Roosevelt would like to have a meeting with him in a convenient and quiet place, perhaps 'some lonely bay or other'. The Prime Minister was soon on the transatlantic telephone, momentarily forgetting to use the scrambler which would have made his conversation secure. It was duly agreed that the two statesmen would meet off the coast of the British colony of Newfoundland, as near as possible to a halfway point between London and Washington. The ideal spot was Placentia Bay, where the Americans had recently been given permission to build a naval base, making it, in a sense, neutral territory. Moreover, Newfoundland was not yet part of the dominion of Canada. Churchill was grateful for Canadian participation in the war but he did not want a visit from Prime Minister Mackenzie King to complicate his one-to-one with Roosevelt.

Next morning, Churchill got the Cabinet's approval for the trip. He wrote to King George VI telling him of his plans. He was going to take with him two of the three Chiefs of Staff of the armed forces, leaving military activity in the hands of Sir Charles Portal of the Air Ministry and General Ismay of the

Ministry of Defence (more correctly known as the Defence Secretariat of the War Cabinet Office since there was no ministry as such). The leader of the Labour Party, Clement Attlee, would be left in charge of political affairs. Churchill had high hopes for the meeting and told Queen Elizabeth, 'I do not think our friend would have asked me to go so far for what must be a meeting of world-wide notice, unless he had in mind some further forward step.' A hint perhaps at an increase in military aid through lend-lease, a tougher line against the Japanese in the Pacific, greater co-operation against the U-boats in the Atlantic, or perhaps even an American declaration of war. But Churchill rather hedged his bets by adding, 'In fact the meeting will be a forward step in itself.'

★ ★ ★

In the meantime, there was work to do at home. Churchill was due to address the House of Commons on war production on the 29th, and his speeches were always carefully prepared. His young typist Elizabeth Layton had been in the Prime Minister's service for nearly three months, having returned from Canada in a cargo ship and being sent to the job from a typing school where she had been a star pupil. She was put to work as he drafted and redrafted and was in 'an *awful* hurroosh'. After working half the night, she and Churchill's private secretary John Martin ended up foraging for scones in the kitchen. Up till now she had found it very difficult to adjust to the Prime Minister's speeds of delivery, his eccentric pronunciation, his moods and the constant hurry. At last she was beginning to feel that she could cope in this strange environment. Next day was 'terrific'. The whole speech was typed and retyped in 'frantic spurts' until 11.35, when the Prime Minister set off for the House of Commons supported by his wife and daughter, two private secretaries, two detectives, two typists and his valet.

The speech ended up at 10,000 words, his longest yet. It contained no great inspiration, no ringing phrases, no 'finest hour', no 'fight them on the beaches', no call to arms; instead, it was a thorough and detailed account of what was being done to mobilise British industry from its interwar depression. It had a mixed reception. The Conservative MP Harold Nicolson wrote in his diary of a 'long and careful speech' which did not go down very well. 'There is a sense of criticism in the air.' The *Daily Telegraph* on the other hand called it 'a brilliant debating speech … As an intellectual exercise alone it was sufficiently amazing … the argument was as cogent … as the wit by which it was enlivened was refreshing.' But, it was asked, was it really a good use of the time and energy of the Prime Minister in dealing with these matters?[2]

That Friday Churchill was driven to the PM's weekend residence at Chequers in Buckinghamshire. He did not relax there, for he had invited the Foreign Secretary Anthony Eden, as well as General Auchinleck, who was about to take over as commander-in-chief in the Middle East, and General Ismay, the Chief of Staff of the Ministry of Defence. Ismay advised Auchinleck on how to deal with his troublesome chief:

> He was a child of nature. He venerated tradition, but ridiculed convention. When the occasion demanded, he could be the personification of dignity; when the spirit moved him, he could be a *gamin*. His courage, enthusiasm and industry were boundless, and his loyalty was absolute. No commander who engaged the enemy need ever fear that he would not be supported. His knowledge of military history was encyclopaedic, and his grasp of the broad sweep of strategy unrivalled. At the same time, he did not fully realise the extent to which mechanisation had complicated administrative arrangements and revolutionised the problems of time and space; and he never ceased to cry out against the inordinate 'tail' which modern armies required.[3]

Ismay advised Auchinleck not to be irritated by Churchill's endless messages, and to remember Nelson's dictum that 'no captain can go far wrong if he places his ship alongside that of an enemy'. For Churchill, offensive action was everything. Meanwhile, according to Eden's private secretary, the Prime Minister was 'in the highest spirits at the idea of his jaunt'.

★ ★ ★

Churchill was excited with the idea of a voyage, for personal as well as political reasons. He was by far the most travelled of British prime ministers before the jet age. In his youth his parents often left him behind on their journeys, but as a young man he soon found that army life at Aldershot was too boring. He got leave to become a war correspondent for the *Daily Graphic* in Cuba, where he picked up or reinforced his habits of smoking cigars and taking an afternoon siesta. In 1896, at the age of 21, he sailed with his regiment to India and saw action on the North-West Frontier, both as an officer and as a correspondent. In 1898 he combined the roles again during Lord Kitchener's expedition to reconquer the Sudan, and at Omdurman he took part in the British army's last great cavalry charge. Then, quitting the army, he was a very active correspondent and prisoner of war in South Africa during the Boer War.

15

Later, as a politician and government minister he never missed a chance to travel in the course of his business, especially as Under-Secretary for the Colonies from 1907, when he journeyed to the Mediterranean, West Africa, the Sudan and Egypt. As First Lord of the Admiralty, just before the First World War, he lived for much of the time on the Admiralty yacht *Enchantress*, visiting British and foreign naval bases and incorporating a voyage to the Mediterranean. During the war he spent much time in France as a minister and as an army officer on the Western Front.

After the war he favoured the French Riviera for holidays, and made many lecture and research tours while out of office in the 1930s. His hobby of painting was a spur to travel to picturesque places such as Italy and Morocco. Returning to the Admiralty in 1939, he visited military forces in France. As wartime Prime Minister, he made four unsuccessful aerial trips to try to persuade the French government not to surrender to the German onslaught. On the last of these, on the same day as the Germans entered Paris, he landed on the bomb-damaged runway at Tours and spent some time looking for the retreating French government. A subsequent trip by cruiser was cancelled while Churchill was on the train to Southampton. The Battle of Britain was about to begin and now he had to concentrate on national defence, while seeking allies in the struggle.

His relations with America were ambiguous. His beloved mother was an American heiress, but she starved him of much-needed affection and squandered her money, and Churchill had little contact with the American side of his family. He loved the country, despite his incomprehension of the policy of prohibition in the 1920s. He made money from several lecture tours, although these were not always happy occasions. In 1929 he was in New York during the Wall Street Crash, in which he lost a good deal of money. While he was away his Conservative colleagues decided to support self-government for India, which was anathema to Churchill. Two years later he was injured in a car accident in New York, heralding the themes for his wilderness years in the 1930s – near bankruptcy, political isolation and poor health.

Churchill's compulsive travelling contrasts with other national leaders of the day. Previous British prime ministers rarely strayed far from the homeland. Neville Chamberlain had not done the European grand tour like his elder brother Austin. His main overseas activity came during the 1890s in the family business, growing sisal in the Bahamas, a venture that ended in catastrophic failure. As a government minister he was entirely concerned with home policy until he became Prime Minister in 1937. Whereas Churchill had flown in various capacities since 1913, Chamberlain's first aeroplane flight was when he went to Munich to meet Hitler in September 1938. Hitler himself rarely travelled outside Austria and Germany, except during his military service in the First World War and on occasional visits to occupied territories in the second; he never stepped outside Europe. Stalin spent less time in exile than his late Bolshevik colleagues, although he did attend a Bolshevik conference in London in 1907. Since then, he had hardly ever left the Soviet Union. His only flights were to and from the Tehran conference in 1943, when he was terrified. President Roosevelt had been an invalid for twenty years and rarely left the United States.

There had been previous international conferences – the Congress of Vienna in 1815 after the Napoleonic War, the Congress of Berlin in 1878 to regulate European colonial expansion, and Versailles in 1919, which had ended the First World War and totally failed to establish lasting peace. But these were rare events, about once in two generations. As a rule, prime ministers had relied on diplomats or foreign secretaries to deal with foreign powers.

Churchill was also elated at the idea of an escape from the besieged fortress that Britain had become, even if it meant a long voyage in very uncomfortable conditions in a warship, and arrival at a spot that was the exact opposite of the bright lights. It would have been impossible for him to leave at any time in the preceding fourteen months, after France was defeated and Britain stood alone. His role as Prime Minister made all the difference between a deal with Germany and fighting on in June 1940. More than any other leader, he symbolised the war effort, and his broadcasts to the nation, his resounding phrases and his presence in bombed areas or air force bases were essential to morale. His effectiveness in actually running the war is controversial and some in his closest circle suggested that he interfered too much, often with disastrous results. But he did galvanise the armed forces and the nation, he supervised and assessed the rival needs of the different services with an experienced and shrewd eye, and provided an overall direction for the war effort. If Churchill could be portrayed as fleeing the country it would be a catastrophe for national morale. If he was lost in the U-boat-infested waters of the North Atlantic his country, and the rest of the world, would face an uncertain future.

Churchill had already decided to travel by sea. The day after the telephone call to Roosevelt he wrote to the King:

I have received an invitation from the President to meet him somewhere off Newfoundland ... The Cabinet strongly approve of my

17

going, and if Your Majesty would graciously consent, I should propose to sail from Scapa on the evening of the 4th ... I can of course return by flying-boat from Newfoundland in a few hours, but I cannot foresee any cause likely to make this necessary.[4]

Like many major decisions, the reasons for this are not revealed in the papers, so we cannot be sure of the logic. Certainly transatlantic air travel was in its infancy, although there were flying boats, such as the three Boeing Clippers owned by the British Overseas Airways Corporation, which could carry a Prime Minister in some comfort and reasonable safety. The terms of the meeting suggested that both Roosevelt and Churchill were to be based in warships of their respective nations, but it would still have been possible to send a British warship to Newfoundland in advance and fly Churchill there to join the ship. But space was limited in a flying boat and Churchill needed a large staff. Perhaps he also saw the voyage as something of a rest from his efforts, and equally a chance to get back in touch with the Royal Navy.

Dozens of ships were lost in the North Atlantic every month, but it was not as dangerous as it might appear for a major warship. A modern battleship could sustain a speed of more than 20 knots on the open ocean in reasonable weather, whereas a U-boat could only do 17 knots on the surface or 7½, for very short periods, submerged. Most U-boat successes in the Atlantic were against merchant ship convoys which rarely did more than 10 knots. The U-boat's only chance against a fast battleship was if it appeared directly ahead of the target, but that was not likely to happen. British signal intelligence could detect the position of most submarines at sea, either by decoding their orders or plotting the direction from which their radio signals were emitted.

The decision to go by sea was probably made on the spur of the moment, but the next question was what ship to go in. None of the great Atlantic liners was available, for they were being used as troopships between Australia and the Middle East. A voyage in a normal merchant ship might take two weeks each way and was fraught with danger. The smallest possible warship was a cruiser, such as the *Kent* which took the Foreign Secretary Anthony Eden to the Soviet Union in December. This would have matched the USS *Augusta* which would bring Roosevelt to the meeting, but Churchill aimed to travel in something much grander. The new battleship *King George V* had already taken Lord Halifax to Washington as British ambassador in January that year. Her sister ship *Prince of Wales* was the newest battleship in the British fleet, having been completed just four months before. At 42,000 tons, she was four times the size of Roosevelt's *Augusta,* and ten years younger. There was no immediate threat from German ships of similar size to the *Prince of Wales.* The great *Bismarck* had been sunk in May, and it was known that her sister ship *Tirpitz* was not yet ready for action.

★ ★ ★

The trip was soon codenamed Operation Riviera. Churchill's personal travel arrangements were made by his naval aide, Commander C. R. Thompson. Apart from his naval interests Thompson was, like Churchill, an early enthusiast for flying. At the beginning of the First World War he applied to join the Royal Naval Air Service but was turned down on a technicality by a letter bearing the signature of the then First Lord of the Admiralty – Winston Churchill. Instead he served as a submarine captain for thirteen years, but ran the *Oberon* aground. This put a black mark against his name at a time in the early 1930s when the navy was at its lowest point and competition for promotion at its most intense. He missed the vital step to commander, but found a new career as flag lieutenant to successive admirals, organising their social lives and travel arrangements with great skill. He gravitated towards the Admiralty and a new post of Flag Lieutenant to the Board of Admiralty was created for him. Churchill found him there when he became First Lord of the Admiralty on the first day of the Second World War, and kept him on when he was elevated to Prime Minister in May 1940. Thompson was soon promoted to commander and was invariably seen in his uniform. His rather simian features (Brigadier Dykes called him 'toad-like') appear in many wartime photographs of Churchill, alongside the long, lugubrious face, crowned with a trilby hat, of his namesake Detective-Inspector Walter Thompson, the Prime Minister's chief bodyguard.

If Commander Thompson handled the details, the general travelling arrangements bore the signature of Colonel Leslie Hollis of the Royal Marines. He was the second most senior officer in the Ministry of Defence, an organisation created largely to facilitate Churchill's personal control of the war effort. By 1 August, two days before departure, it had been established that 28 people were going on the trip. The seven in the Prime Minister's party included Harry Hopkins and the two Thompsons. There were four officers from the Admiralty, as naval co-operation between the two countries was high on the agenda; three from the army and two from the Air Ministry. Hollis himself was accompanied by his Ministry of Defence colleague, Lieutenant-Colonel Ian Jacob.

The party was completed by office staff and male stenographers. Women were not allowed to travel on a warship, even though one of the typists, Mary Shearburn, had made the short journey to France by destroyer in January 1940 and claimed to be the first woman to undertake a voyage in a naval ship during the war. There was a single Royal Marine orderly but none of the travellers brought their domestic staff. Instead, a group of more than 30 stewards, cooks, clerks and signallers was selected from the naval and marine barracks and ordered to report to the *Prince of Wales*. They were headed by Chief Petty Officer Steward Pinfield.

Hollis's instructions ordered the travellers to report to Marylebone Station in London by 12 noon on 3 August. Boxes containing secret documents were to be collected by Colonel Jacob and would be put on the train by a special guard of one NCO and four marines. They were to be labelled from A to F to indicate the department from which they had originated. Personal baggage should be put on the train and marked with the owner's name. No special dress was needed, but jerseys and greatcoats were advisable, and civilians in the Prime Minister's party were asked to bring dinner jackets. On board ship Churchill's immediate circle would mess in the admiral's spacious cabin, and other service officers would eat in the wardroom. The civilian clerks and stenographers and Inspector Thompson would be in the warrant officers' mess, where he might expect to meet men of similar background, who had risen from humble beginnings to positions of authority. The uniformed other ranks – two sergeants and two corporal stenographers – were to be put in a special mess.

Obviously communication between the party and Whitehall would be severely restricted, but some form of contact was to be maintained. A morning signal, consisting of 'a summary of operational news and Military Situation Reports', would be compiled in the War Cabinet Offices and despatched by ten every morning. A summary of political, foreign and other governmental matters which the Prime Minister needed to know about would be sent off in the afternoon. A special cipher was arranged by the Admiralty to prevent the enemy decoding the messages. Outward signals from the ship would be more difficult, as the transmission might give the position away. The plan was for one of the escorting destroyers to receive the message by flashing light, then send it on by radio from a position a hundred miles or so away. Messages for the Prime Minister in person would be codenamed Abbey, and his outward signals would be Tudor. Messages to and from other members of the party were coded Sloane and Avenue. The ship would also receive general broadcasts to the area, giving information, for example, on U-boat movements.

For security reasons the Prime Minister's departure would be kept secret and only announced when it was a *fait accompli*, after he had returned or was on the way back, and the purpose of his trip made clear to all. A photo was taken of him on the steps of 10 Downing Street, buying a flag for a charity event that would actually take place a week later.

★ ★ ★

Meanwhile Churchill's friend Brendan Bracken, the newly appointed Minister of Information, was adding to the party. He wanted a full account of the meeting for the press and for posterity, so he contacted two well-known writers and asked if they would be able to make themselves available at very short notice. According to Bracken, H. V. Morton was 'what journalists call a fine descriptive writer'.[5] He was summoned to the offices of the Ministry of Information on Saturday 2 August, where he met Bracken:

> I have an extraordinary proposition to put up to you. I want you to leave England for three weeks, but I regret to say I can't tell you where you are going or what you will see when you get there. I can only say that if you go you will see history in the making and be present at one of the great moments of the war. Will you go?[6]

Morton agreed instantly and went home to Hampshire to pack. He knew that he was not off to the tropics or the Arctic, but he took every type of clothing for temperate weather, including his Home Guard uniform.

Howard Spring was contacted by telephone at his seaside home in Cornwall. Formerly a reporter with the *Manchester Guardian*, he had been brought to London by Lord Beaverbrook as a book reviewer on the *Evening Standard*. In the last few years he had entered the best-sellers list himself with his novels *My Son, My Son!* and *Fame is the Spur*. He received Bracken's call at the worst possible moment. His teeth had just been taken out, as was quite common at the time, and he had not yet been fitted with dentures. Not knowing what was involved, he took the train to London expecting to return that evening, but in any event he agreed to answer the summons, 'clothesless and toothless, going, God knows where'. With strict clothes rationing in force, it would have been impossible for him to buy new ones. When the two writers met in the ministry on the morning of Sunday 3 August, it was not just the nature of their luggage that made a contrast. Morton was dapper, elegant, balding with a dark moustache. Spring was very thin, long-haired, clean-shaven, toothless and his only suit seemed to hang off him.

They were driven to Marylebone Station where Morton was pleased not to need a ticket or travel warrant, but his name was ticked off on a list as he arrived. He walked the length of the train at platform number 4. He was not aware that it was Churchill's personal transport, as naturally that was not publicised in wartime, but he could see that it was for someone very important. He noticed the sleeping cars and deduced that they must be for a trip to Scotland. Where else could they go, leaving London at midday and needing overnight accommodation?

He was right, but for the wrong reasons. In fact Churchill's train was a mobile hotel, office and communications centre, designed to facilitate his visits to British towns and military bases without compromising security. Rather than sleep in a hotel with all the complications that might involve, he often spent the night in a railway siding, perhaps moving into a tunnel if an air raid threatened. The train had been assembled in mid-1940 by Sir Harold Hartley, a director of the London, Midland and Scottish railway company which operated the long-distance royal trains. At its core were two 'semi-royal' coaches, numbers 803 and 804. These had been built at the beginning of the century as part of the royal train, to carry courtiers and officials while the King and Queen travelled in their own larger and even more luxurious vehicles. No. 803 remained as built, with small saloons, one bedroom, two lavatories and space for an attendant. No. 804 was modified to have a large open lounge in the centre, with the Prime Minister's bedroom and bathroom at one end and an office for a private secretary and typist at the other.

The rest of the train included sleeping coaches and conventional passenger coaches. There was a dining car with a long table and twelve seats for the dignitaries of the Prime Minister's party, while the other end was used by the humbler passengers such as detectives, engineers, stenographers and photographers. There was a diesel generator, and a special communication system which could be hooked up to an adjacent telephone line when the train was stopped, allowing instant contact with London. As the waspish MP and diarist 'Chips' Channon wrote during another trip, 'How luxuriously the PM lives, a most lavish lunch and a grand train.'

The train was due to pull out of the station promptly at 12.30, but with six minutes to go the party was still awaiting the arrival of Brigadier 'Dumbie' Dykes, the Director of Plans at the War Office. He arrived a minute later with vague excuses and the train left on time. One of the other passengers was Sir Alexander Cadogan, the intellectual and aristocratic Under-Secretary of

State, the chief civil servant in the Foreign Office. He was not an obvious suburbanite, but in the early 1930s he had commuted between Rickmansworth and London. Now, as the train passed through Wembley and Harrow he was appalled at how suburban sprawl had overtaken them in the last few years, but reassured himself that they were 'the encampment of the anti-Bolshevist horde'.

After an hour the train came to a halt at Wendover station, near the Prime Minister's weekend residence at Chequers, and the purpose of the trip became clearer. Morton looked out of his sleeper window to see an excited group of passers-by on one platform. On the other stood the Prime Minister himself, wearing a blue suit and a yachting cap and smoking a cigar. He was with a large party, some in army, naval or air force uniform, and several distinguished-looking civilians – 'a retinue that Cardinal Wolsey might have envied', according to John Colville who was not going on the trip. They boarded and the train pulled out of the station. Morton claimed that Colonel Hollis then told him that the Prime Minister was 'rather like a boy who's been let out of school suddenly'. The straight-laced marine denied this hotly; he would never talk about the Prime Minister that way in any circumstances, but the remark simply reflected the mood of the staff. To Colville he was 'as excited as a schoolboy on the last day of term'.

The Chiefs of Staff, the professional heads of the armed services, were there as well. Churchill was determined that the army, navy and air force should work better together than in past wars, and the three chiefs each had an 'individual and collective responsibility for advising on defence policy as a whole'. They met almost every day and spent at least fifteen hours a week in one another's company, discussing all aspects of the war. Churchill had not yet assembled the ideal team, as he would by the end of the war. Admiral of the Fleet Sir Dudley Pound was no one's first choice for First Sea Lord and Chief of Naval Staff. He only got the job because of the untimely death or ill health of several other candidates. He was a mild-mannered man of unremarkable appearance, competent enough for the job. Conscientious to the point of obsession, he tended to fall asleep during Chiefs of Staff meetings and wake up when the navy was mentioned. According to Colville, 'He wore a lugubrious air and his mere entry into the room made the occupants feel grave.' Neither he nor his political chief, the First Lord A. V. Alexander, provided the fire for the naval war. That came from the commanders-in-chief in the various stations, particularly Sir Andrew Cunningham in the Mediterranean, Sir Max Horton in charge of submarines and Sir Bertram Ramsay, who had organised the evacuation from Dunkirk.

General Sir John Dill, Chief of Imperial General Staff, had restored order to the War Office and given the army some self-confidence after the defeats of the previous year, but he was exhausted from his efforts, and did not know how to handle Churchill. When an enraged Prime Minister had demanded 'a court martial and a firing squad' after a defeat in the Middle East, Dill knew that he should have replied, 'Whom do you want to shoot exactly?' but he did not think of that until it was too late. Churchill was rapidly losing respect for him and his name led on easily to the nickname of 'Dilly-Dally'.

Air Chief Marshal Sir Charles Portal was indeed an excellent Chief of Air Staff, but he was staying at home to mind the shop, the most senior military officer in a country engaged in a world war. For this trip he would be represented by his deputy, Air Chief Marshal Sir Wilfred Freeman, who was a great expert on aircraft production but knew less of the wider responsibilities of the Vice Chief of Air Staff.

Churchill sat down to lunch in the dining car with Cadogan, Pound and Dill at his table. In the midst of wartime rationing, which usually applied even to the highest in the land, Cadogan enjoyed the 'unlimited quantities of very good sirloin of beef and delicious raspberry and currant tart'.[7] Among the new passengers Morton had recognised 'a tall unsmiling man', the Prime Minister's chief scientific adviser. Born as Frederick Lindemann in Germany in 1886 (to a father named Adolf) he had much to live down; but he had recently been ennobled and adopted the quintessentially English title of Baron Cherwell of Oxford. He had been a close friend of Churchill for many years and in 1932 the pair visited Germany to research Churchill's books on his ancestor the Duke of Marlborough. It was then that they became aware of the menace of the Nazi party, even before it came to power. 'The Prof' was a brilliant physicist with an ability to explain complex matters in simple terms, but he lacked humour and made many enemies amid the intense office politics of Oxford University.

Cherwell could provide amusement in his own peculiar way. At the end of lunch Churchill stood up and asked him across the dining car, 'Prof, what is 24 times 365?' Cherwell produced his slide rule and gave the answer as nearly 9,000. This, Churchill claimed, was the number of bottles of champagne he had consumed in 'a well-spent life'. He wanted to know what size of swimming bath that would fill. After more calculations the Prof replied that it would easily fit into the present compartment. Disappointed, Churchill commented, 'I do not think much of that. I shall have to improve on that in the future.' The train stopped at Leicester to change engines. The driver of a shunting locomotive recognised the Prime Minister as he passed the train, and raised his oily cap with a cry of 'Good old Winston!' At 4 o'clock Churchill retired to his compartment for his afternoon nap and the rest of the party relaxed, or continued their business.

Colonel Hollis finally told the two writers about the purpose of the trip. According to Morton:

> 'I've been talking to the Prime Minister's secretary,' he said, 'and he agrees with me that it's nonsense for you both to remain in the dark any longer. We're going to Newfoundland to meet the President of the United States. We are to cross the Atlantic in the *Prince of Wales*. While the President and the Prime Minister confer together, the three Chiefs of Staff will meet with their opposite numbers on the American side. So now you can sleep in peace.'
>
> 'How close a secret is it?' I asked.
>
> 'The best-kept secret I can remember in Whitehall,' he replied. 'It has been put about that that the Prime Minister is going North to inspect an operation, which is quite a normal proceeding. Only one or two men in London know that he is really leaving England …'[8]

This account was 'approximately true in substance' but 'of course, highly coloured'. Hollis commented later: 'I wonder why these authors when they have a good story to tell have to invent these things.' Bracken had found his 'fine descriptive writer'.

However, Bracken's purpose in taking the two scribes had already been undermined. Even before the train left, he knew that there would be no journalists in the American party. The last thing the British wanted to do was to upset the American press, so the activities of Spring and Morton would have to be curtailed. Bracken had to beg Churchill to let them go anyway, in view of the inconveniences they had suffered. 'It would therefore be a great pity if they are turned away at the eleventh hour on the grounds that the President had parted from the journalists who usually accompany him on his travels. If the President has achieved the miraculous by freezing the American press and is content to record your meeting by a short and jointly-agreed statement, the two journalists who accompany you will not be allowed to publish anything about your visit.'

★ ★ ★

Late in the afternoon Churchill reappeared in the saloon wearing his famous 'siren suit', a tattered one-piece garment in Air Force blue which had seen him

25

through many an air raid. The train continued on its way, making the characteristic clicking sound as it passed over the joints in the track, its engine belching smoke and soot, and often emitting a distinct smell of burning coal. Churchill put in a few more hours of work:

> Mr Churchill sat with a shaded reading light at his elbow. He had ceased to draw on a cigar which had gone out. He wore a pair of reading glasses. On chairs round about him were dispatch cases and boxes which gushed a river of papers and documents. While he picked up one of them, read it, discarded it or made a note or two in the margin, he was dictating to two secretaries who sat near with notebooks on their knees. In the background was a gleam of gold lace on the cuffs of the First Sea Lord and a glow of red tabs and war ribbons on the tunic of the Chief of the Imperial General Staff.[9]

At eight it was time for dinner, and the rules of wartime rationing still did not apply. Colonel Jacob thought that it was even better than lunch, with better food than he had seen in weeks – travelling in the kind of train seemed to be 'one long meal'. It was dark by the time the train stopped at Edinburgh for another change of engine, guarded by squads of policemen. Morton went to bed after that, but was too intrigued to sleep well.

He awoke at six to see hilly country with crofts and sheep, but the station names were blacked out and the steward would tell him nothing. Eventually they arrived at Thurso on the north coast of Scotland, the end of the line, to be greeted by a column of female sailors (Wrens) standing to attention in the rain. A fleet of cars took the party a few miles to the tiny port of Scrabster. The destroyer *Oribi* was waiting offshore, accompanied by the escort destroyer *Croome*. The party was taken out in two fishing boats, one called *Smiling Morn*, and the dignitaries climbed up to the destroyer's deck. The *Oribi* was a new ship and her officers, headed by Lieutenant-Commander J. E. H. MacHeath DSO, were tremendously proud of her. The visitors were offered the comforts of wardroom and cabin but most, including Churchill, preferred to stay on the bridge, some to see as much as possible, some perhaps for fear of seasickness. Pound, of course, was at home there, Dill let down the chinstrap of his cap to stop it blowing away. Then the 40,000hp engines of the *Oribi* roared into life, carrying her across the troubled waters of the Pentland Firth, where the tides of the North Sea meet those of the Atlantic.

If anyone was still in the dark, there could now be no doubt that the party was heading for the great naval anchorage of Scapa Flow among the Orkney

Islands, the scene of so much history in and after the First World War. During the war the fleet had spent almost four years of enforced boredom there. After the Armistice the German fleet was interned in the Flow and scuttled itself in June 1919 to avoid humiliation – some of the wrecks were still on the bottom. In the present war it was still a major fleet base, although great battle-fleets were less important than in the past. It provided shelter for the ships which had fought unsuccessfully against the German invasion of Norway in 1940, which had chased the *Bismarck* in the following year and were now covering the convoys to Russia. Young sailors, who rarely had a deep interest in archae-ology or wildlife, saw it as a bleak, barren spot with few opportunities for entertainment.

Cadogan watched with interest as naval boom defence vessels opened the gates in the huge underwater nets which guarded Hoxa Sound, the southern entrance to the Flow, against submarines. It took about an hour, and then the destroyer rounded the island of Flotta inside the natural harbour, to find the three-funnelled cruiser *Dorsetshire* exercising, and the great modern battle-ships *King George V* and *Prince of Wales* at anchor. The *Oribi* headed for the *Prince of Wales* and came alongside at ten minutes before noon. The crew on deck spotted the familiar figure smoking a cigar on the *Oribi*'s bridge and the whisper went round, 'It's Winston!' The Prime Minister and his party climbed up the gangway on the side of the battleship as the bosun's pipes played their shrill tune – not for Churchill, who was not entitled to such a salute, but for the First Sea Lord.

On deck, Churchill found Harry Hopkins, who had arrived by air from Moscow after a meeting with Stalin and was 'dead beat'. He had been extremely weak from illness and fatigue when he arrived at Scapa two days before by Catalina flying-boat, and had been nursed back to some kind of health in the Commander-in-Chief's cabin. Morton watched the 'thin man of extraordinary pallor and fragility', with 'a loose American overcoat of tweed blowing about him.' Churchill greeted him and said 'Ah, my dear friend, how are you? And how did you find Stalin?' They shook hands and linked arms as Hopkins replied in 'a slow, wonderfully weary American voice', and the two went below to discuss matters. Churchill's first task was to telegraph Roosevelt about him before the ship left. 'We shall get him in fine trim on the voyage. We are just off.'

II
Voyage to Placentia

Morton thought that the great battleship looked beautiful, 'full of power, strength and pride', as she came into sight through the northern mists. Not everyone would agree. Certainly she was not ugly like the *Nelson* and *Rodney*, seen by the navy as bastard progeny of the Washington arms-limitation treaty of 1922 and nicknamed the 'pair of boots' by the sailors of the lower deck. But she was not nearly as good-looking as the late, lamented battle-cruiser *Hood*, which had been described as 'the most beautiful steamship that man ever devised'. The *Prince of Wales* was much more angular, for her high bridge structure was designed as plainly as possible to avoid trapping enemy shot. Her two funnels were equal in height, tall and perfectly straight, for her designers believed that a raked funnel could be used by the enemy to assess the angle of the ship. Her main deck was almost completely flat, for the Admiralty had decreed that she should be able to fire her guns directly forward, and this meant that she had no raised bow to meet the waves. Her four-gun turrets looked odd to a naval eye which expected to see no more than three guns side by side, and her designers seemed almost apologetic about it, placing only two guns in upper forward B turret.

On the face of it, a British battleship was the safest place on the high seas, protected by more than 12,000 tons of steel armour nearly 15 inches thick in places, a vital component of the greatest sea power in the world. Yet if the passengers had any such illusions, they would soon be shattered as they stepped on board. It was less than three months since the *Prince of Wales* had fought the great German battleship *Bismarck*, and watched the pride of the Royal Navy, the largest warship in the world for 20 years, 'the mighty *Hood*', disappear in a huge explosion. The *Prince of Wales* suffered seven hits from the *Bismarck's* 15-inch, 800kg shells, and seven out of her ten guns were out of action for a time. She had spent a month under repair, but still bore scars. Above the wardroom bar was a piece of steel 'curled round and hung from the roof like a wood shaving', left there as a memento of the action.

The *Hood* was not the only capital ship to be lost recently. A few miles across the Flow was the wreck of the *Royal Oak*, torpedoed by a U-boat in the second month of the war with the loss of 786 lives. Three more British capital ships would be sunk, out of a total of twenty, and other nations suffered losses on a similar scale. For all their strength, capital ships presented very desirable targets and the enemy was likely to make special efforts to sink one, even if it was not carrying the Prime Minister and the leaders of the armed forces.

The faults of the *Prince of Wales* and her four sisters of the *King George V* class were not just in appearance, as Churchill was well aware. He had been out of office in 1936 when the ships were planned, but he had conducted a lengthy correspondence with the First Lord of the Admiralty about them, particularly the decision to fit 14-inch guns as the main armament. Ever since the 12-inch of the *Dreadnought* of 1906, he had been familiar with the increasing size of battleship guns. Indeed, Churchill himself had been instrumental in having 15-inch guns fitted to a total of 13 ships built thereafter, all of which were still in service at the beginning of the Second World War. The *Rodney* and *Nelson*, built in the 1920s, went further and used 16-inch guns. The proposed 14-inch guns, Churchill believed, were a retrograde step, but the government was hoping that a new arms limitation treaty would restrict the size of naval guns, and meanwhile they had to plan the new ships well in advance.

The crew of the *Prince of Wales* got her ready for sea that afternoon. At 4.20 p.m. the cable holding her to No. 6 buoy was slipped and the ship began to gather speed. She passed slowly through the Hoxa Gate and turned west. By 6 o'clock she was clear of land and began a variable course to confuse enemy submarines. She adopted Zigzag No. 8 from the official manual, intended for use by ships 'in open waters where submarines have not previously been operating, but where they may appear'. The ship started by steering 25 degrees to the starboard of her main course. After four minutes she turned 50 degrees to port, and after a further eight she went 25 degrees to starboard again, and so on over a pattern which lasted for two hours. It helped to put off the aim of any undetected U-boat but it did not waste too much time, for the ship would cover 93 per cent of the distance she would have done without zigzags. She was escorted by three of the best destroyers in the fleet, the *Havelock, Harvester* and *Hesperus*, which had originally been ordered to a high specification for the Brazilian navy but had been taken over on the outbreak of war. They were on loan from Western Approaches Command, so their crews had plenty of experience of the Battle of the Atlantic. Unlike the *Prince of Wales* they were fitted with Asdic to detect submarines underwater (though not at the high speeds at which the ships were travelling), and depth charges to attack them.

★ ★ ★

The passengers were shown to their cabins. Morton was taken below by Lieu-tenant Dyer-Smith:

> As battleship cabins go, it was almost luxurious. The bunk was built into the white curve of the ship's side, and there was a writing desk with side drawers and a lot of cupboards. There was a wash basin with hot and cold water, and there were plenty of electric lights. But the place shook like an aspen, and there was a steady roar like thunder.
>   'A bit noisy, isn't it?' I remarked.
>   'It's over the propeller shaft,' said Dyer-Smith, 'But I expect you'll get used to it.'

Dyer-Smith admitted that it was his own cabin he was giving up, presum-ably to sleep elsewhere in a hammock, but he did not mind. 'It's a great privi-lege to be taking the Prime Minister to sea, sir ... We're all tremendously proud of it ...'[1]

That evening the middle-ranking passengers settled down to dinner in the wardroom where most of the officers had their dining and sitting room. According to Morton it was

> a large room some sixty feet in length ... You stepped straight into it from the quarterdeck. It was divided into two parts: on the port side was the ante-room, furnished with easy chairs, a club lounge, a book-case containing Chambers Encyclopaedia and a number of novels and other works ... and on the starboard side was the dining room. In the dining room were two long tables and a hatch where Royal Marines in white mess jackets served the food. Above the mantelpiece hung an irreverent Gillray caricature of the Prince Regent ... At the end of the ante-room was a small bar, which was opened before lunch and dinner, where gin was sold at 3d and whiskey at 5d a glass.[2]

Again they were well fed. They had taken on some grouse in Scotland and had good-quality beef, as well as 'masses of butter and sugar', according to Cadogan. Howard Spring saw the poignancy of the occasion:

> The double scuttles [portholes] of the ship are closed – the inner ones black – and the curtains are drawn across them. The long black room is brilliantly lit. On four or five rows of chairs such officers as are not on duty are sipping their after dinner drinks, wearing the stiff winged

collars and black bows of the ceremonial evening hour. It is a whole
congregation of specialists. Threading the gold lace on their cuffs are
the colours that tell of their callings: the surgeons' red, the paymasters'
white, the engineers' purple, the schoolmasters' hopeful blue. In front,
the screen has been put up. All is warm and bright and a little sophisticated as the mess-servants of the Royal Marines, in their white
jackets, move here and there. Then an imperceptible tremor, or a
sudden slight cant of the room, reminds you of the reality beyond this
appearance.[3]

After dinner they settled down to the evening's entertainment. Film was
Churchill's sole recreation during the war, for he painted only one picture
during that period. As he wrote to Clementine during a later voyage: 'The
cinema is a wonderful form of entertainment and takes the mind away from
other things.' Of course he was not one of the 32 per cent of the population
who went to the cinema at least once a week, or the 38 per cent who went
occasionally, for as Prime Minister he had the films brought to him. He did
not miss the huge screen, the lively local crowds and the elaborate decorations
of the great theatres of the day. He was just as likely to be moved in a small
room at Chequers, or indeed the wardroom of a battleship, hearing the whirr
of the projector and smell of the film acetate. His taste was not for what
became known as 'art' films – he had recently walked out on a showing of
Orson Welles's *Citizen Kane*, admired by cineastes world-wide. Although not
all of his entourage shared this preference, most officers of the armed forces
were tolerant of it. They often had to organise entertainment for troops on
out-of-the-way stations, and needed a nodding acquaintance with popular
culture. But senior civil servants were chosen for a highly developed brain
and had no need to be concerned with what their juniors did after work.
Cadogan haughtily gave Churchill's films scores ranging from 'fairly
amusing' to 'appalling slapstick'.

Churchill had made sure that he had a stock of the latest films with him.
The majority were American, even if some had a strong British interest, for the
national struggle for survival was the great story of the day. Churchill was
quite happy to share his pleasures with the officers of the *Prince of Wales*, and
on the first night at sea those off-duty gathered in the wardroom.

At nine o'clock the Prime Minister entered, wearing the mess dress of
the Royal Yacht Squadron of Cowes. He was followed by Harry Hopkins,
the Chiefs of Staff and the rest of the immediate entourage. The audience
rose as the great man entered, still chewing a cigar which had gone out. He

sank into a deep leather armchair near the front and the lights were dimmed.

The chosen entertainment that night was the conspicuously British film *Pimpernel Smith*. Leslie Howard, whose gentle, understated manner made him popular on both sides of the Atlantic, played a Cambridge archaeology professor who was secretly helping political prisoners escape from Nazi Germany on the eve of war. It celebrated British culture through the verse of Lewis Carroll, which the brutish Nazis totally failed to understand. The central character even had echoes of Lord Cherwell, who as an Oxford professor rescued a number of Jews from Nazi tyranny by finding them jobs in the university. Cadogan grudgingly rated it 'not too bad', if a little long. Howard Spring was deeply moved, especially with the finale when the audience is left wondering whether Smith has been shot at the frontier or not, and a 'very voice of Doom' rings out, 'We shall come back. We shall all come back', expressing the hopes of occupied Europe and the persecuted minorities in Germany itself.

The performance over, Churchill rose and said goodnight to the company. It was not long after midnight but he decided to turn in, much to the delight of his staff. 'He's actually going to bed. I can hardly believe it. Now I can go to bed too! After a film he generally settles down to work half way through the night.'

Spring had not yet overcome his emotion and went to walk on the quarterdeck just outside the wardroom:

> The night was black. Not a glimmer showed in the great ship or in the ships of the escort. To know that they were out there racing with us through the darkness required an act of faith rather than reason; and it was comforting. God knows, I thought, this ship is like our land: rushing through a darkness in which no gleams are yet apparent, beset with enemies below, above and around. We can do with comrades. A glimmer of white water, flowing back in a V from the driving bows, was all the light in the inky midnight hour.[4]

He turned in a few minutes later.

★   ★   ★

The passengers soon discovered that the ship's officers had not made that great a sacrifice by giving up their cabins to them. One design flaw in the *King George*

V class was that the tracks of the propellers overlapped, creating vibration at high speed. Morton found it intolerable, but could think of no alternative and lay awake for most of the night:

> Two o'clock, three o'clock, half past three; and I was still awake; then, chewing up some paper from my note-book and plugging up my ears with the pulp, I managed to exclude some of the noise and I fell asleep, but only for half an hour. A bugle sounded. A fierce and mighty voice magnified by a loudspeaker outside my cabin was chanting a queer couplet straight from the eighteenth century:

> Heave-ho, Heave-ho, Heave-ho
> Lash up and stow …

The seamen were being ordered to take down their hammocks as the ship began a new day.[5]

Howard Spring showed more initiative and had himself transferred to the ship's sick bay, where he was joined by Thompson the detective. Both men were cared for by the sick-berth attendant who waited on them hand and foot, and there was a small four-berth isolation ward where they could be kept separate from the two dozen men on the official sick list.

The Prime Minister was no more satisfied with his large cabin in the stern. At first he paid no attention when he saw objects flying about, for he had spent many a rough night in the London Blitz. But eventually he summoned a young officer who arrived to find the great man looking 'like an enraged cherub' in his night attire. In this case there was an alternative. The young man led the Prime Minister by torchlight though a maze of passages, impeded by the watertight doors which had to be kept secure at sea in wartime. He passed through foetid overcrowded mess-decks and squeezed under the bodies of scores of seamen sleeping tightly packed in hammocks. After covering almost two-thirds the length of the ship, they began to ascend through five decks.

Warships are designed to be occupied by fit young men, not 66-year-old, overweight, hard-drinking and heavy-smoking prime ministers. Churchill struggled on the way, almost getting stuck in some of the hatchways. When his companion offered help he was rebuffed. 'Young man, do you imagine I have never climbed a ladder in my life?' Immediately Churchill bumped his head on a piece of steel, and said no more. Eventually they reached the admiral's sea cabin just under the bridge – vacant, as there was no flag officer on board. It was small, only nine feet square, and interrupted by a large communication tube passing through it, but it boasted a settee bunk with draws underneath, a wardrobe, a chest of drawers, a desk and a few chairs. It was not obvious at that hour of the night, but it also had a fine view of the bows of the ship, and of the Atlantic Ocean. Churchill accepted the cabin and soon fell asleep, to enjoy his best night's rest since the war started.

★ ★ ★

One person who did not appear at the nightly entertainments was Captain John Leach, who had commanded the *Prince of Wales* since her completion that spring. There might have been some friction between Churchill and the captain, for in May Leach had turned away from the *Bismarck* after the *Hood* was sunk. Churchill was enraged on hearing the news and compared it with the time in the previous war when Captain Troubridge had failed to pursue the German battlecruiser *Goeben*. But this was before he knew the full facts – that the *Prince of Wales* was a brand new ship whose crew was not yet fully worked up, that she had suffered heavy damage and most of her guns were out of action. Later he assessed Leach as 'a charming and lovable man and all that a British sailor should be'.

Leach was aware of the enormity of the task now placed on him, to conduct the Prime Minister and most of the country's war leaders across a dangerous ocean. He took his responsibilities very seriously and had the traditional naval officer's inability to delegate. He would spend practically the entire voyage on the open bridge of the *Prince of Wales*, snatching an occasional nap in his sea cabin just aft, or poring over charts in the charthouse aft of that with the navigating officer, Lieutenant-Commander G.W. Rowell. Leach was 'a tall, elegant figure' with 'that definite air of ownership which captains assume upon their own quarterdecks'. Like most regular naval officers, he had entered Dartmouth College in his early teens more than 30 years earlier, and spent his life in the service. He was a gunnery officer like many of those in the higher ranks, but that had left him slightly deaf. Broad-shouldered and athletic, he was fond of squash and tennis. His prominent nose earned him the nickname of 'Trunk' on the lower deck, but he was a popular captain who respected his crew and got the best out of them. Colonel Jacob thought that the *Prince of Wales* was a happy ship and that Leach had a good reputation with his men.

That was not the whole story. The ship's reputation had suffered after the *Bismarck* action and her crew was taunted by the marines of the cruiser *Norfolk*. Still dogged by mechanical problems, she was sent off to defend a Malta convoy as soon as her repairs were finished, making her work harder than any other newly completed ship. She had a high proportion of Hostilities Only seamen about her decks, recruited and often conscripted for service only in wartime. They were hastily trained and often disorientated in their first weeks at sea, and many of them came from social and political backgrounds from which the navy would not have recruited in peacetime. Ordinary Seaman D. F. Watson commented that some of them 'came from that stratum of society which had good cause to resent the "gaffers" and upper class generally'. There was friction between them and the regular officers and petty officers.

Officially Leach had a complement of 63 officers and 1,375 men, not including Fleet Air Arm personnel to man and service the ship's two Walrus biplanes, and the civilian canteen staff who sold soft drinks and other goods to the crew. Almost certainly, extra men such as radar ratings had been added to operate new equipment. A ship of this size was normally run in two watches; so almost half of the 497 able or ordinary seamen, 64 leading seamen, 52 petty officers and five chief petty officers of the seaman branch were on a four-hour spell of duty at any given moment. Not much was heard during the voyage of the men below commissioned rank, the 'lower deck' of the navy. Howard Spring was faintly aware of 'eyes ceaselessly watching, ears fixed to telephones, a complication of instruments under everlasting regard', but the passengers lived alongside the officers of the wardroom. Inspector Thompson, from a working-class background, was the main contact with the lower deck. Sensing he was more approachable than the others, the seamen asked him for Churchill's cigar butts as souvenirs.

On the bridge with the captain and the navigation officer was the officer of the watch, who used a clock to control the zigzag pattern, ordering a turn at the right moment and communicating it to the destroyer escort by signal flags or blasts on the siren. He was accompanied by 'an Armament officer, two midshipmen of the watch, a leading signalman who transmits signalling orders to the signal deck bridge which is situated on the after part of the Bridge structure'. Also on duty were 'about a dozen people … continuously keeping watch though binoculars over the air, and the whole surface of the sea'. The seamen operated the guns and their control systems, kept a lookout and manned the ship's boats, two of which were always kept ready in case a man fell overboard. There were also more than 20 signallers who used flags, semaphore or Morse code to communicate with the escorting destroyers. The 30 men of the wireless telegraphy branch worked hardest at the given hours when the coded messages came in from London, but they had to stand by for any urgent warning that might arrive, as well as for general broadcasts to ships in the region.

Below decks in the engine room, a three-watch system was in operation. There was always at least one commissioned officer and one warrant officer on duty, with a third of the engine-room staff. The four huge 26,000hp turbines in the engine-room proper were manned in each watch by highly skilled engine room artificers or ERAs, the most privileged members of the lower deck, equivalent to chief petty officers and with their own messes. There were also less skilled stokers, who did not shovel coal as their title suggested, for the *Prince of Wales*, like all modern warships, had oil-fired boilers. Instead they monitored numerous gauges and dials, lubricated key points, changed filters and kept the machinery in order. More than 70 men were on duty deep in the hull. Often they knew little about what was going on above, though Captain Leach had a good reputation for keeping them informed by loud-speaker. At 9.45 that evening he announced what everyone must have known already, that the Prime Minister and the Chiefs of Staff were on board, and he revealed that they were heading for Little Placentia Bay, Newfoundland, for a meeting with President Roosevelt.

After leaving Scapa, Leach took the ship due west for several hours at a speed of 23 knots, until the Butt of Lewis lighthouse had disappeared astern. Then he turned slightly more to the north to 303 degrees, perhaps to take him farther away from the U-boat areas, perhaps to persuade any witnesses that he was heading for Iceland where there was an important British base. For most of the voyage the ship would be about 100 miles north of the ideal track for Newfoundland. The northern latitude would also give more daylight at this time of the year, making it more difficult for U-boats to operate.

As the passengers watched the last reel of the film in the wardroom, they began to notice that the ship was rolling more. On the bridge Leach felt the wind rising, from a gentle force 2 as they left Scapa, to a gale force 8 after nightfall. It was coming round to the north-west, almost ahead of the ship, which made conditions difficult for the smaller, more delicate ships of the destroyer escort. By midnight the force had to reduce speed to 18 knots, and Leach faced a serious decision. Should he proceed at the slower speed to allow the escort to stay in company? Or should he utilise the greater seaworthiness of the battleship and let the destroyers fall behind, leaving the *Prince of Wales*, carrying the most important set of passengers ever to cross the Atlantic, alone on the great ocean? It was not dangerous in the short term, for no U-boat could operate in these conditions. But what would happen when the wind moderated and the battleship was left alone and vulnerable? She had no asdic of her own to detect a submarine underwater, although her radar could detect one on the surface. Leach had no choice but to consult with his superior, the First Sea Lord, who was a cautious man. But at one in the morning the decision was taken. The three destroyers were allowed to part company and the battleship's speed was increased to 23 knots.

★ ★ ★

How dangerous was the ocean? U-boat tactics were determined by two main factors, both in the battleship's favour. First, the submarines operated at comparatively slow speeds, of 17 knots on the surface and about 7½ knots, for short periods, underwater. They were effective against merchant ship convoys which normally moved at between 7 and 10 knots, but the *Prince of Wales* was capable of 20 knots or more, except in bad weather. A shadowing U-boat would not be able to call in support, and there would be no time to move other boats into position to form a patrol line ahead of her as was done when a convoy was known to be in the area. Any U-boat that got within torpedo range would have to attack her straight away, as she would be out of sight very quickly. Even if there was an advance warning and a patrol line could be formed, it would have to be much more concentrated than was customary. Normally the boats were 15 to 20 miles apart, so that they could radio one another on sighting a convoy, and then move into position. There would be no time for that in this instance, and the boats would have to be close enough to get a shot in right away.

A U-boat torpedo had a range of up to 14,000 metres in extreme cases, but there was no guidance system and the chance of hitting a fast-moving, zigzagging target at that range was tiny. Realistically, the U-boat would have to be within about 3,000 metres of the target to have a reasonable prospect of a hit. This meant that the boats in a patrol line would have to be about 6,000 metres apart, instead of 15 miles. A patrol line of, say, a hundred miles would require 27 boats. It would be impossible to form it up close to the beginning and end of the battleship's route, where Allied air reconnaissance was intensive. In mid-voyage the possible routes covered an area more than 3,500 miles wide, so there would only be one chance in 35 of finding the target, without previous intelligence or reconnaissance.

If a patrol line was formed up after a sighting by an aircraft, normal U-boat practice was to assume the possibility of the convoy altering course by up to 30 degrees in either direction; the boats would then form a curved line about 180 to 200 miles ahead of the reported position. But even if there was time to form a line against a fast ship, it would have to be around 200 miles long, comprising more than 50 boats. In fact, no patrol line of any kind was likely to be formed without the British knowing something about it.

The second factor to the battleship's advantage was that U-boats relied heavily on long-range radio communication with their bases. It proved impossible to appoint a leader for a U-boat pack at sea, for he would often need to submerge and lose control of the situation. Very few boats left port with detailed orders, which were issued by radio once the boat was approaching an operational area. Moreover, unknown to the Germans, these Enigma signals could be decoded by the British, using the secret method known as Ultra. Unless the Germans had something very special and very secret up their sleeves, any attempt to intercept the *Prince of Wales* would quickly be detected.

As an extreme example, one might consider the possibility of the Germans knowing something about the voyage in advance and sending out a special force that would maintain radio silence and take up its positions. This would assume an intelligence source close to the centre of British affairs, which the Germans certainly did not have; and it would necessitate some knowledge of the route, which would be difficult since that was known to only a very few people and was continually subject to change in practice. Furthermore, the U-boats would have to leave well in advance, for at a maximum travel rate of 180 miles every 24 hours, submerged during daylight, it would take them at least five days to reach a possible interception position for the *Prince of Wales*. Any attempted mass exodus of boats from their bases would be spotted immediately by British reconnaissance aircraft and noted by resistance movements in France and Norway. It was not a realistic possibility.

There was always the very remote chance that the *Prince of Wales* might stumble across an isolated U-boat which had not sent a radio signal for some time. It would not be able to attack on the surface without being detected by radar, so it would have to get its shot in very quickly at as close a range as possible. But the naval authorities believed that even this could not sink the *Prince of Wales*. She had been designed with an anti-torpedo defence known as Side Protection System (SPS). Energy-absorbing compartments were fitted on each side under the waterline, filled with oil alternating with air, to absorb the blast of any torpedo. The admirals were confident that a battleship such as the *Prince of Wales* would need at least six torpedo hits to sink her, whereas a U-boat could only fire four from her bow tubes without retiring to reload. SPS had been tested on a rig in Portsmouth harbour in 1934 but it had not been tried in action.

★ ★ ★

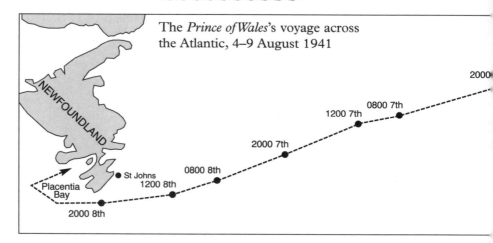

The *Prince of Wales*'s voyage across the Atlantic, 4–9 August 1941

For once, Churchill was ready to relax and he had brought some leisure reading matter with him. Oliver Lyttleton, now Minister of State in Egypt, had recommended the Hornblower novels of C. S. Forester, set in the Napoleonic Wars. He gave Churchill the omnibus edition *Captain Hornblower RN*, containing the first three books in the series, *The Happy Return*, *A Ship of the Line* and *Flying Colours*, and he read them in the tiny cabin high up in the *Prince of Wales*. All had been published before the war so none was a conscious allegory of the present circumstances, but it would be surprising if Churchill did not see parallels in them. The hero, Captain Horatio Hornblower, is a 'man alone', according to the author. He is usually to be found in command of a ship on a special mission, has little or no contact with higher authority, and so has to make his own decisions. His subordinates are loyal, brave, hard-working but unimaginative, and only his own resourcefulness and initiative can lead to success.

In *The Happy Return* the hero has to co-operate with *El Supremo*, a histrionic and sadistic Latin dictator, until a reversal of alliances in Europe enables him to overthrow him. In the next volume Hornblower's men raid the Spanish coast like World War II commandos taking the war to the enemy, and although he supports guerrillas, rather along the lines of resistance movements in occupied Europe, they are only successful under his leadership. In *Flying Colours* he recovers from defeat and isolation, as Churchill did in the 1930s. Napoleon Bonaparte, a far more powerful, cold-blooded and efficient tyrant than *El Supremo*, orders Hornblower's execution in a fit of spite, but the hero escapes and returns home in triumph. He marries a tall, intelligent and well-connected woman not unlike Clementine Churchill. There is still a war to be fought but Hornblower is now in a good position to conduct it.

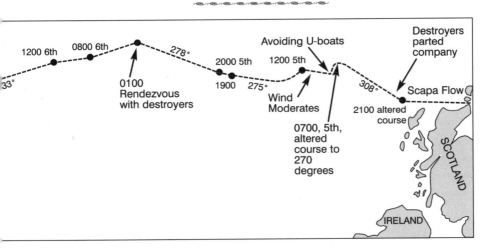

One thing that disturbed Churchill in his cabin was the constant calling over the ship's Tannoy or loudspeaker. This continued during the night, for example when a new watch was summoned to duty at midnight and 4 a.m. He asked Commander Thompson to look into it, but the Tannoy was needed to raise the men from their hammocks. 'The only alternative as far as this ship is concerned would be a large number of bosun's mates and call boys who would have to go round the mess decks waking men up.' For safety reasons it was not possible to cut off the Tannoy in Churchill's cabin, so the officers agreed to reduce the amount of broadcasting as far as possible. But Churchill needed the Tannoy himself. In the absence of his valet Sawyers he tended to use his bodyguard in the role and the call 'Inspector Thompson aft to the Prime Minister's cabin' was often heard throughout the day.

For meals and recreation, the Prime Minister's inner circle took over the warrant officers' mess, situated near midships, and Churchill found that it was without doubt 'the most comfortable place in the ship'. The warrant officers themselves were displaced into the wardroom, so Inspector Thompson's segregation was nullified. Churchill tried his hand at playing darts in the mess, but those provided were not to his satisfaction. He bought new ones from the shop on board and presented them to the mess.

Churchill also found time to do a little work. During the voyage he drafted a memo on petrol rationing. Civilians issued with extra fuel were obliged to keep a log of its use, or face prosecution. Was it wise, he asked the Home Secretary, to criminalise respectable members of society in this way? He queried the tables produced by the Minister of Aircraft Production, urged General Ismay of the Ministry of Defence to take action for the defence of aerodromes, and wrote to the Chairman of the Import Executive about ways to make the maximum use of shipping space.

A replica of the Map Room in the Cabinet War Rooms off Whitehall had been set up in the ship's staff offices by Captain Richard Pim, a former Northern Ireland civil servant who was also a commander in the Ulster Division of the part-time Royal Naval Volunteer Reserve. He had been attached to the Admiralty at the beginning of the war and on his second day as First Sea Lord, Churchill ordered him to set up a room close to his office in which he could follow the progress of the naval war. Pim was promoted to captain in May 1940, and almost immediately joined Churchill in Downing Street, extending his activities to the air and sea war. Wearing his naval peaked cap, Pim was tall and handsome, though the bald head concealed under it was hardly fashionable at the time. He was to accompany Churchill on most of his long-distance voyages, and would be with him at his last moments as wartime Prime Minister.

The Map Room was much admired by H. V. Morton:

They had taken over an office in the ship for the purpose. An enormous map of the Atlantic Ocean occupied one wall. It was lit by strip lights. The opposite wall bore large maps of the Russian front. The officers in charge were busily engaged all day in filing war cables and marking up the maps to correspond with them. The position of every ship, warships and merchant ships alike, and the position of every known U-boat, were plotted hour by hour upon the huge map of the Atlantic Ocean … Most impressive to see were the great convoys crossing the Atlantic, sixty or seventy little red ships escorted by grey ships lying in a wide space of open water.

Captain Pim would read a message, bring it over to the map, work out the longitude and latitude, and quietly place a couple of black coffins in the path of the convoy … It was interesting to follow the fortunes of, say, a convoy approaching England.

Churchill visited the Map Room each day after his afternoon nap and he surprised Morton, who had just referred to a U-boat being sunk. 'Only British submarines are sunk,' he said with a smile. 'German U-boats are – *destroyed*!'[6]

★ ★ ★

The wind began to moderate during the morning of Tuesday 5 August. At 6.20 there was a report of a U-boat 40 miles ahead, disguised as a sailing ketch. This is a little mysterious, though it was believed by many people, including the *Prince of Wales*'s navigating officer. Disguise was not a common tactic of U-boats at that time. Exactly how did it go about it? Where did it find the masts and sails that it would need? How would it crash-dive in the event of being spotted by an aircraft? What, in any case, would a small sailing vessel be doing in the middle of the ocean in wartime? Or was it all part of a complex scheme to disguise the fact that it had been detected by Ultra, the decoder of German signals? This was the best-kept secret of the war, and of those on board the battleship, only Churchill and the Chiefs of Staff were privy to it.

Certainly there was real evidence of a U-boat there, and it had to be avoided. The *Prince of Wales* turned west, then three hours later to the south and finally back to the south-west to give it a wide berth. But British intelligence knew that there were not many U-boats in the north at that moment. Most were heading for positions off the coast of Spain and Portugal to attack the convoys to Gibraltar. Convoy OG 70 was already passing that way and later OG 71 would be heavily attacked and lose seven ships, an event described vividly by Nicholas Monsarrat in *The Cruel Sea*.

Churchill rose late at 9.30 that morning, but 'seemed quite content to forget about what is going on elsewhere and simply to enjoy himself'. The Chiefs of Staff assembled for their daily meeting an hour later, joined by Hollis and Jacob from the Ministry of Defence. A telegram had been received, mostly containing political matters which were of no interest to the Chiefs. A second one arrived in the morning, containing a news bulletin that was short and to the point. After lunch and a short nap the Chiefs resumed their deliberations at four in the afternoon. The Prime Minister joined them, 'in very skittish form'. He and Harry Hopkins settled down at one end of the room and listened to the 'dulcet tones' of the BBC announcer Bruce Belfrage. Jacob was not impressed with progress as they stopped work at 7 o'clock, having done very little work.

There was, however, one urgent matter. It became clear to those left behind that the news of the voyage had leaked out through German sources in neutral Portugal. Their Transozean Radio announced that Churchill and Roosevelt were to meet somewhere in the Western Hemisphere in the near future. This was vague enough, and there was no real chance of moving extra U-boats into the area concerned during the outward passage. The battleship *Tirpitz* was another prospect with her 15-inch guns and a speed of 29 knots. It did not worry Churchill, who rather hoped the enemy might come out and 'have a dart at him' – though in fact she was not ready for action.

After dinner there was the usual film show. It began with footage of Harry Hopkins arriving in Moscow, which Churchill greeted with a cry of 'Oh, there you are, Harry. Bravo! Bravo!' The main film, *Comrade X*, was an unfortunate choice in the circumstances. It had been made in 1940 before the German invasion turned the Soviets into allies and heroes. Based on the success of the comedy *Ninotchka* starring Greta Garbo, it featured Clark Gable as an American reporter in the Soviet Union and Hedi Lamarr as a traditional communist who not surprisingly falls in love with him. Cadogan 'had to apologise to HH for any reflection on his new friends', though for once he was silent about the quality of the film. Churchill, however, 'displayed great enthusiasm throughout'.

★ ★ ★

Early in the morning of Wednesday 6 August, Captain Leach ordered an alteration of course to the west-south-west, to meet three destroyers which had been ordered out from Iceland. Cadogan was on deck by 18.35 to see three Canadian ships, the *Assiniboine*, *Restigouche* and *Ripley*, which had succeeded in finding them at a prearranged rendezvous, despite fog that had come down during the morning. Cadogan was impressed. 'They were 3 mins. ahead of time, and found us in mid-Atlantic, in a patch of fog!' In the more expert opinion of Lieutenant-Commander Rowell, it was 'an achievement reflecting credit on the destroyers' navigation'. Course was altered to 233 degrees to give a more direct route to Newfoundland and the ships groped through the fog for the rest of the day.

With destroyers in company, it was possible to send signals again. Churchill drafted a message to the Deputy Prime Minster, Clement Attlee. He was not concerned about the leakage of news of the voyage, but ministers should be vague if asked questions about it. He was equally sanguine about German attack on the way home, for he relished the prospect of a naval battle, however remote. 'About *Tirpitz* I fear there will be no such luck. Have no doubt Roosevelt will see us out to sea on the return journey.' In addition, the Foreign Secretary was to be 'very stiff' about Free French demands in the Middle East.

Churchill wandered about the decks during the day, and found more to criticise in the design of the *Prince of Wales* and her sisters. She was equipped with hangars and a catapult for launching two low-performance Supermarine Walrus aircraft, which could be used for reconnaissance. Churchill was concerned that they were sited near the centre of the ship, undermining the concept of a heavily armoured area round the engines, guns and magazines. 'Merely for the sake of having a couple of low quality aircraft, the whole principle of the citadel so well exemplified in the *Nelson* and the *Rodney* has been cast aside ... Although it looked very progressive to be able to fly two aeroplanes off a battleship, the price paid in the rest of the design was altogether excessive.'

The Chiefs of Staff continued to meet in what became a very long day, as the clock was put back half an hour at 2 p.m., 5 p.m. and 7 p.m. The only compensation was that extra tea was served. When not on deck or in his cabin, Churchill continued to sit at the other end of the room listening to the radio with Hopkins and Cherwell. Jacob was still unimpressed with the work done, though he conceded that the Chiefs of Staff would benefit from a good rest. At other times Cherwell strolled the deck wearing a yachting cap at an unusual angle and occasionally buttonholing one of the Chiefs for a long discussion of figures, when the officer concerned merely wanted to go off for his afternoon sleep. He was 'not entirely popular'.

Over dinner that night with the Prime Minister's party, Harry Hopkins produced a tub of 'admirable caviare' given to him by Stalin. That was combined with grouse to produce 'a very good dinner', satisfying even the sophisticated palate of Cadogan. Churchill commented, 'It was very good to have such caviare, even though it meant fighting with the Russians to get it.' When Hopkins refused a second brandy, the Prime Minister referred to America's recent history of prohibition. 'I hope, as we approach the U. S., you are not going to become more temperate.'

The film that night was *The Devil and Miss Jones,* which had rather less political relevance than the previous ones. The *Prince of Wales* had no skilled cinema operator and the performances were not entirely slick. There was only one projector, so there was always a gap as reels were changed. During these intervals Churchill turned to those nearest to him and said 'Jolly good', or asked 'What do you think about it?', or had popular records such as *Mad Dogs and Englishmen* and the more recent *Franklin D. Roosevelt Jones* played on the wardroom gramophone. He sang along, and knew every word. Often there was further delay as a reel was put in wrong and the characters appeared upside-down or in reverse. The film itself was a light comedy to Churchill's taste. A fabulously rich man, played by Charles Coburn, takes a job in one of his own department stores to find out more about trade union activity. Critics were much kinder to the film than they had been to *Comrade X,* and it had two Oscar nominations. Cadogan was not impressed. 'Bad,' he wrote tersely in his diary. Even the more generous Morton felt that it 'did not impress all of us', despite Churchill's evident pleasure and relaxation.

★   ★   ★

The fog continued during 7 August, and that afternoon the *Prince of Wales* had to alter course to avoid a ship which had been detected by radar. The Chiefs of Staff met again that morning for an hour and three quarters, during which Sir Dudley Pound slowly read out a statement on discussions between the British, Dutch and Americans at Singapore. Dill showed his discontent by asking questions ranging from 'What kind of aeroplanes have the Japanese got?' to 'What is the food like in the wardroom?' After that they decided to give themselves a free afternoon. At seven that evening the fog finally cleared, to give good visibility for the rest of the passage. By this time Churchill was keen to press ahead at full speed and reach Newfoundland the following evening, which was within the ship's capacity. Sir Dudley Pound was more mindful of naval protocol and the danger of arriving too early. According to Cadogan he was 'equally (but silently) determined that we *shan't!*'

Meanwhile Morton took the opportunity to find out more about the ship. The whole philosophy of his writings was based on the belief that technology was corrupting mankind, so he was sceptical about the *Prince of Wales's* equipment.

> I came upon young men in duffel coats sitting before a bewildering array of instruments: dials, clocks, handles, levers, bell-pushes and the like. That is modern war ... It is a place where, on the principle of ringing for afternoon tea and with no greater effort, a young man can pull a lever or press a button and send several tons of high explosive into the sky. The labour-saving devices of Death are remarkable. While Nelson's seamen, stripped naked to the waist, man-handled their tethered guns and lit them with fire, the modern gunner picks up a telephone, receives his orders and presses a button. No more physical effort is involved in firing a broadside from the *Prince of Wales* than in ringing the vicarage bell.

He was more impressed to hear that, moments before the action with the *Bismarck* began, the captain had allowed the chaplain to read a famous prayer over the Tannoy:

> O Lord, Thou knowest how busy we must be today, if we forget Thee, do not Thou forget us; for Christ's sake. Amen.[7]

Morton looked in on 'Captain's Requests', where men came forward one by one to ask for various privileges. He was mystified when one sailor asked for 'Permission to grow, sir', until he was told that he wanted to grow a beard. He went to the ship's bakery where 1,500 loaves were produced every day, and was shown the ship's cats, for she had been infested with rats since her dry-docking after the *Bismarck* affair.

After the quietest day of the trip the wardroom settled down to watch *The High Sierra* starring the up-and-coming Humphrey Bogart. It was 'Awful bunk', according to Cadogan. After it ended in a bloodbath, Churchill rose from his seat with the ambiguous comment, 'And a good time was had by all!' Colonel Jacob had thought they had reached rock bottom with the last film, but this one was worse.

★   ★   ★

As the sun rose at six in the morning of 8 August, the hands were called to action stations as usual. Two hours later Lieutenant-Commander Rowell plotted the ship's position, 240 miles from Cape Race on the south-eastern tip of Newfoundland. The course was altered to 242 degrees to bring the ship closer. Soon the waters became congested with stragglers from convoys which had recently left Halifax, and the *Prince of Wales* had to alter course several times to avoid them. Fortunately the weather was still clear and there was no serious risk of collision.

The passengers were also aware of the approach to land, and what they would have to do after the ship anchored. The bad news was broken to Morton and Spring that they would not be allowed to report the voyage as they had expected. Spring took it philosophically; Morton felt that to remain silent about such a dramatic story would be 'desperately hard'.

That afternoon passengers and crew were involved in a rehearsal for the President's arrival on board the *Prince of Wales*. Sir Alexander Cadogan took on the role of Roosevelt, and was rather diffident in it. He had to stand at the top of the gangway and raise his hat to represent the moment when he arrived on board. About a hundred of the ship's Royal Marines were drawn up in ranks, and the band played *The Star-Spangled Banner*. The ceremony was carefully arranged to take account of Roosevelt's extreme difficulty in walking. The Prime Minister shook his hand first, followed by the Chiefs of Staff; then every officer down to the rank of commander was to march up to him one by one and shake his hand. It took a long time to get it right, and the ship's speed of up to 27 knots created a bitterly cold wind. Inspector Thompson, still combining the role of valet and bodyguard, was concerned about the effect on the Prime Minister and went to his cabin to get his overcoat.

After some time it was judged that all was well, the marines were dismissed and the party broke up.

For the last night of the voyage out, Churchill returned to the naval theme. He had chosen his favourite film – Alexander Korda's *Lady Hamilton,* starring Hollywood's hottest couple of the day, Laurence Olivier and Vivien Leigh. He had already seen it four times since June, and it might have been more. On his last night at Chequers before embarking on the voyage, he had suddenly exclaimed after dinner, 'I don't want to do any more tonight. I want to see that film again of Nelson and Lady Hamilton!' The cinema operators had already been sent home, but Churchill ordered that the local police be contacted to recall them. He was unsuccessful and instead he worked until 2 a.m.

Howard Spring was not impressed with the film, which he saw as 'a tribute to Hollywood's skill in grafting a whole body of illusion on to a bone or two of fact'. It tended to get tiny details right, such as the name of the hotel Nelson stayed in after his return to London from the Mediterranean, but it was wildly inaccurate in many other ways. It showed Big Ben chiming 50 years before it was built. It had Nelson covering up his blind eye to avoid offending Lady Hamilton, in a way that he never did. Lady Hamilton appeared as 'a beautiful woman who looked, all through the film, about twenty years old', instead of 'a loose woman well past her prime'. Her husband Sir William was grossly caricatured and nothing was shown of Nelson's great regard for him. Worst of all in Spring's eyes, Nelson's blameless and loving wife was shown as 'a thin-lipped shrew and prig from whom any man would be glad to escape, not as a woman whose life had known much sorrow and suffering, not the least through Nelson's acts'.

It is a little odd that Churchill, a happily married man whose wife was a great support to him, should be so fond of a film which celebrates adultery. He was a historian himself but tolerant of the film's inaccuracies. At one stage Nelson addresses his superiors on the Board of Admiralty:

Napoleon cannot be master of the world until he has smashed us up – and believe me, gentlemen, he means to smash us up. You cannot make peace with dictators. Wipe them out![8]

The passage was so Churchillian that the scriptwriter had to deny that it was written by the great man himself, and the director was summoned before a Congressional Committee to answer accusations of being a British agent. Fortunately by the date set, December 12, the world had changed.

Most of all, however, Churchill was affected by the fine acting, the tragic love story set against great events and the defence of Britain against a continental tyrant. Everyone close to him in the room noticed that tears were streaming down his cheeks as the distraught Lady Hamilton was told of her lover's death at the Battle of Trafalgar.

The film ended, the lights went up and Churchill rose. There are several versions of what he actually said to the wardroom, but as a civil servant used to taking minutes, Cadogan must be considered the most reliable witness. 'Gentlemen, I thought this film would interest you, showing great events similar to those in which you have been taking part.' The audience dispersed, equally moved. Churchill stayed up playing backgammon and lost seven guineas (£7.35) to Harry Hopkins.

★ ★ ★

As usual, Captain Leach was on the bridge dealing with the hazards as they approached Newfoundland. The ship was south of Cape Race by nine on the evening of the 8th, and altered course to the west soon afterwards. At three in the morning of the 9th it turned to the north-north-west to head direct for Placentia Bay and by 6 a.m. it was off Cape St Mary where an escort of American destroyers was expected. They arrived an hour and a half later and an officer came on board with berthing details in the bay. It was half an hour before the reason for the apparent lateness was understood – the American ships were operating in a different time zone, an hour and a half behind Newfoundland time. It was awkward, but the huge battleship had to turn through 180 degrees in the narrow channel and steam backwards and forwards to kill time. Obligingly, the British ships put their clocks back an hour and a half, making another long day.

At last, at 8.40 in the new time, the group of ships entered what looked to many rather like a Scottish loch, guided appropriately by the American destroyer *MacDougall*. Although Roosevelt had come in a humble cruiser, he had brought other ships with him including the battleship *Arkansas*, the cruiser *Tuscaloosa* and a flotilla of destroyers. They were anchored in lines and the Americans seemed at home opposite their half-built naval base. The destroyer led the *Prince of Wales* to an anchorage opposite the *Augusta*, but the Americans were still prepared to defer to the British in the matter of protocol. Their ships' boats flew the Stars and Stripes from their sterns, which they only did in a foreign harbour.

Churchill took up his position with the Chiefs of Staff aft on the quarterdeck, wearing his quasi-naval blue suit and yachting cap. Roosevelt stood in a

49

less traditional but more prominent position under an awning just forward of the bridge, where his light brown 'Palm Beach' suit stood out among the mass of blue uniforms. The Royal Marine band struck up *The Star-Spangled Banner* and the American ships replied with *God Save the King*. Captain Leach ordered the release of the cable and with a rattle of chain and a splash the anchor entered the water, which was 14½ fathoms deep at that point. Churchill's first wartime voyage outside Europe was complete.

III

Good Voyage, Churchill

As soon as the *Prince of Wales* was anchored, Roosevelt's aide, Captain Beardall, arrived on board to discuss arrangements; then Harry Hopkins went to the *Augusta* to report to the President. There was a hitch when the Americans heard about the presence to the two writers, and it had to be explained that they were not allowed to publish anything. Churchill left the ship at 11 a.m. in one of the boats, to go over to the *Augusta*. He was well aware that he was only a head of government while the President was a head of state, so he bore a letter of introduction from the King, offering best wishes and expressing the hope that Roosevelt would agree that Churchill was 'a very remarkable man'. The Prime Minister was led into another slight diplomatic error, when he acted as if it was the first time the two had met. In fact they had already met in 1918 when Roosevelt was a junior navy minister, which Roosevelt remembered and Churchill did not. After being introduced to various dignitaries such as General Marshall of the US Army and Admiral Stark of the Navy, the Prime Minister went off for a private lunch with the President. Roosevelt found him 'a tremendously vital person' and, lunching alone with him, 'broke the ice both ways'. That evening the Prime Minister and the Chiefs of Staff returned to the *Augusta* for dinner, during which Harry Hopkins discussed his visit to Russia and helped persuade both leaders that aid to the beleaguered country was a priority. Churchill then delivered his overview of the war, not at his best as an orator but impressing his audience with the range of his thinking.

Next day was Sunday and it was the British turn to act as hosts. At eleven there was a combined church service on the quarterdeck of the *Prince of Wales*, conducted by a British and an American naval chaplain. British and American sailors mingled, and the flags were draped over the pulpit. Even the hymns were perfectly balanced – *Onward Christian Soldiers* for the armies, *Eternal Father Strong to Save* for the navies, and *O God Our Help in Ages Past* to offer 'hope for years to come.' Churchill associated its words with John Hampden, the seventeenth-century defender of English liberty and an ancestor of British and American democracy. He was not particularly religious but regarded the service as 'a deeply moving expression of the unity of faith of our two peoples'. As a journalist, Morton had watched many great events including the victory parade after the First World War, the funeral of King George V and the coronation of his successor. He rated this among them. 'Now, as the voices rose and fell, a situation that was almost intolerable in its uncalculated emotionalism reached breaking point.'

When they got down to business, it soon became obvious that Roosevelt was not going to offer anything dramatic. As Churchill reported: 'It was clear at once that, on consideration, the President had decided that he would be unable to give an assurance that he would go to Congress for authority to give armed support.' He had proposed, however, some kind of joint declaration of principles, which Churchill considered a 'most hopeful suggestion'. They duly began work on a document that became known as the Atlantic Charter.

Churchill confirmed that Britain had no major secret deals with other countries, a practice that had bedevilled peacemaking after the last war and was anathema in America. By the morning of the 11th the two had agreed a document with seven clauses. Neither power was seeking any territorial gain from the war, which was important in view of American suspicion of the British Empire, and Churchill's enthusiasm for it. Territorial changes would be in accordance with the wishes of the peoples concerned. They would 'respect the rights of all peoples to choose the form of government under which they will live', which was carefully worded to avoid causing the immediate dissolution of the British Empire. They would allow free access to markets, they would work towards safety on the high seas, and pledged that the future world would 'be guided in the spirit of the abandonment of the use of force'. Most important of all in Churchill's eyes, the document looked towards 'the final destruction of Nazi tyranny' and the days when all nations would live in peace and security within their own boundaries.

Paragraph 4, on free access to markets, caused the most difficulty, as it might be interpreted as contrary to the Ottawa Agreement about free trade within the British Empire and Commonwealth. Churchill had the clause 'with due respect to their existing obligations' added, and 'trade' substituted for 'markets' to tone it down. Lord Beaverbrook, the newspaper owner and Minister of Supply, arrived by air on the same day. As a Canadian the issue was of great importance to him, and he later implied that he had some part in the changes, although his late arrival suggests that this was unlikely.

Apart from the Atlantic Charter, Churchill wanted a firm joint declaration against Japanese expansion in the Pacific, but Roosevelt was not prepared to make a direct threat of war. Instead they produced a system of 'parallel communications' that also involved the Dutch government-in-exile, which claimed control of Indonesia. It threatened only 'counter-measures which might lead to war'.

Churchill was more satisfied with another aspect of the talks. It was agreed that the United States Navy would take over convoy escort in the western Atlantic, freeing more than 50 British and Canadian ships for other work. Privately Churchill also hoped it would lead to an act of provocation by the Germans, to which the Americans would have to respond. Furthermore, if the Germans moved into Spain and Portugal, an Anglo-American force would seize their Atlantic islands, which would make very valuable bases. Meanwhile the British Chiefs of Staff discussed military matters with their American counterparts, and voiced contradictory opinions on how ready the Americans were for war.

In the afternoon Churchill went ashore to the beautiful but sparsely populated coast with a small party. He was in a playful mood again, climbing over rocks, throwing stones down a cliff and collecting a bunch of wild flowers, until the party came back on board at 5.45 after being caught in a short, sharp shower of rain. Spring and Howard went ashore next day, with the Paymaster-Commander of the ship. They had become intensely bored, for they were not allowed to visit the *Augusta* and were tired of watching ships' boats going to and fro. Howard believed that the health of a society was centred in its villages, but that was strained in the wastes of Newfoundland. 'The shops of Placentia … were nothing more than wooden shacks or the bottom storeys of ordinary houses with nothing inside one could possibly require. There were not more than six or seven of them. Nearly everything in the shops came from the United States or Canada.'

Churchill felt he needed the support of the War Cabinet for the Atlantic Charter, and it had to be done quickly if he was to sail on the 12th as he intended. He therefore demanded a maximum effort from the Admiralty to decode his telegrams during the next 24 hours. The text of the charter was complete by two in the afternoon (5.30 London time), but it was midnight before it had been coded, transmitted and then decoded. Most of the Cabinet had gone to bed but an emergency meeting was convened. Anthony Eden, the Foreign Secretary, was wakened at two in the morning by a telegram bearing the words 'Attend to at once!' He was furious to read: 'A terribly woolly document full of all the old clichés of the League of Nations period.' There was some discussion on paragraph 4 and an amendment was sent. Churchill thanked the War Cabinet for their 'amazingly swift reply'. He put the amendment to Roosevelt who preferred to stick to the original, although Churchill could not see any real difference. The President agreed to an extra clause on social security inserted by the Cabinet, where the Labour members were predominant in the absence of Churchill and Beaverbrook. The agreement was signed early in the afternoon of the 12th. Churchill returned to the *Prince of Wales* at 3 o'clock, and the ship made ready to sail. Ian Jacob had feared that they might be there for several more days awaiting the Cabinet response, and was pleased to be off.

★ ★ ★

Relieved of the pressure of preparing for the conference, Sir Dudley Pound began to take increasing interest in planning the voyage home, which Ian Jacob suggests led to some conflict with the captain – traditionally an admiral should leave the running of his flagship to the captain, and only intervene if he felt something was seriously wrong. It was clear that the Germans knew about the meeting, and some action might be expected against the return voyage. On the 10th a Sloane signal had reported that little was known about U-boat movements since the attack on convoy SL 81 from Freetown in West Africa to Britain, when five ships out of 18 were sunk. Radio direction finding had identified two boats some way to the south of Iceland in the last 36 hours, so it was possible that an attack was being built up on the northern route from Newfoundland, possibly with the *Prince of Wales* in mind. In view of that, it was preferable to go still farther north of the convoy routes, passing close to Iceland. As well as evading the known U-boats, this would make it easier to provide destroyer escorts which could refuel in Iceland. The signal left open the possibility of a visit to Iceland itself, which was an important British base. But on the 13th, prior to leaving, Churchill telegraphed his deputy Attlee to say that he was sailing for 'Iceland (C)'. Some time ago he had decreed that the C should be included in all signals, to prevent confusion with Ireland, which had an R after it.

There was great activity on the decks of the battleship on the afternoon of the 12th, as she got ready to sail. Boats were hoisted in, skylights were closed and all the preparations for sea were made. At five in the afternoon, the *Prince of Wales* began to weigh anchor, under a cloudy sky with some drizzle. The marine guard and band fell in on the quarterdeck, along with all the seamen who were not immediately needed for setting sail. Salutes were given and the band played 'various tunes to enliven the occasion'. The *Prince of Wales* quickly got up to a speed of about 20 knots, but reduced it when passing an anchored destroyer. A couple of following American destroyers were not informed about this and came within a hundred yards of the stern of the battleship before swerving violently. Then there was 'another excitement' when the helm of the Canadian destroyer *Reading* jammed and she headed towards the battleship's bows. Captain Leach ordered his engines put in full astern, and the two ships missed by 40 or 50 yards – 'a narrow squeak', according to Jacob.

The group got out of the bay and turned on to a course of 220 degrees to take it clear of the island. The ships' clocks were put forward two hours as soon as they sailed, so it was dinnertime almost immediately after afternoon tea. Two American destroyers, the *Rhind* and *Mayrant,* steamed ahead with Franklin D. Roosevelt Jr on board as liaison officer. In view of American neutrality they were not regarded as a protective screen. The official story was that they were on the way to Iceland anyway, to support American troops there. Their instructions were complex and ambiguous. They were to 'Consider any submarine or other potentially hostile forces contacted, visual or sound, to be a threat unless positive evidence to the contrary apparent. Destroy hostile forces that threaten action addressed. Do not take part in action concerning only belligerents' – i.e. an attack on the *Prince of Wales* or her escorts that did not involve any threat to the American forces. They were to steam 5,000 yards ahead by day, and drop back to 2,000–3,000 yards by night, forcing any enemy submarines to get down as they approached. The actual escort was provided by the Canadian destroyers *Reading, Ripley, Assiniboine* and *Saguenay.*

The wind was a moderate force 2 which caused no difficulty to the passengers, but zigzagging was too much for the destroyers and it was abandoned during the night. On the 13th the captain broadcast to the ship's company, telling them that they were going back via Iceland, and warning them to keep a specially good lookout against submarines and aircraft, as the Germans probably knew that they had sailed. There were no meetings that day, and the army officers Jacob and Dykes had a tour of the ship conducted by Captain Schofield of the Admiralty Trade Division. Jacob was impressed by the bridge, the galley with its well-arranged steam coppers, oil-fired ovens, and vegetable steamers, and the bakery with its electric baking ovens.

Churchill rested again during the voyage back. His constant climbing of ladders to the admiral's sea cabin had damaged his leg and he later developed a cold. When Surgeon-Commander Quinn of the ship's medical staff was called on to treat him, he advised, rather obviously, that he had been smoking too many cigars. He had known that for years, replied the Prime Minister. He summoned the young stenographer Patrick Kinna to his cabin on the 16th to take dictation. He began: 'This is a melancholy story', and the stenographer, thinking he was making general conversation, said, 'I am so sorry.' Churchill barked at him to take it down; it was the beginning of a letter to the Air Ministry and the Ministry of Aircraft Production about the supply of Grumman aircraft to the navy's carriers. He also found time to comment at length on a speech by General Franco that suggested an increasingly anti-British policy in Spain; the difficulties of the commando regiments; and the design of future battleships in the light of his experience in the *Prince of Wales*. He spent time playing backgammon with Harry Hopkins again, and lost 32 Canadian dollars. Hopkins commented, 'The Prime Minister's backgammon game is not of the best. He likes to play what is known to backgammon addicts as a "back game". As a matter of fact, he won two or three very exciting games from me by these tactics. He approaches the game with great zest, doubling and redoubling freely.'

The films were, if anything, more lowbrow than last time, and they had an unfavourable reception from much of the audience, at least in their private accounts. Perhaps the low point was on the night of the 13th when the Surgeon Commander began to wonder if he should have kept Churchill longer in bed as he watched Laurel and Hardy in *Saps at Sea*. Jacob concluded that Laurel and Hardy should never be allowed to make a long film. Cadogan (who in fact had chosen it as an alternative to the drama that Churchill liked) considered it 'appalling slapstick'. The Prime Minister ended the evening by announcing it was 'a gay but inconsequential entertainment', and went straight to bed.

★   ★   ★

This time the danger from U-boats was greater than ever, for German intelligence was expecting the return voyage. The ship steered quite a complex course on the way to Iceland. One priority was to spend as little time as possible in the 'air gap' when cover from aircraft based in either Labrador or Iceland was not available. This meant steaming north-east for a time in the general direction of the southern tip of Greenland, on a course of 20 degrees. The ship altered course to 57 degrees in the morning of the 14th, before the most dangerous period began early that afternoon. It went on to 36 degrees at half past six that evening because of the latest U-boat intelligence. This was in addition to the usual zigzags. Sometimes standard patterns as laid down in the book were used, sometimes the ship was kept turning for two to four minutes until she was heading 30 degrees on one side of the course, then the process was reversed. Thus she was never on a straight course, and a torpedo fired at long range would take several minutes to reach its target. The destroyers often had difficulty with the zigzags and were sometimes allowed to steer a straight course.

There was a good deal of expectation among the passengers as some kind of naval action seemed more than possible. Morton was not happy at the thought of another six days in cabin 27, but that was only part of his worries:

I also wondered how my nerves would stand up to a naval action, for everyone was now anticipating with some pleasure a battle on the way home; at least, everyone except myself. Some thought U-boats would lay in wait for us; others thought long-range bombers; a few enthusiasts thought U-boats and long-range bombers, and I was inclined to throw the *Tirpitz* and a few cruisers in as well.[1]

He made a point of wearing his life-belt, which he called his 'Mae West', though it was not the same type as the garment worn by the RAF and named after the raunchy film star. The naval life-belt was worn round the waist and Morton found that he could keep it under his waistcoat, 'the slight abdominal swelling hardly noticeable'. He practised 'abandon ship' in his cabin, 'flinging off my dinner jacket and inflating my Mae West until I was encircled by a warm and consoling tyre'. But British intelligence knew that the *Tirpitz* was still working up in the Baltic, and either Ultra or photo reconnaissance would quickly tell them if there was any change.

On the night of the 14th, at the most dangerous point of the voyage, the officers settled down in the wardroom to listen to a radio broadcast by Clement Attlee, the Deputy Prime Minister. For the first time they heard the terms of the Atlantic Charter which was the main outcome of the trip. Attlee was deliberately misleading when he said that the President and Prime Minister had met somewhere at sea, and this was hailed with cries of 'No!' and 'We don't believe it!' Then he read out the clauses of the charter, and as Morton observed:

Faces grew long with disappointment as Mr Attlee proceeded, and the exciting rumours set about by Mr Churchill's Atlantic journey were all deflated in an atmosphere of anti-climax … What we had all subconsciously hoped for, and not, perhaps, entirely subconsciously, was a declaration that America was coming into battle with us; the only thing that seemed to us to justify the dramatic encounter in the Atlantic between the two statesmen. In comparison, words, no matter how admirable, were a disappointment.[2]

Some of the officers tried to keep up their spirits by suggesting that the agreement was like an iceberg, with its largest part invisible.

The ship went back to close to its old course of 58 degrees at 6.39 in the morning of the 15th. It was soon joined by a new escort, the destroyers *Tartar*, *Punjabi* and *Escapade*, out of Iceland. The Canadian *Assiniboine* and *Saguenay* stayed with the group. By this time they were approaching the end of the air gap, for a fast ship such as the *Prince of Wales* could pass through it quite quickly. A friendly Catalina flying-boat was sighted to the south-east at 12.50, followed by another at five to three in the afternoon.

★ ★ ★

Everyone in Europe and America knew that the Atlantic was the ocean upon which Britain's survival depended, that the supplies had to get through despite the efforts of the *Luftwaffe* and the U-boats. Even in peacetime, imports made up about half of Britain's food requirements, and in war she needed vast quantities of oil to keep her ships, tanks and aircraft operational. Military supplies from America, provided under lend-lease, were already essential to Britain's war effort. On average some 15 convoys were crossing the ocean at any given moment to this end. It was Captain Pim in the Map Room who first noticed that the *Prince of Wales* was coming close to one of them. A reconnaissance aircraft was ordered to look for it and found it at the second attempt.

Convoy HX 143 had left Halifax, Nova Scotia, in the afternoon of Tuesday 5 August, just as the *Prince of Wales* was settling down to its first night alone at sea. It was a relatively fast convoy, with a speed of 9 knots, so the voyage was neither as long drawn out nor as dangerous as one of the slower ones which did 7 knots. The convoy had not been attacked by U-boats, but Captain Shuttleworth, in charge of the naval escort, had some cause for frustration. His own ship, the armed merchant cruiser *Wolfe*, was a large converted merchantman fitted with a few 6-inch guns, and was too slow and clumsy to pursue U-boats. Traditionally the Royal Navy's greatest rivalry was with the merchant fleet, and a regular officer like Shuttleworth might be expected to share that feeling. But in fact the 72 merchant ships of HX 143 had behaved rather well. A few had to drop out because they were too slow to keep up, or because of steering defects. The commodore of the convoy had to warn three offenders about making too much smoke, and the *Empire Opal* showed an unauthorised light on the poop for two hours one evening, but on the whole the ships of the convoy had kept their stations. On the other hand, his warships, the corvettes *Mayflower*, *Levis* and *Agassiz*, and the ex-American destroyer *Burnham*, were fighting an ocean war they had not been designed for. They tended to pitch and roll almost uncontrollably in the Atlantic swell. They were crewed by hastily trained conscripts of the Royal Canadian Navy, which was in the process of expanding from a peacetime strength of 3,500 regulars and reservists, to more than 30,000 men by May 1942. One conventional British naval officer referred to them as 'travesties of warships', which were 'unbelievably dirty and unseaman-like' and whose discipline was 'weird and wonderful'. They were very different from the crack Canadian destroyers which had found the *Prince of Wales* so easily in a fog. The *Levis* had been become separated and had only rejoined that morning. The *Mayflower*'s anti-submarine installation was defective and she was not much use. Captain Shuttleworth found that the warships' signalling was slack, and their lookout was even worse.

It is not recorded who in the convoy first sighted a ship astern early in the evening of 15 August. It was soon identified as the British destroyer *Tartar*, and a much larger ship, the *Prince of Wales* herself, was soon in view with her complete escort of destroyers. The officers of the merchant ships were not briefed about what was happening. In the Bank Line ship *Aymeric*, fog had just begun to clear as an Indian lookout ran up to the officer of the watch. 'There emerging from the light fog on the starboard quarter was a battleship. She seemed huge and infinitely menacing but since the convoy was holding its course … and we had no orders I assumed she was friendly.'

The warships closed fast at a relative speed of 13 knots, and within an hour and a half the battleship was just astern of the convoy. (It might have been more appropriate, incidentally, had it been its predecessor, HX 142, which was escorted by the Canadian destroyer *Churchill*.) The Prime Minister had ordered a slight alteration of course so that the *Prince of Wales* could pass through the ships, between the columns which were 500 yards apart. It was not long since he had visited the bombed-out citizens of London and Bristol, the pilots of the Battle of Britain, the soldiers defending the country against invasion, and the men and women of aircraft factories and dockyards. Now his attention was focused upon the unsung, unseen heroes of the Atlantic, the men of the merchant navy.

Both Cadogan and Morton were reminded of an industrial town as they approached the convoy, with dozens of funnels pouring out a carefully controlled amount of smoke to avoid giving the position away. Meanwhile Churchill considered how to greet the crews. He wanted to make a flag signal saying 'The Prime Minister wishes you the best of luck', but there was no signal for 'Prime Minister' in the International Code which would be understood by merchant ships. 'The Chief Minister of State' was wide of the mark.

Commander Thompson suggested using the separate words 'church' and 'hill' but that was anathema to the Chief Yeoman of Signals, a petty officer of the old school who was in charge of the *Prince of Wales*'s flags. He recommended the three-letter hoist PYU which meant 'Good voyage', and the use of nine single-letter flags to spell out the word 'Churchill'. The Prime Minister himself stood on the bridge, waving his hat and making the famous V-sign with the fingers of his right hand. The ship entered the convoy between columns eight and nine, towards the starboard side of the twelve-column formation.

The merchant navy crews were already crowded on deck to see the great battleship come so close, and they reflected the Allied struggle as well as that of the British Empire. There were ships from the Netherlands, Norway and neutral Sweden. As well as British seamen there were lascar deckhands from India, Africans who worked in the engine rooms, Chinese who manned laundries. The officer of the *Aymeric* was aware of the differences in dress. 'My old cap and stained duffel coat were in sharp contrast with the impressive array of gold braid, full uniform, collar and ties.' The crews were even less formal. In contrast to the regular naval uniform to be found on a battleship, they were dressed in shirt sleeves or oily boiler suits, with battered blue peaked caps of the sailor, or the cloth caps of the industrial worker. They waved and cheered loudly as soon as they realised who was greeting them, though the words could not be heard in the *Prince of Wales*. The ships replied to the flag signal as best they could. Some tried to make the Morse letter V (dot dot dot dash) with their sirens but faltered on the dash. Some simply hoisted the V flag in the International Code, others dipped their ensigns.

The *Prince of Wales* sailed between the columns at a speed of 23 knots, 14 faster than the convoy. She passed close to ships like the *Empire Whale* owned by the Ministry of War Transport and carrying scrap steel to Manchester, and the Dutch *Gaasterkerk* of 8,679 tons. The tiny Norwegian cargo ship *Carmelfjell* of 1,334 tons had been forced to drop out of line the day before and was proceeding to Iceland alone. In striking contrast was the *Southern Empress* of 12,398 tons owned by the whaling company Salveson of Leith, which had been used as a factory ship and was now carrying fuel oil. The *City of Cardiff*, belonging to the Ellerman Line of London, had entered service at the end of the last war and during the great depression of the 1930s she had been laid up in the Gareloch off the Firth of Clyde with many other ships. A year from now she would be torpedoed and sunk off Cape Finisterre. Several of the ships, too, were visibly carrying American-built aircraft on their decks.

Having reached the head of the convoy, the *Prince of Wales* began a wide 180-degree turn to pass through again, between the fourth and fifth columns.

Morton thought this was for the Prime Minister's indulgence, but in fact he wanted the other half of the convoy to have an opportunity to see him. The process was thus repeated, although this time the battleship and her escorts were on an opposite course. They reached the end of the line, passing between the Swedish *Sydland* carrying iron ore to Loch Ewe, and the *Novelist*, a sister of the *Politician* which had sunk off the Scottish island of Eriskay earlier that year carrying a cargo of whisky. Like two other ships in the convoy she was fitted with a Hurricane fighter which could be catapulted into the air to shoot down enemy reconnaissance aircraft – a rather desperate measure brought on by the shortage of aircraft carriers.

Then, after half an hour in company with the convoy, the warships resumed their original course of 52 degrees, zigzagging again because of the U-boat menace in the vicinity of a large target. As they parted, some reflected on the dangers the convoy still faced. Cadogan wrote: 'It is disturbing to see what a target they offer, and how little protection they have.' Captain Shuttleworth enjoyed a certain amount of satisfaction when the First Sea Lord signalled to compliment the ships on their station keeping.

★ ★ ★

Several more friendly aircraft were seen during the night of the 15th to 16th, giving some reassurance. At 4.20 in the morning of the 16th, the coast of Iceland was sighted and three and a half hours later the ship prepared to enter the harbour of Hvalfjord 15 miles from the capital, Reykjavik. Even before the *Prince of Wales* had anchored, Churchill transferred to the *Assiniboine* for a tour of the island. He had recovered his energy after his illness and he crammed a great deal into a ten-hour visit. He was greeted at the quay at Reykjavik by the British Minister, Charles Howard Smith, and then in the summer sunshine he was driven through tumultuous crowds into the city. The islands had been occupied by the British in 1940 to forestall a German takeover, and their troops were not popular with the islanders, unlike the Americans who were beginning to relieve them. Apparently the unpopularity did not apply to Churchill. His private secretary recorded: 'There were crowds in the streets and remarkable enthusiasm, with cheering and clapping, said to be unusual among these stolid, undemonstrative people.' Churchill was taken to the Althinghaus, or parliament building, to be received by the Regent and Cabinet. He went on to the balcony to address the crowd and pay tribute to Iceland's thousand-year parliamentary tradition:

I am glad to have an opportunity to visit the nation which for so long has loved democracy and freedom. We, and later the Americans, have undertaken to keep war from your country. But you will realise that if we had not come others would.[3]

Again he had a tumultuous reception. Continuing the Anglo-American theme, he reviewed a parade of British and American troops with Franklin D. Roosevelt Jr standing by his side. Then he was driven round some of the sights of the island, including the hot springs which would some day be used to warm the capital. He took tea in the forces' headquarters and at 5.30 he again boarded a destroyer to visit the battleship *Ramillies* anchored in the harbour – she was a veteran of the First World War and a sister of the lost *Royal Oak*. The crew was roused from its afternoon rest and ordered to change into best blue uniforms. Churchill came on board 'stumping solidly forward' to the forecastle where the men were assembled. He called for a soap-box and spoke for a quarter of an hour, telling them that

the war would last for another three years at least and that hard times lay ahead. He told us we were carrying out one of the most vital jobs of the war in ensuring that the food and supplies without which Britain could not survive reached us from North America. He would not deny that this was one of the bleakest times in British history, but he was confident that we would survive, and with right on our side and help from our allies – a glance to the ensign here – we should win through to a great and glorious victory.[4]

There were cheers as he left the ship, but Churchill's anti-trade-union past was not forgotten. One Welsh sailor, a miner in his past life, said 'in a voice full of venom', 'There goes the bastard, back to his bloody brandy.' But perhaps he recognised Churchill's new role as a war leader, for he added, 'And the best of bloody luck to him.'

He also found time to visit the destroyer *Churchill*, with which he had a distant link. The ship was named after the town on Hudson's Bay in the Canadian province of Manitoba, but that in turn derived from his ancestor John Churchill First Duke of Marlborough; he had written a four-volume biography of him in the 1930s.

Meanwhile Morton and Spring went ashore to see the capital and were relieved to get away temporarily from the confinement of the ship. They were amazed at the sophistication of the city. It was not full of 'frozen inhabitants chewing blubber and driving reindeer', as they had expected, but seemed like 'a dazzling mixture of Paris and New York'. They found large numbers of bookshops, and fashionable blonde girls wearing silk stockings which were unobtainable in Britain. The sailors who got leave and could afford it stocked up on gifts for home.

★ ★ ★

Churchill came back on board the *Prince of Wales* at 7.55 in the evening, and the ship sailed nine minutes later to head for Scapa Flow. This time they went east, almost parallel to the coast of Iceland, and then headed south-west towards the Outer Hebrides, zigzagging as usual. That afternoon the Prime Minister visited the ship's 14 midshipmen in the gunroom where they lived, and answered questions about the war:

'Is Turkey coming into the War, sir?'
'What about the French Fleet, sir?'
'What do you make of Reynaud, sir?'
'Do you think America is coming in, sir?'
'What did the President say about …?'

Churchill employed his politician's skill and 'replied to some questions without actually answering them, but leaving the questioner with the happy impression that they had been answered'.

Early next morning they sighted their old friend Convoy HX 143, still making its way towards British ports by the northerly route. There was plenty of air cover that day as the ship altered course to avoid floating mines, and passed over the shallower waters of Bill Bailey's Bank. The Butt of Lewis lighthouse was sighted just after one in the morning and clocks were put forward to Greenwich Mean Time an hour later, as the *Prince of Wales* returned to familiar waters.

On the final morning of the trip, Captain Leach took the opportunity to exercise the ship's great 14-inch guns, and perhaps demonstrate them to a Prime Minister who was sceptical about their power. A tug towing a target had been sent out from Scapa to meet them. Traditionally Y turret in the stern was manned by the Royal Marines, and Colonel Hollis was proud to invite Jacob to watch his corps at work. Unfortunately someone failed to follow procedure and cordite charges, each weighing about 100 lbs, had to be hauled up by hand through complicated passages. They could only be got up for two of the guns, so only half those in the turret could fire. Hollis was particularly mortified because of the presence of Jacob. The turret crew was equally embarrassed, and Jacob thought it would be a long time before they heard the last of it. However, shooting did start at 0716 and went on for eight minutes. Jacob was told that it was very accurate and was surprised to feel no blast within the turret, unless the breech of one of the other guns happened to be open at the time.

It was rather noisier on the bridge where Morton was given cotton wool to use as ear plugs. Even so, he heard a noise like 'the Day of Judgement' as 'tongues of hot light shot from the forward fourteen-inch gun turret, followed by clouds of white smoke'.

They passed through the Hoxa Gate at 8.45 into Scapa Flow and dropped anchor half an hour later. The Commander-in-Chief boarded to greet the distinguished guests and destroyers came alongside to take them off. Churchill addressed the crew rather briefly, referring to his predecessor Benjamin Disraeli and the Congress of Berlin of 1878, though it is doubtful if many seamen were familiar with it:

> Many years ago there was a statesman who came back from a European Conference and said he had brought 'Peace with Honour.' We have not sought Peace on this occasion; and as for Honour, we have never lost it. But we have brought back a means of waging more effective war and surer hope of final and speedy victory.[5]

Destroyers took the party back to Thurso where the train was waiting, almost exactly two weeks since they had left London. Lady Sinclair, the wife of the Air Minister, was waiting and promised grouse. A long lunch was served in the tradition of the train and Churchill finished it with a Benedictine. Ten minutes later he called for a brandy and the attendant reminded him he had already had a Benedictine. Churchill replied, 'I know: I want some brandy to clean it up.' Cadogan's sensitive palate was offended again next morning, when he found Churchill eating cutlets and bacon for breakfast. They arrived at King's Cross Station soon afterwards, where the Prime Minister was kissed by his wife and greeted by most of the Cabinet.

★　★　★

At the time Churchill was careful to keep expectations from the conference low. He broadcast to the British people on 24 August and admitted that the results were symbolic. Later he placed great store in paragraph six of the Charter:

> The fact alone of the United States, still technically neutral, joining with a belligerent Power in making such a declaration was astonishing. The inclusion in it of a reference to 'the final destruction of the Nazi tyranny' ... amounted to a challenge which in ordinary times would have implied warlike action.[6]

Perhaps the most important result of the conference was to establish the personal friendship between Churchill and Roosevelt, which gave the Prime Minister great influence in Washington. But when the attack on America finally came, it was not in the way that Churchill had expected.

IV
The Dull Pounding
of the Great Seas

Relaxing at Chequers one Sunday evening in December 1941, Churchill heard some momentous tidings, in the strangely casual way in which the British sometimes become aware of great events. He was sitting round the table with John G. Winant, the American ambassador, and Averell Harriman, the President's representative, when he turned on the radio for the nine o'clock news. At the end of a fairly routine broadcast was tagged an extra announcement:

> The news has just been given that Japanese aircraft have raided Pearl Harbor, the American naval base in Hawaii. The announcement of the attack was made in a brief statement by President Roosevelt. Naval and military targets on the principal Hawaiian island of Oahu have been attacked. No further details are yet available.[1]

This was just beginning to sink in when the butler Sawyers arrived and confirmed the story. 'We heard it ourselves outside. The Japanese have attacked the Americans.' Churchill immediately got on the transatlantic telephone to Roosevelt and asked him about the attack. Roosevelt replied, 'It's quite true. They have attacked us at Pearl Harbor. We are all in the same boat now.' The Prime Minister sent off messages to various other governments that night, and received a report that the Japanese were also attacking British possessions in the region. He was elated with the news:

> No American will think it wrong of me if I proclaim that to have the United States at our side was to me the greatest joy ... Being saturated and satiated with emotion and sensation, I went to bed and slept the sleep of the saved and thankful.[2]

Elizabeth Layton arrived early for work at Downing Street next morning, and was soon called into the Cabinet Room where Churchill was pacing about:

> He looked keen, enormously alive, on top of his job. After all, things had just taken a turn, so that he could now feel more than confidence

in Britain's survival and eventual victory – it was now a sure prospect. He said, 'Shorthand', and continued walking about muttering 'Letter to the King.' But what was I writing down? 'Sir, I have formed the conviction that it is my duty to visit Washington without delay ...', asking for Royal approval of his sudden plan to cross the Atlantic immediately. This letter was followed by a directive to General Ismay, giving instructions as to who was to be included in the party and what arrangements made.[3]

As a political secretary Layton was not used to being privy to this level of secrecy. 'I staggered out to my typewriter, eyes bulging, feeling this heavy secret could probably be read from my countenance.'

Despite Churchill's elation, the world situation was not necessarily to Britain's advantage in the short term. The Americans had suffered heavy losses at Pearl Harbor and their fleet was crippled. Moreover, Churchill needed to persuade them to pursue the war against Germany rather than Japan. The Germans themselves obliged here by declaring war on the USA on the 10th, for once carrying out the terms of a treaty – to Hitler, the United States was a mongrel nation dominated by Jews, and a natural enemy. But that still did not ensure active American participation. It was Japan that had carried out an outrageous and unannounced attack, it was Japan that immediately threatened American interests in the Pacific. Consequently, many Americans were resolved to pursue the war there as a main priority, which would leave Britain in danger again if supplies from America dried up.

Even in his most elated moments Churchill had forecast 'terrible forfeits in the East' but these would merely be 'a passing phase'. They proved to be far worse than expected, as the Japanese advanced inexorably across the Pacific and towards British Hong Kong and Malaya. On the morning of the 10th he was in bed opening his dispatch boxes when Sir Dudley Pound telephoned and spoke in an odd, hesitant voice: 'Prime Minister, I have to report to you that the *Prince of Wales* and the *Repulse* have both been sunk by the Japanese – we think by aircraft.' This was a terrible personal blow to Churchill. It was not just that the *Prince of Wales* had recently been his transport to Newfoundland and he and his staff had formed personal

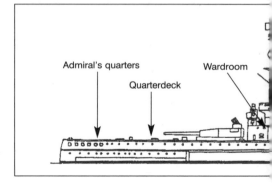

friendships with many of the officers. It was Churchill who, against the best naval advice, had ordered the ships' departure to the Far East to act as a deterrent. They had obviously failed in that role, and now they were lost in the Royal Navy's greatest humiliation for centuries. Unlike the sinking of the *Hood*, this loss would not be avenged a few days later.

All this was fresh in Churchill's mind as he addressed the House of Commons on 11 December. He acknowledged that 'A great many things of far-reaching and fundamental importance have happened in the last few weeks. Most of them have happened in the last few days ...' He talked for some time about the situation in North Africa, before turning at last to the area everyone wanted to know about. 'A week ago the three great spheres, Libya, the Atlantic and Russia, would have almost covered the scene of war with which we were concerned. Since then it has taken an enormous and very grave expansion.' He went on to one of his most rousing perorations:

> Not only the British Empire but now the United States are fighting for life; Russia is fighting for life, and China is fighting for life. Behind these four great combatant communities are ranged all the spirits and hopes of all the conquered countries of Europe, prostrate under the cruel domination of the foe. I said the other day that four-fifths of the human race were on our side. It may well be an understatement. Just these gangs and cliques of wicked men and their military and party organisations have been able to bring these hideous evils upon mankind. It would indeed bring shame upon our generation if we did not teach them a lesson which will not be forgotten in the record of a thousand years.[4]

★ ★ ★

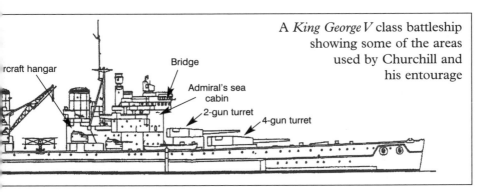

A *King George V* class battleship showing some of the areas used by Churchill and his entourage

rcraft hangar

Bridge

Admiral's sea cabin

2-gun turret

4-gun turret

Churchill's enthusiasm for an early trip to Washington was not shared by everyone. Foreign Secretary Anthony Eden and his private secretary Oliver Harvey were horrified. They were on the way to Russia and it would not be a good idea for Churchill and Eden to be out of the country at the same time. Moreover, they 'both felt that he would not be wanted in America at such a moment and there was nothing for him to do there if he went.' Harvey wrote in his diary: 'Really the PM is a lunatic: he gets in such a state of excitement that the wildest schemes seem reasonable. I hope to goodness we can defeat this one.'

Roosevelt read Churchill's message with dismay, for his government was preoccupied with the sudden and unexpected transition from peace to war, the need to mobilise the armed forces and get civilian industry on a war footing. His first instinct was to put Churchill off and he drafted a telegram asking for a delay 'until the early stages of mobilization complete here and situation in Pacific more clarified'. He changed this to 'My first impression is that a full discussion would be more useful a few weeks hence than immediately.' At one stage he suggested a January meeting in the West Indies, but this was too late for Churchill. Finally he relented and sent a reply. 'Delighted to have you here at the White House ... My one reservation is great person [sic] risk to you – believe this should be given most careful consideration for the Empire needs you at the helm, and we need you here too.' Churchill replied:

We do not think there is any serious danger about a return journey. There is, however, great danger in not having a full discussion on the highest level about the extreme gravity of the naval position, as well as upon all the production and allocation issues involved.[5]

He suggested Bermuda as a possible meeting place, but that had no attraction for Roosevelt who had to remain close to the White House during such a crisis. But Churchill had got his way again. Despite the shortage of serviceable battleships, it was decided to use the *Prince of Wales*'s sister ship, the *Duke of York*.

★ ★ ★

By this time Churchill was building up a regular entourage for such trips. His inner circle on every voyage included at least one of his four private secretaries. They were very different animals from the typists who took down his letters – generally women, with few prospects of promotion. Private secretaries were bright young men in the highest class of the civil service, usually from distinguished families and with good degrees from Oxford or Cambridge. According to one of them, 'There was never a day or night when at least one Private Secretary was not with Winston Churchill – that is to say capable of being physically present at his desk or at his bed-side within a couple of minutes, or on the same train, ship, aircraft or car and able to comply with any request, reasonable or not, on the telephone or in person.' As a humble typist, Elizabeth Layton was alarmed by 'these elevated gentlemen', though she came to respect their qualities. 'Their work called for the highest degree of care and responsibility, and their first rate education and high office combined to give them plenty of self-confidence.' They regarded the post as a step that would lead on to higher things, and none of those employed by Churchill in wartime were to be disappointed: men like Eric Seal, Leslie Rowan, John Martin and John Colville would all go on to high offices in government and commerce. On this occasion, as on the Newfoundland trip, the selected secretary was John Martin. Born in 1904, he was a classics graduate of Edinburgh University and Corpus Christi College, Oxford. He started his career in the Colonial Office dealing with the thorny problems of Palestine and became the principal private secretary in Downing Street in May 1941. According to his colleague John Colville he 'had a shy and retiring disposition combined with a ready wit, a delectable sense of humour and a conscientious devotion to the public service ... he was too law-abiding to keep a diary. That is a pity as his writing is as agreeable as his conversation.'

Commander Thompson, the organiser of the trips, was an essential companion. He was efficient in his way, but often did not make a good impression on those around him. According to Colville he was 'more esteemed by Churchill than by his staff', and the British ambassador in Moscow thought him unimpressive. Churchill's family found him clinging. When a goose began to follow Churchill round his estate at Chartwell, it was nicknamed 'the naval aide de camp'. Ian Jacob of the Ministry of Defence and Leslie Rowan, another of the secretaries, collected examples of his minor sins of omission on the trips, which they called 'Tommy muck-ups'. Their dislike of him was intense. Jacob was shocked that a great figure like Churchill should be attended by an 'insignificant', 'selfish' and 'undignified' figure like Thompson, who was only interested in getting the best accommodation for himself and making sure that others did all the work. But they recognised that their indignation was futile, and he was held in high regard by Churchill.

Ian Jacob of the Ministry of Defence was one of the most regular travellers. He looked nothing like the stereotype of a British army officer, with his wiry frame, intent eyes, balding head and round glasses. Certainly he was more intellectual than most members of the army, but as the son of a field marshal and the grandson of a general his career path was laid out for him. He joined the Royal Engineers, the most technical branch of the army, and built roads in Waziristan on the North-West frontier of India. But his main talent was as a staff officer for the Committee for Imperial Defence, and then in the Ministry of Defence directly under Churchill from 1940. His superior General Ismay reported:

> He is exceptionally quick to seize the essential features of a complicated situation and to reach a sound judgement upon them. His reports and appreciations are models of what such papers should be. He has the capacity to work long hours at high speed without loss of accuracy or efficiency, and even at the worst moments of the war, I have never known him ruffled.[6]

In other words he was the ideal staff officer. Colville nicknamed him 'iron pants' because of his devotion to duty and he was 'a sharp observer of people and events'. He kept detailed diaries of the voyages he was on, not all of which have been published. His intellect made him gravitate towards the private secretaries within the entourage, and he was an increasingly influential figure.

One important addition to the group was Sir Charles Wilson (later Lord Moran), the Prime Minister's personal physician. After distinguished service in the medical corps in the First World War, he combined a successful Harley Street practice with building up St Mary's Hospital in London, and he became President of the Royal College of Physicians in 1941. He had already been appointed as Churchill's doctor on the recommendation of Brendan Bracken and Lord Beaverbrook, who were among his patients. Clementine had urged Winston to take Wilson with him on the first voyage to Placentia, and not to rely on the ship's doctor; but that did not happen and this was to be his first trip. He did not fit in easily with the Churchill entourage, mainly because he was not in daily contact with the others at home; and as a rule he had little to do during voyages and conferences. Colville wrote: 'Lord Moran was never present when history was made, though he was quite often invited to lunch afterwards.' As 'a roundhead among cavaliers', and he became the butt of many jokes.

Inspector Walter Thompson of Scotland Yard came from a very different background to the others. Born in 1890, he was one of a family of thirteen in the East End of London. He joined the Metropolitan Police in 1913 and was soon involved in Special Branch work, keeping tabs on suffragettes in peacetime and suspected German spies in war. He was Churchill's bodyguard between 1918 and 1931, retiring from the police force in 1936 to run a grocery shop, but being recalled to serve Churchill in 1939. Ambassador Kerr thought him 'very true to type' – in appearance and manner he was rather like the plodding Scotland Yard detective of contemporary popular fiction, constantly outsmarted by the talented amateur. On foreign trips he sometimes appeared in a naval cap or open-necked shirt, but he only looked comfortable in his dark suit, raincoat and trilby hat. Thompson had a strong sense of duty and worked the long and unpredictable hours the job demanded. Churchill had as great a variety of enemies as anyone in history, and Thompson protected him from Irish Republicans and disgruntled French aristocrats in addition to the more obvious threats from the Nazis.

As stenographer and typist, Churchill brought along Patrick (or Peter) Kinna, who had already had his baptism of fire with the Prime Minister's dictation on the way back from Newfoundland. Kinna was a very small man, a 'midget typist', who weighed only 115 lbs. Churchill joked that he would not make a very good meal in the desert. He was 'bright, intelligent and alert', according to Colville. With him was Geoffrey Green, a 22-year-old RAF Flight-Sergeant who had served until recently as personal clerk to the Chief of Air Staff. He did not work directly for the Prime Minister, who 'didn't accept new faces' but took shorthand and did typing for other members of the party. Kinna wrote that he was a 'tall, slim, pleasant young man'.

This time Churchill did not trust naval servants and brought his own butler and valet, Frank Sawyers, who had worked for him since before the war. He was 'a little, baldish Cumbrian with a round, florid face, piercing blue eyes, and a pronounced lisp ... Something of a wag, he had a way with Mr. Churchill that no one else dared to emulate.' Colville thought 'he was a considerable character, and would have made a fortune on the stage'. Churchill greatly valued his resourcefulness during his travels: 'He is absolutely honest, capable of attending to a great many personal details as a valet, and always rises to the occasion ... He waits well at table, and also has an admirable manner with visitors. He has a good memory and always knows where everything is.' That was a great asset, for Churchill often carried up to 30 pieces of luggage on his trips, and his dress requirements were unpredictable.

★ ★ ★

Almost as significant was the list of people who did not go on Churchill's travels. He did not take journalists again after the problems with Morton and Spring, though sometimes he took official photographers and newsreel cameramen. He never took any of the service ministers – the First Lord of the Admiralty or the Secretaries of State for War and the Air – but preferred to deal directly with the Chiefs of Staff. Occasionally he invited a minister directly concerned with the affairs of the conference, such as Anthony Eden or Lord Beaverbrook; but he never took anyone connected with home affairs, such as Clement Attlee, (Deputy Prime Minister), Herbert Morrison (Home Secretary) or Ernest Bevin (Minister of Labour) – it is probably just coincidence that all of them represented the Labour Party.

This selection might be justified in terms of the work in hand, but it gave a very distorted image of British life and politics. The chosen group was led by the aristocratic and imperialistic Churchill. It included large numbers of red-tabbed generals and gold-braided admirals (though the air force cultivated a more modern image). It might admit ministers such as Eden and Harold Macmillan, who had radical ideas of their own but projected an image of old-fashioned conservatism; or arch-capitalists like Lords Beaverbrook and Leathers. Civil servants included the aristocratic Cadogan and the very superior private secretaries. The supporting detectives, typists and valets of humbler origins were never part of any decision-making process. To an American reared on Hollywood films, or a Russian brought up on the works of Marx and Lenin, it much resembled a cross-section of British society as they perceived it.

The entourage, in fact, said nothing of a new and meritocratic Britain in which men such as Bevin had risen from very modest origins to the highest posts in the land, in which the junior officer ranks of the army were open to all classes as never before, in which the aircrews of the RAF, recruited largely from the lower middle class, had saved the nation in the Battle of Britain. The travelling party conveyed very little of the fact that the British were reduced to a kind of rough equality by food rationing and conscription, that all classes were united in a common effort in a people's war. The stately homes of the aristocracy had largely been taken over as military headquarters or training camps. Bombing could affect many different people in the big cities. In London, even Buckingham Palace was hit and the Queen commented, 'Now I feel we can look the East End in the face.'

Industrial and military conscription applied to all classes, including women under 40, and well-connected young ladies might find themselves working in factories. Young men of all classes might be obliged to work in the coal mines, without any option to join the armed services where they would have prospects of becoming officers. Food rationing produced a basic and very plain diet, in which oranges, for example, were a great luxury. Clothes rationing led to a certain level of uniformity even among civilians. The socialist George Orwell wrote: 'Since no real structural change is occurring in our society, the mechanical levelling process that results from sheer scarcity is better than nothing. ... If the poor are not much better dressed, at least the rich are shabbier.'

★ ★ ★

Perhaps the most important person to accompany Churchill on this trip was Lord Beaverbrook, the great newspaper magnate and now Minister of Supply, who was a great influence on the Prime Minister. Churchill and Beaverbrook had a good deal in common, though they had been born in very different backgrounds – Churchill was the grandson of a duke, Beaverbrook, by his own account, was 'descended from eight or ten generations of agricultural labourers'. Both were born in the 1870s, Beaverbrook being five years younger, in the heyday of the British Empire, for which they exhibited great enthusiasm – Churchill mainly for India, Beaverbrook for the white dominions and especially Canada. Both were independent, buccaneering conservatives and both were of transatlantic origin: Churchill's mother was American, Beaverbrook was brought up in Canada by Scottish Presbyterian parents. Both achieved prodigies before they were 30, Churchill in war, journalism and politics, Beaverbrook in finance and industry. Uniquely, both served in high government office in two world wars. Both could work with almost superhuman energy, alternating with bouts of illness; and their personalities were mercurial, often difficult and demanding of their subordinates. Both owned country houses south of London that were admired more for their views than their architecture; and their round, baby-like faces were beloved of cartoonists. Both had made many enemies on the way to the top, but they were largely forgiven in the heat of war.

There were also great differences. Unlike Churchill, Beaverbrook never relished a fight and was a conciliator rather than a combatant. In contrast to his rival newspaper owner and sometime collaborator Lord Rothermere of the *Daily Mail*, he did not support Fascism in the 1930s. Beaverbrook's newspapers were relentlessly optimistic even in the gloom of that decade. After the Munich Crisis of 1938 the *Express* famously proclaimed, 'Britain will not be involved in a European war this year, or next year either', and it continued to support this view until August 1939. Even after war started the *Express* of 12

75

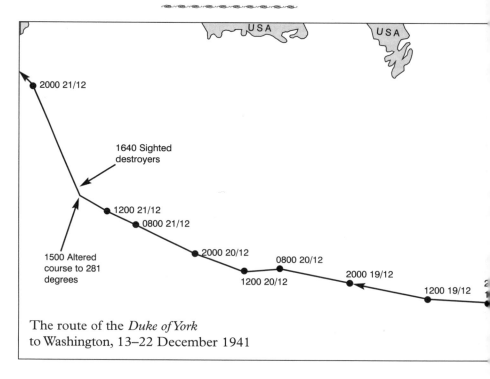

2000 21/12

1640 Sighted
destroyers

1200 21/12
0800 21/12

1500 Altered
course to 281
degrees

2000 20/12
0800 20/12
1200 20/12
2000 19/12
1200 19/12

USA

USA

The route of the *Duke of York*
to Washington, 13–22 December 1941

September carried the headline, 'Nazi Army Tired Out'. A month later, after the conquest of Poland, Hitler was said to be 'pale with anger' as pessimism spread among his high command, and to be making his will and agonising about what to do next.

Beaverbrook now brought his own entourage with him, which according to Brigadier Dykes exceeded even that of Churchill. His staff included his very superior valet, Nockels (who was never addressed by his Christian name of Albert). Tall, balding and immaculately dressed, he never tired of reminding his employer that he had once served Her Royal Highness Princess Arthur of Connaught. If ever there was one, he was a model for Jeeves in the books of P. G. Wodehouse.

Averell Harriman, another of Roosevelt's special representatives, was one of the guests on this occasion. Born in 1891, he was the son of a fabulously rich railway magnate, and then he made a highly successful business career of his own. Harriman was abrasive and intolerant and did not express himself well on paper, but he was also clever and determined and succeeded at almost everything he turned his hand to. He was in London to organise supplies to Britain through lend-lease, and he required a good deal of skill to keep his organisation out of conflict with the American Embassy. The ambassador,

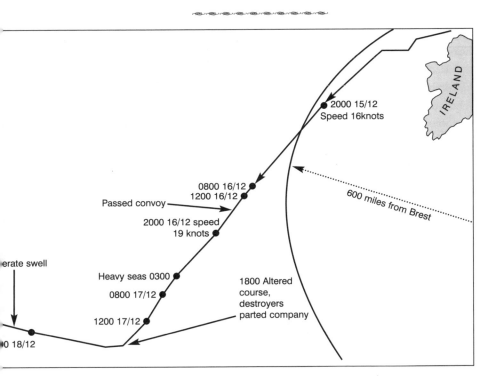

John G. Winant, had served as head of the International Labor Organisation and represented one side of Roosevelt's inclusive national administration, while Harriman stood for capitalism. It was similar in a way to Churchill's employment of the trade union leader Ernest Bevin along with the newspaper magnate Beaverbrook.

The final addition to the party was the new Chief of Air Staff. Air Chief Marshal Sir Charles Portal, known as Peter to his friends, was a tall, dark man whose lined face was dominated by his great beak of a nose. Anyone who saw him with his beautiful wife might conclude that he must have some great mental qualities to attract and retain such a woman. Indeed this was true, though he wore them lightly – according to Colville he was 'quiet, unforthcoming and not easy to converse with' but 'shrewd in his judgement … Although he displayed no goods in his shop window, he was universally respected and admired.' More intellectual than many of his colleagues, he was studying at Oxford with a view to becoming a lawyer when he was swept up by the outbreak of war in 1914. He served as a corporal despatch rider in France, then transferred to the new Royal Flying Corps as an observer. Retraining as a pilot, he was in command of a bombing and reconnaissance squadron by 1917. He flew more than 900 sorties, and his abilities in other directions were noted, so he stayed on in the new Royal Air Force after the war.

Between the wars Portal was a highly successful squadron commander and staff officer at the Air Ministry, and he had a seat on the Air Council when the war began. He was chief of Bomber Command for a time, until October 1940 when Churchill singled him out as 'the accepted star of the Royal Air Force' and had him promoted to head it. He had a quick brain and worked hard in his new job, steering the air force through the years when it made its mark on world history, enjoying its greatest prestige at the end of the Battle of Britain. It was his responsibility to deal with the night bombing of British cities, to struggle to retain some RAF control of Coastal Command, and to build up forces for the bomber offensive against Germany.

★　★　★

The party was seen off by a large number of people at Euston Station in London. The Prime Minister wore his blue boiler suit again, and one of his secretaries reminisced about how he had last seen him in it on the floor of No. 10 with Lord Beaverbrook, playing with a model of the new Churchill tank. Churchill's son Randolph came with Averell Harriman's daughter. Sir Charles Craven of the giant armaments firm Vickers was sipping crème de menthe and remarked about the *Duke of York*, 'Watch out for Y turret. It's not very good' – a strangely revealing comment from the chairman of the company that had designed and built it.

Apart from Beaverbrook and his entourage and Portal, the party was similar to the previous one. Pound and Dill were there, though the latter was about to leave his post as Chief of Imperial General Staff and his very competent successor, Sir Alan Brooke, was already in the office and was staying at home to settle into his new job. Dill would soon begin a new and highly successful career as British military representative in Washington.

For security reasons it was put about that Lord Beaverbrook was the head of the party. The ruse was quite effective and some of the passengers on the special train were amazed to find that the Prime Minister was on board. Churchill's daughter Mary, serving as a junior NCO with the anti-aircraft artillery, came north with him, as did his chief typist, Mrs Hill.

Lord Beaverbrook was rich enough to afford his private saloon, and it was attached to the train. The journey north was relatively simple this time, for the ship was to leave from the Clyde rather than Scapa Flow. Brigadier Jacob slept very well, for he had been working day and night to get the papers ready for the conference. The special train pulled into the station at Princes Pier in Greenock and the party, with the usual extensive luggage, was ferried out to the waiting battleship. Churchill boarded at 10.50, wearing a yachting cap and a double-breasted blue jacket.

The party had very strange feelings on boarding. Brigadier 'Dumbie' Dykes wrote: 'The layout of the ship is very similar to the poor old *Prince of Wales*, but more staff accommodation aft.' His friend Ian Jacob commented in more detail:

> The *Duke of York* is a sister ship to the *Prince of Wales* and *King George V*: there is hardly any difference in characteristics. It was hard to remember that it was not the *Prince of Wales* which we were once more to travel in, and harder still to realise that the great ship we had so much admired was now at the bottom of the seas. Every day on board brings home the bitterness of that blow.[7]

This time Churchill knew to head straight to the admiral's sea cabin. He told his wife, 'I have a lovely cabin in the bridge structure as well as my apartments aft. These latter are unusable owing to the noise and vibration. Here it is cool and quiet and daylight.' Beaverbrook and Pound were also found cabins in the bridge, and had their meals in the warrant officers' mess yet again. According to John Martin, 'It was remarkably spacious and comfortable quarters ... I never enjoyed a fortnight's meals more ... I have never eaten so much caviare ...' Jacob found himself allocated to the wardroom as usual. It was 'the same shape, but better supplied with tables and chairs'.

The ship weighed anchor at ten minutes past noon and headed out of the Clyde escorted by three destroyers, *Faulkner*, *Foresight* and *Matabele*. The recent history of British battleships gave some cause for thought. The old *Barham* had been sunk in November, the only capital ship to be lost at sea to a U-boat. True, the circumstances were very different from those facing the *Duke of York*. She had been patrolling up and down in the much narrower waters of the Mediterranean, where enemy air reconnaissance was far more effective. A U-boat penetrated her poorly trained destroyer screen and put four torpedoes in her port side from the very close range of 400 yards. All struck within the narrow space between the funnel and the after turrets, blowing in a large area of the hull and 'opening her vitals to the sea'. That was enough to cause her to capsize, but in addition the poorly protected 4-inch magazine seems to have caught fire and it spread to the 15-inch magazine. She rolled over and there was little chance for the men clinging to her sides to escape as she blew up with the loss of 862 men, nearly two-thirds of the crew.

It was not completely relevant to the *Duke of York*'s voyage – there was little chance of a U-boat getting within 400 yards to launch such a concentrated attack, and her escorting destroyers were far more experienced in anti-submarine work. Also, the *Barham*'s system of underwater protection consisted of bulges fitted to the outside of the hull after construction, and was considered far less effective than the Side Protection System of the *Duke of York* and her sisters. But now, the loss of the *Prince of Wales* was beginning to raise questions about that. Inquiries had not yet been completed but they would show that the ship had been lost mainly because of five hits from Japanese air-launched torpedoes. Already that was one less than the experts had predicted, but there was worse to come. It seemed that the first two hits, during an attack by the second wave of bombers, had done most of the damage. One had hit near a propeller shaft, destroying the watertight integrity of the bulkheads round the shaft passage. This was a vulnerable area in any ship, and could not be easily remedied – the *Bismarck* had been crippled by a hit in the same area. The second torpedo had apparently struck around the after funnel. The SBS system proved far less effective than predicted, and many compartments were flooded. The protected area was not deep enough to cope and the ship was already sinking when more torpedoes hit on the other side. Fortunately the Germans had not developed the art of torpedo bombing, so that was not an immediate threat. But it did raise the possibility that a couple of lucky strikes by a U-boat could finish off the battleship and put most of the British war leadership in danger.

Fortunately again, the U-boats were not in a position to launch such an attack, for the submarine war was going through a relatively quiet phase. Naval intelligence showed that there were only five U-boats in the North Atlantic, apart from a concentration of ten boats off Gibraltar and Portugal, with a general movement toward the Mediterranean. This time the battleship was going on a far more southerly route, for after clearing the north of Ireland she took up a course of 252 degrees, heading approximately south-west.

★ ★ ★

The winds were already strong as the ship and her escort lost sight of Ireland, and speed was reduced to 10 knots by the early morning of the 14th as the vessel was shipping heavy seas over the forecastle. By the afternoon, as the ship was still only a hundred miles or so from Ireland, the wind was up to force

9, severe gale, and speed was reduced to 7 knots, and then to 6. Yet another fault of the *King George V* class was becoming apparent. The Admiralty had specified a low bow so that the main guns could fire directly forward, but this allowed the great Atlantic waves to break continually over it, and the ship rolled violently. The passengers were confined below decks. Churchill managed to avoid seasickness but that did not stop him talking about it over dinner, and at one point Sir John Dill had to leave. Brigadier Dykes 'staggered up to see Dill for about one hour before lunch but could not face more than a cup of tea'. According to John Martin, 'The PM dosed me most tenderly with Mothersill, which he finds an unfailing remedy ...'

Weather forecasting had developed fast in the last few decades, as more accurate predictions were needed for air travel and increased use of radio made them possible. Meteorologists understood the structure of the travelling depressions that formed off Newfoundland and moved eastward, dominating the weather in the North Atlantic and British Isles. They knew that the winds in them rotated in an anti-clockwise direction. South of the centre of the depression was a warm front, which would be signalled well in advance by an increasingly low cloud, a dropping barometer and rain. The passage of the front itself would lead to a change in wind direction and the onset of warmer, humid weather. It would be followed by the cold front with sudden heavy rain, another change in wind direction and cold weather.

The theory was excellent, but the means to use it were rather sparse, because of the shortage of information from the North Atlantic. The Americans had a chain of weather ships west of longitude 65 degrees west. The British had set up two ships in their own area, but these were withdrawn in July 1941 due to enemy action. Ordinary warships and merchant ships could not radio weather reports without giving their position away. Coastal Command aircraft could record weather information but could only report it after the flight. Two specialised meteorological trips set off every day, 300 miles out from Aldergrove in Northern Ireland and St Eval in Cornwall. Apart from that, the weather in the North Atlantic was only known intermittently.

The *Duke of York* carried her own meteorological officer in the person of R. A. Bennett-Levy, who spent most of his career in Royal Naval Air Stations. He was rather junior in the rank of sub-lieutenant, and was overawed when Commander Thompson ordered him to produce a forecast for the First Sea Lord. Due to wireless silence and a shortage of information he could say very little but predicted gales, which happened to be true. Like weathermen in all ages, Bennett-Levy came in for a good deal of criticism, but his position was more difficult than most.

During the 14th and 15th the ship made very slow progress off 'Bloody Foreland' in the north-west of neutral Ireland. The gale was met head on and the destroyers struggled to keep up. Speed was reduced to as low as 5 knots on occasion, with an average of about 10 knots. By the evening of the 15th, after more than two days at sea, the *Duke of York* was only 300 miles from the coast of Ireland, and 3,000 miles from her destination in Washington. It was dangerous territory, for 30 German Focke-Wulf Condor long-range bombers were based in Bordeaux and made constant sweeps over the Atlantic between there and Stavanger in Norway. An attack by a single bomber was not likely to be fatal to the *Duke of York* – it had taken 80 Japanese bombers and torpedo bombers to sink her sister *Prince of Wales* and the *Repulse*. More likely the Condor would radio the position of the large capital ship and have U-boats meet her in her path. That danger would not be over until the ship was west of 20 degrees, which happened about midnight on the 15th.

Some sources suggest that the ship had to make constant changes of course to avoid U-boats. That is not borne out by the log, which shows a steady course of 252 degrees until the evening of the 14th, then gradual alterations to keep on a great circle track. The only exception was zigzagging, which was carried out during the daylight hours. They did not see much on the way. Hands were called to action stations on the morning of the 14th while off the north of Ireland, but it turned out to be a friendly aircraft. An east-bound convoy was sighted in the afternoon of the 16th, but there was no time to make passes through it as with HX 143.

★ ★ ★

Churchill's spirits recovered quickly from the loss of the *Prince of Wales* and *Repulse*, and Sir Charles Wilson found him strangely happy at the start of the voyage:

> The P.M., I suppose, must have known that if America stayed out there could only be one ending to this business. And now suddenly the war is as good as won and England is safe; to be Prime Minster of England in a great war, to be able to direct the Cabinet, the Army, the Navy, the Air Force, the House of Commons, England herself, is beyond even his dreams. He loves every minute of it.[8]

Beaverbrook was much less pleased. He had probably crossed the Atlantic more often than anyone else on board, but mostly in the comfort of a luxury liner, or with the speed of a Liberator bomber, as on his last trip. He was not used to playing second fiddle to anyone, even Churchill. 'At Cherkley [his country house] he is king.' As Wilson noted, 'He hates the hours we spend round the table when lunching or dining. The P.M. does the talking, of course, and Max does his best to listen. It is not easy for him; his life has not prepared him for this sort of thing.' Beaverbrook worshipped brevity above all, and Churchill's conversation, rather like his writing, seemed to him 'interminably long-winded'. Confinement below decks made the situation even worse. No one liked being 'battened down for eight days, listening to the dull pounding of the great seas on the ship's ribs', but according to Wilson, 'Everyone here takes whatever comes as it comes, save Lord Beaverbrook, whose undisciplined spirit chafes at the confinement.'

The nightly films did not help. They had been chosen by the Ministry of Information to reflect Churchill's taste, and Beaverbrook considered them 'a series of the most juvenile screen plays in the repertoire' – though inevitably they included *Lady Hamilton*. Churchill himself watched them 'wearing a dressing-gown over his pyjamas which made him look like a monk belonging to some easy-going order' and 'presided with droll delight'. One night, after a western with a particularly high death toll, he got up and remarked, 'Now I think we will have a little peace and get back to the war.' Beaverbrook loved films as much as Churchill and had his own private cinema at Cherkley, but he liked to make his own choices, and to talk loudly through the performance. The best one on the voyage, according to Jacob, was *The Private Lives of Elizabeth and Essex* which included a fine performance by Bette Davis. Again Churchill found resonances. When Queen Elizabeth was seen refusing to pay for more ships against the Spanish Armada, he turned to Harriman and said:

You see, the British have always been the biggest damn fools in the world. They are too easy going and niggardly to prepare. Then at the last minute they hurry around and scrape together and fight like hell. Good luck has pulled them through. If the good Lord once forgets them, they will be finished.[9]

For reading matter Churchill brought another C. S. Forester book, *Brown on Resolution,* in which a seaman single-handedly holds up the progress of a major German warship until help arrives; and *Forty Centuries Look Down* by Frederick Austin, published in 1936. It dealt with Napoleon's relations with his wife Josephine, and his expedition to Egypt in 1798. Although Bonaparte might have been regarded as a continental dictator and potential invader of

Britain, Churchill did not equate him with Hitler and sometimes used his memory to help his case with the Free French. His armies 'had a theme. They carried with them the surges of the French Revolution. Liberty, Equality and Fraternity – that was the cry.' In contrast, Hitler brought 'naught but mania, appetite and exploitation'.

Churchill found plenty of time to work on this trip. He made many comments on detailed matters such as the use of skilled manpower in the armed services, the manning of aircraft carriers, the defences of Singapore, the appointment of Labour peers to the House of Lords, the formation of a Polish division in the army and on methods of dealing with submarines. But his greatest effort went into a magisterial summary of the state of the war so far which would form the basis for discussion in Washington. His first sentence got to the root of the matter. 'Hitler's failure and losses in Russia are the prime fact in the war at this time.' The Germans had recently failed to take Moscow, and the Soviets had launched a counter-attack against them. Churchill dealt with each front in turn – the Atlantic which included North Africa and Russia in this context, and the new front in the Pacific. He considered the needs and resources of Britain, the US and the other Allies, and balanced the land, sea and air wars in each theatre. History would show that he was over-optimistic in some areas – 'We may expect the total destruction of the enemy force in Libya by the end of the year [presumably 1942].' And he acknowledged one failure so far: 'Our own bomber programme has fallen short of our hopes', and predicted 'We expect … that Singapore island and fortress will stand an attack for at least six months.'

Again no women were taken on the trip, as it was not considered seemly to have them on a warship at sea. Patrick Kinna acted as stenographer again, and one morning he was very uncomfortable taking the Prime Minster's dictation, as the rolling of the ship combined with Churchill's cigar smoke to produce a very unpleasant effect in the confined space. Worse, Kinna could hear some sailors whistling outside. He knew that Churchill could not bear it and indeed he ordered him to go and stop it. The diminutive Kinna approached the seamen with great trepidation, but they stopped before he reached them.

★ ★ ★

On the morning of 16 December the wind began to moderate from Force 7, a near gale, to Force 4, a moderate breeze on the Beaufort Scale. The passengers were allowed on deck after two days under hatches. Wilson strolled with the Prime Minister who remarked, 'This is a new war with Russia victorious, Japan in and America in up to the neck.' The ship's speed increased to 19½ knots, but there were heavy seas breaking over the forecastle again early in the morning of the 17th. The wind was only force 4, but a swell had been built up by gales elsewhere. During the day it was suggested that they might make for Bermuda, which was only 1,800 miles away, then proceed by air. An investigation showed that it would save a day at most and would need a great deal of organisation.

By six in the evening of the 17th the ship was about 130 miles from the most northerly of the Azores islands, held by neutral Portugal. The U-boat danger was much reduced by this point, and the destroyers left. It was now time to head more directly for Washington, and the *Duke of York* altered course to 262 degrees; she made good progress, with a steady speed of 20 knots over the next 26 hours. Then the barometer began to fall again, and the weather worsened. Ian Jacob felt the effects of the tremendous sea, hearing the great ship shake as her bows bored into a big wave. Then she pitched and rolled 'like a cork' but he suffered more from the stuffiness of the atmosphere than from seasickness. Speed was reduced to 13 knots, but this storm was shorter and sharper than the last. By midday on the 19th, the ship was travelling at 20 knots again and was 450 miles south of Newfoundland.

At last, at three in the afternoon of the 21st, there were signs that the voyage was nearing an end as course was altered to 281 degrees, heading straight for Washington. Then at 16.40, some destroyers were sighted in the distance. Within half an hour they had been identified as the American vessels sent out to meet them, and by 6 o'clock the United States ships *Bristol, Trippe* and *Warrington* were forming station as a screen, for now America was at war and there was no more need for pretence.

Jacob was delighted to wake on the morning of Monday 22nd to find the ship 'sailing steadily toward land in mild sunlight, in a smooth sea'. A boat had been waiting since seven in the morning, but it was 37 minutes past one before it was able to put the pilot on board the *Duke of York*, to conduct her through the shallow and devious waters and the protective minefield in Chesapeake Bay. The pilot was so obviously surprised to see the Prime Minister that it was clear there had been no security breach. The ship arrived off Hampton Roads just after four and dropped anchor in 22 fathoms of water.

Despite their initial lack of enthusiasm for the visit, the Americans had made careful preparations and two naval officers came on board with the pilot bearing 'the most complete and carefully worked out plans for our arrival', which had been wrecked by the delays. Roosevelt wanted the party to transfer to a destroyer and be taken up to Washington through the relatively shallow waters of Chesapeake Bay and the River Potomac, but time was too short. The Americans had laid on a special train near Hampton Roads, but even that was not fast enough for Churchill. He asked Roosevelt for an aircraft, and a Lockheed was prepared for him at a nearby airfield. Taking Beaverbrook, Portal, Harriman and Wilson with him, he flew directly to the capital. The doctor was delighted to see the lights of Washington, a contrast to blacked-out London. On landing he saw Roosevelt propped up against a car and was struck by his large head and his thin legs after his paralysis. The President soon used his famous knack to put him at his ease, and they talked about casualties at Pearl Harbor until they were whisked off by car to the White House.

The rest of the party went ashore to join the train and were put up on a special railroad car by the Vice-President of the Baltimore and Ohio Railroad. They were fed on hard boiled eggs and salad with coffee and fruit. They played bridge with the Americans and arrived in Washington at 1.15 in the morning to be met by embassy officials and taken to their hotels.

Churchill and Roosevelt soon reached some conclusions on war policy. American troops retreating in the Pacific might be used to defend Singapore and Australia. American bombers would be stationed in England for the air offensive against Germany. The first American troops sent to the United Kingdom would be stationed in Northern Ireland. As well as relieving British forces for the war in the Middle East, this would mean that any enemy move against neutral Eire would be countered by the Americans, not the hated British army.

On Christmas Day the party went to the historic Foundry Methodist Church and celebrated Dill's birthday in the afternoon. There were some signs of dissension among the various leaders – Secretary of State Hull objected to Gaullist forces taking over the island of St Pierre et Miquelon in the St Lawrence estuary; General Marshall was annoyed about the commitment to use US troops to defend Singapore; and on the British side the Chiefs of Staff were shocked by General Marshall's proposal to set up a unified command. At eight in the evening they began a dinner of over 60 people in the White House, organised by Eleanor Roosevelt. It ended cordially, though Churchill had to finish preparing his speech for the following day.

On 26 December Churchill addressed both Houses of Congress and won them over by telling them, 'if my father had been American and my mother British, instead of the other way round, I might have got here on my own'. That night there was the first of many scares about his health, when he had a mild heart attack. Wilson knew that the proper treatment was six weeks of complete rest, but that was not possible – it would mean publishing to the world that 'the P.M. was an invalid with a crippled heart and a doubtful future'. Not for the last time, he had to compromise between best medical procedure and national need.

Churchill continued his meetings, agreeing with General Marshall that General Sir Archibald Wavell was the best man to command in the Middle East. He sorted out various shipping policies with Roosevelt, and agreed that the Pacific war would be directed from Washington, and the war in Europe, on the Atlantic and in North Africa from London. On the 30th he travelled to Canada by train. Addressing the Parliament in Ottawa, he deployed General Weygand's remark that he had mentioned to Charles Eade before his first North American trip. 'In three weeks England will have her neck wrung like a chicken.' With perfect timing he declaimed, 'Some chicken! – some neck!' to thunderous laughter.

Back in Washington Roosevelt and Churchill had a moment of surprising intimacy, when the President entered the bathroom to find the Prime Minister standing naked. But Churchill was never shy about these matters, and according to Inspector Thompson he said, 'Mr President, I have nothing to hide.' After dressing, he and Roosevelt prepared a declaration on behalf of the 'United Nations', those states at war with Germany. They discussed war production, then it was time for a rest, for Churchill's schedule would have strained a man in good health. He flew to Florida in General Marshall's aircraft, to spend five days in a villa at Pompano near Miami, bathing in the warm sea. John Martin wrote: 'I think that the main reason for our visit to Pompano was to provide a break for the President, exhausted by the PM's late nights and flow of talk.' Mrs Roosevelt confirmed that the President needed several days to catch up with his sleep after one of Churchill's visits. According to Wilson, 'The air is balmy here after the bitter cold of Ottawa – oranges and pineapples grow here. And the blue ocean is so warm that Winston basks half submerged in the water like a hippopotamus in a swamp.' Even then his work did not cease, and back in Washington he and Roosevelt agreed on an Anglo-American landing in North Africa. By 12 January it was time to go home and the President parted from Churchill with the words, 'Trust me to the bitter end.'

V
A Flying Hotel in the Fog

A fter the horrors of the outward passage, the Prime Minister and his party were keen to avoid another long and hard sea voyage. It was decided that they should be flown out to the British island colony of Bermuda to join the *Duke of York* there. This was a useful way of saving time, but British naval intelligence also knew that American waters were becoming more dangerous. The U-boats were building up for an offensive off the east coast, where the convoy system was not yet in use and shore lights could be used to pick out passing ships. Three Boeing 314 Clipper flying-boats were provided to transport the party, one in British ownership and two from Pan American Airways.

A planning meeting was held on 13 January in the British Embassy Annexe, chaired by Air Marshal Arthur Harris who was soon to take charge of the air offensive against Germany and gain the nickname of 'Bomber'. It was attended by Tommy Thompson and Ian Jacob of the travelling party, as well as British and US naval representatives. A special train was to leave Seventh Street Station in the evening of the 14th, carrying the remaining 92 persons, for Dill and his staff were to stay on in Washington. It would head for Norfolk in Virginia, where it would meet the flying-boats. Elaborate security was needed. Passengers were warned to say nothing to the hotel staff, drivers or anyone else about the move. Each was to prepare his own hand baggage, the test being that he could carry it himself. Other items were to be labelled with the owner's name and nothing else. They would be collected centrally and colour coded according to the aircraft they were to be loaded on. The *Duke of York* had already sailed for Bermuda, giving the impression that the British party had departed. The three flying-boats would leave from their usual base at Baltimore, the BOAC crew making a great show of clearing customs as if they were on a regular trip to Bermuda; but in fact they would land at Norfolk where the party could be embarked in relative secrecy in the naval air base. From there they would be escorted by two US Navy flying-boats.

★   ★   ★

The Boeing 314 (known as the Clipper in its service with Pan American Airways) was a remarkable aircraft, the first in the world designed mainly for crossing oceans and offering great comfort to passengers who could afford it. The Atlantic was the greatest challenge for the pioneers of aviation, as it had been for steamships a century earlier. The Pacific was larger, but it had many islands for stopovers. The North Atlantic linked the two great civilisations of Europe and North America, with so much culture, history and economics in common, but it was notorious for unpredictable weather, strong winds and an unforgiving sea. The British pioneers Alcock and Brown flew across relatively quietly from Newfoundland to Ireland in 1919, but Charles Lindbergh became an international celebrity when he crossed single-handed in 1928. In the 1930s, the setting up of a transatlantic air service became a matter of national prestige. British and French individuals made many heroic flights, but their governments were not very interested – they had no wish to undermine their dominance on the sea routes. Their civil aviation was directed towards their empires, with flights to Asia, Africa and Australia which had different demands. The Germans, always leaders in airship design, began a service to Brazil with the *Graf Zeppelin* in 1930. A service to New York came to a disastrous and spectacular end when the *Hindenburg* caught fire in 1937 with the loss of many lives. The Italians under Air Marshal Balbo sent out a mass flight of 24 aircraft in 1933, but that was essentially a publicity stunt which led nowhere. It was the Americans who found a practical solution with the Boeing Clippers. When they first set up a regular service on 28 June 1939, fewer than 100 aircraft had crossed the Atlantic successfully, and 50 more had failed in the attempt. Now they planned to operate a scheduled weekly service. But the war intervened and it was suspended in October after three months.

Pan American used flying-boats, but not because they were expected to land in the middle of the Atlantic – the ocean was far too rough for that. The simple reason was that the infrastructure of transatlantic aviation, the great concrete runways, had not yet been created. Very few British airfields had hard surfaces of any kind in 1939, and even fewer were long enough for huge aircraft carrying a heavy load of fuel. The sea, on the other hand, was free. A good sheltered stretch of water was needed, but there were plenty of these on both sides of the Atlantic, such as New York harbour in the USA and Plymouth Sound and Poole harbour in Britain. But the designers paid some penalty for this. The aircraft needed the lower part of the fuselage shaped like a speedboat so that it could reach the high speeds it needed for take-off. This was a most unsuitable shape in the air, and would tend to slow it down. That was not a major issue when the great majority of aircraft were slow and had drag-creating fixed undercarriages, but by 1941 almost all modern aircraft had retractable undercarriages.

One unusual feature was that the Boeing 314 had no wingtip floats, which most flying-boats used to give some stability on take-off and landing. Instead it had short wings, known as sponsons, at water level. These were slightly heavier than wingtip floats, but they gave a little extra lift. They also allowed the flying-boat to be brought in against a pier or jetty, so that passengers could walk over them into the cabin, without having to be taken out by boat, as with most flying-boats.

Churchill and Beaverbrook had already heard a great deal about the Boeing flying-boats. In 1940 Harold Balfour, the dynamic Under Secretary for Air, purchased three of them in the United States. Technically this was the job of the Ministry of Aircraft Production, not the Air Ministry, and Beaverbrook was furious: he himself was no respecter of rules, but he did not appreciate his own tactics being employed against him. Balfour was also rebuked by the Chancellor of the Exchequer, and by Churchill himself: 'I really do not see how the government could be carried on if such unauthorised commitments were to be countenanced.'

Nevertheless, the aircraft were there and were soon found to be useful. They were taken over by British Overseas Airways Corporation, the state-run airline, for as civil aircraft they could visit neutral countries such as Portugal and the United States. Externally, they lost the silver paint which had conferred a surprisingly attractive appearance, in favour of green and grey wartime camouflage. RAF roundels were not carried on civilian aircraft but the registration letters on the side of the fuselage were underlined in red, white and blue and a large Union Jack was painted under the cockpit. The Boeing 314 could carry 74 passengers in seats for daytime flights, or 40 in bunks for night voyages. Balfour was lucky to get hold of them, as only twelve were ever built, nine for Pan American Airways and the three for BOAC. They were given the names *Berwick*, *Bangor* and *Bristol* after towns to be found on both sides of the Atlantic.

The idea of a flight across the ocean had already been considered for Churchill's party on the way out, but on 10 December BOAC management was sceptical. 'It is doubtful whether a Boeing 314 can fly from Foynes [the flying boat base in Ireland] to Bermuda with a payload of 1,500 lbs (say 6 or 7 passengers). Everything depends on wind condition and navigational problems involved.' The Air Ministry was also doubtful, though it did believe a return trip might be possible with the prevailing winds in its favour.

One constant difficulty in those days was the height at which to fly. Very few aircraft had pressurised cabins, in which the air pressure at low level was maintained at high altitudes. The Americans experimented with the Boeing Stratoliner of 1938 but it never entered mass production and the technology was still very new. The famous B-29 bomber, when it came, was urgently needed for operations against Japan and only the parts occupied by the crew were pressurised. In other aircraft, the pressure within the cabin would reduce with height and oxygen would become scarcer. A normal individual could fly at 10,000 feet in this state without risk, but above that an oxygen mask would be necessary. Churchill was in poor health for most of the war, and even 10,000 feet was on certain occasions too high for him. But high-altitude flying was often necessary, to get over mountains or in rough weather.

★ ★ ★

The special train arrived in Norfolk at 4.30 in the morning of the 16th and the passengers were allowed to sleep on. BOAC sent a staff of two pursers and two baggage handlers to load the suitcases efficiently. Around 6.30 Churchill and his party embarked in the BOAC aircraft *Berwick*, registration G-AGCA. There were 22 passengers including the Prime Minister, Pound and some of his staff, Wilson, the two Thompsons, Sawyers, Kinna and various other clerks and typists, as well as Lord and Lady Knollys, the Governor of Bermuda and his wife who had come out to meet them. Passengers and baggage were carefully weighed – Churchill was not quite the heaviest passenger at 210 lbs, for Captain Brockman of the navy weighed two pounds more; but he did have by far the heaviest luggage – 200 lbs, more than a fifth of the total amount in the aircraft.

They took off and soon reached a height of 8,000 feet which was maintained throughout most of the journey. Churchill had breakfast alone in his cabin, the 'bridal' or 'honeymoon' suite towards the rear. He was hungry and 'went through the whole menu, which consisted of grapefruit, cereal, hot scrambled eggs on toast with fried sausage, tomato and bacon, hot rolls, tea and coffee'. The term 'full English' was not in use at that time but Churchill obviously relished it, especially in contrast with the American food of the White House and the meagre rations at home.

Then Churchill was shown round the aircraft by the captain of the BOAC crew, John Kelly Rogers. He was a large 36-year-old Irishman who had started off as a sailor in the training ship *Conway* in the River Mersey at the age of 14. He became an officer in the Royal Naval Reserve but joined the RAF in 1927 and served mainly in army-co-operation aircraft. From 1935 he worked for Imperial Airways, the forerunner of his current employer. He had flown the first British air mail to the US in 1939 and rescued a flying-boat from a Congo swamp; and he had made the airline's last flight over Europe before war conditions rendered it impossible.

Churchill was impressed with the aircraft and soon began to regret the harassment of Balfour over its purchase. The interior was essentially on two levels, for a flying-boat needed a deep fuselage to lift its engines clear of the spray. Forward on the upper deck was an extensive flight deck, not just a cramped cockpit as on most aircraft then and now. The pilot and co-pilot sat well forward, only partly segregated from the flight deck itself, which had a large chart table and stations for the flight engineer and radio operator. Aft of that was a small office for the captain, and a baggage compartment which was also used for sleeping and recreation quarters for the crew. The wings were deep enough to allow an internal catwalk, along which the flight engineer could walk to reach the engines. Churchill was interested in this, and Kelly Rogers told him how it had been used occasionally to carry out repairs in flight. There was a central 'navigation turret' or astrodome for the navigator to take fixes on the stars, and when not in flight it could be opened to allow access to the storage compartment.

Below, the space in the bulbous bow was only accessible from the crew's compartments above. It was known as the anchor room and was used for mooring gear and so on, as well as more baggage and crews' bunks. The passenger compartments began aft of the bulkhead. There was a stateroom with seats for eight people, which could be converted into four bunks if needed. Next came a kitchen on the port side, with a gent's toilet on the other side, containing perhaps the only standing urinals ever used in the air. Another similar stateroom led into a large dining room under the wings, with seats for twelve at a time. There followed two more staterooms and finally the rear passenger lounge, or 'bridal suite' with even more luxurious accommodation. There were only a few concessions to wartime austerity on the aircraft in BOAC service. For example, the partitions between the cabins were removed to save weight and replaced with stretched canvas.

The titles 'flying-boat' and 'clipper' were not empty, for the Boeing 314s were run rather like ships. The title of 'captain' for the chief pilot of an airliner was already well established, and civil aircrew wore dark blue uniforms which were more reminiscent of the merchant navy than the air force, but the Boeings went much further than that. With a standard crew of ten, they had enough men to operate on two watches on long flights, while the others rested. Almost uniquely among civil aircraft of the day, they had fully trained navigators who could use the stars to fix the position over the ocean. Officers were trained by long apprenticeship and could not expect to take command until they had many years' service. They knew almost as much about seamanship as they did about flying, for they often had to alight and moor up in difficult conditions. The flight engineers knew every detail of the aircraft, and could carry out repairs, and even make spare parts, in any out-of-the-way station. The stewards knew how to cook gourmet meals as well as serve them.

Churchill soon made friends with John Kelly Rogers, 'a man of high quality and experience'. He entered the cockpit smoking his usual cigar, and Kelly Rogers waived the rules and let him continue, even allowing him to strike a match when it went out. He tried the controls of the huge craft, as Kelly Rogers whispered into the co-pilot's ear, ordering him to apply corrections only if it looked as if the plane was getting out of the Prime Minister's control. The Boeing 314 cockpit was a good one for him to practice in, for it was unusually spacious. The engine controls were down either side rather than in a central column which would have impeded access. Each pilot had a set of the six basic instruments in front of him and there were other dials in the centre, but it did not have the bewildering array of instruments that was already beginning to bedevil cockpit design, as the engine controls were mostly in the flight engineer's compartment.

Churchill was allowed to do a couple of slightly banked turns, and was photographed by one of the official cameramen. He talked about his own flying career which had begun in 1913 when he founded the Royal Naval Air Service, and compared the Boeing Clipper with the primitive aircraft he had known then. When Kelly Rogers made radio contact with the Pan American planes, Churchill asked if he could speak to them, but the captain ruled that out as too much of a security risk.

Churchill was beginning to see other possibilities, and he asked the captain, 'What about flying from Bermuda to England? Can she carry enough petrol?' Kelly Rogers was enthusiastic. 'Of course we can do it. The present weather forecast would give a forty miles an hour wind behind us. We could do it in twenty hours.' This seemed very appealing after the horrors of the outward voyage in the *Duke of York*. Moreover, Churchill was anxious to get home quickly as the war situation deteriorated in the Far East and he was facing increasing criticism in Parliament and the country.

After about four hours they arrived at Bermuda and Kelly Rogers offered a sightseeing flight around the islands. The Prime Minister was summoned from his seat below and he and the Governor came on the flight deck to view the sights. Then they landed inside Darrell's Island, the main flying-boat station in Bermuda. The two photographers jumped ashore to take shots of the dignitaries arriving.

The passengers in the two Pan American aircraft had far less enjoyable flights. They were all crammed into compartments in order to get a suitable weight distribution for take-off. There was no attempt to 'differentiate between the relative ranks or importance of the passengers', so Beaverbrook and Portal had to share space with ordinary marines. They were kept waiting for an hour on the water with no explanation and all the hatches and doors closed, and a promised breakfast never materialised despite repeated requests. Eventually two sandwiches were issued per head with the promise of coffee later, but the water boiler broke down and that did not arrive. The planes flew at 1,500 feet all the way, causing continuous bumping. They were supposed to lead the way into Bermuda for the benefit of the crew of *Berwick*, but there was no sign of them until they arrived an hour late, from the wrong direction, having made a navigational error. Beaverbrook and Portal were 'speechless with rage' after the landing, although Portal apparently recovered his voice sufficiently to tell the story to Kelly Rogers. The big Irishman enjoyed it, for he was no lover of Pan American. He noticed that the American crews kept out of the way in Bermuda, because 'their faces might be red'.

★ ★ ★

After landing at Bermuda, Churchill consulted the Chief of Air Staff about flying on, but Portal considered the risk 'wholly unjustifiable'. Pound backed him and referred to the comfort and safety of the *Duke of York* which was awaiting them – a rather unappealing offer after the voyage out. Churchill asked, 'What about the U-boats you have been pointing out to me?' Pound said that they were no threat to a 'properly escorted and fast battleship'. Sensing that Pound and Portal thought they might be left behind, Churchill told them, 'Of course there would be room for all of us.' After that, according to Churchill, their attitude changed visibly:

> Two hours later they both returned, and Portal said that he thought it might be done. The aircraft could certainly accomplish the task in reasonable conditions; the weather outlook was exceptionally favourable on account of the strong following wind ... Pound said that he had formed a very high opinion of the aircraft skipper, who certainly had unrivalled experience. Of course there was a risk, but on the other hand there were the U-boats to consider.[1]

Meanwhile Kelly Rogers was consulting with Squadron-Leader Gordon Store about possible routes, when he was summoned to Government House. He met Portal on the way and the Prime Minister (apparently in a tactile mood throughout this trip) clapped him on the shoulder and invited him to a conference, which also included Pound and Martin the Secretary. Churchill stated the position:

> Outside lies the 'Duke of York' waiting to take me to England, which I can reach in seven to nine days. During that time I have ears to hear but no lips with which to speak. On the other hand, Captain Kelly Rogers assures me that in the aeroplane in which we have flown to Bermuda today we can fly to England tomorrow in not more than 22 hours. This is many days saved, and during that time many things may happen. Two important battles may be fought, and one major decision.[2]

It was, he added, a 'war convenience' to go, not a 'war necessity'.

The conference soon turned into a grilling of Kelly Rogers, who was asked 'every conceivable question' about the performance and reliability of the aircraft, the route, alternative destinations in case of trouble, meteorology and aerodynamics. The easiest one, he claimed later, was when the Prime Minister asked what he would do if 'the British Isles were covered in one continuous sheet of fog reaching up to 25,000 feet with severe icing'. Squadron-Leader Store supported Churchill, Portal was obviously in favour of flying but was relentless in his questioning, while the First Sea Lord remained quiet. Eventually Churchill turned to the others and said, 'He seems to have all the answers, doesn't he?' Kelly Rogers replied that this was a result of long experience and that the projected voyage, despite its great importance, was 'an everyday occurrence' to him. It was decided to go on the next morning, though the final decision would be up to Kelly Rogers. If the weather made it impossible, Churchill would return by the *Duke of York*.

Beaverbrook, although not invited to the meeting, had already made up his own mind. He told Kelly Rogers, 'Wild horses won't drag me aboard that submarine the "Duke of York." ' If the Prime Minister went by sea, Beaverbrook planned to wait in Bermuda until the next commercial flight via Lisbon was available.

There was a good deal of jockeying for position among the entourage when it became known that Churchill was planning to complete the voyage by air. There were only places for seven passengers given the necessary fuel load, so many had to be left out to return by sea. Hollis got wind of it and rang John Martin the secretary, pointing out that he had to prepare and distribute the reports of the meeting as soon as possible and that would not be possible if he went by sea. Thompson the bodyguard 'protested violently' at being left out and Churchill added fuel to his flames by declaring, 'The Inspector is very sore that

Right: Churchill in Downing Street with his secretary John Martin and Detective-Inspector Walter Thompson. (IWM HU 90347)

Below: Churchill reading papers and dictating on his special train. (IWM H 10874)

Left: Churchill with Captain Leach and Admiral Sir Dudley Pound on the deck of the *Prince of Wales*. (IWM A 4859)

Opposite page, top: British and American sailors mingle on the decks of the *Prince of Wales*, with the USS *Augusta* in the background. (IWM A 4803)

Below: Roosevelt coming aboard the *Prince of Wales*. (IWM A 4807)

Opposite page, bottom: Churchill with Roosevelt and his son, Captain Elliot Roosevelt. (IWM A 4821)

Above: The signal sent to the convoy – 'Good voyage, Churchill'. (IWM A 4990)

Below: The *Prince of Wales* in Hvalfjord, Iceland. (IWM H 12911)

Right: Chequers in wartime, protected by barbed wire and other defences. (Coward-McCann)

Right: Churchill walks on the deck of the *Duke of York* with his secretary, Mrs Hill. His daughter Mary and Averell Harriman walk behind. The ladies did not go on the voyage. (IWM A 6905)

Right: Lord Beaverbrook holds his ears during gunnery practice on the *Duke of York*. (IWM A 6911)

Above: A Boeing publicity picture for the peacetime Clipper service. The spaciousness is only slightly exaggerated, and most of the luxury survived into wartime. (CPL)

Above: *Berwick* takes off, with a crewman sitting in the nose to watch out for floating debris. (IWM CH 14069)

NCI8601

DE LUXE COMPARTMENT

LADIES ROOM

PASSENGER COMPARTMENT

BERTHS

PASSENGER COMPARTMENT

NAVIGATION TURRET

BRIDGE

CATWALK

SEA

MENS ROOM

Below right: Captain Kelly Rogers (second from left) with his crew for a delivery flight of a Boeing 314 to Britain. (Boeing Aircraft Co.)

Above: Churchill at the controls of the Boeing 314 on the way to Bermuda. (IWM H 16645)

Below: Bermuda in the 1940s.

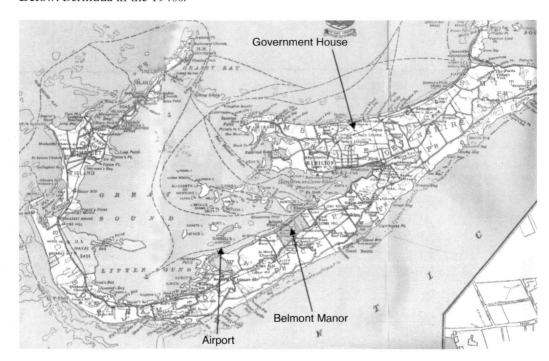

he is not coming with me.' Sir Charles Wilson had a stronger case. Churchill came up to him and put his arm through his, saying,'We are returning by air. They are fixing up the details now. But we cannot all go in the flying-boat. I am sure, Charles, you won't mind returning in the ship.'

Wilson, however, did mind. He recalled Churchill's numerous small accidents during his travels and the heart attack in the White House, and pointed out that he had been given leave from his normal job as President of the Royal College of Physicians to look after him. How would it look if Churchill arrived back home without him? He disengaged his arm and walked towards the house, bursting into a Chiefs of Staff meeting to state his case forcibly and with success. This meant that someone else had to be displaced and Tommy Thompson was now considered the least essential. It was suggested he might toss up with John Martin if Kelly Rogers could be persuaded to take one more, but the captain was adamant. In the middle of the night Thompson had the idea of supplanting one of the stewards, but Kelly Rogers turned this down too – the steward had safety as well as domestic duties. Hollis sent a message to Jacob: 'In a world of Bedlam, I have at last established that the Prime Minister is going by air, and I am going with him.'

★ ★ ★

Kelly Rogers had decided to take the maximum amount of fuel for the journey, 5,000 gallons. This would put the aircraft slightly over the weight limit imposed by BOAC, though not above that recommended by the manufacturers. Boeing had suggested a limit of 88,000 lbs, and the loaded aircraft came in at 87,644 lbs. This would make take-off more difficult, but the captain believed that it would not impose any undue strain on the aircraft.

As to the route, it was decided to fly south of Ireland and land in Pembroke Dock in the south-west corner of Wales. A flight to Cornwall or the south coast of England would have taken the plane too close to enemy activity, while a flight round the north of Ireland with a landing in Scotland would have been slightly longer. Alternative destinations were chosen in case of accident or bad weather – Horta in the Portuguese Azores, Gibraltar, Foynes in Ireland and Stranraer in Scotland. Surprisingly, Kelly Rogers chose a rhumb-line route which meant maintaining the same compass course all the way through, even though slightly longer than a 'great circle' route.

A report from the Meteorological Office suggested a strong tail wind throughout the flight, reducing its time from 22 hours to 17 hours and 25 minutes. It was best to fly in the night-time and land by daylight, so it was decided to postpone the departure until later in the morning. Kelly Rogers went to Squadron-Leader Store's office to get the secret codes for his flight. He chose the RAF rather than the Atlantic Ferry system of flying control. This meant that his flight plan would be communicated to three stations – Bermuda while he was west of 55 degrees, Gander in Newfoundland for the middle part of the journey and Prestwick in Scotland when he was east of 30 degrees. He would transmit his call sign once an hour and the station would use it to plot his position roughly, giving him any new information on hazards, routeing or weather forecasts. Apart from that, he would only use his radio if he was more than 50 miles off the projected track.

The stop in Bermuda was an enjoyable interlude by any standards. The island had a pleasant climate, warmed by the Gulf Stream, and was a stark contrast to freezing London. It was one of the oldest of Britain's colonies and about a third of the population of around 35,000 was of British descent. The Governor's mansion offered fine accommodation for Churchill, and there were plenty of good hotels for the more junior members of the party. A naval base with a large floating dock in its deep harbour, the island was virtually untouched by wartime austerity. Ashore, Kelly Rogers socialised with Portal and Beaverbrook, who mocked Tommy Thompson's anxiety to go on the trip, and made amusing comments on the 'character and ability' of members of the party. He took Portal to see the weather forecast in the Meteorological Office, and was surprised when the Chief of Air Staff admitted that his knowledge of the subject was 'very limited'. But there was still some doubt about the flight. The weather in England was beginning to get worse and a cloud base of 1,000 feet was forecast, with visibility of four miles. Catalina aircraft making regular trips from Bermuda were not allowed to fly if the cloud base was lower than 800 feet, and the forecasters told Kelly Rogers that this was a borderline case. He saw it differently, for cloud could offer protection against enemy aircraft, and his crew was far more experienced than those of the Catalinas. He was supported by the Director of the Meteorological Office, and decided to go.

Churchill was well aware of the risk he was taking, not just to himself but in carrying two of the Chiefs of Staff and a member of the War Cabinet in the same aircraft. Kelly Rogers discovered that the King had specifically forbidden this, but Churchill found a way round it. He left instructions with the Governor that a message should be sent home about the decision to fly, and ordering the special train to be got ready. But it was not to be sent until the aircraft was at least halfway across the Atlantic, beyond the 'point of no return' after which it would make no sense to order it to turn round. Kelly Rogers sensed an air of 'naughty boy' about the passengers, though this is easier to imagine in Churchill and Beaverbrook than in Portal and Pound. They felt 'they had done the right thing' but 'they had nevertheless broken the rules in doing so'. Churchill, who loved snap inspections of factories, offices and military posts, said gleefully, 'They'll get quite a surprise when I turn up five or six days earlier than expected.'

★ ★ ★

Kelly Rogers had an experienced crew. His co-pilots, J. S. Shakespeare and Anthony Lorraine, both used the title of 'captain' because they had commanded aircraft in their own right. Lorraine was a very experienced aviator. Born in 1910, he had served an apprenticeship with the de Havilland aircraft company while qualifying as a pilot. He started with Imperial Airways in 1931 and served on the South African, Middle East and Far East routes. He conducted experiments in air refuelling on the Atlantic service in 1939 and flew a French mission into Leopoldville in the Congo, the first flying-boat to land there. He had been in at the beginning of BOAC's transatlantic service. The navigator, R. G. Buck, took on a great deal of responsibility during the trip. The chief engineer was H. Clark, assisted by L. A. Coates. H. D. Danger-field was the chief radio operator, his second A. H. Stewart. The purser was H. F. Good. Chief Steward E. W. Smith was the best flight attendant Kelly Rogers had ever come across, and he would look after the Prime Minister's needs during the flight; his assistant was Steward Partridge.

The chosen passengers turned up early on the dockside at ten in the morning of the 17th, to inspect the airport and take their ease in the sun. There was confusion when it was found that the Prime Minister's baggage was on board a tug on the way to the *Duke of York*. He confronted Sawyers and 'in no uncer-tain terms he expressed his opinion of the usefulness of valets, secretaries and detectives who he said in spite of the fact they surrounded him could still succeed in losing his luggage' – rather unfair as the fault was traced to the flag lieutenant attached to the local commander-in-chief. Time was getting short and the Prime Minister agreed that if necessary he would fly with only his deed box, which was still with him and contained the papers he was working on at the moment. But the baggage was returned just in time, and was quickly loaded on board.

At last all was ready and the giant aircraft cast off from the jetty six minutes late, at 11.36. It taxied out across the water, leaving Thompson inconsolable on shore, 'lamenting as bitterly as Lord Ullin in the poem', as Churchill put it. Kelly Rogers invited Portal to the flight deck and began his take-off run. The flying-boat lifted from the water after 57 seconds and Kelly Rogers felt vindicated about his decision to take so much fuel. He saw the *Duke of York* below and rightly

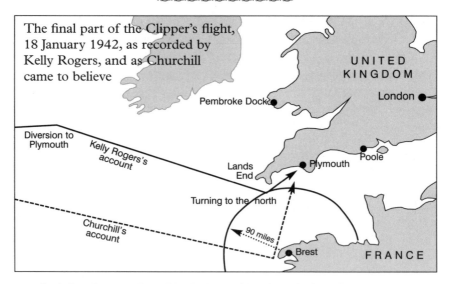

The final part of the Clipper's flight, 18 January 1942, as recorded by Kelly Rogers, and as Churchill came to believe

UNITED KINGDOM

London

Pembroke Dock

Diversion to Plymouth

Kelly Rogers's account

Lands End

Plymouth

Poole

Turning to the north

Churchill's account

90 miles

Brest

FRANCE

surmised that those on board looked up with mixed feelings. Jacob watched the Boeing passing overhead and was content to settle down for a quiet and restful voyage home, with no work to do.

The flying-boat climbed rapidly to 8,000 feet and settled on its course. Because of the extra fuel Kelly Rogers could fly at the relatively high cruising speed of nearly 200 miles an hour through the air, with any tail wind added to that. At such a speed the aircraft would fly more level, which increased the passengers' comfort. The height of 8,000 feet was safe for the Prime Minister, and it kept the plane above four weather fronts that would be encountered on the way.

Lunch was served soon after take-off and the Prime Minister decided to have it in the saloon with the other passengers – Beaverbrook, Pound and Portal, Hollis, Wilson and Martin. Churchill declined champagne and cocktails as he 'did not like fancy drinks' and settled for a whisky and soda. First Officer Buck and Radio Officer Stewart were both amateur photographers, and took shots that later appeared in the *Daily Telegraph*. Then Churchill retired to his cabin for his afternoon nap while the others settled down in the lounge. Kelly Rogers took the chance to explain his ideas on flight-crew training to Portal and felt that he was 'definitely interested' even though the needs of airlines were obviously different from those of the air force. The puritanical Sir Charles Wilson surprised the First Sea Lord with his skill at card tricks. Beaverbrook questioned the captain incessantly, despite Portal's attempts to shield him. Both the First Sea Lord and the Chief of Air Staff took an interest in the navigation of the aircraft. Later Kelly Rogers climbed into one of the bunks that had been set up for the crew in

Compartment C, but he failed to get any sleep and went back to the flight deck to relieve Lorraine. The flight continued at 9,000 feet, and the aircraft never ventured higher than 10,000 feet, cruising mostly between two layers of cloud, which increased security but made navigation more difficult.

★ ★ ★

That evening Churchill dined with the rest of the party and the captain. As usual on his voyages, the passengers sat down to a sumptuous meal, 'a festive affair consisting of cold consommé, shrimp cocktail, filet mignon with fresh vegetables, sweet, dessert, coffee, champagne and liqueurs'. At ten in the evening Greenwich Mean Time, Captain Kelly Rogers issued a typewritten bulletin to the passengers. They were at a height of 9,000 ft, 7 hours and 12 minutes away from Bermuda, and expected to arrive home in a further 9 hours and 10 minutes, but they had enough fuel for 15 hours. They were making a speed of 199 mph through the air, but the tailwind increased that to 207 mph. He noted optimistically, 'If present speed is maintained, it will be necessary to slow down so as not to arrive too early.' Reading it, Churchill put his hand on Wilson's knee and said, 'Do you realise we are 1,500 miles from anywhere?' Wilson quoted the Elizabethan mariner Sir Humphrey Gilbert – 'Heaven is as near by sea as by land.'

Most of the passengers retired to bed after that. One of the saloons, Compartment F, had its six bunks fitted for sleeping during the entire flight, and the occupants' names were marked on them. Churchill already had a bed in the after cabin. Hollis and Wilson enjoyed long and deep sleeps, while Martin had to conform to the Prime Minister's routine. Churchill was up and down several times during the night, spending long periods on the flight deck. At one stage he expressed doubt about the ability of the plane to withstand icing-up of the wing. Kelly Rogers waited until Churchill and Beaverbrook were on the flight deck together, and demonstrated the de-icing 'boots' on the leading edge of the wing, which vibrated to break up the ice as it formed. Churchill, despite his indifference to danger, found something else to worry about when he noticed brilliant flames belching from number three engine. Kelly Rogers reassured him that they were harmless, and invisible in the daytime.

The only passenger who did not sleep was Beaverbrook. He read some of the time and engaged the captain in conversation as much as he could, as Kelly Rogers later explained with a certain amount of tact: 'If I had not known Lord Beaverbrook to be an air traveller of many years standing and the maker of several trans-Atlantic flights, I would have thought him a nervous passenger, but I knew his anxiety was entirely on the Prime Minister's account.' Kelly Rogers shared this anxiety. In fact he had not slept or eaten properly since the idea of the transatlantic voyage was first suggested, having 'thrown away any mental pretence that the flight was a routine affair'. His frame of mind was not improved by Beaverbrook who kept talking about the risk to Churchill as if he was the only one who cared, and stated, 'If we lose Churchill, we lose the war.'

Churchill came on deck to see the dawn around 8 o'clock. The sky was suddenly clear of clouds and this conveyed a feeling of insecurity. Kelly Rogers posted lookouts in all directions but Churchill asked the obvious question – What would he do if an enemy aircraft was sighted? Kelly Rogers pretended not to hear.

★ ★ ★

Around this time, according to the most commonly accepted view, things began to go wrong with the flight. Churchill's account, written for the third volume of his *Second World War*, is the most often quoted:

> Later on I learnt that if we had held on our course for another five or six minutes before turning northwards we should have been over the German batteries in Brest. We had slanted too much to the southwards during the night. Moreover, the decisive correction which had been made brought us in, not from the south-west, but just east of south – that is to say, from the enemy's direction rather than that from which we were expected. This had the result, as I was told some weeks later, that we were reported as a hostile bomber coming in from Brest, and six Hurricanes from Fighter Command were ordered out to shoot us down. However they failed in their mission.[3]

The story was clearly attractive to Churchill, who was always drawn towards danger even if, as in this instance, it was unwitting. It was also meat and drink to journalists, and the *Daily Telegraph* serialised that part of the memoirs in April 1950. It was not acceptable, however, to Kelly Rogers, now working for Aer Lingus in his native Ireland, who had already learned of its serialisation in the American papers. He wrote to the *Telegraph*:

> Mr. Churchill displayed exceptional skill in navigating the world through the uncharted seas of war, but in the course of this and subsequent

flights over the Atlantic with me I felt he appeared to take no more than a layman's interest in the art of aerial navigation, and was inclined to dismiss the whole thing as a bit of a mystery.

We know he thought little of his own safety in the presence of the enemy and in consequence it is understandable that he should lightly dismiss the matter of his close proximity to the German guns in Brest.[4]

Kelly Rogers had a very different account of the final part of the trip, both in the remainder of his letter and in his report to the BOAC management, written a week or two after the flight, long before he had any idea that his navigation might be questioned.

★ ★ ★

At dawn, with the aircraft still west of Ireland, Kelly Rogers received signals that the weather was closing in over his proposed landing place at Pembroke Dock in Wales, where the Prime Minister's train was waiting. The alternative landing site at Poole was also covered in fog, while Plymouth had good visibility under thick cloud at 1,000 feet. It was decided to divert there. He planned to approach it from the south to avoid the balloon barrage over one of the most heavily bombed towns in Britain. They began a gradual descent from 10,000 feet and 50 minutes later they were at 1,000 feet and close to Land's End, though they were not sure whether they were to the north or south of the promontory as fog descended on them. Kelly Rogers rose to 1,500 feet to get above it, but he had no view of the ground. So far he had not needed any radio bearings, but now he called the station at Land's End and found that the aircraft was just to the south. A second call a few minutes later allowed a cross-bearing and showed how far they were from land, so they turned about 50 degrees to the north to pass just off the Lizard, the most southerly point in England. At no time, according to Kelly Rogers, were they within 90 miles of Brest. Churchill, with his amateur navigation, was confused as he sat in the co-pilot's seat with the nervous Beaverbrook standing beside him. As Kelly Rogers put it:

Although I assured them that we were very close to the coast all that was visible was a rolling expanse of fog, and they could not therefore appreciate the fact that we were following a definite plan of action, which was made visible to us by the radio bearings received but remained invisible to them.

Churchill, by his own account, had no knowledge of the danger at the time, although he noticed, 'It was evident from the discussions which were going on that we did not know where we were.' It was Portal who declared, 'We are going to turn north at once', after looking at the chart and discussing it with the captain.

★   ★   ★

Churchill's story of the supposed crisis begins when he had been sitting in the co-pilot's seat for two hours since dawn – though according to Kelly Rogers's account he interrupted that to go below and have breakfast with the other passengers. In any case, he began to sense a feeling of anxiety. There is no surprise about that, for Kelly Rogers was highly stressed. Churchill's statement that 'We were supposed to be approaching England from the south-west, and we ought to have already passed the Scilly Isles, but they had not been seen through any of the gaps in the cloud floor' means no more than that the weather was too bad to get a good visual position. He claims that the crew had only had one sight of a star in the last ten hours; but that is misleading in at least two ways. Firstly, Churchill appears to confuse 'sight' with 'fix'. A sight was a measurement from a single star, which would only indicate that the aircraft was on a certain line on the chart. A fix requires at least two sights, and the place where the position lines cross gave a reasonably accurate position on the chart. Secondly, Kelly Rogers claims far more fixes than that. Possibly Churchill was remembering the time when he joined Beaverbrook on the flight deck in the early hours, and was told that there had been no sights for some hours. According to Kelly Rogers, the two dignitaries 'showed no inclination to go below until the sky finally cleared and the stars became visible'. He does not say so, but it would be very surprising if he did not use the 'brilliantly starlit sky', which appeared at that point to update the position. Anyway, Churchill and Beaverbrook seemed reassured and they surprised Kelly Rogers by telling him that they envied him his job.

Churchill implies that wireless communication was not used, but in fact it had been deployed hour by hour throughout the flight to give Bermuda, Gander and Prestwick an indication of their position, and Kelly Rogers used it again to get a bearing from Land's End. Churchill's statement that 'we did not know where we were' was at best a half truth. The crew knew as well as anyone could in the circumstances before the radio fixes, and quite accurately after them. When Portal announced, 'We are going to turn north at once', that might well have meant an alteration through about 50 degrees to bring the aircraft's heading from south-east to north-east. Kelly Rogers also claimed that the control centre at Prestwick had been plotting their position, presumably from radio and radar fixes, during the whole of the approach to England. He spoke to Wing-Commander Jeffs next day and was told that 'from their point of view the flight had gone well in all respects and they particularly appreciated our close adherence to the agreed schedule'. Unfortunately the Operations Record Book of Prestwick only reports the fact of the flight, with no details.

Churchill's 'five or six minutes' from the German batteries at Brest is clearly not credible. At a speed of 200 knots that meant about 17 miles. Taken literally, the aircraft would already have been on the Brittany coast by that time. If we interpret it to mean 17 miles from the coast itself, then they would have been over the off-lying island of Ushant. Even if they were 17 miles from Ushant, it is difficult to believe that they would not have been picked up by German radar some time previously. But in fact the story may have originated elsewhere, in a Fighter Command headquarters.

★　★　★

It was a busy day for Air Commodore H. V. Rowley. He was in temporary charge of No. 10 Group RAF Fighter Command at Rudloe Manor near Bath, responsible for the air defence of England and Wales between Southampton and Milford Haven. If that was not enough, Headquarters had telephoned him the night before to say that a VIP flight would be coming into his area that morning – the emphasis on the letter 'V' left him in little doubt about who was on board. He was in the control room early next morning to supervise the operation personally and provide fighter cover against any intruders from the south. Most of his twenty squadrons were grounded by the same fog that had caused the *Berwick* to be diverted. The Operational Record Book of 87 Squadron, stationed at Colerne near Bristol, gives a flavour of the days from 13 to 23 January:

This was a period of continuous bad weather. The winter really started and heavy snow with frost cut out all flying. There was plenty of work to be done keeping the runways clear of snow, but otherwise activity was nil.

However, it was not so bad all over the command. It was first light at 8.40 at RAF Ibsley near Bournemouth when three Spitfires from No. 234 Squadron took off to patrol the area. Four more from No. 188 Squadron took off at 9.15 to fly around Swanage in case there was a landing at Poole, where they believed the

Prime Minister might arrive in a Sunderland flying boat. No. 130 Squadron at Perranporth in Cornwall was also on the alert:

The normal state would have been '30 minutes' but B flight was brought to 'Readiness' because of the return of Mr Winston Churchill from America. They were scrambled to patrol Plymouth which was done while the Prime Minister landed there. The weather was foggy throughout the morning.

Meanwhile, Rowley had identified another problem. His radar had detected an aircraft 30 miles west of Brest and slightly to the north. It was likely to be an enemy bomber, and four Spitfires of 310 (Czech) Squadron were scrambled at 9.05. The Air Commodore's worries intensified as there was still no sign of the VIP Boeing, perhaps because at a height of 1,000 feet it passed under his radar. He began to believe that the mystery aircraft was the Boeing itself, and that he had sent a patrol of fighters to destroy it. As he wrote some years later: 'Fighter pilots at that time were apt to be light on the trigger, and the Boeing was not a very well-known type of flying boat.' Fortunately they did not find it.

The plot of this aircraft was shown to Portal some time later, and also to Churchill. Both came to believe that navigational error had taken them close to flying over Brest, that they had made an alteration of course in the nick of time, and had narrowly avoided being shot down by the RAF. But in fact there is another perfectly satisfactory explanation. Lockheed Hudson serial number AM 692 of 224 Squadron, piloted by Squadron-Leader Lynn, had taken off from St Eval on the Lizard peninsula at 8.24 that morning to carry out a routine anti-shipping patrol off Brest. It had radio failure and was forced to turn back after less than an hour in flight. Half an hour's flying south at the Hudson's standard cruising speed of 170 knots would have put it very close to the position described by Rowley. If it turned back around 9 o'clock, it would have shown up on Fighter Command radar as an unidentified aircraft approaching the coast from the Brest area. Communication between RAF commands was far from perfect, and it is not difficult to believe that the aircraft's return was not reported to Rudloe Manor.

★   ★   ★

It is significant that none of those who tell that story about nearly flying over Brest was a very reliable eye-witness. Churchill was there, but by his own admission he did not know what was happening. Hollis and Wilson were probably asleep and were certainly not in the cockpit, while Beaverbrook left no coherent account, and Portal's evidence was at best circumstantial; he was a knowledgeable, calm and level-headed observer who was not likely to get things out of proportion, but his interest in the navigation of *Berwick* was desultory to say the least. In three separate letters to Churchill he denied that he had given any orders or instructions to Kelly Rogers, though in one of them he also admitted that he might have done so if they had not turned to the north. He defended the Churchill story in 1950 but denied that he had been Churchill's source for the account. He disclaimed any special knowledge of astro-navigation and recounted how he was approached by 'an officer whom I took to be the navigator on duty', which suggests that he was not intimately connected with running the aircraft.

Portal was worried during the last hour of the flight, but that was unsurprising as the RAF of the time would not have attempted to fly in such weather. He wrote: 'I remember observing how much better to hit Ireland than Holland.' A flight to Holland would have involved a navigational error of spectacular proportions, and it implies that Portal was not thinking of that but of diversions due to fog – that he would rather turn back and try to land in neutral territory than over-fly the whole of southern England and find every landing place was closed. When the turn to the north was made, he 'omitted to notice how long elapsed between our making the turn and sighting the Devon coast'. He thought the time was consistent with the Brest story, tending to prove 'that we had been in a position which involved some risk of contact with enemy fighters'. That would have involved about an hour's flying time from Brest to Plymouth rather than half of that from the Lizard. But in Portal's state of tension, such a mistake was easy to make. Nor did he explain the other flaw in the Brest story. If they had very little idea of their true position when nearly over Brest, how did they manage to find Plymouth so easily, apparently without another major alteration of course? Portal's story depends heavily on the plot shown to him some time afterwards by Rowley, the only piece of concrete evidence he presented in 1950.

Taken in these terms, Kelly Rogers's two statements are by far the most reliable. The first one was written before he had any knowledge that he was accused of such reckless navigation, so it is unbiased and has no sign of any defensive tone. In the second account, after Churchill published his version, Kelly Rogers maintained the same story in private and in print.

Kelly Rogers's letter did nothing to scotch the story about the flight near Brest. Leslie Hollis's biography, ghost-written in 1956, is even more alarming than Churchill's. He places the aircraft 'within one and a half minutes of coming out into a cloudless sky over Brest', where 'the *Berwick* would not have stood one chance in a million against the German anti-aircraft guns'. The story was clearly gaining some momentum of its own. How could Hollis, or anyone else involved, have known if the sky was cloudless over Brest? Why had the Germans not sent up fighters to intercept them before they got that close to the city? He ended, 'Thanks to Rogers's skill, however, all was well.' This is rather difficult to understand, except as an attempt to placate the captain of the *Berwick* – for the Churchill camp could never understand why Kelly Rogers should be upset about the story.

The next attempt to deny the story is to be found in *The War and Colonel Warden*, written by Gerald Pawle in 1963 and based on the papers of Tommy Thompson. The latter was of course not on board the Boeing, but he had been on the circulation list for Kelly Rogers's account and Pawle paraphrases his version of the approach to Plymouth. Nevertheless, the Brest story was repeated in 1966 by Sir Charles Wilson, who was probably asleep at the time it happened. It is accepted without question in many Churchill biographies.

The real danger came, not from flying over Brest, but from the difficulty in landing. In Bermuda, Kelly Rogers had accepted conditions which the weather forecasters considered 'borderline'. These got even worse before he arrived, with Pembroke Dock and Poole closed, and Plymouth very difficult. What would he have done if conditions became slightly worse at Plymouth? He does not say what his answer was to Churchill's question as to what would he do if 'the British Isles were covered in one continuous sheet of fog', but it is clear that he was pushing his experience and knowledge to their limits.

★ ★ ★

In any case, the last stage of the approach to land was made with guidance from the radio transmitter at Plympton just east of Plymouth. Captain Shakespeare was keeping a lookout ahead when he spotted the coast through the fog. Kelly Rogers looked down to see the unmistakable Mewstone rock to the east of Plymouth Sound, followed by Staddon Heights and the RAF flying-boat station at Mount Batten to the north. He circled over the Sound and saw that the barrage balloons were down at the moment. Making a mental note of the positions of anchored ships, which he would have to avoid when landing, he started his descent, but at 300 feet he found that his horizontal visibility was lost in the fog, so he climbed above it. He circled and approached again, this time keeping the cliffs of Staddon Heights in sight on his right. He spotted the breakwater at the entrance to the harbour and crossed it at 50 feet, noting that he could see Drake's Island a mile ahead, but not Plymouth Hoe which was slightly farther away. He pulled the throttles back and touched down, to come to rest close to RAF Mount Batten. The station Operations Record Book recorded the time as 9.49, which is probably more reliable than Kelly Rogers's 8.59, as he admits he did not have logs and other documents to hand when he wrote his account.

The RAF station was ready despite the short notice and launches were sent out to meet them. As Churchill debarked from the aircraft, Kelly Rogers turned to him and said, 'I never felt so much relieved in my life as when I landed you safely in harbour.' Churchill later took this as evidence that they had been close to Brest, but it simply confirmed the captain's stress under the great responsibility placed on him.

They were taken ashore at Mount Batten and Churchill inspected a rough-and-ready guard of honour. He declined a breakfast which had been prepared for him, as he wanted to get on. His own train, of course, was still in Pembroke Dock, but the local railway authorities had hastily assembled some coaches at North Road Station, sufficient for the seven men in the party, plus some bodyguards. There was no time for proper goodbyes to Kelly Rogers and the crew, which both Churchill and Beaverbrook regretted and tried to make amends for later. Churchill was on the way within an hour of landing and reached London at 3.15 in the afternoon after an absence of more than a month. General Brooke was there to meet him, along with 'a queer crowd of Cabinet Ministers in black slouch sombreros and astrakhan collars'.

★ ★ ★

The story of Churchill's flight was very newsworthy, for he was the first prime minister to fly the Atlantic, and indeed the first world statesman to do so. It was quickly taken up by all sections of the press, from their respective angles. Churchill encouraged this. When a vague press release was being drafted he interrupted, 'To hell with the West Country port – say Plymouth!' Some papers stressed the great size of the American flying boat, the '*Queen Mary* of the air', and speculated about the future of civil aviation after the war. The *Sunday Dispatch*, edited by Churchill's friend Charles Eade, called it 'The most daring flight of the whole war', though of course no one mentioned any risk of flying over Brest. On the contrary, one report had the subheading, 'All tickety-boo, dead on course and right on time.' Most papers headlined the fact that Churchill had flown the plane himself, while the more popular ones highlighted the homely story, confirmed by Kelly Rogers, that the steward had warmed Churchill's shoes in the galley. Kelly Rogers found on arrival that his wife and young daughter were seriously ill, which was also featured in the papers; they did not record his resentment that it was partly caused by stress, and that no one had seen fit to tell his wife about his movements.

At the time, Churchill and Beaverbrook had no doubts about Kelly Rogers's skill, or that of his navigator and crew. The passengers subscribed £2 each to present him with a silver plate engraved with their signatures. To make up for their neglect in saying goodbye, he was invited to London and had lunch in Downing Street with Churchill, his wife and his daughter Mary, 'one of the most charming family meals I have ever attended'. The Prime Minister told stories about the flight and Mrs Churchill was deeply grateful for her husband's safe return. The ladies retired as was usual in an old-fashioned household and over the brandy and cigars Churchill confided, 'We are now winning the war! I could not have said that 12 months ago or even six months ago but I can say it now.' When Kelly Rogers eventually left, planning to stay in the Royal Aero Club, he found another invitation, this time from Lord Beaverbrook. He was taken to Cherkley by car and found the accommodation extremely comfortable, though the dinner party was less to his taste. He was rather overawed by the company of industrialists, newspapermen and politicians. Next morning he was finally able to return to his sick wife and daughter in Beaulieu, Hampshire. It was not the last time he would fly Churchill across the Atlantic.

Churchill was facing troubles of his own, for he returned as the Far East campaign went from bad to worse. As the Japanese advanced overland along the Malay Peninsula, he learned for the first time that the defences of Singapore were all on the seaward side – perhaps a penalty he paid for being away for so long. Sensing a mood of public criticism, he demanded a vote of confidence in the House of Commons. Only the tiny pacifist Independent Labour Party failed to support him and two of them had to act as tellers, so he won by an impressive 464 votes to 1. But the Japanese took Singapore in mid-February and forced the surrender of more than 50,000 British, Australian and Indian troops. Meanwhile the Germans had altered their Enigma code machines, so that source of intelligence dried up and the Atlantic became much more dangerous for British shipping. The year 1942 would be very testing for Churchill, although that did not reduce his urge to travel.

VI
The Longest Flight

The 12th day of June 1942 should have been a red letter day for General Sir Alan Brooke, the Chief of Imperial General Staff and professional head of the British Army. For months he had been planning a visit to the Farne Islands off the north-east coast of England. They were perhaps best known to the public for the story of Grace Darling, the Victorian lighthouse-keeper's daughter who had rowed out in a storm to rescue passengers from a sinking steamer. To Brooke, a keen bird-watcher who ranked among the most knowledgeable amateurs in the country, they were the breeding grounds of the Arctic tern, which lay their eggs in their thousands during May and June, and defend their nests fiercely against any intruders.

Brooke managed to escape from a Cabinet meeting on the 11th, when the Prime Minister was 'in good form and carried Cabinet with his proposed policy that we do not land in France in strength except to stop there, and that we do not go there unless German morale is deteriorating'. He flew north in the afternoon to inspect the 42nd Division at Catterick Camp, then on to Northumberland where he stayed with friends and found time to catch two trout after dinner. Next morning he arrived near the small port of Seahouses with Lieutenant-General Eastwood of Northern Command to be met by a naval captain and two sailors in a small dinghy. The weather was foul and there was a heavy sea. Eastwood stepped aboard and the boat capsized, taking Brooke's camera and films with it. They were fished out and a larger craft was found to take them out to a naval motor launch, which took them to the islands. But the camera was out of action and drizzling rain made photography difficult in any case. They returned to the mainland disconsolate, and flew back to London in the evening.

There were some in the army who might have been amused by the general's discomfiture. He had taken on the job of CIGS in December as Dill went to Washington, and many regarded him as an austere, frightening figure with a formidable intellect and few close friends. To a junior officer he was 'a thickset general, obviously of high rank, wearing enormous horn-rimmed spectacles', whose very presence caused 'an extraordinary current of physical energy, almost of electricity'. To a journalist he was a man of 'demanding and abrupt efficiency' who knew 'when to scold, when to encourage, when to protect. Men admired him, feared, and liked him: in that order, perhaps. He became, in peculiar, the conscience of the Army: a dark, incisive, round-shouldered Irish eagle ...'

Those who feared him had not had the chance to read his personal diaries, which reveal a shy and sensitive man, with far more self-doubt than he could show in public or at the War Office. He was born in 1883 in the south of France to an aristocratic Northern Irish Protestant family. He did not really enter British culture until he joined the Royal Military Academy at Woolwich at eighteen. As an artillery officer he rose from lieutenant to lieutenant-colonel during the First World War, and was a star pupil and then an instructor at the Imperial Defence College. He commanded a corps during the German invasion of France in 1940 and had to escape twice over the Channel. He was put in charge of the defence of southern England against the German invasion, until Dill's removal created a vacancy at the top.

Brooke was a very efficient officer, perhaps the best of the wartime chiefs of staff of any of the British services. His relationship with Churchill was often stormy and he described him as 'a prima donna of a Prime Minister, suspicious to the very limits of imagination, always fearing a military combination of effort against political dominance'. He could stand up to Churchill, who wrote: 'When I thump the table and push my face forward towards him, what does he do? Thumps the table harder and glares back at me.' Sometimes Brooke envied the position of his American opposite number General Marshall, as Roosevelt had no illusions about his own knowledge of military affairs and left it to the generals and admirals. But Brooke was determined to stay in the job and do his duty, unlike Beaverbrook, who was said to resign almost every day. In 1942 he even turned down the highly prestigious command in the Middle East because he felt he was needed in Whitehall. In the end he came to respect Churchill's great value as a war leader: 'Throughout all these troublesome times I always retained the same unbounded admiration, and gratitude for what he had done in the early years of the war. One could not help being filled with the deepest admiration for such a genius and super man.'

Brooke was back in his office on the 13th, the day after the Farne Islands fiasco. He was visited by Lord Louis Mountbatten, the young and well-connected Chief of Combined Operations who had just returned from Washington, where he had had a six-hour meeting with the President. Brooke was also called by the Prime Minister, who was becoming alarmed about the situation in the American capital. There was an essential strategic dilemma during 1942. Churchill had to keep the Americans interested in the war in Europe rather than the Pacific, but at the same time he was sure that the western Allies were not ready for an invasion of France – the armies were not well enough trained, there was a shortage of landing craft and a lack of experience. For the Americans, on the other hand, this was very frustrating. The tide was now turning in the Pacific and on 4 June they sank four Japanese aircraft carriers and prevented an invasion of Midway Island. Two months later they would go on the offensive with the invasion of Guadalcanal. Meanwhile there was stale-mate in Europe and strong pressure to send more forces to the Pacific.

Churchill's answer to this reflected British concern with the war in the Middle East and the Mediterranean which was not shared in Washington or Moscow. He wanted to invade the territory in North Africa held by the pro-German Vichy French. This would be combined with a British advance from Egypt in the east and would free the Mediterranean for Allied shipping and remove any threat to the Middle East. But it had to be sold to the President. In his telephone call to Brooke, Churchill 'considered Roosevelt was getting a bit off the rails and some good talks as regards the western front were required'. A trip was indicated, and Brooke was soon at his tailors being measured for a warm-weather uniform, as he knew that 'the temperature in Washington in June is like a Turkish bath'.

Churchill had already begun to consider the possibility of a trip by the 11th, while Brooke was inspecting the troops in the north. He set up a simple code for use on the telephone, in which the date of any meeting was 'date of leaving for London', Churchill was 'Colonel White' and the President was 'the General'. On the 13th he began to inform his staff:

> The Prime Minister has had a long talk with Mountbatten on his return from the United States and, in the light of his report, is now satisfied that it is his duty to pay another personal visit to Washington. Only so can he settle all the many points outstanding between ourselves and the Americans on the highest level, which cannot be dealt with by correspondence.[1]

It is not clear when Churchill decided to go by air, but the advantages were clear. The return in January had shown that it was perfectly possible, if hazardous. It would be rather easier with proper planning, and in midsummer rather than January. It would take one or two days of travelling each way, rather than six to eight. Churchill could get to Washington almost instantly, and only needed a week or ten days out of the country. There was no great threat from U-boats at that moment, as they were being driven from the American east coast and had not yet deployed elsewhere, but it would be a bad moment to take a capital ship out of its normal service. The *Barham, Prince of Wales* and *Repulse* had been lost at the end of 1941, the *Queen Elizabeth* and *Valiant* were seriously damaged in Alexandria harbour, while the *Anson* and *Howe* of the *King George V* class were delayed in the builders' yards and were not quite ready. Meanwhile the *Tirpitz* was now fully operational and based in the Norwegian fjords to raid convoys to Russia.

On the other hand, there were dangers in flying. Apart from the normal hazards, Churchill and Wilson had now heard the story that they had almost flown over Brest (although there is no sign that they confronted Kelly Rogers and gave him a chance to deny it). Yet Churchill's faith in the Irishman had clearly not been dented and he asked for him again as pilot. Of course there were possible medical problems, so Sir Charles Wilson was needed. John Martin sounded him out, and he replied that he had no great wish to go, but that 'there would be a real risk in undertaking such a journey without a medical attendant' and he would hold himself ready if necessary. Wilson himself wrote: 'The P.M. is always a little apprehensive in the air and our "narrow squeak" flying back from Bermuda has not helped matters. He asked me whether I minded flying. But before I could answer, I saw that he was thinking of something else.' Churchill himself was concerned enough to take the unusual step of writing to the King, to inform him that 'in the event of my death on this journey I am about to undertake ... you should entrust the formation of a new Government to Mr. Anthony Eden ... who is in my mind the outstanding minister in the largest political party in the House of Commons'.

Churchill was unusually diffident when he telegraphed Lord Halifax, his ambassador in Washington, for he was not sure if the visit was welcome. 'Mr Churchill does not know the President's intentions as regards accommodation and does not wish to impose on his hospitality, but accommodation of himself and complete personal staff in White House with office there would of course be most convenient.' It was revealed that Roosevelt would be in his country house at Hyde Park from 19 to 21 June, so much of the meeting would be held there.

It was decided to fly from Stranraer on the south-western tip of Scotland. There was a railway station for the Prime Ministerial train and nearby Loch Ryan offered a good take-off area for a flying-boat. Kelly Rogers was told that for security reasons it would be best if he could make it to Washington in one hop, though they would fly the northern route via Newfoundland which would take them well away from enemy air activity and allow a refuelling stop if necessary. The main question now was the weather. Head winds across the

Atlantic had to be avoided in view of the length of the voyage, and so too with depressions and fronts, for it would not be possible to fly over the top of them at perhaps 10,000 or 15,000 feet, in view of the Prime Minster's delicate health. From the 16th onwards the weather was monitored through Portal and the Air Ministry. A forecast was telephoned to the Prime Minster's staff at 8.15 each evening, with others at 9.00 and 10.15 each morning. A flying-boat was standing by at Stranraer, and the train was kept ready to leave. It would have to depart by 12.15 in the afternoon to allow the plane to take off that evening.

There was the usual indecision about exactly when to go. Brooke was at Downing Street with the Prime Minister late in the evening of Monday the 15th, when Churchill almost decided to start at 11.00 next morning. Brooke was relieved when it was postponed to Wednesday at the earliest. On Tuesday he had another fitting for his new tropical uniform and was about to dine with his cousin when the news arrived that they were leaving tomorrow. Clothing was rationed even for generals and an ordinary civilian suit used up 26 coupons, more than half the allowance of 48 per year. It would be intolerable to waste the coupons, so he had his unfinished uniforms delivered to Euston Station next day. The final decision to go was taken after the 10.15 forecast on Wednesday 17 June, and they boarded the train at 12.15.

Brooke had not travelled on it before and found it 'very comfortable'. He took his meals alone with Churchill, as he was the only person of his rank on board. This allowed him to 'settle many points in anticipation of talk with Roosevelt'. They arrived at Stranraer at 10.30 and Churchill used the train's special communications to catch up with the latest news. As he walked down the jetty he hummed the First World War soldiers' song 'We're here because we're here', and Wilson wondered if it was to keep his spirits up. A motor boat took them out to the *Bristol* which was virtually identical to the *Berwick*. Brooke was enchanted to find a 'huge flying-boat beautifully fitted up with bunks to sleep in, dining saloon, stewards, lavatories etc'. They took off at 11.30 that night.

This time Kelly Rogers had been persuaded to take a total of ten passengers. As well as the Prime Minister and the Chief of Imperial General Staff, they included the standard travelling party of Wilson, John Martin as secretary, Commander Thompson, Inspector Thompson, Kinna as clerk and typist, and Sawyers the valet. Major-General Sir Hastings Ismay, the Chief of Staff of the Ministry of Defence, was also there. One look at his face would explain his nickname of 'Pug' and according to John Colville, 'when he was pleased one could almost imagine he was wagging his tail'. He was the main instrument of Churchill's control of the war:

Nobody did more to oil the wheels on the sometimes bumpy road between the service chiefs and the politicians and it was due to him more than anyone else that the confrontations between the two in World War I were avoided in World War II.

The tenth member of the party was Brigadier G. M. Stewart, Brooke's staff officer.

They flew across the top of Ireland and Brooke saw a little bit of the coast before they climbed through the clouds to 5,000 feet, where they would remain for most of the journey to preserve Churchill's health. Ismay began to enjoy the flight, for 'Our Boeing flying-boat was the acme of comfort – plenty of room, full length bunks, easy chairs and delicious food.' Most of the party went to bed and the CIGS woke up at 11.00 GMT next morning, 8 o'clock local time, to see only clouds until 12.30, when they flew over a convoy of 35 ships. An hour later, after 14½ hours' flying, they were over Newfoundland with a wonderful view of the country. They came down to 1,500 feet and circled over the new airport being built at Gander, but they had no need to refuel and flew on. The cloud came down again over Nova Scotia, and then there was heavy fog and bumpy conditions until they reached Cape Cod.

Four hours out from Washington Churchill called Tommy Thompson and said, 'It is nearly eight o'clock, Tommy, where's my dinner?' Thompson explained that it was only about 4.30 local time and they were having dinner in the British Embassy that evening. Churchill was not appeased and answered that he went by 'tummy time' not sun time, so the party was given a meal – 'and a very good dinner it was!' according to Ismay. They had planned to take a look at New York but there was no time for that now, and they flew on to Washington. Churchill noticed that they were approaching at the same height as the top of the Washington Monument and remarked to Kelly Rogers that 'it would be peculiarly unfortunate if we brought our story to an end by hitting this of all other objects in the world'. The captain assured him that he would 'take special care to miss it'.

Brooke saw the 'beautifully laid out town in the hazy light of the evening' and wondered if they could really alight on the Potomac, 'a small silver ribbon running through the middle of it, so small at that height that it seemed quite impossible for the large Clipper to find sufficient space to accommodate it'. But after nearly 27 hours in the air it 'slid down on the water like a great swan'. Brooke 'found it hard to realise that in one hop I had moved from Stranraer Loch to the Potomac'. For Kelly Rogers it was the longest flight he ever did in wartime and he found it 'pretty tedious'. The passengers disembarked at

Anacostia naval air force base just outside the city and stayed overnight in the British Embassy.

★　★　★

Next morning Churchill flew north in an American aircraft to Roosevelt's country home at Hyde Park on the Hudson River above New York. At Hackensack Field he had 'the roughest bump landing I have ever experienced'. The President then drove him around his estate in a special car which could be operated without the need for feet on the clutch, accelerator and brakes. Churchill was careful not to interfere too much with his driving on the banks above the Hudson, but they talked business. It was not difficult to persuade the President that a landing in France that year would be a disaster. Churchill also came to believe that they discussed plans for an atom bomb in Roosevelt's tiny office, but it seems that he was mistaken: all the evidence suggests it was on a later visit.

That night they went by Presidential train to Washington and next morning Churchill was in Roosevelt's office when a piece of paper was brought in for him. The fortress of Tobruk had surrendered. Twenty-five thousand men were believed to have been taken prisoner and the way was open for Rommel's *Afrika Korps* to advance into Egypt. This was the only front in which British land forces were engaging the Germans, and it was a disaster.

On the 24th the disconsolate Churchill and Brooke were flown to South Carolina where they saw a demonstration of mass parachute jumping by the soldiers of the US Army. Sawyers asserted himself when the Prime Minister was about to get out of the plane wearing his zip suit and a Panama hat turned up at the brim, looking, according to Brooke, like 'a small boy in a suit of rompers going down to the beach to dig in the sand'. Sawyers blocked his way until he had turned the brim down. Meanwhile Brooke got to know the key American politicians and generals, as well as Roosevelt himself. Since Churchill had brought only a small personal staff with him, much work fell on the British Embassy in Washington to decode his messages and tend to his needs.

★　★　★

On the evening of 25 June it was time to depart after a visit of just under a week. Averell Harriman, Roosevelt's envoy, and Ian Jacob were added to the party for the return. The President came to see them off as they boarded the

Clipper at Baltimore where it was 'drawn up against the quay like a ship'. Churchill was experiencing a good deal of criticism as the war was going badly, and he remarked to Harry Hopkins, 'Now for England, home and – a beautiful row.' That was not the only hostility he faced. A disgruntled and mentally disturbed airport worker armed with a gun was heard muttering, 'I'm going to get that fucking Churchill. I'm going to kill him.' He was dealt with by the American secret service, who wrestled him to the ground. Churchill heard about it as he boarded and later remarked with his usual *sang froid*, 'Crackpates are a special danger to public men, as they do not have to worry about the "get away".'

They took off at 11.00 p.m. and saw the lights of Baltimore below. Brooke had a good night's sleep again and woke at 6.30, an hour and a half before the aircraft was due to reach the flying-boat base at Botwood in Newfoundland to refuel. He noticed the swampy countryside before landing on a lake near 'a small village of wood houses and a wooden church'. They took off again after refuelling and a breakfast of lobsters, which proved too much for Harriman's stomach, still on American time. Over the Atlantic, Brooke mused on the success of the visit and the wonders of air travel. Kelly Rogers approached him and said, 'We have just passed the point of no return.' Brooke thought of the air pioneers and what they must have felt at that point. Later he was in the cockpit with Churchill as they approached Ireland. 'Beautiful moon shining on a sea of clouds, as the moon was nearly full the scene was beyond words.' The pilot said that they should see a lighthouse soon if their navigation was accurate. 'And then suddenly flicking out of the darkness was a small spark of light! We had crossed that vast expanse of water and struck the exact spot we had hoped for.' Churchill and Brooke were both enchanted, and the general looked down as they flew over Northern Ireland, to see Lough Erne, where he had fished for pike, Colebrooke the family seat, and the industrial city of Belfast 'wrapped in all the morning mist, pierced with columns of smoke'.

They landed at Stranraer at five in the morning where the train was standing, with the secretary Robert Peck and 'a mass of boxes' full of papers awaiting the Prime Minister's attention. The newspapers reported a staggering government loss in a by-election at Maldon in Essex, and increasing criticism of the Prime Minister. Wilson planned to make his way to the sports day at his son's school at Sunningdale in Berkshire and the only way to do it was to take the plane which had brought up the mail. Churchill rebuked him. 'Now why, Charles, do you want to break up the party like this?' But he was allowed to go, and had a bad moment when the plane had to make a forced landing near Worcester. He arrived just in time to see young Geoffrey compete in his first race.

Churchill brooded for a time on the train, looked through his papers and then had his nap. 'What a blessing is the gift of sleep!' On arrival he was met as usual by the War Cabinet and was soon back at work. It was the shortest and most painless of his long-distance wartime trips, but the situation at home was far less comfortable.

★ ★ ★

On 1 July Churchill entered the House of Commons to face a vote of confidence. The defeats at Singapore and Tobruk and the retreat in the desert war were beginning to tell against him and Aneurin Bevan, the great Welsh Labour orator, declaimed, 'The Prime Minister wins debate after debate and loses battle after battle.' Soon the opposition began to unravel. Some were pacifists, some wanted to unseat Churchill, others wanted to keep him as Prime Minister but take away his detailed control over the war. Sir John Wardlaw-Milne, tabling the motion, made the incredible suggestion that the Duke of Gloucester should be put in charge of the armed forces. Churchill made a rousing speech and won by a majority of 475 to 25. But he still had to answer Bevan's taunt by winning some battles.

VII
Vanderkloot Brings It Off

There was another way to fly across the Atlantic besides the Boeing flying-boats, and Beaverbrook himself had set it up. By mid-1940, many aircraft were being produced in the United States for Britain and they were shipped across by sea, as Churchill had seen on the decks of Convoy HX 143. The voyage itself took about ten days, but convoys had to be assembled, ships loaded and then unloaded at each end, so the whole process might take weeks. This conflicted with the picture being painted for the Americans, that the planes were desperately needed in Britain for national defence. Many of them were long-range bombers for the RAF's Coastal Command, and Beaverbrook realised that they could be flown across from Newfoundland to Northern Ireland or Scotland, perhaps with extra fuel instead of armament. The RAF was chronically short of pilots at that time, so Beaverbrook assembled a strange collection of men from elsewhere. Some were from the airline interests of the Canadian Pacific Railway which managed the scheme. Some were ex-flying instructors in Canada, and more were from the United States, lured by the promise of $500 per flight and at least two flights per month. They included ex-servicemen, airline pilots, crop dusters, amateur pilots and barnstormers who travelled around the country with 'flying circuses'.

Among a collection of adventurers and extroverts, Bill Vanderkloot stood out as a quiet, studious man. He was a true air enthusiast, having earned flights by doing odd jobs on the aerodrome at his home town of Lake Bluff, Illinois. He did his first solo at the age of sixteen and persuaded his parents to send him to Air College in East St Louis instead of law school. He was beginning a career as an airline pilot when he was attracted by Beaverbrook's Atlantic Ferry Organisation, or Atfero. In April 1941 he was rated highly by Atfero staff and recommended for captain of an aircraft. He soon recognised that good navigation was the key to survival in this business, and he had a natural bent for it. As well as ferrying aircraft, he was employed to make a study of landing grounds around the main one at Prestwick in Scotland, in case aircraft had to be diverted. He was sent south to the West African coast to explore ways of sending aircraft to the war in Egypt while avoiding enemy territory in North Africa.

Initially, ferry pilots were sent back to North America by ship, which took several weeks as the fast Atlantic liners were in use elsewhere. Meanwhile, six

Consolidated B-24 Liberator bombers became available. They had been ordered by France, but went to the RAF after that country was defeated. The Liberator was a fine aircraft, though overshadowed by its American counterpart the Flying Fortress, and the British Lancaster which had a similar layout. The Liberator's greatest single advantage was its range, of 2,100 miles in the standard version compared with the Lancaster's 1,600 miles. This made it very suitable for Atlantic operation, and the first six in British service were used to take ferry crews back after completing their missions. Many of them found this the worst part of the process. Twelve or fourteen men were crammed into the bomb bay for a fourteen-hour trip and sat on inward-facing seats with no space, no view, no heating and not enough oxygen masks to go around. It was too noisy for conversation, and the passengers had no control over the aircraft. It was also dangerous – two Liberators crashed when leaving Scotland during August 1941, while the *Prince of Wales* was on her voyage to Newfoundland. Forty-four men were killed in all, including M. K. Purvis, Chairman of the British Supply Council in North America, a loss that Churchill described as 'most grievous'.

This was at the opposite end of the scale from the luxury of the Boeing flying-boats, but it had its attractions for government officials who wanted to get to and from North America quickly. Beaverbrook himself used it to join the Argentia conference in August 1941 – he preferred a few hours of terror to days of boredom on a ship. In June 1942 Lord Louis Mountbatten, the head of Combined Operations, wanted to get back from Washington in a hurry. A standard Liberator, serial number AL 504, was taken off the production line and converted to a slightly higher standard than normal ferry aircraft. It had two small shelves that could be used for bunks, and six seats. Air Commodore 'Taffy' Powell, head of the ferry service, flew it over himself.

★　★　★

Despite his success in two votes of confidence, Churchill's political position remained uneasy for most of 1942. Even with the accession of two of the most powerful states in the world as allies, victories remained few and far between and defeats were all too common. Churchill needed a clear-cut success to re-establish his position, preferably on land, and his eyes turned towards Egypt. The desert war had veered to and fro several times since 1940, but now the enemy was less than 70 miles from Alexandria, and the British high command were making plans to evacuate Egypt in an emergency. Churchill believed that only a personal visit could restore impetus, and ensure that the right people were in charge. Moreover, he wanted to go to Russia to talk to Stalin, and break the news that, despite requests from the Soviets and a vigorous campaign in Britain, the 'second front' against Germany in Northern Europe was not going to be launched that year. A flight around the north of Norway would be difficult and dangerous and in any case it was not encouraged by the Soviets; but it would be quite natural to fly on to Moscow from Egypt across Persia, which Allied troops occupied in August.

Churchill was already considering a trip to Egypt and the Soviet Union almost immediately after his return from Washington. When Kelly Rogers visited Downing Street, Churchill asked him about a visit to Gibraltar and remarked that 'it was very desirable to have a personal meeting with Mr Stalin'. He seemed keen to travel in the *Berwick*, as 'he had obviously learned of the discomfort to be endured by travelling in Service bombers or flying-boats'. Tommy Thompson examined ways of getting to Egypt. The Mediterranean was closed to normal sea traffic and even a convoy to relieve Malta could only get through at great cost in ships and lives. The voyage round the Cape of Good Hope would take several weeks, and would not be free from danger. Thompson consulted Kelly Rogers about the use of the flying boats but was not encouraged by his answer. They could fly to Bathurst and Lagos in West Africa, then across French Equatorial Africa to land on the Nile at Khartoum. It was a journey of 7,000 miles and three days, which would be wearing even in the luxury of the Boeing Clipper. The return journey could be worse, as the plane might be forced by the wind pattern to make a double crossing of the Atlantic, taking nearly a week in all. Worse still, a stopover in Sub-Saharan Africa would involve many inoculations, and Sir Charles Wilson was not sure if the Prime Minister's health would stand them. The alternative was to use the route the RAF had developed to deliver fighters across central Africa, with many stops on the way, which was even worse. But by July 1942, the Prime Minister was determined to go. Wilson was summoned to Downing Street:

> The P.M. has decided to fly to Cairo. From Gibraltar he will fly south to Takoradi on the Gold Coast, and so across Central Africa to Cairo. It means about five days in the air, landing at places where malaria and yellow fever are rife. The P. M. wanted my advice about inoculations. I did not like the plan and gave my reasons.[1]

Portal, however, had already found another solution. The Air Ministry had asked Taffy Powell of the Ferry Service for a suitable pilot for a long distance

VIP flight, and he soon came up with 'a young American, equally well quali-fied in navigation', a 'quiet unassuming man' who had 'made a special study of radio facilities in the United Kingdom' and whose 'instrument flying was superb'.

★ ★ ★

In July Bill Vanderkloot was between flights and staying in some luxury at the Savoy Hotel in London. Possibly he was there because his friend Duke Schiller, a very different character from the reserved Vanderkloot, had got them evicted from the nearby Strand Palace Hotel, but the Savoy's high prices were no bar to young men making at least a thousand dollars a month. One night Vanderkloot was dressing for an evening out with his crew when the phone rang and he was summoned to the Air Ministry. He was ushered into the office of Sir Charles Portal himself. After some small talk, Portal told him he had a VIP assignment for him and began to ask questions. He soon estab-lished that Vanderkloot was not some transatlantic braggart or daredevil, but a serious and intelligent man. Shown a map, he soon identified a possible route across North Africa:

> Setting out from here, I would fly directly to Gibraltar, in one hop. On the next evening, I would proceed eastward along the Mediterranean until last light, before cutting across Tunisia and so on to Cairo, with the hope of reaching the Nile shortly after dawn. In that way, we'd have the protection of the night against any enemy aircraft we might possibly meet along the way. It would involve two very long hops, but with the Liberator's range, I don't think that would present too much of a problem.[2]

Portal would later claim that a similar route had been used by RAF pilots since May, but gave Vanderkloot credit for providing a graphic demonstration of its viability and safety. Portal questioned him about other matters, particu-larly the reliability of his flight engineers, and thanked him for his opinions. He dismissed him but told him to stand by the telephone.

Vanderkloot had no idea which VIP he was to carry, until two evenings later when an RAF staff car collected him from the Savoy. He was surprisingly confused about directions during the short trip from there, and did not recog-nise the street he was dropped off at – possibly it was the annexe in Great George Street rather than Downing Street, as he came to believe. The driver told him to 'walk down this street until you find a door on your right, where you will see a very dim light. You are to knock on that door and identify yourself when it is opened to you. You are being expected.' He obeyed and was ushered into a room where to his surprise he found none other than Winston Churchill, wearing a blue dressing gown and smoking a huge cigar. 'Sit down, Captain Vanderkloot ... I understand we're going to Cairo! Do you care for a drink?' 'It took about two minutes to pick my jaw up when it dropped to the floor. Here was the greatest man in the world, and I was going to be associating with him as his pilot.' Churchill asked when he would prefer to leave for Egypt.

Well, sir, if I had the choice ... I'd like to leave as closely as possible to midnight and in as bad weather as it is practical to fly in. A midnight take off should bring us into Gibraltar at about the right time, with most of the flight under cover of darkness. Bad weather here over the British Isles might cut down our chances of running into enemy aircraft during this critical stage of the flight.[3]

Churchill agreed to give him a margin of four days to pick the night, and they parted.

★   ★   ★

Wilson was in the cabinet room in Downing Street after his consultation with Churchill about the inoculations. He was discussing the problem with Sir John Anderson the Home Secretary and Sir Stafford Cripps, the Leader of the House of Commons, when a beaming Prime Minister burst in and unfolded a large map on the table. 'Vanderkloot says it is quite unnecessary to fly so far south. He has explained to me that we can fly in one hop to Cairo. Come here and look.' Churchill traced the route with a pencil, reaching the Nile and turning sharply north. 'This changes the whole picture,' he added. Wilson asked who Vanderkloot was and was told that 'he had just crossed the Atlantic in a bomber', which rather understated his achievements. Anderson and Cripps were convinced and 'pored over the map like excited schoolboys', which was uncharacteristic of these austere gentlemen. Wilson was unconvinced as 'the party broke up without a word of warning or remonstrance about the risks the P.M. was taking in flying over hostile territory in an unarmed bomber by daylight. The P.M. gets his own way with everyone with hardly a murmur.' Wilson 'wondered why it was left to an American pilot to find a safe route to Cairo, but that did not seem a profitable line of speculation'.

As to security, the operation was codenamed Bracelet and the usual series of telegrams was arranged – Tulip coming out from London and Reflex from the party travelling. It would not be necessary to communicate with aircraft in flight, as messages could be sent through the British embassies in the countries concerned. The stopover at Gibraltar was always going to be a problem, but Churchill thought he had a solution. One of his assistants found him standing before a mirror in Downing Street wearing 'a long bright red beard and luxuriant side-whiskers', looking like 'a figure which might have stepped straight from the world of Walt Disney'. 'A very effective disguise, you will agree? I think I shall go and see the King in this this afternoon.'

It was decided to test Churchill and Cadogan for their reactions to low pressure at great height and in the afternoon of 31 July they arrived at the Royal Aeronautical Establishment at Farnborough. They were tested for blood pressure and took turns to go into a pressure chamber. Mrs Churchill watched through a porthole as the pressure was reduced to simulate 15,000 feet of altitude while her husband breathed through an oxygen mask. He complained about pain, but it was found that his mask was badly fitted. After a quarter of an hour with reduced oxygen he came out and was passed fit. Cadogan suffered from deafness and a slight pain in the head after his test, but he too was fit and it was decided to start next day.

★   ★   ★

Wilson's unasked question about 'why it was left to an American pilot' was an apt one, for the RAF had neglected navigation between the wars. Air transport had been used to link the British Empire rather than cross oceans, so in peacetime it was done in short hops across Europe and Africa to India. Pilots were expected to do the navigation themselves, though most regarded it as a diversion from their real duties. In the military field, it had been assumed that day-bombing of cities would win the next war, and the RAF was taken off balance when that did not work and it had to learn to attack by night. In mid-1941 it was found that only one in five bombers dropped its load within five miles of the target. The specialist navigation branch, with its own badge, was not set up until 1942, but navigator training still lagged a long way behind that of pilots. The Americans knew little more. Flights across country were guided by radio beacons, and there was no official standard for air navigation. Only Pan American Airways needed it for its oceanic flights, and set up its own training school. But as Churchill's first transatlantic flight had shown, accurate navigation was as important as anything else in ensuring the Prime Minister's safety.

Basically, there were three ways of navigating an aircraft before the advent of electronic aids. The simplest was to follow features on the ground, which worked well in good weather over land. Many pilots followed railway lines, known as 'Bradshawing', after the well-known railway guide of the time. In 1936 *Flight* magazine recognised the difficulties: 'At no time does one feel so helpless or realise the limitations of a normal aeroplane so well as when one is unable to recognise a town or railway-crossing during a cross-country flight in thick weather.' It recommended painting the name of the town on prominent features such as gasholders, but that was not likely to happen in wartime. Bill Vanderkloot did not consider this as proper navigation and called it 'air pilotage' whereby 'flying is carried out without the full analysis of the factors governing the direction of the aircraft's movement across the ground'. Before the war it was by far the most common method of finding the way in the air.

The second method was by dead reckoning. This had long been used by sailors, and John Mitchell, Churchill's navigator for the last two years of the war, wrote that 'the RAF was still ingeniously adapting the time-honoured methods of the marine navigator to the speed and environment of the aircraft'. In dead reckoning, the aircraft's course was found from the compass, the distance travelled through the air from the airspeed indicator. But the wind would also be pushing the aircraft from behind or ahead or from either side, so that had to be taken into account too, and it was not easy to predict or measure, especially in the North Atlantic.

Dead reckoning worked reasonably well with marine navigation because speeds were much lower, and because the main effect came from the tides and currents, which were predictable. According to the RAF's *Air Navigation* manual: 'The D.R. [dead reckoning] position is, however, always open to doubt, and it is consequently rather a misnomer.' Bill Vanderkloot thought that dead reckoning was the basis for all true air navigation: 'Broadly speaking, navigation consisting of dead-reckoning is navigation constantly checked by the use of three main navigational aids' – objects on the surface, radio signals and the stars.

The great problem was to calculate the effect of the wind on the aircraft. The manual listed a dozen different ways of measuring sideways movement or 'drift', but most of them relied on a fixed and identifiable point, which was not always available over the sea or the desert or in bad weather. The RAF manual recommended 'exercising acute observation while in flight' by which a navigator would be able to 'acquire a wealth of experience, constituting almost a sixth sense'. John Mitchell was well on the way to developing this, and he had a thorough knowledge of practical meteorology. He would work

> from in-flight calculation of past wind components and visual observation of the weather around us, cloud formations, turbulence, outside air temperatures, etc. These taken together could often give us some idea of the movement of weather systems as they affected our route, perhaps meeting a weather front sooner than forecasted, or finding that a front that looked threatening on the weather chart had in fact died away.[4]

The third method of navigation was by using the sun, moon and stars. Again, this had been used for centuries by mariners, and the invention of the chronometer in the eighteenth century had made it practicable for any navigator with enough mathematical skill. The air navigator had one advantage here, in that he could usually get above the clouds by about 15,000 feet to get a clear view of the heavens (though not necessarily when Churchill was on board and his doctor would not allow him to fly so high). Above the clouds the navigator would probably lose sight of the horizon, so he had to use a 'bubble' sextant which had a kind of spirit level and allowed him to measure the angle of the star above the horizon. VIP pilots and navigators preferred the night, not just for security reasons but because it allowed them to take constant observations of the stars, and the RAF almanac provided details of the more easily identifiable ones.

The navigator would usually plot a star from the aeroplane's astrodome, shaped like half a goldfish bowl. Some believed that it was better to take the observation from an open hatch, but Bill Vanderkloot was not among them. He had 'found that the errors in the glass are very small' and was 'of the opinion that sights taken through the glass in comfort are generally more accurate than sights taken through an open hatch much to the navigator's, and the rest of the crew's, discomfort'.

It might take a few seconds to measure the angle of one star. During the taking of the sight the aircraft would have moved several miles, but the navigator needed at least two and preferably three to give a 'fix'. He then had to apply various corrections for the time travelled during the observation, for the refraction of the atmosphere, the height of the aircraft and so on. Finally he went back to his chart table to plot the position. The exact position of each star had to be found from the almanac, and this gave a circle on the earth's surface a certain number of miles from the position directly under the star. Having plotted several of these and found out where they intercepted, the navigator could now say with confidence where the aircraft had been ten or fifteen minutes ago when he began the process. Even then it was not likely to be accurate within about ten miles.

A navigator on a long flight had to work hard taking fixes, estimating the speed of winds and often assessing the various pieces of contradictory information. Vanderkloot warned him against exhausting himself in the first few hours:

> Usually for the first half or two-thirds of the flight they work very hard, with the result that they are tired when they should be working the hardest. A flight of 10 hours can be said very quickly, and it does not appear to be a very long period of time, but if it is analysed further, it is longer than a normal working day. It is obvious that energy must be conserved.

Vanderkloot believed in careful pre-flight planning, which was one of the secrets of his success. A navigator should check that all his tools and instruments were available and working:

> As soon as the navigator knows that he is going on a flight, there is a great deal of essential work to be done. He must calculate the track and distance and divide it into zones for ease of handling the weather forecast. Over long distances the forecasts are usually made for about 200-mile intervals. He must obtain all the information possible about the various navigation aids that he will have: the location, frequency and services of the various radio stations, both direction finding and broadcast, and the position and times of marine beacons. It is well to study a star chart to ascertain what stars will be visible and to locate the visible planets ... When the weather forecast has been obtained, the navigator will be able further to plan his flight in that he will know whether he can obtain drifts, radio or astro, at various times along the route ... The charts should be of a suitable scale and have the tracks laid off before the flight commences.[5]

Very little of this would happen on the flight he was about to undertake.

★ ★ ★

At some stage it was decided to send an RAF navigator as well, the only Briton and the only serviceman in the crew. Charles Kimber had no idea why he was selected for the task, but he speculated that he had recently flown Liberator AL 505 across the Atlantic, and someone in the Air Ministry might have mistaken this for AL 504, *Commando*. But in fact the RAF had few navigators with his level of experience. His career symbolised the confusion of navigation policy over the last decade and a half. He joined the RAF as a ground crew apprentice at the age of sixteen in 1928, and trained as a metal fitter on airframes before converting to engines. He spent 190 hours flying as a gunner, during which time he did a certain amount of navigation, or at least air pilotage, in an open-cockpit biplane:

> Flying as navigator in the Hind involved the use of a Bigsworth board; a simple pair of hinged boards, one of which was transparent. The map was sandwiched between the boards, and a graduated straight-edge, combined with a protractor, enabled the navigator to draw tracks and courses on the transparency. The navigator sat with his back to the pilot, exposed to the blast of the slipstream on the upper half of his body. He obtained his instrument readings, airspeed, height, temperature and compass, by standing erect and looking over the pilot's shoulder.

In 1937 he took the observer's training course as a corporal:

> Lectures, flying, analyses and remedies followed in rapid order. Each meticulously discharged. The only light relief, though full of meaning, were the *ad hoc* competitions in stripping and reassembling a Lewis gun – blindfold … Lectures were well organised and thorough, and I learned much of the theory of bombing and navigation.

Kimber soon developed a love of celestial navigation:

> The navigator enjoys a close intimacy with the stars; to him they are not millions of light years distant, but his friends and neighbours. When he brings a star down into the optical sights of his sextant, he feels on terms with it; Arcturus becomes Archie; Alpheratz – Alphy; Dened – Debby.[6]

He was commissioned in 1940 but as an air gunner rather than a navigator, and took part in missions over France and Germany. He did an advanced navigation course at Port Albert in Canada in 1941 and became the chief navigation officer of 44 Group, Bomber Command, with the rank of squadron-leader.

Now Kimber was sent to RAF Lyneham and told he was going on a special mission but he did not know where, so it was impossible for him to find the right charts and do his pre-flight planning. He thought it might be South Africa, in which case he would need thirteen volumes of Air Navigation Tables to cover the different latitudes involved. He met Vanderkloot and his co-pilot casually in the mess, but did not make any association from that. Then there was an unfortunate start when he was summoned to a hangar for briefing, but denied entry by the security officer. Eventually Tommy Thompson sorted it out and before any more could be said, the Prime Minister himself entered with his party. Kimber was introduced to them and then sought out Vanderkloot.

For all his navigational expertise and meticulous planning, Vanderkloot seemed amazingly vague. He told the navigator that the destination was Gibraltar, and indicated a route in his Midwest accent. 'I wanna go thissaway for 400 miles, then thataway for 500 miles, then thissaway for 300 miles to Gibraltar.' In other words, he planned to make a wide sweep out into the Atlantic to avoid the attentions of enemy fighters and reconnaissance aircraft based in France. Kimber sensed that Vanderkloot was not happy about having an outsider in his crew. Years later, when his biography was written by a Canadian journalist, Kimber did not rate a mention at all.

Kimber was not any happier when he boarded and reached the flight deck. It was already overcrowded with two pilots, two engineers, a radio operator and Wing-Commander Roland Winfield, the RAF's expert in oxygen supply, who had conducted the test at Farnborough. Kimber demanded that the wing-commander and one of the flight engineers leave. Even worse, the chart table was loaded with clothing, briefcases and other items. The engines had already started, but he insisted in having it cleared – he would need to be up and down throughout the flight, taking star sights every twenty minutes or so and then plotting them.

For all his confidence in front of Portal, Vanderkloot too was beginning to feel the strain:

There was the prime minister boarding the plane after being escorted every foot of the way from 10 Downing Street to the airport. But when the door slammed shut, all the guards got back in their cars and left! It was now our responsibility. You could go crazy thinking about it, so I decided not to think about it any more than I had to.[7]

It was a horrible feeling, the thought of losing Churchill. I would think, 'Here am I, a civilian, and an American civilian at that, with the safety and very life of the prime minister of Great Britain in my sweaty hands.'[8]

The plane took off at 10.28 in the evening of 1 August, watched by Mrs Churchill:

It was both dramatic and mysterious standing in the dark on that aerodrome while your monster bomber throbbing, roaring and flashing blue light taxied away into the blackness – it seemed a long time taking off – Finally we saw its huge dim shape airborne against the row of 'glim' lights which I suppose are there as a guide to planes.[9]

Churchill went into the cockpit to watch the first stages of the flight, as the aircraft flew low over south-west England in order to be recognised by the anti-aircraft batteries. On leaving the coast it began a wide sweep over the Atlantic. During the flight Churchill had a conversation with the pilot:

'You know what Hitler would do to me if he ever got his hands on me, don't you, Vanderkloot?'

Vanderkloot nodded.

'But you're not going to let him do that, are you Captain?' Churchill said, with a twinkle in his eye.[10]

Later co-pilot Jack Ruggles increased the tension by remarking, 'This fellow is England, and if we ever dunk him in the drink ...'

Leslie Rowan, another of the private secretaries, was making his first overseas journey with Churchill, just as the Berlin–Rome Axis was at the height of its powers at this very moment. British armies in the Middle East had been pushed back almost to Cairo. The Germans were advancing in Russia and the battle for Stalingrad, the bloodiest conflict in world history, was about to begin as the Germans moved towards the city. Leningrad was besieged and Axis power still seemed unbeatable. The journey would be the longest one Churchill undertook in the war, 17,000 miles round the fringes of the enemy strongholds.

Mountbatten was only 42 at the time when he first flew in *Commando*, and as a serving naval officer he was reasonably fit and accustomed to hardship – it was just over a year since he had spent hours clinging to a liferaft, half blinded by oil, after the sinking of HMS *Kelly* – the episode later portrayed by Noel Coward in *In Which We Serve*. Churchill was to find the Liberator a very different matter. The accommodation was unheated at this stage. The two shelves were furnished with mattresses which according to Wilson had been 'dumped' there. It was cold at that height even in the summer air, but the fuselage was not windproof and the aircraft was flying at around 200 miles per hour. Blankets had been crudely tacked onto the sides to prevent draughts but they did not go all the way round. Wilson managed to sleep reasonably well as he usually did, but Churchill hated draughts and persisted in wearing his light night clothes. He commented:

> This was a very different kind of travel from the comforts of the Boeing flying-boats. The bomber was at this time unheated, and razor-edged draughts cut in through many chinks. There were no beds, but two shelves in the after cabin enabled me and Sir Charles Wilson, my doctor, to lie down. There were plenty of blankets for all.[11]

Inspector Thompson was surprised that Churchill would put up with such conditions, but underneath it all the Prime Minister saw himself as a soldier on active service, ready to endure almost anything before returning to luxury in the officers' mess. Wilson, still sceptical, thought it was 'a feckless way of sending him over the world when he is approaching his seventieth year'. But Churchill too fell asleep, 'fortified by a good sleeping cachet', as he put it. He was in good fettle in the morning.

★ ★ ★

Commando reached Gibraltar after a relatively simple part of the journey, although in thick cloud it was mostly done by dead reckoning. The airstrip had been built out into Algeciras Bay and it was only 5,000 feet long, so that any deviation to the left or right would put the aircraft in the sea. To Vanderkloot it was 'like landing on an aircraft carrier'. The Liberator was never easy to land, and one British pilot complained that it could not be 'floated' onto a runway like other aircraft. It 'had to be motored until it touched, and the rate of descent had to be controlled by carefully judged applications of power'. Worse, it was only yards from neutral Spanish territory where German spies were known to be very active. There was no doubt that the arrival of a strange Liberator would be reported to Berlin, and its passenger might well be identified by local gossip if not by actual observation.

After landing, Churchill was whisked off to stay with the Governor and tour the Rock, although his red beard was not deployed. Charles Kimber

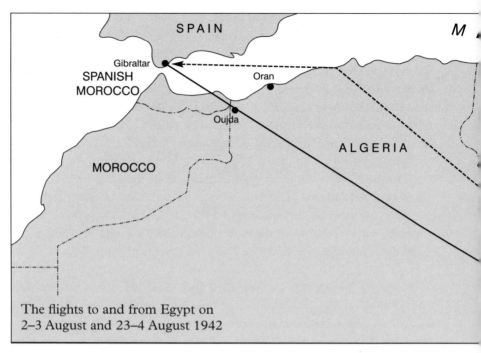

The flights to and from Egypt on
2–3 August and 23–4 August 1942

began to worry about the onward journey. 'I reasoned that if the next stage was eastwards, it was most unlikely to be along the Mediterranean because of enemy activity in Malta. I assumed it would be inland from the North African coastline.' He selected charts accordingly, and drew out navigation graticules – the network of lines of latitude and longitude on a chart. They would allow him to reach a specified destination by means of celestial navigation, provided its latitude and longitude were known. The charts did not include any ground features, but these were few and far between on a desert flight in any case. Vanderkloot was sworn to secrecy and requests for more information brought no response. As Kimber observed: 'Security may be so secure that essentials to the success of an operation may be jeopardised.' Vanderkloot's own ideas on pre-flight planning were being ignored. At last, just as the passengers were boarding, Kimber was handed a sheet of paper. He gave a sigh of relief. 'The route was eastwards within the latitude limits I had estimated.'

★ ★ ★

The Liberator took off at six minutes past four in the afternoon of 2 August and headed across the Mediterranean. The general plan was to go south-east to a point in the Libyan desert 400 miles south of Tripoli, then turn east in two

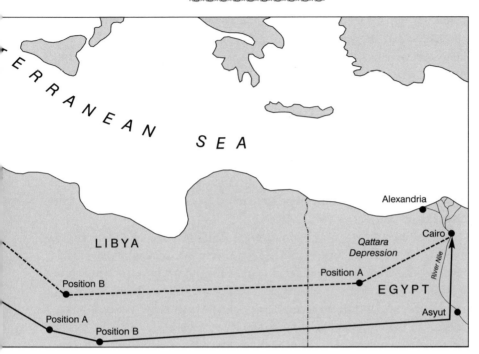

stages to meet the Nile 200 miles south of Cairo. This would involve different problems for each stage, as the aircraft passed over different kinds of territory, both neutral and enemy.

The chances of a lone bomber being shot down by night in these circumstances were very small indeed, as Churchill knew better than anyone. It was only eighteen months since the *Luftwaffe*'s night blitz of Britain, when they had flown many thousands of sorties with a loss rate of about 1.5 per cent. This was in an area about an eighth of the size of Libya alone, defended by a large and highly trained air force supported by a chain of radar stations and later with radar-equipped night fighters. None of these conditions would apply over the Sahara desert.

The aircraft was escorted by four RAF Beaufighter twin-engined fighters for the first part of the journey and it crossed the North African coast at 4.50 in the afternoon, close to the town of Mellila in Spanish Morocco. This was one of the strangest features of the journey, for crossing Spanish territory saved only a very small amount of time. The risk of being shot down was small. British intelligence was aware that the Spanish Air Force had a mixed collection of obsolete aircraft left over from the Civil War – German, Italian and even some antiquated and unserviceable Russian ones. It was believed that seventeen of them were based in Spanish Morocco, but shortage of fuel had virtually grounded the air force for several months and prevented training. It was considered that 'the fighting value of the Spanish Air Force is negligible'. More important were possible diplomatic consequences. If such a blatant violation of neutrality was revealed, it would give ammunition to the war party in Fascist Spain – a declaration of war would be disastrous for Britain, probably neutralising Gibraltar as a base, providing new airfields for the *Luftwaffe* and sealing off one end of the Mediterranean. It was a huge risk for such a small gain in distance. The Liberator was mainly flown by a civilian crew, but its number, AL 504, put it on the books of the RAF and it wore the famous roundels. It would be difficult to pass it off as a civil aircraft, either in the air or in a court of law. The Beaufighter escort only drew attention to it, and undermined any flimsy claims to civilian status.

The Liberator was now flying alone at 9,500 feet and passed over Oujda in Vichy French territory by 5.15. There were no qualms about violating neutrality here, for Britain did not recognise the puppet government. Kimber, however, had another concern, as he looked down and saw French aircraft on the ground, and wondered if there had perhaps been some secret diplomatic agreement to permit the flight. He would have preferred to carry out this part of the journey in darkness. He also wanted to fly due south to get farther away from areas where unfriendly aircraft might be encountered, but that was not allowed. Again, the Vichy French air force was not strong. British intelligence believed that it had one naval squadron of twelve Dewoitine 520 fighters at Port Lyautey on the Atlantic coast 150 miles west of the route, and two air force squadrons, with a total of 49 planes, at Oran, which was more than 100 miles to the east. The Dewoitine, however, was quite an effective fighter, which claimed more than a hundred German aircraft during the invasion of France. About 70 per cent were believed to be serviceable at any given moment, morale was good, but training was poor, again due to petrol shortage.

Meanwhile Kimber had work to do, calculating the wind velocity from observations on the ground while there was still enough light. At last, after just over two hours of flight, darkness fell without any intervention by the Spanish or the Vichy French. A fix at 8.23 showed them to be on track to the southeast, and around nine that night they crossed the border of the Italian colony of Libya.

They were now technically in hostile territory, though the desert was sparsely populated and occupied and there was still no sign of the enemy. By an intelligence report dated on the last day of July 1942, the Italians had a total of 340 fighters in North Africa, of which 210 were in Egypt behind the main battle area. Of the 65 in Libya, only one flight of perhaps six aircraft was believed to be south of the coastal area in Hon, which was in the desert 200 miles north of the route. The Italians were believed to have 20 full aerodromes, 66 landing grounds and 58 emergency landing grounds in Libya, but the great majority of these were concentrated on the northern coastal strip, to take part in the land war, to attack British convoys heading for Malta and to protect their own supply routes across the Mediterranean. It was difficult to operate aircraft from the desert, where roads to bring in fuel were practically non-existent, and water was scarce except in a few oasis areas. A few airfields were quite close to the Liberator's route. Emergency Landing Ground No. 3, for example, was just 20 miles north of the track and the aircraft passed close at around 1.30 in the morning, but no aircraft were normally based there and according to intelligence reports it 'had some facilities, but reported in September, 1941, the petrol pump had been rendered useless'. More dangerous was the field at Sebha which was only 60 miles away from the route and near the first turning point. It had hangar accommodation, radio communication and some kind of fuel store, but again there was no evidence of any aircraft operating from there.

In truth, the navigation was not particularly difficult for this stage of the journey. It was only necessary to head east to reach the unmistakable feature of the River Nile, then follow it north to Cairo. There was no need to zigzag or take evasive action, as a bomber over heavily defended enemy territory would have to do. The only danger (apart from mechanical failure or detection by the enemy) was in straying too far north into German and Italian territory, but that would take a course error of at least 30 degrees, and neither Vanderkloot nor Kimber was capable of such negligence.

The squadron-leader worked hard throughout the night, taking fixes from the stars and revelling in the clear visibility. As he had predicted, he was constantly bobbing up and down between the astrodome and the chart table, and took more than a dozen star sights during the night, on Polaris, Altair, Aldebaran, Arcturus and Vega. He had to stand on a box to use the astrodome. Occasionally he was interrupted by the Prime Minister, who had to pass through a hatch below to enter the cockpit, and knocked on it to have Kimber remove the box. He was working almost continuously for four hours up to 3.30 in the morning, and was not able to use his oxygen mask while taking a sight, which made it very exhausting.

The Liberator's four engines still 'purred happily', to Churchill's relief – though it is difficult to imagine that any cat could make a noise resembling that of four Pratt and Whitney Twin Wasps each generating 1,200hp. Churchill went on: 'It would have been tiresome to make a forced landing on neutral territory, and even descent in the desert, though preferable, would have raised problems of its own.' On the whole the travellers were more worried about engine failure than enemy action, and Portal had questioned Vanderkloot intently about the quality of his two flight engineers. The engines needed a good deal of attention. According to a British pilot, 'The complications of the B-24 included turbo-blowers, fuel booster pumps, intercoolers for the blowers, inverters for the electric dopers for engine starting, integral control locks and ashtrays in the pilot-seat armrests … for every 30 minutes in the air we seemed to spend an equivalent time going through the cockpit drill, setting up the boost for each engine separately on the turbo-blower controls, creeping along the runway to get the nosewheel straight, and unlocking and checking the control surfaces.'

At 10.40 Vanderkloot's Liberator began to turn on to the easterly course at 27 degrees of latitude north of the Equator, and a fix after midnight showed them to be less than 300 miles south of the Gulf of Sirte, the closest they would come to the Libyan coast where the enemy was most active. At half past midnight a position line taken from the star Aldebaran showed that they had crossed the border into Egypt, but that did not guarantee safety. They passed 300 miles south of the position at El Alamein, where the Eighth Army of British, Australian, South African and New Zealand troops was holding the line against Rommel's triumphant German *Afrika Korps*. The Liberator was flying about 150 miles south of the Qattara Depression, an impassable desert area that restricted both armies to a narrow coastal strip.

The *Luftwaffe*, of course, was by far the most formidable unfriendly air force in the region. Fortunately its main priorities were elsewhere, for it was fully engaged on the Russian front, and on defending the Reich against increasing air attack from Britain – three raids of a thousand bombers each had already been staged that year. British intelligence believed that there were about 144 German Me-109F single-seat fighters in North Africa, but these would not have been much use at night. The most lethal force for the Liberator was *Zerstorer Gruppe 26* with its 30 Me-110 night fighters, but it was the only German force of the kind in the Mediterranean region and had to spread itself very thinly. Intercepted signals told the British of the plight of the German air force in North Africa. These revealed almost daily complaints about shortages of ammunition, of pilots, of fighter aircraft and of fuel as British submarines and torpedo bombers sank oil tankers. There were difficulties of division of command between the Germans and Italians. The new Me-109F fighter had serious engine problems. Meanwhile, contradictory orders were issued to the squadrons. On July 23 the *Luftwaffe* was to carry out night harassment of enemy land forces, but also to give priority to transport of personnel for the army. On 31 July the army commanders complained of heavy losses to coastal shipping and on 1 August, as Churchill set out from RAF Lyneham, they were ordered to transport a paratroop battle group from Crete. On 3 August Rommel requested that they concentrate on attacking Allied supply lines and protecting Axis supplies. On August 6, a night fighter unit was transferred to Belgium to fight the British bombers. The vast and empty lands far to the south were nowhere on their list of priorities.

★ ★ ★

Churchill was up several times during the night to visit the cockpit, and Kimber was not surprised that he was on hand half an hour before dawn. He witnessed 'the changing spectrum of colours running round the eastern horizon as the sun steadily climbed from its nadir below the horizon, reaching a climax when the sun tipped the horizon and, to the west, night giving way to the unequal struggle for supremacy'. He was still there at 4.25 when the Nile came into sight. 'Often I had seen the day break on the Nile. In war and peace I had traversed by land or water almost its whole length, except the "Dongola Loop", from Lake Victoria to the sea. Never had the glint of daylight on its waters been so welcome to me.' They reached the river just north of Asyut and turned north to follow its course towards Cairo. Kimber had Vanderkloot fly along the west bank to give Churchill a view of the railway from Cairo to Aswan, and was impressed with the span of the Prime Minister's life, and how much must have changed since his cavalry charge in 1898. He had used Greenwich Mean Time throughout the flight and by that reckoning it was 5.30 when they landed. In local time, it was 7.30. Sir Charles Wilson's scepticism evaporated as they touched down on Landing Ground 224. 'Vanderkloot has brought it off.'

VIII
To Moscow with an Atlas

In Cairo, Churchill stayed with Ambassador Sir Miles Lampson in 'princely' accommodation with an air-conditioned bedroom and study. He spent much time with General Jan Smuts, the veteran South African Prime Minister, a man of great experience and wisdom. He visited the front line near El Alamein and flew over the British positions. He found the army was 'almost double as strong as the enemy' but 'baffled and bewildered by its defeats'. He decided to replace General Claude Auchinleck as head of the Eighth Army and focused on Lieutenant-General William 'Strafer' Gott as the man to do the job. The tall, saintly-looking officer had risen from the command of a battalion at the beginning of the war to lead the 13th Corps, and his promotion through three ranks had all been earned in battle. He had an unconscious knack of leadership, and was just the man Churchill needed. No sooner, however, than he had telegraphed his decision on a complete reorganisation to the War Cabinet in London, when he received the news that Gott's plane had been shot down and he was dead. He had been travelling in a slow and anti-quated Bristol Bombay transport aircraft, taking him from the headquarters at Burg El Arab back to Cairo, when it was pounced on by six German Messerschmitt 109 fighters. The pilot somehow managed to land the burning aircraft but the rear door was jammed and most of the passengers, including Gott, were trapped. The incident highlighted the dangers of air travel in wartime, even if it was not directly relevant to Vanderkloot's trips across the desert. When Churchill wrote of Gott's death 'in almost the same air spaces through which I now flew', he was referring to his short flights to the front line, not to the lengthier journey from Gibraltar to Cairo.

A new commander had to be appointed and Churchill sent for General Sir Bernard Montgomery, a far less popular man. 'If he is as disagreeable to those about him he is also disagreeable to the enemy,' he wrote to Clementine.

★　★　★

Egypt was technically neutral in the war and ruled by King Farouk. British and Commonwealth troops were stationed there in large numbers under the terms of a treaty of 1936 and Cairo was the headquarters for the British army and air force in the Middle East. Cairo was a vibrant and cosmopolitan city of more than a million people on the east bank of the Nile, with all the sights, sounds and smells of the Orient. The desert army included divisions from Australia, India and New Zealand as well as from England and Scotland. The city was accustomed to dealing with service personnel and a locally produced wartime guide had advertisements for cinemas, bookshops, military tailors, hostels, the Waterloo Club, which was reserved for senior NCOs, and the Biba Troup cabaret which was 'in bounds to other ranks'.

Off duty in the city, Kimber did not socialise with Vanderkloot's crew but went to Tommy's Bar, which 'had the reputation that any officer of the armed forces dropping in would meet someone he knew', and this turned out to be true of his visit. He also found time to take a trip on an Arab dhow and visit the pyramids, but there was a pressing need.

Neither Vanderkloot nor Kimber knew that they were to be sent on another, even more challenging flight, until after they landed at Cairo, and were informed they were to go on to Moscow with the Prime Minister and his party. Vanderkloot had mixed feelings: 'I didn't know if the airplane could go that far and into such a foreign country.' He chose the route, and Kimber began his navigational planning, in circumstances that were even more bizarre than those of the flight to Cairo. Clearly the need for security was paramount, but the Air Ministry might at least have sent out a set of what charts it possessed for the area, perhaps in a sealed envelope. There was no such foresight, and Kimber toured the offices of Cairo looking for something to guide him on his way. At air force headquarters Wing-Commander Taylor told him he had nothing. When he turned to the army, a brigadier produced three very small-scale maps with a projection that was unsuitable for air navigation. Kimber accepted them in desperation and began to plot new navigation graticules for any likely route to Moscow: those for the desert flight would not do because part of the forth-coming flight would be to the north, and there would be a change of scale on the latitude measurement. Eventually he hunted down a commercial Phillips Atlas, and plotted the latitude and longitude of all major towns along the routes. He sketched in the outlines of the Caspian Sea and the Ural and Volga Rivers, as well as railway lines which might provide some indication of direction. This was improvised 'Bradshawing' on a grand scale.

★ ★ ★

They were to travel via Tehran for refuelling. Vanderkloot decided to plan the journey so that they would pass over the Zagros Mountains of Persia in daylight, but there was much confusion about timings. According to Ian Jacob, someone had told Churchill that he should see the sunrise over Baghdad. This became an obsession, and timings were changed to allow for it, though Churchill did not take any account of how it would disrupt the timings and delay the arrival in Tehran.

The Liberator took off from Cairo at eleven in the evening GMT, which Kimber continued to use for navigational purposes. He was pleased to find that security was at last given some priority. The aircraft flew to the south-west, apparently heading towards Cape Town; then, after 50 miles it turned to the north-east, seemingly making for Palestine or Syria. It crossed over the Bitter Lake on the route of the Suez Canal at 20 minutes past midnight, and altered course to 70 degrees, towards Iraq. Kimber did two fixes from star sights and found that they were slightly north of the planned track, so course was altered to converge with it. At 1.25 Ruggles spotted the depression of the Dead Sea.

Averell Harriman was among the passengers for this leg, and he was not impressed with conditions on board: 'It was converted for passengers in the most primitive manner, without insulation, and with two rows of hard benches facing each other. The noise was so great it made conversation impossible. Our only communication was by passing notes to each other, some on important subjects, some trivial.' Thus the purpose of personal contact was undermined. Harriman thought that Commander Thompson had 'a delightful personality' but was amused as he incurred the Prime Minister's wrath. Churchill selected a ham sandwich from the lunch basket, and asked for mustard. There was none, and Churchill responded, 'How could you have forgotten the mustard? No gentleman eats ham sandwiches without mustard.'

The crew continued to work hard. Kimber managed to get in a last star sight just before the sun rose at 0244 hours GMT, and less than an hour later they were crossing the Euphrates just south of Baghdad. They altered course to 069 degrees to head straight for Tehran. Vanderkloot planned to cross the Zagros Mountains at 9,000 feet, but Churchill looked at the map and spotted that there were several peaks of 11,000 or 12,000 feet, with a more distant one of 18,000 feet which was not on the track. He recognised that 'so long as you are not suddenly encompassed by clouds, you can wind your way through mountains with safety'. Nevertheless, in an uncharacteristic moment of caution, he insisted in climbing to 12,000 feet and oxygen masks had to be fitted. His amateur navigation was not always so successful. As they descended to Tehran he pointed out that the altimeter showed 4,500 feet and suggested that Vanderkoot might have it checked. The captain told him that the airfield was 4,000 feet above sea level. They touched down on one of the concrete runways of Tehran airport at 0550 GMT, or 8.50 local time. It was too late to start for Moscow that day, so Churchill went to lunch with the Shah in his palace and had a long discussion with Harriman (formerly a railroad magnate) about running a train service through Iran to Russia.

The Foreign Office had asked the Russians to send any maps that might be available on to Tehran, but there is no indication that this happened. Kimber tried to make contact with the air attaché in the Embassy, but he was unavailable. In any case, Kimber was not unduly concerned. He did not know the chosen route to Moscow, but he was confident that it would lie within the boundaries of his improvised charts.

The Liberator took off at 0600 GMT, 9 o'clock local time, to fly the remaining 1,700 miles. They had to follow a route somewhat to the east of Moscow, to avoid the front line as the Germans advanced fatefully towards Stalingrad. The first task was to get round the Elburz Mountains which rose to 12,000 feet north of Tehran. As they flew east, Commander Thompson was enchanted with the snow-capped peak of Mount Demavend in the distance; and Kimber found that the Quizl Uzung valley was 'wild and exhilarating country' as they skirted peaks rising up to 10,000 feet. They turned north at Khazvin and headed for Resht, on the shore of the Caspian Sea. Thompson was amazed as 'the scene changed dramatically and we saw green, fertile slopes, almost tropical in their luxuriance, stretching away to the shores of the Caspian.'

Crossing the inland sea, Kimber was impressed with its splendour after the clouds cleared just south of Baku: 'It was a brilliant day and the Caspian reflecting the sky, was a brilliant sapphire blue. Somewhere in its depths lurked the sturgeons from which the Western world sought caviare.' They passed the peninsula of Baku and thereafter the land was littered with oil derricks, a 'glittering prize' for the Germans should they capture the area. From then on the visibility was perfect, there was no heat haze and 'the whole panorama of the scene was breathtaking'. Kimber came out of his reverie to take a sun sight and calculate the winds – there was no sideways drift, but a headwind of 27 knots reducing speed over the ground to 145 knots. They made a landfall on the north coast of the Caspian and continued to head north following the course of the Ural River. According to Kimber, it was 'the easiest country to fly over with my do-it-yourself charts'.

The city of Kuibyshev was the point at which they were scheduled to turn off and head for Moscow; but here they were victims of a misunderstanding. In the expectation that the distinguished visitors would land at

Kuibyshev, a party led by the President of the Soviet Republic was waiting with an official welcome and a huge lunch. But the Liberator simply flew on, over more difficult terrain. Soviet security demanded that they descend to less than 2,000 feet to be recognised by the anti-aircraft batteries, which made map reading harder as there was less time to view the ground. Winds were now more variable, and visibility was poorer. Kimber had pinpointed a railway line identified on his Phillips Atlas, five miles east of the town of Arzamas, but tension mounted inside the plane as the aircraft approached. 'Twenty minutes before the estimated arrival time at the railway line all faculties were concentrated ahead and downwards. There were some false sightings made on streams and tracks, but fifteen minutes later the railway line came into view, thence a turn due west brought us over Arzamas.' But they successfully followed the line west to Murom where a Russian fighter escort was waiting to convey them onward. 'At about five o'clock,' according to Churchill, 'the spires and domes of Moscow came in sight. We circled around the city by carefully prescribed courses along which all the batteries had been warned.' Finally they landed at Moscow airport to be greeted by the Foreign Minister Molotov and 'a concourse of Russian Generals and the entire Diplomatic Corps'.

★ ★ ★

Commando was not the only Liberator heading for Moscow that day. Squadron-Leader Llewellyn was in command of aircraft no AL 911, carrying what Jacob called 'the four big beasts' – Sir Alan Brooke, General Wavell, Air Marshal Tedder and Sir Alexander Cadogan. Brooke was sceptical as to the need for such a group:

> Our party was unnecessarily large, as Winston on these occasions loved to accumulate a large number of Generals, Admirals and Air Marshals who were not much concerned with the work in hand, but I think felt increased his dignity. On this trip there was little reason for Wavell's or Tedder's presence.[1]

The passenger arrangement was different from *Commando*, but even less luxurious, and Ian Jacob found there was not much room to spare. There were four bunks in the bomb bay, two per side. The compartment was only about 4ft 6in high, so it was difficult to sit on a bunk, and there were no windows. Aft of that was another compartment, also windowless and even smaller and

3 ft higher, in which two people could lie out on either side of the gangway. This led to the wireless operator's compartment, while the rest of the fuselage tapered towards the rear gunner's compartment. He was, however, reasonably comfortable on one of the bunks in the bomb bay.

Brooke crawled up to the rear of the Liberator and was able to see out, but after about an hour one of the variable-pitch propeller blades stuck in place and it was necessary to turn back. Brooke was uneasy as he saw 'Winston's plane disappearing into the distance as it headed for Moscow whilst we turned back to Tehran! I did not like seeing him go off out of my sight on these occasions without knowing we were going to follow him.' They flew out next morning, stopping over at Kuibyshev, where they enjoyed the meal of 'masses of hors d'oeuvre, including caviar' that Churchill's party had missed the day before. They were then put into a Russian-manned Douglas airliner which Brooke found surprisingly comfortable after the Liberator. It was 'beautifully fitted up inside with 8 armchairs and two couches, also large table'. When they finally landed at Moscow that evening, they discovered that Churchill had already done a good deal of business without them.

★ ★ ★

The crew members of *Commando* found plenty of entertainment during their three and a half days in Moscow, for the Russians, when not suspicious to the point of paranoia, were incredibly generous. The hardship endured by the Russian people became all too obvious when some of the crew visited villages that had been ravaged by the Nazis, and were told, 'We Russians don't hesitate to sacrifice a hundred men to stop a German tank.' Despite this the visitors were treated to meals they could only dream of in Britain. Charles Kimber shared a hotel room with the co-pilot Jack Ruggles, but saw little of Captain Vanderkloot except in the evenings. Some of the party visited the ballet in the company of a Soviet Air Force major – a production of *Don Quixote* and of *Les Sylphides*, which was very different from one that Kimber had seen back home; and there was a very convivial evening after which at least 85 per cent of the guests needed help to leave, and Vanderkloot arrived in his room with a mysterious red star pinned to his jacket.

Churchill was taken to the Kremlin, where he met Stalin for the first time. Writing his *Second World War* volume nine years later, at the height of the Cold War, he was rather guarded about his impressions. Brooke did not meet Stalin until the following day, but was 'impressed with his astuteness, and his crafty cleverness. He is a realist, with little flattery about him, and not looking for

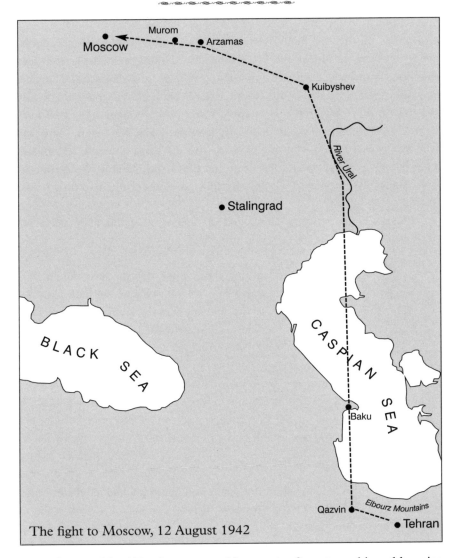

The fight to Moscow, 12 August 1942

much flattery either.' For the moment his past was forgotten – his ruthless rise to power; the forced industrialisation of the Soviet Union involving the elimination of a whole class, the Kulaks; the show trials and executions of many of his former Bolshevik colleagues and the assassination of his great rival Trotsky; the Nazi-Soviet Pact of 1939, his invasion of Poland; and the purge of his generals on the eve of the German invasion.

Churchill found Stalin in a sombre mood. He broke the bad news that there would be no cross-Channel invasion that year, and 'Stalin's face crumpled into a frown'. Churchill explained the situation in some detail, and emphasised the importance of the projected landings in North Africa, and above all the bomber offensive, which he said would 'shatter almost every dwelling in almost every German city'. Stalin seemed placated and the mood improved. It turned far worse on the second day when Churchill was subjected to many taunts about British courage. His patience finally snapped and he delivered a spontaneous and very eloquent address: 'I have come round Europe in the midst of my troubles – yes, Mr Stalin, I have my troubles as well as you – hoping to meet with the hand of comradeship; and I am bitterly disappointed. I have not met that hand.' Even without translation, Stalin was impressed with Churchill's passion and the two men talked until 2 a.m.

The series of meetings concluded on the night of the 15th. Churchill described the events in his telegram to Attlee:

At 8.30 when I got up to leave he asked when was the next time he was going to see me. I said that I was leaving at dawn. He then said, 'Why do not you come over to my apartment in the Kremlin and have some drinks?' I went and stayed to dinner to which M. Molotov was also summoned. M. Stalin introduced me to his daughter who was a nice girl and kissed him shyly but was not allowed to dine. The dinner and ... communiqué lasted till 3 a.m. this morning. I had a very good interpreter and was able to talk much more easily. The greatest goodwill prevailed and for the first time we got on to easy and friendly terms. I feel that I have established a personal relationship which will be helpful.[2]

There was no time for sleep that night and Churchill had a bath and then went to the aerodrome. Despite torrents of rain, a guard of honour stood to attention and a band played.

★ ★ ★

It had been decided to fly back to Tehran on the same track as on the flight out. Kimber was at least able to do some pre-flight planning this time, though it could not be considered complete without a weather forecast. Boarding the aircraft early in the morning of 16 August, he found two Russian officers who, Ruggles informed him, would be travelling with them to Tehran. The Prime Minister's party arrived and as the aircraft taxied to the runway Ruggles spoke to Kimber through headphones, which the intruders were not wearing. The

Russians, he said, were supposed to be returning to their embassy in Tehran, but more likely they were there to keep an eye on the crew, and make sure they did not fly over prohibited areas.

The Russians turned out to have their uses. Kimber noticed that they were examining some charts of their own, well printed and at a scale of one inch to 15 miles. He was allowed to see them, taking care initially that they were the right way up, because he could not read the Cyrillic script. He was able to identify towns, marking them up using their original script in his navigational log. They passed close to Orekhovo Zuyevo, and flew over Kuibyshev. After they landed at Tehran at three in the afternoon, Churchill had another audience with the Shah, but Cadogan understood little of what was said, being a little deaf after flying.

Sitting on the floor of the other Liberator, amid the usual noise, General Wavell composed *The Ballad of the Second Front,* one verse of which summed up their feelings on the way back:

Prince of the Kremlin, here's a fond farewell;
I've had to deal with many worse than you.
You took it, though you hated it like hell;
No Second Front in 1942.[3]

The flight from Tehran to Egypt was also relatively simple and followed the old track, though without the evasive manoeuvres round Cairo. The aircraft landed at Heliopolis instead of LG 224, where they had landed last time, and nearly a week was to be spent in Cairo. The secret of Churchill's visit to the Middle East was now out, so it was possible to make somewhat more open visits to the troops in Egypt, including Churchill's old regiment, the 4th Hussars, who had swapped their horses for armoured vehicles before the war. He was impressed with the effect that Montgomery, already known as Monty, had made on the army in a few days. 'The P.M. spoke of it as an astonishing transformation; he said it was plain that Monty knew the secret of preparing his men for battle.'

Ironically, it was Sir Charles Wilson who was taken ill with a stomach bug, known to the British as 'Gyppy tummy', and Churchill enjoyed himself. 'Sir Charles has been a terrible anxiety to us during the night, but I hope we'll get him through!' Over dinner on the night of the 20th he talked about Sir Charles's favourite subjects, medicine and psychology, most of which was 'pretty good nonsense', according to Cadogan. He ended, 'My God, I do have to work hard to teach that chap his job.' With the weight of replacing

Auchinleck and meeting Stalin off his mind, Churchill was in 'terrific form' and 'enjoyed himself like a schoolboy'.

★ ★ ★

The flight back across the desert was even more daring than the one out. The main part would be at 28 degrees north instead of 27 degrees, bringing the aircraft 60 nautical miles, or 69 land miles, nearer to the enemy positions on the coast. They started off by flying south-west to skirt the Quattara Depression, then turned west on reaching a prearranged point. Kimber found that the stars were ideally placed for navigation, but he also used the moon to obtain position lines. When they reached the second turning point at 14 degrees longitude, they turned to 309 degrees to head for the coast of Vichy French Algeria. This took them within a hundred miles of the coast south of Tunis, but they were not concerned. Gott's fate notwithstanding, it seemed clear that a single bomber was unlikely to be detected at night in this vast area. They crossed the coast at Tenes west of Algiers and then headed for Gibraltar.

Navigation was slightly easier now, because for the first time in the trip they were able to use radio beacons on the Rock to guide them in. Churchill was in the cockpit with Vanderkloot as they approached Gibraltar:

I must say it looked very dangerous. All was swathed in morning mist. One could not see a hundred yards ahead, and we were not flying more than thirty feet above the sea. I asked Vanderkloot if it was all right, and said that I hoped he would not hit the Rock of Gibraltar. His answers were not particularly reassuring, but he felt sufficiently sure of his course not to go high up and stand out to sea, which personally I should have been glad to see him do, We held on for another four or five minutes. Then suddenly we flew into clear air, and up towered the great precipice of Gibraltar, gleaming on the isthmus and strip of neutral ground which joins it to Spain ... After three or four hours flying in a mist Vanderkloot had been exact.[4]

Yet again Charles Kimber's contribution went unrecognised. The aircraft went in to make a good landing.

★ ★ ★

Churchill had telegraphed ahead to inform Gibraltar that his party, including Harriman and Brooke, would arrive on the morning of the 24th:

> Essential utmost secrecy should be observed. There should therefore be no reception. Suggest only one car should meet each of the aeroplanes on arrival to take me and a few others off at once and that no unessential persons should be allowed near the aircraft till we have left. Cars for remainder can then come down later.[5]

Security, however, was never going to be tight at Gibraltar and Charles Kimber was worried when he heard that they would be flying off again in a few hours, which meant they could be over the Bay of Biscay in daylight, with no certainty of cloud cover to protect them. He had flown in obsolescent Blenheim bombers over the North Sea early in the war, and knew that the only real protection in these circumstances was to stay at wave-top height, which posed dangers of its own. He protested, but was even more alarmed when he was told that a fighter escort would be provided. First, this would necessitate coming closer to enemy territory to cater for the shorter ranges of the fighters. Secondly, it would attract undesirable attention to the transport aircraft. Thirdly, as an ex-air gunner in bombers in the early stages of the war he had no faith in such protection in daylight:

> If the enemy attacks in force, it has greater freedom of action than the escort, since the latter is held to the aircraft it is protecting. Further, the enemy can checkmate the escort by flying two or three aircraft *in close formation* with the escorted aircraft and defy the escort to open fire for the obvious reason that the escorted aircraft may be struck.[6]

When he questioned it he was told that orders had come from the 'top of the Rock'. He found that the rest of the crew had carried out a briefing without his knowledge. He enquired if there had been any safety briefing for passengers for the flight over water and one of the engineers answered, 'I guess so.' As the passengers boarded at 11.15 he asked Commander Thompson to ensure that they wore lifejackets for the flight.

They took off 25 minutes later and headed out past Tarifa on the Spanish coast. Kimber was pleased that there was plenty of cloud below them as they flew at 4,200 feet. He took radio bearings from a station at Corunna in north-western Spain and carried out a running fix. This involved taking one bearing, flying a determinable distance and taking another one. The position could be calculated with a reasonable degree of accuracy from this data. By four o'clock there was cloud above and below, giving a good 'funk-hole' in case of attack. By six they had bearings from three separate radio stations to give a good position but were flying blind in cloud. They were over the coast within 40 minutes, but contact with the ground was infrequent and the land below could only tentatively be identified as South Wales; but once they spotted the mouth of the River Severn their position was established. They landed at Lyneham at 7.43 that evening.

The Liberator carrying the 'big beasts' came ten minutes later. It had hit thunderstorms and the radio failed to function. The coast that could be seen though the clouds was identified as Cornwall by some of the passengers, but in fact it was Wales. At last, with the daylight almost gone, the pilot made an excellent landing at Lyneham. A substantial group was there to receive both parties, including Mrs Churchill and their son Randolph, Sir Charles Portal and Averell Harriman's daughter Kathleen. Thompson had already telegraphed ahead to ask for 'the train, usual composition with breakfast' to be ready at Dauntsey near Lyneham. The nature of the meal had to be changed as the party arrived much sooner due to the early take-off from Gibraltar, but they enjoyed dinner in unaccustomed comfort and safety before arriving in London at 11.15.

★ ★ ★

As they arrived, Brooke wrote 'a deep felt and agonised prayer' in his diary, 'I pray God that the decisions we arrived at may be correct, and that they may bear fruit.' General Smuts had no such doubts and wrote to Churchill:

> I have read your Moscow message with deepest interest and congratulate you on a really great achievement. Your handling of a critical psychological situation was masterly and final effect on my mind is that you have achieved even more than you appear to realise and have firmly bound Russia to us for this war at least …
>
> After your recent HERCULEAN labours I implore you to relax. You cannot continue at the present pace. Please follow Charles Wilson's advice as you expect nation to follow yours.[7]

General MacArthur, the American commander-in-chief in the Pacific, focused on another aspect when he talked to his British liaison officer. 'A flight of 10,000 miles through hostile and foreign skies may be the duty of young pilots, but for a Statesman burdened with the world's cares it is an act of inspiring gallantry and valour.'

After the return, Churchill's praise for the crew was tempered by the poor conditions on board. Tommy Thompson wrote to Vanderkloot:

Dear Van,

The Prime Minister has asked me to write to say will you make sure that the windproofing of the aircraft around the beds is completed before your next trip.

He suggests that the way you have fixed the blankets is all right as far as it goes, but that similar protection should be fixed round the head ends of the beds as well as up to the roof. He also suggests that some kind of windproof fabric might be better than blankets.[8]

The operation had been a great political and military success. Churchill had re-energised the desert army, and appointed a new commander who would soon bring success. He had broken the bad news to Stalin without a rift in the anti-Nazi alliance. But there remained grave doubts about the wisdom of undertaking the voyage in these conditions. Wilson was quite accurate in describing it as 'feckless' from a medical point of view, but he did not know the whole truth, which was far worse. There was serious tension and lack of communication within the crew, the navigator was not able to carry out a pre-flight preparation and had to improvise his charts in almost incredible fashion. It was one of the most dangerous of Churchill's voyages, as well as the longest and least comfortable, but arguably it was one of the most profitable.

IX
Agreement in Casablanca

If Churchill's voyage to Moscow was the most dangerous, his trip round North Africa and the Mediterranean early in 1943 was in many ways the most complex of his wartime travels. It involved eight separate destinations with varying accommodation and security problems, 24 flights by five different aircraft, a ship, and at one stage a party of almost 150 people. There were changes of plan due to bad weather, frequent changes of mind by Churchill, and one major tragedy.

The idea originated as a three-power conference on strategy, for there were still many differences between the British, Americans and Russians even after Churchill's Washington and Moscow visits in 1942. The Anglo-American landings in North Africa in November 1942 had been completely successful. General Montgomery had won the Battle of El Alamein, and Allied advances from east and west would soon clear enemy forces from North Africa except for their last enclave in Tunisia. On the advice of Brooke, Churchill was becoming increasingly doubtful about an invasion of northern France even in 1943, but he did have other visions.

A landing in Norway would compensate for the defeat there in 1940, but more importantly, it would clear the northern route to Russia, where the ships of the Arctic convoys were suffering terrible losses. But that was soon ruled out as impracticable, and Churchill came up with another idea. The enemy would soon be out of North Africa and Allied forces would invade either Sardinia or Sicily, opening the Mediterranean for shipping. Italian morale had never been high and it was now crumbling even further, so it would not be difficult to knock the country out of the war. Churchill also hoped to bring in Turkey, opening up a new and much safer supply route to the Soviet Union and providing bases for bombing German oil resources.

His allies saw this differently. Stalin still wanted a true 'second front', an invasion of northern Europe as he felt he had been promised for 1943, and considered everything else as a diversion. The Allied bombing campaign against Germany, although rapidly gathering momentum, was a poor substitute. The Americans wanted either to go for the German jugular as soon as possible, or to switch more forces to the Pacific where they were now on the offensive and hopping from island to island. The path to victory seemed obvious there, though strewn with bloodshed and difficulties.

The notion of a tripartite conference fell through in mid-December when Stalin announced that he was unable to leave the Soviet Union while the Battle of Stalingrad was being fought to a victorious conclusion: 'I must say that things are now so hot that it is impossible for me to absent myself ever for a single day. The battle is developing on the Central Front as well as Stalingrad. At Stalingrad we have surrounded a large group of German armies and we hope to achieve their final liquidation.'

Roosevelt and Churchill decided to go ahead. Casablanca had recently been taken over from the Vichy French by American troops during the North African landings and seemed a good neutral site. Roosevelt stated that he would rather meet in 'a comfortable oasis' than on 'a raft on the Tilsit' – as Napoleon Bonaparte, Tsar Alexander I of Russia and Frederick William III of Prussia had done in 1807. He first proposed Khartoum or somewhere south of Algiers, but Casablanca was surveyed by General Bedell Smith and seemed an ideal location. It was certainly acceptable to Churchill who had happy memories of Morocco, and it could serve as a stepping-stone to other parts of Africa. The contemporary film starring Humphrey Bogart and Ingrid Bergman had no effect on the decision. Rather, the movie benefited from the free publicity afforded by the conference.

There was a mood of optimism in the British camp as they bade farewell to the difficult year of 1942, and Brooke wrote:

We start 1943 under conditions I would never have dared to hope. Russia has held. Egypt for the present is safe. There is hope of clearing North Africa of Germans in the near future. The Mediterranean may be partially opened. Malta is safe for the present. We can now work freely against Italy, and Russia is scoring wonderful successes in Southern Russia. We are certain to have many setbacks to face, many troubles, and many shattered hopes, but for all that the horizon is infinitely brighter.[1]

★   ★   ★

Ian Jacob, now a brigadier, was sent to North Africa to do a reconnaissance of Casablanca from the British point of view. He flew out on Christmas Day, and an American officer recommended the Hotel Anfa, five miles west of the city. It stood in the centre of a roundabout which was itself in an area that could be sealed off easily. There were surrounding villas which could be used for members of the party. The hotel was a mile from the beach and two miles from the airport, which was suitable for Liberators except in very rainy weather. The only alternative was the Miramar, a good hotel but without the surrounding villas.

Jacob was careful not to recommend the alternative town, Marrakech. He knew that Churchill would favour it, for he had spent a very successful holiday there in 1932 and regarded it as 'the Paris of the Sahara'. But it was a hundred miles inland and far removed from communication facilities, which would have to be provided by ship. Nevertheless, it too was mentioned as a possible alternative venue, or a place to which the conference could move if security at Casablanca was threatened.

This time security was tighter and more complex than ever. The operation was codenamed Symbol and Churchill was to be known as Air Commodore Frankland, or just 'the air commodore'. The general plan was 'to conceal the departure of the Air Commodore by air and to maintain for as long as possible the impression that he is still in the country'. That could not be maintained for long, and once his absence had been admitted, the impression was to be given that he was somewhere else, perhaps in Washington.

Getting the Liberator AL 504 ready would be a sign that something was happening, but Averell Harriman was persuaded to go on the trip, using the cover story that he was travelling via Casablanca to investigate a possible route to Cairo, where he would take part in a conference. The Liberator itself was to be known in signals as AM 500, and Captain Vanderkloot was referred to as Squadron-Leader Jones. On the day, Churchill would leave Downing Street for Chequers. He and Wilson would leave that evening in separate cars, and after half a mile would join up and be driven to the RAF station at Benson south of Oxford, entering by a side gate. Harriman would already be on board ready for take-off.

Meanwhile, everything possible would be done to conceal Churchill's absence. Engagements, including meetings with neutral diplomats and jour-nalists, would be entered in his diary, then cancelled at the last minute. It was assumed there was little communication between the staffs at Downing Street and Chequers, and the hope was that each would believe that the Prime Minister was at the other place. At other times it would be casually suggested that he was on a tour of inspection somewhere in the country.

To cover the absence of other members of the party, it was given out that Lord Leathers, the Minister of Shipping, was also investigating a route via Casablanca to relieve congestion at Gibraltar airport. The Chiefs of Staffs' deputies would have their letters signed 'per pro', giving the impression that they were still in the country. They too would enter engagements in their diaries, and concoct plausible stories for their families.

★ ★ ★

On 7 January 1943, the Chiefs of Staff were still discussing how to travel to Africa. Churchill wanted to go by cruiser but Pound ruled that out because of the submarine threat. They had recently broken the German codes again after a gap, but 'Special Intelligence', as it was coyly known, was still late and incomplete. It did, however, show more than 30 U-boats in the Biscay–Azores–Madeira–Gibraltar area, massing for an attack on the supply lines to North Africa. If the air option were chosen, Churchill had planned to travel by Liberator rather than the more commodious Clipper. Perhaps he felt that the former would be better suited to the somewhat shorter voyage, and that there would be less discomfort, now that the accommodation in the aircraft was improved. Or perhaps he had lost some confidence in Kelly Rogers after the alleged flight close to Brest and his negative views on the trip to Cairo; certainly he had built up a corresponding faith in Vanderkloot and his men. More importantly, he wanted to keep his options open. At the back of his mind was the possibility of a trip onward to Cairo and Turkey, for which the Liberator was far more suitable.

It was originally planned for the rest of the party to travel via Gibraltar, and officers were despatched there and to Casablanca and Marrakech to make preparations. In the event, it was decided to fly the party to Casablanca in a Boeing Clipper piloted again by Kelly Rogers, which was standing ready at Poole. But much depended on the weather and Air Ministry meteorologists stood by to pass messages to Portal and to the Prime Minister's staff, and to the American Embassy for Harriman.

Departure was set for 11 January, but the weather at Gibraltar proved unsuitable for landing a flying-boat. So the decision was made to take the airborne party in four Liberators instead of the Clipper. *Commando*, carrying the Prime Minister's party, would leave from Benson and the others from Lyneham in Wiltshire.

In view of the size of the group that was considered necessary, and the uncertainty about accommodation and signalling facilities in newly liberated Casablanca, it was decided to send out the headquarters ship *Bulolo*. She was the first Landing Ship Headquarters in the world, designed as a control centre for amphibious assaults. Formerly an Australian passenger ship of 6,400 tons, she was converted in 1942. She had extensive signalling facilities as well as a certain amount of space for passengers, and cabins that could be used for accommodating members of the party in Casablanca. The vessel had taken part in the landing in North Africa in November, controlling an Anglo-American force which took Algiers and thus proved the value of the amphibious concept. The *Bulolo* was to carry women for the first time – a dozen officers from the women's services who were to act as shorthand-typists for the Chiefs of Staff. To the disgust of Miss Joan Bright of the Cabinet Office, however, it was decreed that no civilian women could be carried in warships.

The ship sailed from Greenock on 5 January carrying a party of fourteen navy, army and air force officers from major-general downwards, twelve women officers, fourteen ratings and other ranks as stewards, batmen, clerks and typists, and three civilian security officers. There were 64 marines under two officers to act as guards and orderlies. During the voyage the administrative staff began to plan for their roles, trying out the typewriters and duplicators they would use during the conference. A float of £100 sterling was carried for expenses, along with £1,000 in British Military Authority currency. Captain Pim of the Map Room was delighted to be allocated a large cabin in which he could hold bridge parties and avoid the overcrowded wardroom. On Sunday the 10th he conducted a church service but was interrupted as the escorting destroyers dropped depth charges on a suspected U-boat, with no result. The *Bulolo* arrived off Casablanca later that day and was escorted towards the port by small American warships, to moor alongside the Mole de Commerce in the large artificial harbour built by the French.

★   ★   ★

On this occasion Squadron-Leader Kimber was not invited to form part of the crew; neither was any other member of the RAF. Kimber had clearly not fitted in well with Vanderkloot's men. He had been interviewed by Portal about the Moscow trip at the end of August 1942, when the Chief of Air Staff expressed amazement at many features of the flight. He had assumed that Kimber rather than Vanderkloot was responsible for starting off in daylight from Gibraltar; moreover, he was surprised that Kimber had been told nothing about the destination until the last minute, and that his protests had been ignored. This probably strengthened Portal's determination to appoint an RAF crew for Churchill's subsequent flights.

In the meantime, however, Churchill had formed a liking for the North Americans and he paid very little attention to the man from the RAF. The

Americans and Canadians were awarded decorations from the Order of the British Empire, yet Kimber received only a letter of thanks from Thompson, which rankled for many years afterwards. When Kimber, therefore, was ordered to stand by for a special trip in January 1943 he immediately thought 'Oh no! Another "thissaway!"' But in fact his mission was to fly some Russian officers from Scotland to Moscow. This time *Commando* had the usual crew of Vanderkloot as captain, Ruggles as co-pilot, Russ Holmes as radio operator and the flight engineers Ron Williams and John Affleck; and Vanderkloot would do his own navigation.

★ ★ ★

Brooke was packed and ready to go for 5.30 on the 11th as planned, but at a quarter to five the weather was judged unsuitable and it was put off for another day. On the 12th it was better, though still not suitable for a flying-boat at Gibraltar, so the three Liberators at Lyneham were to be deployed. The airfield was kept secret even from members of the party, who left by car at 7.30 in the evening to travel the 90 miles.

The deception on the Prime Minister's arrival at Benson airfield was rather less successful than hoped. Churchill's convoy of vehicles attracted attention with bright headlights, sirens and high speed. The air commodore in charge remarked to Harriman, 'Good God, the only mistake they made was that they didn't put it in the local newspaper. No one could make that much noise except the Prime Minister.'

The Liberator took off soon after midnight in the morning of the 13th. It flew across the south-western peninsula of England, avoiding the great cities of Bristol and Plymouth but passing over the smaller town of Taunton before crossing the coast at Newquay in northern Cornwall. It continued out into the Atlantic until 49 degrees north, 10 degrees west and 200 miles from the enemy airfields near Brest. It turned to a more southerly course across the Bay of Biscay area, then due south off the north of Spain, to continue about 120 miles from the coasts of Spain and Portugal, well away from any spies sheltering in neutral territory.

The interior of the Liberator had been improved since the last trip. The passengers were now accommodated in the rear part of the fuselage, with the flight deck forward and a large fuel tank in the centre between the wings. The bomb bay below was used for luggage but had a passageway to allow communication between the passengers and the flight deck. It also served as a cellar, from which Sawyers could produce wines as requested. The main accommodation was right aft and consisted of six reclining seats, three on each side of the gangway – the first pair faced aft, the next pair faced forward to allow conversation and the last pair also faced the front. Forward of the seating compartment were two narrow bunks. There was even a primitive heating system. Churchill and Wilson went to sleep on their mattresses, but in the middle of the night the doctor awoke

> to find the P.M. crawling down into the well beneath, where Portal was asleep. When he shook him vigorously by the shoulder, I thought it would be well to find out what was wrong. Winston said he had burnt his toes against some metal connections of the improvised heating arrangements at the foot of the mattress. 'They are red hot,' he explained. We shall soon have petrol fumes bursting into flames. There'll be an explosion soon.[2]

It seemed simplest to turn the heaters off, and Wilson woke up later to find the shivering Prime Minister trying to attach blankets to the side of the plane to keep out the draught. 'The P.M. is at a disadvantage in this kind of travel, since he never wears anything at night but a silk vest. On his hands and knees, he cut a quaint figure with his big, bare bottom.'

Brigadier Jacob had a very different dress as he followed in one of the three Liberators from Lyneham. He had to don flying kit against the cold, which he found tedious but amusing. It consisted of zip-up fur-lined flying boots, trousers, jacket, helmet and gloves. For safety, each passenger had to wear a 'Mae West' life jacket and a parachute harness and carry a small packet

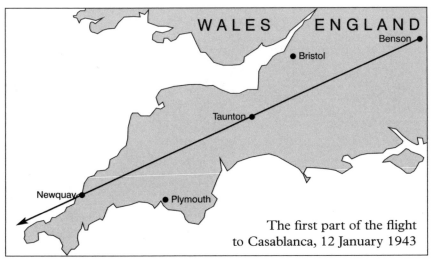

The first part of the flight
to Casablanca, 12 January 1943

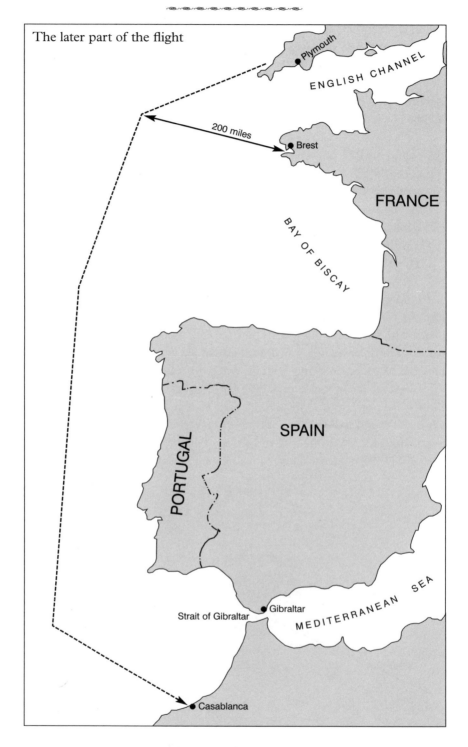

The later part of the flight

Plymouth

ENGLISH CHANNEL

200 miles

Brest

FRANCE

BAY OF BISCAY

SPAIN

PORTUGAL

Gibraltar

Strait of Gibraltar

MEDITERRANEAN SEA

Casablanca

with maps, emergency rations, a compass and some money in case of a forced landing. He felt like a stuffed turkey but laughed inwardly as he watched the indignity of 'the whale', Sir Dudley Pound, and 'Pug' Ismay. 'Some people seem to truss more easily than others.'

Conditions on board were 'pretty grim' due to overcrowding. Brooke and Mountbatten had to share a mattress on the floor of one of the Liberators, and the CIGS was not comfortable. 'I did not find him a pleasant bed companion, as every time he turned round he overlay me, and I had to use my knees and elbows to establish my rights to my allotted floor space!'

Commando flew south until it reached a position at 36 degrees north and headed south-east towards Casablanca. Commander Thompson was looking out as Morocco was sighted:

As the sun rose we sighted the African coast. What a contrast to the chill, wet England we had left a few hours before. Above us was a cloudless sky; below, the brilliant line of the coast, shimmering in the hot sun.[3]

The Liberator landed at Mediouna airport at 10.20 in the morning, to be followed by the other three aircraft by 11.05. Churchill came out wearing his RAF uniform and stood waiting for the others to land. According to Thompson, one American major remarked scornfully to Harriman, 'Fancy dressing up a little guy like that in R.A.F uniform and expecting us to believe he's Winston Churchill.' Oddly enough General Ismay stepped down from his plane and made a similar remark in jest. 'Anyone can see that is an air commodore disguised as the Prime Minister.' He greeted the new arrivals with a cry of, 'Now, tumble out, you young fellows, and get on parade.' Onward transport to Anfa consisted of one command car, 15 motor cars departing at three-minute intervals, 7¾-ton trucks for the luggage, 11 motor cyclists and 2¾-ton ton trucks carrying American troops for security.

★   ★   ★

Casablanca was largely a European town, mainly built since the French protectorate was established over most of Morocco in 1912, though it had a small and crowded Arab quarter or Medina near the harbour. Before the war it had more than 70,000 Europeans, including a thousand British, in its population of a quarter of a million. It boasted the finest port in Morocco, largely an artificial creation by the French in the preceding 30 years.

Churchill was accommodated in the Villa Mirador, which was very comfortable apart from one initial difficulty. The hot-water system was 'rather like an under-engined car'. By the time Churchill came to use it at 11 a.m., several people had taken baths and no hot water was available, to his fury. 'You might have thought the end of the world had come. Everyone was sent for in turn, all were fools, and finally the Prime Minister said he would not stay a moment longer, he would move into the Hotel or go to Marrakech.' Somehow teams of plumbers were assembled and Churchill was satisfied. On the 15th he wrote to Clementine:

This, as you know, is a very attractive part of the world. The weather is bright, with occasional showers, and like a nice day in May for temperature. The hotel is taken over by the American Army, who keep open house there and allow no British to pay for anything ... I have a nice villa ...

The food here is very good, especially on the points where we are weak. There are plenty of eggs and oranges, but of course the milk is not safe so we have to have it out of tins. Most of our stores have been

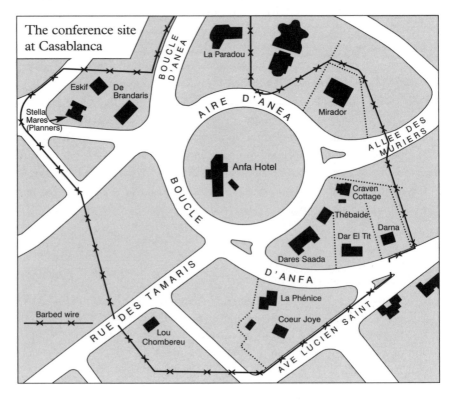

The conference site at Casablanca

brought from England, but fresh meat and vegetables abound here. The countryside is verdant with lush grass in the meadows and many fine trees, some of which are palms. Around the whole circle of villas is drawn a circle of barbed wire, ceaselessly patrolled by American sentries, and around that again is a circle of anti-aircraft guns.[4]

Among those who arrived in the city from various directions was Churchill's misfit son Randolph, serving as a captain in a commando brigade in Egypt. Churchill sent Captain Pim to meet him, telling him not to mention his own presence as he hoped to keep it a surprise, but Randolph already knew. Churchill credited Mountbatten with arranging the visit, though there was evidently some prompting from Churchill. Not everyone would thank him for it, and Cadogan regarded Randolph as an 'incubus' on the party.

Ian Jacob was delighted to share a room with Brigadier 'Dumbie' Dykes, who had nearly missed the train to Scapa in 1941, and had been based in Washington since Churchill's first meeting with Roosevelt there. Friends since they had been at the Royal Military College together, they stayed up late at night like schoolboys mocking their teachers, as Dykes perfected his mimicry of General Brooke:

I have never met a man who so tumbles over himself in speaking. He is incapable of reading aloud intelligibly. He cannot move his brain slowly enough to fit his speech or his reading, especially when his interest is strongly engaged. All this, together with his constant habit when talking of shooting his tongue out and round his lips with the speed of a chameleon, which made him an easy prey to Dumbie's imitative wit.[5]

The object of the wit was busy during the conference, but he too found a little spare time. Major-General Sir John Kennedy, the Director of Military Operations, was a fellow birdwatcher and the two wandered the beach each morning – 'Delightful 1½ hours, during which we saw goldfinch, stonechat, warblers of all sorts, white wagtail and several kinds of waders on the seashore, such as sanderlings, ring plover, grey plover and turnstones!'

Vanderkloot and his crew had much less to do for the moment, but they were delighted when the American aircraft arrived and found that the pilots included Otis Bryan, an old friend from the Ferry Service, and Milo Campbell from Vanderkloot's airline days. The crew enjoyed sightseeing in the streets of Casablanca, which had been laid out in grand style by the French colonialists with tree-lined avenues and street cafés. They were plagued by shoeshine boys and even cobblers, one of whom changed the soles of Jack Ruggles's new shoes before he was able to say no.

★ ★ ★

Churchill kept his distance from the Chiefs of Staff meetings during the early stages of the conference, allowing them to reach their own conclusions but reporting to him every day. The main issue was what to do with the armies in North Africa after the Germans and Italians were driven out, which was expected soon. Mountbatten favoured an invasion of Sardinia, which was an easy target and could be done quickly. Brooke was far more persuasive and preferred Sicily, which was more directly on the route to Italy and would contribute more to freeing the Mediterranean for Allied shipping. Churchill eventually supported Sicily as he considered Sardinia 'a piddling little operation'.

Churchill's needs to keep constantly in touch with home had greatly increased since the days of the Argentia voyage, and even the activities of *Bulolo* were not sufficient for him:

> The first three days of the conference were enlivened by the bellows, as of a wounded buffalo, of the Prime Minister for more news. It happened that there was not much going on in the great world at the time. But a can of petrol was poured on the flames of the Prime Minister's wrath by the fact that he got no detailed account of the big raid on Berlin, which took place on the night of January 16/17, until about 6 p.m. on the 17th. There were various technical hitches to account for the delay, but the Prime Minister dispatched a series of 'winged words' to the Private Office, to Jo Hollis, demanding more information and blasting them for their failure to keep him informed. The result was such a stream of stuff, much of it of little importance, of course, but sufficient to keep him quiet.[6]

The Americans were inexperienced at travelling to conferences and had brought a much smaller party – just the President, Hopkins, and nine officers who must have 'rattled like peas in drums' in their two C-54 transport aircraft. They had no Map Room, because according to Captain Pim they knew that they could use Churchill's. Instead they had a large security staff, an 'entourage of gunmen and thugs', according to Jacob, and they could rely on their local troops for a certain amount of administrative support, but that was not enough to cover the needs of planning complex operations. As a result the British took on the work of producing the facts and figures, typing the drafts and sending the signals. This gave them a great advantage, although it was hard work. Jacob had been horrified at the size of the British party, but in the end he accepted that it had earned its keep.

Having decided upon Sicily, the British now set about convincing the Americans, which proved surprisingly easy. According to Ismay they were 'at sixes and sevens amongst themselves' and had not agreed any plans in advance. At first the Americans were highly suspicious that they were being outsmarted, and led away from a quick invasion of northern Europe, but Field Marshal Dill was respected by both sides, and managed to allay the American fears. When the British paper was accepted with a few modifications in the afternoon of the 19th, Brooke could hardly believe their luck.

A secondary object was to reconcile the two French leaders, General Giraud and General de Gaulle. Admiral Darlan, the ex-Vichy High Commissioner of Morocco and Algiers, had been assassinated in December. Giraud, who had recently escaped from captivity in Germany, had been appointed in his place with American support. This infuriated General Charles de Gaulle, whom Churchill had backed since 1940 as the leader of the Free French despite his infuriating arrogance and lack of loyalty. According to Churchill, 'He might be Stalin, with 200 divisions behind his words', rather than a refugee whose country had collapsed. De Gaulle was eventually persuaded to come to Casablanca, despite his annoyance that French territory had been invaded without consulting him. He was forced to shake hands with Giraud in front of the cameras, but no real reconciliation was reached.

Another issue was the bomber offensive against Germany. The Americans had already built up a force of 500 bombers in England, but they had not yet begun their projected daylight operations over the Reich. Churchill wanted them to join the RAF in night bombing, while some elements back in America wanted them withdrawn for other work. General Arnold of the US Army Air Force was able to persuade Churchill to give them a little more time, and on 27 January they launched their first major raid against Wilhelmshaven.

During the later stages of the conference Brooke and some of the other delegates found time to visit the harbour to inspect the *Bulolo,* and look at the French battleship *Jean Bart* which had been sunk by the American bombardment during the landings. Later they went to Fedala to see the site of one of the American landings, and confirm Brooke's fears about an invasion of France. 'It was most interesting, and quite evident that, if the French had put up any real resistance the landing could not have been carried out.' He saw three storks on the way back and did some shopping in the Galeries Lafayette. Jacob was delighted with the results of the conference:

When I came to write the final document indicating the decisions taken and the agreement reached on all the separate matters dealt with, I found that if I had written down before I came what I hoped the conclusions would be, I could never have written anything so sweeping, so comprehensive, so favourable to our ideas.[7]

The conclusion of the conference was less happy for the British. Roosevelt and Churchill addressed a press conference, with journalists seated on the grass around them. They had discussed the idea of only accepting the 'unconditional surrender' of Germany and Japan, but Roosevelt apparently got carried away as he made his announcement. He remembered the story of the American Civil War general U. S. Grant, who had demanded unconditional surrender of Fort Donelson in Tennessee in 1862 – though not of the main Confederate Army under Robert E. Lee in 1865, as Roosevelt apparently thought. He announced:

The elimination of German, Japanese and Italian war power means the unconditional surrender by Germany, Italy and Japan. This means a reasonable assurance of future world peace. It does not mean the destruction of the population of Germany, Italy and Japan, but it does mean the destruction of the philosophies in those countries which are based on conquest and the subjugation of other people.[8]

Continuing with his rather shaky Civil War history, he used the analogy that Grant had accepted Lee's surrender, then allowed the Confederates to take their cavalry horses home to plough the land.

Churchill was said to be in 'high dudgeon' at the timing of the announcement, though he was forced to defend its substance. It remains controversial. Did it make it more difficult for the less fanatical elements in the countries concerned to propose peace? Did it ensure that the Germans fought to the last? In any case it became the most memorable result of the conference.

The Americans were impressed with the idea of holding conferences on neutral ground, as Jacob reported:

If the conference is held in Washington or London, the home team are unable to strike themselves off duty, so as to give undivided attention to the conference ... Except for formal meetings, and formal meals, there is little contact. At Casablanca it was quite different. Everyone fed, slept and worked together in the same building or group of buildings. British and Americans met round the bar, went for walks down to the beach together, and sat about in each other's rooms in the evenings. Mutual respect and understanding ripen in such surroundings, especially when the weather is lovely, the accommodation is good, and food and drink and smokes are unlimited and free.[9]

★ ★ ★

The conference ended with 'everybody dispersing in different directions', according to Brooke – 'Marshall for Algiers and back to America, Dill for Algiers and on to Delhi, Arnold also for Delhi and on to Chungking from there. Portal Algiers, Malta and home. Dudley Pound Algiers and home.' Jacob continued with his schoolboy theme: 'it was exactly like breaking up at the end of term. Each aeroplane party left the hotel in cars, with their luggage, and we said goodbye as if we were separating for the holidays.'

The mood soon changed. Liberator AM 913 was approaching the British coast from Gibraltar at about 7.30 in the morning of the 30th, when the outer starboard engine caught fire. The pilot cut off the fuel supply and deployed the automatic fire extinguisher with little success. The engine fell off into the sea, taking a piece of wing with it. The plane flew on with three engines until the coast of Pembrokeshire was sighted. The pilot came down to 2,000 feet to look for an airfield and was about to land near Haverfordwest when the other starboard engine cut out. It was difficult to keep on a straight course and the plane was losing height. It hit a mound and the tail was knocked off. Most of the passengers and crew survived, but Brigadiers Dykes and Stewart, still asleep in the bomb bay, were killed. Even more than the death of Gott five months earlier, this was a reminder of the dangers of air travel, for this time they were following a route and in an aircraft very similar to that used by the Prime Minister's party. It was also a personal tragedy for Jacob, who lost a close friend. Churchill was not told for the moment, as he was about to embark on another flight.

★ ★ ★

Brooke and Jacob had been ordered to stay with the Prime Minister's party. Churchill had decided to visit Marrakech while he had the chance, and invited Roosevelt to come with him 'to see the sunset on the snows of the

Atlas Mountains'. The two principals were driven 150 miles by road, with American troops lining the way. It was one of the best roads in the country, built by the French since 1912, and for much of its length wide enough for four lanes. It passed over a flat, featureless plain for the first 45 miles, then to a plateau, and over the River of Oued Oum el Rbia. After 124 miles it began to ascend over the Djebilet Hills, then down to Marrakech, which was 1,475 ft above sea level. The two statesmen talked business in the car, but also touched on lighter matters. The party stopped for a picnic to break the five-hour journey. They parked on an area of stony ground and were guarded by a screen of armoured cars and American secret servicemen with sub-machine guns, as fighters patrolled overhead. Meanwhile the C-54s and Liberators took other members of the group to Marrakech. Brooke had 'a lovely fly with an excellent view of the country. It is an amazing sight as one approaches the Atlas mountains to see mile upon mile of snow peaks in front of one.'

Marrakech was a far more typical Arab town than Casablanca – fewer than 7,000 of its 190,000 people were European. Its area was dominated by the great walled Medina, but to the north-west was a modern New Town, with wide tree-lined streets, commercial buildings and many villas. Churchill and Roosevelt were to stay at the one owned by a wealthy American, Mrs Moses Taylor, and lent to the American consul, Kenneth Pendar. According to the prosaic official reconnaissance:

It has first class sleeping accommodations for 8 individuals and reasonably satisfactory accommodations for 12 additional, making 20 for the entire villa. The villa faces the Atlas Mountains with their snow covered peaks forty miles away plainly visible. It has comfortable messing facilities for 14 people. Other staff officers living in the villa can eat at the hotel which is one-half mile distant. There are separate messing facilities for servants.

The Villa has a large living Room and a fair sized library, so arranged that they could be used as offices by the two principals without interference with each other.[10]

This conveyed nothing of the remarkable features of the villa. According to Brooke, it was, 'built in complete Moroccan architecture in the middle of what used to be an olive grove plantation. Very ornate and Moroccan with a wonderful garden around it.' The centrepiece was Mrs Taylor's former bedroom, now used by the Prime Minister. It was done up in Moorish style, the ceiling was a marvellous fresco of green, blue and gold. The head of the bed rested in an alcove of Moroccan design with a religious light shining on either side. The bed was covered in a light blue silk covering with a 6 in wide lace 'entre deux' and the rest of the room in harmony with the Arabic ceiling. And there in the bed was Winston in his green, red and gold dragon dressing gown, his hair, or what was left of it, standing on end, the religious lights shining on his cheeks, and a large cigar in his face!! I would have given anything to have been able to take a coloured photograph of him.[11]

Churchill took Roosevelt up to the tower of the villa and showed him the mountains. They had dinner together in a party of 15 or 16 and sang songs, though Roosevelt was interrupted before he could attempt a solo. Early in the morning of the 25th Churchill came down to the airport to see Roosevelt off, wearing his dressing gown. Captain Otis Bryan of the presidential aircraft was amazed at his dress but Bill Vanderkloot, far more used to the Prime Minister's ways, winked at him.

Churchill should have been content as his business finished. The war was going well on almost all fronts, he had held highly successful conferences with both his major allies and got his way. He had even effected some kind of agreement between the French factions. He was staying in a beautiful villa in one of his favourite spots in the world, with a marvellous view over the Atlas Mountains, and he had his paints to hand. Certainly Brooke hoped for some rest, and the birdwatching was good: 'It is great fun identifying the European specimens in the form of some sub-species with minor variations. For instance I found the ordinary chaffinch, but the cock with a grey-blue head instead of the red-brown of the home specimen.'

But Churchill was still restless. He decided to paint for two hours in the afternoon, then get ready to head off at 6 in the morning. Brooke asked him where. 'I have not decided yet.' On being pressed he answered: 'I am either going to answer questions in the House tomorrow, or I am going to Cairo.' He went up the tower and as promised he painted the view over the mountains.

★   ★   ★

A trip to Cairo would be far less dangerous than the one the previous August, as the enemy had been cleared from most of North Africa. The first stage, however, would cross the Atlas Mountains, which were more than 13,000 feet in places, so Commander Thompson arranged for Vanderkloot to take

Commando up for a reconnaissance of ways through the passes. The War Cabinet in London proved more difficult. They thought that a trip to Turkey was unnecessary and dangerous, and was most likely to result in a diplomatic snub. At last, at noon on the 25th, the Cabinet agreed reluctantly to give Churchill his way.

The party was now reduced to two Liberators, as most of the officers and officials had left by sea or air. Churchill would travel in *Commando* again with his usual party of Wilson, Martin, the Thompsons, Sawyers and his son Randolph. AM 911 was to carry Brooke and Jacob, along with the secretary Leslie Rowan, Lieutenant-Colonel Brian Boyle who was Brooke's Military Secretary, Inspector Thompson's assistant Sergeant Dudgeon, and the typists Kinna and Green.

They took off at 6.30 in the evening of 25 January, and ascended in circles until they reached 14,500 feet when they could cross the High Atlas safely. Churchill telegraphed to Attlee and Eden, 'We are just off over Atlas mountains which are gleaming with their sunlit snows. You can imagine how much I wish I were going to be with you tomorrow on the Bench but duty calls.' Brooke was impressed with the beauty:

> It became bitterly cold, but the view was glorious. The sun was setting, there was not a cloud in the sky, and the horizon all round was lit with a pink glow which was reflected on the snowy peaks. As we passed over the mountains the sun set, and the whole scenery gradually disappeared into darkness, till we were left alone in the dark, driving into the unknown with 2,300 miles of desert in front of us. We then had dinner of boiled eggs and sandwiches. After that we rolled up for the night and packed stacks of blankets on top to keep warm. We had dropped down again to 9,000 feet, which was more comfortable but still very cold.[12]

Churchill was in the cockpit as usual to see the dawn as they approached the Nile. Vanderkloot saw that Churchill was dazzled by the glare so he unpinned the ribbon of his OBE from his tunic and used it to secure a curtain across the window. Churchill was amused that the ribbon of the Order of the British Empire should be thus employed to protect the eyes of its leader. Charles Kimber might have seen it rather differently.

X
Wild Dreams in Turkey

Commando landed in Cairo at 7.10 on the morning of 26 January. Brooke had had an uncomfortable flight, but was pleased to see dawn breaking over the desert. Churchill, who loved snap inspections, had only given the British Embassy twelve hours' notice of his visit, so its resources were strained. Ambassador Miles Lampson greeted him on arrival and Churchill asked, 'Shall we have breakfast now?' This offended Brooke, as he thought the question should have been addressed to the ambassador's wife Jacqueline. Brooke intervened, 'I think we had better first of all get washed and have a shave', but Churchill was insistent. Fortunately breakfast was ready and he was offered a cup of tea, which he declined in favour of a glass of white wine, not his first drink of the day. Brooke commented, 'We had travelled all night in poor comfort, covering some 2,300 miles in a flight of over 11 hours, a proportion of which was at over 14,000 feet, and there he was, as fresh as paint, drinking white wine on top of two previous whiskies and 2 cigars!!'

The onward flight to Turkey brought another difficulty which had not been planned for. The travel instructions issued by the War Cabinet Office had clearly stated, 'Service officers will not require mess dress or plain clothes'; but they could not wear uniform in neutral Turkey. Commander Thompson describes the hunt for suitable garments: 'This started a frantic search for plain clothes as we couldn't wear uniform in a neutral country. The only suit I could buy which anywhere near fitted me was a startling affair in electric blue.' General Sir Henry Wilson's nickname of 'Jumbo' conveys some idea of the problem of finding clothes for him, but 'to our astonishment he eventually appeared in a suit which was too *large* for him'. It belonged to the gargantuan Ambassador. Brooke borrowed his from Lampson's aide, but 'as he was quite 8 inches taller and very long in the leg, I had serious trouble with the trousers. I braced them up till they caught in my armpits and would go no further, and then found that the top fly button appeared above the waistcoat opening and half concealed my tie!' They looked, according to Brooke, 'more like a third rate travelling theatre company than anything else!'

Cadogan, meanwhile, was to be flown out to Cairo to represent the Foreign Office in the meeting with the Turks, despite his hostility to the idea. He flew down to Plymouth on the 26th but the Catalina flying-boat which was scheduled to take him was stuck at Stranraer due to bad weather. 'They might have told us this before we left Hendon,' he complained, and walked round the town to look at the bomb damage, which was not as impressive as he had expected. At 4.30 in the morning of the 28th he got off in a Lockheed Hudson, a landplane which was considerably smaller than the Liberator. Service officers were expected to endure some hardship in the course of their duties, but as a civil servant Cadogan was less prepared: 'Shut up in dark, so I couldn't read, and didn't manage to sleep.' He was mollified by a landing at Gibraltar so perfect that he did not realise they had touched down, but the catering facilities there brought back his gloom again ('the usual meal of a pink sausage, a soggy bit of toast and some tinned beans, all ready mixed with reputed milk and sugar'). A whisky and soda from the station commander was some kind of compensation. After a night in a bed with a pillow so black that he had to wrap it in his shirt, he took off again and landed at Cairo after midnight, to be greeted by Churchill on his arrival at the Embassy.

Turkey had loomed large in Churchill's life in the past. As First Lord of the Admiralty on the outbreak of war in 1914, he had been instrumental in taking over the magnificent battleship *Sultan Osman I* building for the Turks on Tyneside, and renaming it *Agincourt*. The Turks considered this a great insult and, combined with the escape of the German ships *Goeben* and *Breslau* through the Mediterranean and their presentation to Turkey, it was enough to cause a Turkish declaration of war. Churchill's response was to organise the expedition to open the Dardanelles, which foundered due to military incompetence and temporarily ended Churchill's career. The Turks were finally defeated by General Allenby's advance from Egypt and T. E. Lawrence's famous campaign in Arabia. This great empire was dismantled and there was a revolution led by Kemal Ataturk, creating a modern, westernised state. Since then it had progressively reached agreement with most of its neighbours, until the beginning of the war in 1939 raised the threat of Italian and German aggression and brought the country closer to Britain. The Turks agreed to a meeting in their capital, Ankara, but the British, for security reasons, suggested somewhere more remote.

★   ★   ★

Cadogan judged the improved Liberator to be far better than the Hudson he had travelled out in, 'very comfortable, with a saloon with armchairs and windows'. They took off at 10 a.m. and flew over the Suez Canal and past Gaza. Flying along the coast, they were intrigued to see several waterspouts.

They passed off Tripoli in Lebanon and then headed for the small airfield at Adana where they landed at one in the afternoon. Soon they were taken to a railway siding containing a train which Churchill delighted in calling 'an enamel caterpillar'. The political leaders went into a discussion while the military commanders formed a group of their own. Brooke was disconcerted and annoyed to find that the Turks had made no preparation for the meeting, and had no conception of how to organise a modern army for battle. But the talks seemed to go well, the Turks apparently offering some hope of following Churchill's wishes.

Brooke was astonished to be told by the Turkish Foreign Minister how delighted everyone was with Churchill's visit. 'How could you keep an event of that kind secret? Of course everybody knows about it.' The Turks had posted sentries round the trains, but it was raining and each man put a blanket over his head. 'Their primary concern was to keep dry and the security of the PM ranked a very bad second.' Brooke was even more alarmed when he thought he caught Inspector Thompson and Sergeant Dudgeon slacking. Thompson was eating in the dining car, being 'more concerned with his personal comfort than with the PM's safety'. Thompson did not react well to this interference and replied, 'Am I expected to work all night as well as all day?'

The meetings ended with a dinner party which according to Brooke was 'a screaming success'. Churchill managed to communicate by using 'his astounding French, consisting of a combination of the most high flown French words mixed with English words pronounced in French'. He told 'the most complicated stories' by means of this method and was 'quite at his best and had the whole party convulsed with laughter'.

Most of the staff were pleased with the Turkish project. Ian Jacob felt it was 'an outstanding success and a real triumph for the Prime Minister, who had undertaken it against all the advice of the experts'. Brooke came away feeling, 'My wild dreams of bringing Turkey along with us no longer look so wild!' Cadogan was far more sceptical. At the time he thought they were simply relieved at not being asked to do anything concrete for the moment. Later he recollected that he

> never saw men more disinclined to be drawn into a war. They were very friendly and pleasant, and I am sure their sympathies were genuinely with us, but when the conversation began to veer towards anything like practical action on their part it seemed that they had found more than usual difficulty in hearing what was said.[1]

Wilson was quite prescient, as he often was, when he noted in his diary, 'P.M. taken in by the Turks.' Brooke eventually had to admit that his ' "wild dreams" about Turkey unfortunately remained wild dreams', and there was no concrete result from the meeting.

★　★　★

Having shaken off the clutches of the War Cabinet, Churchill felt a new sense of freedom. Wilson wrote of his travels:

> As for the P.M., when he gets away from his red boxes and leaves London, he puts his cares behind him. It's not only that he loves adventure; he feels, too, at times that he must 'let up'; even a week or two away from the unending grind helps. He wants to shed for a little the feeling that there are more things to do in the twenty-four hours than can possibly be squeezed in. Perhaps Roosevelt has that feeling too. It's the instinct to escape, to take a long breath. Besides neither of them, in a way, has ever grown up.[2]

At Adana airfield he showed the enthusiasm of a tourist with no fixed itinerary, changing his mind about where to go next, and came up with the idea of visiting Cyprus. Unlike his other visits, there was no compelling reason to go there. It was not the scene of conflict, it was not threatened by enemy action, there were no world leaders or important military commanders to meet, there were no decisions to be made about it, there were no potential allies to be wooed. Churchill's only reason was to look up his old regiment, the Fourth Hussars, now stationed there, in which he held the honorary post of colonel. But in the afternoon of the 31st he resolved to spend another night with the Turks. He was talked out of this and then decided to go straight on to Cairo instead of Cyprus.

While taxiing *Commando* around the airfield, Vanderkloot misjudged a sharp turn in front of the hangars and ran one of the Liberator's wheels off the runway, where it sank in two feet of soft soil. A crowd soon gathered. The RAF dignitaries were sceptical about the possibilities of getting it out, while Jacob watched with increasing *schadenfreude* – he had no responsibility for what was happening and plenty of time to look on. The Turkish guard of honour was fallen out and a rope was attached to the rear of the aircraft. Some of the soldiers attempted to lift the aircraft while the others pulled on the rope, with no result. A 3-ton lorry was added to the pulling forces. Then it was decided to dig holes ahead of the wheel so that the aircraft could be pulled forward over planks, and the aircraft's own engines were used to assist. By this time Churchill had decided to fly in the other Liberator, 911, and his luggage was transferred. Just then, with the combined effects of the engines, the lorry and the soldiers, the Liberator began to move slowly forward. There was laughter from the crowd as her wheels got back on the runway. But his luggage had been loaded and Churchill decided to stay with 911. Since it was now too late for Cairo, he decided to divert to Cyprus, a flight of 45 minutes.

This gave Ian Jacob his first chance to fly in *Commando*, which he found was more comfortable than the other Liberators, provided no more than eight people were carried. He found that the accommodation was much better than in 911, with comfortable seats and a view from most of them. Brooke enjoyed the view as usual: 'As we rose up and left Adana we had a wonderful view of the whole of the Taurus range of mountains from one end to the other, all covered with snow glittering in the wintery sun. After about half an hour's flying we struck the east end of the island and had a very jolly fly over it with good visibility and lovely evening lights.' They landed at Nicosia airport to be met by the Governor.

★ ★ ★

Cyprus had been a British colony since it was acquired by Benjamin Disraeli in 1878, although the mountainous island had no good harbours and little strategic value, while tension between Greeks and Turks made it difficult to govern. Churchill was to stay at a mansion which had been built at the expense of the islanders, as a punishment for burning down a previous Government House. Next morning Cadogan awoke early to find 'a most suspicious member of the Lepidoptera family on my sheet'. Wilson confirmed that it was a bed bug. For breakfast Cadogan was offered 'Bekanek' which he thought was a local dish but turned out to be a good helping of bacon and eggs.

At the airfield, Vanderkloot and his crew found that the black-painted *Commando* was the subject of much curiosity, and that the locals knew perfectly well who the passenger was. Russ Holmes, the radio operator, tried to cook some lunch on the aircraft's propane stove, placing it under the open astrodome to let the smoke escape. This too attracted attention and the airport fire engine was sent out to deal with it.

Meanwhile, Churchill was taken round the island to view the defences, though there was no particular reason to expect an attack. He inspected the Fourth Hussars, who had almost been wiped out during the Greek Campaign of 1941 and again during the retreat across the desert in 1942, but were reformed in time to take part in the battle of El Alamein and the pursuit that followed it. Their current posting to Cyprus was largely a rest from battle. Churchill inspected them during the 31st, and told them that the half million Allied troops in North Africa would soon be turning north, 'across the Mediterranean, carrying the war to a tense climax'. Brigadier Moffatt was impressed and wrote to his wife, 'Winston was grand. He radiated confidence and made a most stirring speech to the troops.'

That afternoon they flew back to Cairo, and heard the news of Field Marshal Paulus's surrender of the German Sixth Army at Stalingrad. There was a large party for lunch in the Embassy; then Brooke did some shopping and watched newsreel films. Churchill had now decided to pay a surprise visit to the Allied headquarters under Eisenhower, for he was disturbed by the news that the Americans had given increased recognition to General Giraud rather than de Gaulle. As usual on this trip there was doubt about Churchill's intentions and Brooke wrote, 'I only hope he will not suggest any more changes of plan at the last moment! It is high time we started turning homewards, and I shudder at the work to catch up with events when I get home.'

★ ★ ★

They took off for Tripoli at 9.45 in the morning of 3 February. Wilson sat opposite Brooke on the flight, and watched the CIGS totally immersed in Lansborough Thomson's *The Migration of Birds*. However, Brooke did find time to visit the cockpit and look down on the various battle sites, including El Alamein. The Prime Minister's relations with his son were as uneasy as ever, as he removed the cigar from his mouth and advised Randolph to give up smoking. Their bickering could be heard above the noise of the aircraft, but eventually Wilson fell asleep in his chair. As they approached Castel Benito airfield outside Tripoli, Brooke noticed the effect of Italian colonisation – 'settlements consisting of little white cottages, a well and a few palm trees'. Vanderkloot did several circuits to get a closer look, for he could see that the runways had been damaged by RAF bombs. They landed at 4.30 and were met by Generals Alexander and Montgomery, then driven off to Montgomery's camp. According to Wilson, it consisted of 'three caravans, outspanned like those of gipsies on a heath. One is for the P.M., a second for Alex and the third is mine.' Wilson mused that commanders-in-chief no longer lived in châteaux as they had during his own military service in the First World War. 'It is not that they fear attacks from the air, but rather that they dread democracy. They want to persuade the soldiery that their leaders are not lounging in luxury while they grovel in discomfort.'

Tripoli, like Casablanca, was a colonial city and port – about a third of its pre-war population of more than 100,000 was Italian. It was the capital of Libya, an Italian colony since 1912 and the launching pad for their attempt to control North Africa. Montgomery's troops had entered the city on 23 January and they were still employed clearing the damage caused by the fighting and by enemy sabotage. The first large ships had been moved into the port that morning. Commander Thompson was worried about security, as Churchill's route into the city had not been thoroughly searched and was over-looked by houses, but Montgomery was confident.

Commando's crew were intrigued to be in a captured enemy aerodrome, and to have their aircraft housed in a former *Luftwaffe* machine shop. As well as the holes in the runway, they could see much debris. They spotted a German Mauser rifle sticking out from some bushes and fished it out gingerly, fearing that it might be a booby trap. It became a souvenir instead. They were lodged in a former *Luftwaffe* hospital, still with its operating theatres intact.

The arrival in Tripoli was an emotional moment for Churchill and his staff, the first visit to captured enemy territory, as distinct from former neutral territory such as Casablanca. Brooke was impressed with the troops he inspected on the sea front and main square of the city. The inexperienced and pink-skinned men had been transformed into bronzed and victorious warriors, and the 51st Highland Division marched past to the sound of a lone bagpiper playing from the top of Mussolini's triumphal arch. Brooke, who had inspected hundreds of thousands of troops in his time, thought it was 'one of the most impressive sights I have ever seen'. He had a lump in his throat, while the more openly emotional Churchill had tears streaming down his cheeks. To Ian Jacob, 'It was an occasion that made all the disappointments, hardships and setbacks of the Middle East campaign seem to be robbed of their sting. The bitter moment in the White House, when Tobruk fell, was swallowed up in the joy of the morning in Tripoli.'

During the Tripoli visit, Vanderkloot and Churchill continued the tradi-tion of 'short-snorters', souvenirs assembled by the select band who had crossed the Atlantic by air. For each trip, every member acquired a note in the local currency and had it signed by the other passengers and crew. They were then glued together to produce, in the case of a crew like that of *Commando*, a very long document. According to Brooke:

Originally you could only become one if you had flown the Atlantic. It cost you 5/– [5 shillings, 25p] and you were initiated by someone who already belonged to this sect. Your name was entered on a bank note, and you then collected signatures of all other 'short snorters' till you had to gum several bank notes together. Mine consisted of a Russian note, a Turkish note and an American one, and was covered with signatures including President, PM, Hopkins, Harriman, Anthony Eden, Attlee, Inonu, etc, etc.[3]

If a member was unable to produce his notes on demand by another, he had to stand him a drink. On the flight out to Tripoli Churchill had to fetch his from the briefcase on his bunk, although technically that was a breach of the rules. On the second day in the city, he sent a staff car to conduct Vanderkloot to Montgomery's headquarters where he was allowed to collect the autographs of most of the British commanders in the Middle East.

★ ★ ★

Churchill now wanted to go to Algiers where he could confer with General Eisenhower and the British Admiral Cunningham. For this flight, Jacob went in the same aircraft as the Prime Minister for the first time, and he developed sympathy with Churchill's valet who had 'a dog's life' on such trips. He had to cope with 20 or 30 pieces of baggage, and they had to be kept together in case his master demanded a particular item of clothing – his dress requirements were completely unpredictable, and it was dangerous to leave some of the baggage behind, even if only stopping off for a few hours.

Wilson went to bed early that night, while Sawyers produced a drink from the bowels of the bomb bay. Jacob observed that Churchill had difficulties:

It was quite a business hoisting him into his perch and undressing him. At one stage I heard Sawyers say: 'You are sitting on your hot water bottle. That isn't at all a good idea.' To which the P.M. replied: 'Idea? It isn't an idea, it's a coincidence.'[4]

They flew some way south to avoid the last enemy strongholds in Tunisia. Jacob woke in the morning of 15 February to find the aircraft above the clouds. Sawyers produced 'some rather revolting coffee out of thermos flasks in a tea basket, but it was better than nothing'. The plane descended and almost at once it was over Maison Blanche airfield near Algiers. It was a fine feat of navigation, removing any suspicion that Vanderkloot was dependent on the services of Charles Kimber to find his destination.

Admiral Sir Andrew Cunningham had already established his reputation as the greatest British sailor of the war, perhaps since Nelson. He had commanded the Mediterranean Fleet through very difficult times, and then served in Washington before coming home again. Now in the days of victory, he was upset by the short notice of Churchill's arrival, in a city that was not totally cleared of unfriendly elements. 'In vain the War Office in London told him it would be extremely dangerous to come, and that there was a plot to assassinate him. Eisenhower was also strongly opposed to the visit, all of which made Mr. Churchill more determined to have his own way.' Cunningham arranged for the Prime Minister to be picked up from the airport in Eisenhower's special car, which had armoured sides and bullet-proof windows. They went by a circuitous route while Churchill grumbled about the length of the drive.

Jacob had sympathy for those left behind on the airfield, facing neglect, lack of washing facilities and a very poor breakfast. But he himself was getting closer to Churchill's inner circle and had no such problem.

He was taken to the Admiral's house where he was greeted with an excellent breakfast, a bath and a shave. Cunningham described the building to his aunt as

> a very modern house with a cocktail bar in the drawing room ... And you should see my bathroom, several steps up to the bath and a basin with cut-glass bottles all round it, some still filled with exotic scents as the lady apparently left in a hurry when the bombing started. The bed is upholstered in blue satin, and alongside the head of it, let into the wall, is the lady's private wireless set ... the grounds are very secluded and just lovely, with palms, orange trees, syringas and all manner of flowering shrubs and bougainvillea and masses of rose trees which will soon be in blossom.[5]

Jacob was impressed with the organisation of Cunningham's chief of staff, secretary and flag lieutenant, not to mention his coxswain and chief steward. Cunningham was an excellent host, who treated everyone the same. Nevertheless his resources were strained. He wrote to his wife: 'You never saw anything like this house. Every type of hanger-on, detectives, valets, secretaries. The Foreign Office was set up in Roy Dick's bedroom!'

The weather was poor as rain swept in over the city but Churchill was not disappointed. 'You know, there is no reason why we should hurry on from here. No one knows we are here, and I have a lot of business to do. I think we should spend a little time here.' Jacob pointed out that they should take advantage of the weather forecast, if it was favourable, to leave that evening. Churchill spent the morning discussing the military situation with Brooke and before lunch Vanderkloot and the local air force commander were summoned in. After much discussion it was agreed to head out that evening if the weather was suitable, flying directly to England without touching Gibraltar. Meanwhile a fake convoy of cars was assembled outside to create a diversion, and one American officer accidentally fired a burst of machine-gun bullets into the side of the villa.

★ ★ ★

The take-off from Algiers led to one of the most mysterious incidents in Churchill's voyages. The weather had cleared by 9.15 in the evening of the 5th and the party began to assemble at Maison Blanche airfield. They donned the usual costume of flying boots and fur-lined overalls, while Wilson was helped into his bunk with some difficulty, Sawyers went in and out of the bomb bay to fetch whiskies and soda and Churchill sat on one of the seats reading newspapers that had recently arrived from home.

Vanderkloot taxied to the end of the runway and ran up each engine in turn as a final test. The engine had two separate ignition systems, with one spark plug in the rear and one forward on each cylinder. The pilot switched from both magnetos to one, and then to the other to test that both systems were working. Apparently one was not functioning properly. It would be possible to fly for a time on one electrical system, but in the long term it would cause damage to the engine.

The aircraft remained stationary on the runway, and Vanderkloot came down through the trap door to announce to the passengers that he was unhappy about one of the engines. Churchill grunted and Vanderkloot went out. Jacob was dismayed around midnight when Randolph reappeared through the hatchway, for they thought they had got rid of him. He began his usual bickering with his father. Forty minutes later Vanderkloot re-entered to say that the trouble had been traced to a faulty magneto, which would take about three-quarters of an hour to change.

Churchill seemed put out by the news at first, but his mind worked quickly. 'It would be very dangerous to undertake the flight now. We should have to do the last 3 or 4 hours in broad daylight, and that on the most dangerous part of the route. We had better return to Algiers.' This was disputed by the others, who were anxious to get home. John Martin said, 'We are starting only one or two hours later than we intended to start, and we should in any case have done some of the end of the journey in daylight. Surely it would be best to go on.' Churchill thundered, 'You know absolutely nothing about it.' Randolph's intervention was met with equal contempt, and Churchill 'staggered to his feet, and before anyone could say anything further he left the aircraft and was off to Algiers in Admiral Cunningham's car, which fortunately had remained until we actually took off.' According to Jacob, he had spotted a chance to stay longer in Algiers, in a city which he enjoyed. Sir Charles Wilson, half asleep in his bunk, decided to stay there for the night. According to Cunningham Churchill was 'not in the best of tempers' when he arrived at the villa.

In his rather scurrilous account, Harry C. Butcher of Eisenhower's staff claimed that the aircraft had been sabotaged deliberately by one of Churchill's detectives, and later writers implied that this was done on the Prime Minister's orders. Perhaps he had received Ultra intelligence of a possible German attack on his aircraft, and wanted to postpone the flight without giving the secret away. This suggestion was regarded as 'grotesque' by Commander Thompson and denied by the rest of the entourage. Inspector Thompson, the only detective present, also denied it publicly throughout his life. Later, however, he is said to have admitted to his son that he did do it, not by damaging a magneto but by taking the rotor from a distributor cap.

This raises more questions than it answers. One can accept that Thompson had some knowledge of mechanics, and it would have been a relatively simple operation in, say, a motor car. But would he be able to climb out on the wing of a Liberator without attracting notice from its guards? The magneto was situated towards the rear of the engine and low down, so at least a stepladder would be needed, and it might take some time to find the relevant piece in the dark. If Churchill was behind the ploy, would it be reasonable to trust the skills of an amateur mechanic in such a matter of life or death? On the one hand he might fail to sabotage the engine, in which case the flight would go ahead anyway. On the other, the fault might not be discovered until the aircraft was in flight, with even more serious consequences. Would experienced flight engineers such as Ron Williams and John Affleck have been fooled by any of this? A damaged magneto might be passed off as an accident, but a missing rotor arm could only happen through human intervention. Would it not have been far simpler for Churchill to say that he wanted another night in Algiers, as he did in any case? On the whole the evidence is against the deliberate sabotage theory.

★ ★ ★

The Prime Minister spent the 6th in sunshine and rest, playing bezique with Randolph while Jacob and Rowan worked themselves into a mood of indignation about Tommy Thompson's faults and errors. 'Wendy' Holmes, pilot of the other Liberator, was unhappy about the single hop, as his aircraft was less well provided with radio navigation aids. It was agreed that he would leave at two in the afternoon for a stop at Gibraltar, where Brooke wanted to carry out some business in any case. The Prime Minister's party left the villa at 9.30 to find everything ready for them at Maison Blanche. As they settled down, Sawyers produced some drinks and Churchill sat opposite Jacob. After the deaths of Dykes and Stewart in another Liberator, the Prime Minister was morbid and he confided:

It would be a pity to have to go out in the middle of such an interesting drama without seeing the end. But it wouldn't be a bad moment to leave. It is a straight run in now, even the Cabinet could manage it![6]

Sawyers began to prepare him for bed, but his reputation for always knowing where everything was failed him for once. He could not find the Mothersill drug that Churchill used to help him sleep, despite looking in his RAF greatcoat pocket and in various packages. Frustration grew until a fresh supply was found. The aircraft finally took off at 11 p.m.

Jacob slept the night in his chair, to wake in broken cloud which was enough to give the aircraft somewhere to hide, without hampering navigation too much. They sighted the Bristol Channel and were met by an escort of twelve Spitfires. They passed over the port of Avonmouth and landed gently at Lyneham. Churchill congratulated Vanderkloot on 'the best landing you've made in the whole trip'. Mrs Churchill was there; her telegrams to her husband had barely concealed her concern about his flights. Despite Churchill's reassuring messages, she had suffered severe anxiety and tension, and was relieved that the engine trouble at Algiers had been discovered before the flight began. She wanted to arrange a private reunion – 'I like to kiss my Bull finch privately & not be photographed doing it!'

Cadogan, who travelled in the other Liberator, did not forget his discomfort:

Greeted by Portal, who said he hoped we'd had a good trip. Both C.I.G.S and I said yes, but that it was *damned* uncomfortable. I won't be dragged around the world again in these conditions, which are filthy. I don't think the P.M. has ever looked into our 'plane, or realises how beastly it is. Told C.I.G.S. never to cease chasing Portal on Chiefs of Staff Committee. Sure he'll play up.[7]

★ ★ ★

Back in London, Brendan Bracken arranged a film show of what he believed was the newsreel footage of the Casablanca conference. Unfortunately he had made a mistake, and it was the recent Humphrey Bogart movie. Most of the exhausted travellers fell asleep, though Churchill was fully alive as always on these occasions. His reactions to the film are not recorded, but must have been contradictory. Certainly its anti-Nazi message was clear, and its moral was that this was not the time to stand aside or let one's personal affairs get in the way of the world struggle. But it showed a fictional Casablanca which had nothing to do with the city they had just visited. Throughout the film America is constantly referred to as the only beacon of freedom, and Britain is barely mentioned, and then only in a defensive capacity, the Germans having failed to take London. This was the beginning of a trend in American cinema, and it also represented a movement in the balance of power within the Allied camp. As Russian and American military strength grew, Britain's steadfastness and experience would count for less and less.

As often happened, the trip had a contradictory effect on Churchill's health. It gave him a chance for some relaxation in luxurious villas in Marrakech and Algiers, afforded him a certain amount of freedom from daily affairs and provided a good deal of mental stimulus. On the other hand, it was physically exhausting and placed great demands on his over-stretched constitution. A week after the return, Wilson was called into Downing Street to treat him for a cold in the head. Next day he was X-rayed and Dr Geoffrey Marshall of Guy's Hospital confirmed that he had pneumonia. It was his most serious illness so far, and his low mood was not helped when Marshall told him that the disease was 'the old man's friend ... because it carries them off so quickly'. Fortunately his heart was now sound, his temperature fell and he began to recover slowly by the end of February. But it had long-term effects on his travel plans.

XI

The Queen of the Ocean

On 29 April 1943, as the daily War Cabinet meeting drew to a close, Churchill informed its members that the British commanders in India and the Far East – Field Marshal Wavell, Air Chief Marshal Peirse and Admiral Somerville – had been invited to Washington to discuss strategy with the American Chiefs of Staffs. This was enough to awaken Churchill's recurring fear, that the Americans wanted to switch most of their forces to the Pacific. It would be churlish not to let the C-in-Cs go, so he suggested that they should attend but with 'political support' – in the form of himself and the British Chiefs of Staff. He had to make the voyage by sea, because 'his doctors did not regard it as suitable that he should fly at a great height, which might be necessary at this time of year'.

Sir Charles Wilson described the process rather differently:

Before Winston crossed the Atlantic he appeared to go through a period of indecision: one day he would decide to go by sea and the next he was sure that he could not spare the time and must go by air. If he travelled by sea he had a feeling of being out of touch with things; something might happen and he would hear of it too late to do anything. Furthermore, he always had a horror of time wasted; during the war this became an obsession with him and in mid-Atlantic he would say, 'If we had flown as I wanted we should be in London by now and could do business.' On the other hand he disliked flying … Winston, however, was made so he would not give way to fears of this kind; because he disliked the air, he was more likely to fly. On this occasion he credits me with the decision to go by sea, affirming that I did not want him after his pneumonia to fly in a bomber at perhaps ten thousand feet. It may be so, but I had little say in matters of this kind. It was the P.M. himself who weighed the pros and cons; I was never allowed to touch the scales.[1]

In any case, the Cabinet was doubtful. The First Lord of the Admiralty suggested he might look at the chart of U-boats in the Atlantic before he reached a decision, for the submarine war was approaching a climax. Various ministers asked if it was really necessary, but the Prime Minister was adamant and as usual he had his way. It was Lord Leathers, the Minster of Shipping, who suggested the solution in this case – that the party should travel in one of the great Atlantic liners, now being used to ferry American troops to the war in Europe.

★ ★ ★

No ship ever carried the hopes and aspirations of a nation more than the *Queen Mary*. She was conceived in 1930, in the depths of the Great Depression, as a new type of Atlantic liner. For 80 years the Cunard Company had prospered by carrying masses of emigrants cheaply across the ocean. This ended in 1921 when the United States imposed immigration quotas and the older liners such as the *Aquitania* and *Mauretania* were converted and given more luxurious accommodation. The Germans and Italians were launching new ships, and the French government supported the building of a great liner, the *Normandie*. Cunard awarded the contract for a ship of 80,000 tons to John Brown's of Clydebank, already established as one of the world's greatest builders of very large ships. The huge liner, originally known by the yard number of 534, began to rise among the grim industrial tenements. Even the fervent socialist artisans of Clydeside were not put off by her standard of luxury, for unemployment among shipyard workers stood at more than 60 per cent. Thousands of men, however, were laid off when work stopped in 1931 as Cunard faced a financial crisis. The company had to merge with its great rival White Star Line, to secure a government guarantee of three million pounds. When work on No. 534 resumed in April 1934, the town of Clydebank was bedecked with flags, and bagpipers led the workmen back into the yard. Five months later she was launched by Queen Mary and given her name. The BBC covered it with a pioneering radio broadcast, dozens of newspapers published special supplements, huge crowds cheered on both banks of the Clyde and the newsreel footage was shown in every cinema in the land. The great ship was an expression of national characteristics. One French journalist compared her with her rival the *Normandie*. 'The French built a beautiful hotel and put a ship round it. The British built a beautiful ship and put a hotel inside it.'

The *Mary* made many transatlantic voyages before the war ended that trade, and her luxury fittings were stripped out so that she could carry troops, initially from Australia and New Zealand to the war in the Middle East. Cunard built a slightly larger ship, the *Queen Elizabeth*, but she was completed

188

in wartime and went straight on to trooping, so she did not have the same place in public affection. Her German and Italian rivals could no longer venture on the Atlantic in the face of British sea power and the *Normandie* was held in New York at the outbreak of war. She was accidentally burned in 1942 and her capsized wreck remained between Piers 88 and 90, leaving the *Mary* as the true queen of the ocean.

After the American entry to the war she returned to her old route, though in very different conditions. She could now carry up to 15,000 troops at once, sleeping and eating in shifts. She relied on her great speed of nearly 30 knots to keep her safe, for she travelled alone for most of the time – she and the other 'monster' liners were each reckoned as a convoy in herself by the Admiralty authorities. She left the Atlantic again early in 1943, as part of a group of ships carrying 31,000 Australians and New Zealanders back home to fight Japan, when the war in North Africa came to an end. She had returned by the spring, operating from her original home on the River Clyde. She was rather more suitable for the prime ministerial trip than the *Queen Elizabeth*, which had never been fitted out with luxury accommodation. The lavish furnishings of the *Mary* were in store near by for use after the war, and could be taken out for selected areas if needed.

Unlike Royal Navy battleships, the *Queen Mary* was designed specially for Atlantic operation, and did not carry heavy guns which had to be kept low to improve the centre of gravity. She had seven decks above the waterline in the bows, compared with three in the *King George V* class, so they were 65 feet above the waves instead of the 28 feet of the battleships. It was highly unlikely, therefore, that passengers would be kept below decks by waves breaking over the ship. Moreover, she was almost half as long again as a battleship, and 15 per cent wider, so she would be less troubled by rough seas.

The central part of the *Queen Mary*'s main deck, the highest one with passenger cabins, was chosen for conversion. This was one of only two places intended for luxury staterooms, or 'special' rooms, with suites instead of mere cabins. It was more suitable than A deck just below, for it allowed immediate access to the open air on the sheltered promenade deck above. Two hundred workmen were employed for four days on the refit. Extra temporary bunks were removed, cabin doors were replaced, and many luxury items were got out of store. Parts of the deck had to be partitioned off for security, but that was not difficult as the area was already subdivided by fireproof bulkheads.

There were two possible problems. First, the ship was scheduled to carry 5,000 German prisoners of war to America and some thought that this posed an unacceptable security risk, but Churchill agreed that they should remain on board. Secondly, the ship had become infested with bugs which had got into the baggage of the Australian troops at Suez. Gas was used to eliminate them from the VIP quarters, delaying the passage for several days. But they were still in the ship, and no form of security could prevent them creeping back into the protected area.

★ ★ ★

Elizabeth Layton longed to travel, to return briefly to Canada where she had been brought up, to eat American food and to visit cities not under threat of bombing. The prospect of stocking up on clothes from American shops was equally attractive. An adult civilian in Britain was allowed 48 coupons per year, and a woman's cotton dress would take up seven, a woollen dress eleven. Five coupons were needed for a pair of shoes, and three for a pair of silk stockings. People were urged to 'make do and mend' and the population looked increasingly shabby.

Up till now civilian women had been prohibited from travelling on the warships and aircraft that had carried Churchill. Miss Layton soon realised that this could no longer apply on a merchant ship such as the *Queen Mary*. Eventually, 24 hours before departure, she found the courage to ask Mrs Hill if it was possible for her to join the party. The immediate reply was 'If you wanted to go, why didn't you ask sooner?' She rushed home to iron and pack her meagre wartime allowance of clothing. Joan Bright of the Cabinet Office was equally delighted:

> We could not believe our luck. Like many, many others, we had been shut up in the fortress of Britain, blacked out, bombed out, conditioned to austerity. Now we were to sail away from it on a top-secret, top priority meeting. From now on, in our coupon-valued clothes, we would join the ranks of khaki and blue, pack our bags and climb into special trains, aircraft, ships and staff cars. We would be carried from one place to another to open out typewriters, short-hand notebooks, duplicating machines, and try to produce the same standard of work as was expected – and received – in London.[2]

The party was larger than ever, which meant that some sea travel would be, in any case, almost inevitable. As well as Churchill and his immediate entourage of eight, Averell Harriman and Lord Beaverbrook would be travelling with their own followers. Lord Leathers had to come, too, for the provision of shipping resources was becoming one of the main constraints on war activity. He had a modest party of a private secretary and a stenographer. The First Sea Lord was accompanied by six officers including Admiral Somerville, with a petty officer steward and both a naval and a newsreel cameraman. The War Office party had eight officers including the CIGS, Lord Wavell and two others. The Air Ministry sent Portal and five other officers. Mountbatten, the Chief of Combined Operations was ill, but five officers were sent including a WRNS stenographer. The War Cabinet office group was headed by General Ismay and Brigadier Jacob, with two more officers and five clerks and typists.

The operation was codenamed Trident and as usual, elaborate security precautions were devised. Rumours were to be spread by MI5 that important personages were to embark in New York for a conference in London. To add colour, wheelchair ramps were to be fitted in places, hinting that President Roosevelt was to come on board. It was to be put about that the Prime Minister was going to Scotland to view secret operational trials with the First Sea Lord, while Lord Leathers, heading the party, was inspecting the ports of western England and Scotland. More prosaically, General Ismay's staff were to pretend that he was at home with influenza.

At the beginning of May 1943, the U-boats seemed as dangerous as ever. On every other major front, in North Africa, in the Pacific and in Russia, the tide had already turned and the Axis forces were in retreat. American and British bombers were pounding Germany day and night, Italy was heavily demoralised, and troops were training in England for the invasion of Europe. This was not so in the Atlantic, where the U-boats had sunk more than 100 ships in March 1943. Naval intelligence warned that there were 128 U-boats in the Atlantic, more than ever before. Nearly 40 of them were massing south of Greenland to attack convoy ONS 5, which had been delayed by bad weather and had lost much of its escort. The crisis of the Battle of the Atlantic was approaching. Because of her great speed the *Queen Mary* was only in danger if the enemy was able to predict her movements, but that was all too conceivable. Brooke was pessimistic:

Apparently impossible to conceal nature of preparation on the *Queen Mary*, and quite possible news might get over to Dublin. German ambassador there might cable or wireless the news to Germany. We were assured that in either case messages would be intercepted although wireless ones could not be stopped. We should know however and could then change and go by air. Pound also explained that a carrier had been detailed to act as escort in area where Focke-Wulf aircraft might operate. Also cruisers detailed to provide protection on sections of the journey.[3]

* * *

Train travel arrangements were complicated. There were only sleeping berths for some of the party, and those chosen were recommended to arrive at Addison Road Station in West London between 11.35 in the evening of 4 May and half past midnight to stand a chance of a good night's sleep. The train would then be moved out of the area, and return at 5.15 next morning, when the others would have 25 minutes to get on board. Elizabeth Layton was pleased to find she had a sleeping berth. She did not sleep well due to excitement, which was just as well as Churchill kept her up for much of the night anyway. 'In his tiny compartment the only place for me to sit was on the bed, squashed up trying not to land on his feet. Bad moment when I got cramp in one leg.'

At four in the afternoon they arrived at Greenock and boarded the tug *Romsey* which took them out to the *Queen Mary*, moored in the Tail of the Bank anchorage off the town. Elizabeth Layton was slightly disappointed as the tug drew alongside the ship, and she saw her in her 'dirty blue-grey camouflage, three funnels smoking, but not as big as I had imagined'. General Brooke was more impressed, especially after the party was taken up by lift to their quarters on the Main Deck. 'They have done marvels in a very short time, and the cabin I am in must be almost up to pre war standard. A very large double room very well fitted with sitting room, 2 bath rooms, box room and masses of cupboards, arm chairs, sofas, etc, etc.' Miss Layton found 'a sort of Royal suite. Mr. C. has a flat for himself and Sawyers, our office opposite, and palatial rooms alongside in a row for Mr Rowan, Commander Thompson, Peter [i.e. Patrick Kinna] and me.' Meanwhile the tug was taken to a remote anchorage in the Firth of Clyde and kept incommunicado until there was news that the group had arrived safely.

It took a good deal of work and tact to get the accommodation allocated and the offices into shape, as Joan Bright found:

The Administrative Office on 'M' deck became a bedlam of travellers, demanding this and complaining about that. No one wanted to share a cabin, but it had to be done. The girls suffered the most;

Above: The operations room at RAF Rudloe Manor showing the map of the English Channel, seen upside down from this angle. (IWM CH 11887)

Right: General Sir Alan Brooke in his office in 1942. (IWM TR 149)

Above: The Liberator *Commando*, AL 504. (Canada Wide)

Below: Some of the crew for the Cairo and Moscow flights – Vanderkloot, Ruggles, Kimber and Williams. (Wing Commander Charles T. Kimber Archive)

Opposite page, top: Some of the British party at Cairo. Front row: Smuts, Churchill, Lampson and Casey, the British minister. Back row: Tedder, Brooke, Harwood, Auchinleck, Wavell, Wilson and Cadogan. (IWM E 15218)

Opposite page, bottom: Churchill getting out of *Commando* in Moscow. (IWM FLM 1116)

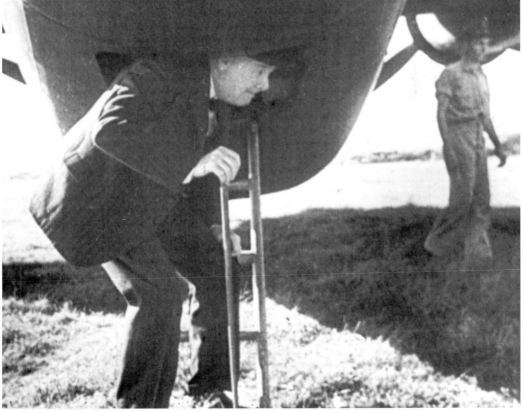

Above: Harriman and Churchill on their arrival in Moscow, with *Commando* in the background. (IWM FLM 1115)

Below: Roosevelt and Churchill address a press conference at Casablanca, as Roosevelt announces the policy on unconditional surrender. (IWM A 14062)

Above: Churchill with President Inonu of Turkey in the 'enamel caterpillar', the Turkish presidential train. (IWM K 3987)

Below: Churchill in the cockpit of the Liberator, soon after the Turkey trip, as the flag of that country is painted on, along with the Soviet flag. (IWM K 4473)

Left: *Commando* arrives back at RAF Lyneham after the Casablanca conference. (IWM CH 8554)

Centre: *Ascalon*, Churchill's Avro York. (IWM ATP 11382c)

Below: Churchill on board the *Queen Mary*, in conference with Field Marshal Wavell and Admiral Somerville. (IWM 17088)

Bottom: The *Queen Mary* in her wartime camouflage. (IWM FL 10021)

Above: The battlecruiser *Renown* in her wartime camouflage.
(IWM A 7322)

Left: Churchill with his wife and daughter on the quarterdeck of the *Renown*, with an escorting destroyer.
(IWM H 32974)

they always shared, four, eight, ten, unless their rare seniority rated them a double. And furniture – everyone wanted furniture. Thinking they were still in Whitehall, perfection-prone officers flew to their office cabins, rushed out, called for more tables, more chairs, more lamps. It was a day of sound and fury which ended in the early hours of next morning as the Administrative Staff – Maurice Knott and I – sat silent and ate our supper.[4]

The aircraft carrier *Indomitable* left the Clyde at four in the afternoon, and she was to scout ahead, flying off constant anti-submarine patrols during the hours of daylight and standing by to shoot down any *Luftwaffe* reconnaissance aircraft that might appear. The *Queen Mary* left at 5.30 to get cover from darkness as she passed north of Ireland. Brooke went on to the bridge with his fellow chiefs of staff and stayed there for two hours, watching the coast of Ayrshire where he had spent holidays with his wife. As night fell they passed the north coast of Ireland and the Giant's Causeway was visible.

Next morning they were 120 miles from Ireland and already making faster progress than the *Duke of York* had done on the last trip. There was a lifeboat drill and the Chiefs of Staff were shown which boat to use in the event of sinking – a routine precaution on a normal voyage, but especially poignant when they were still within the range of U-boats and Condors. It was the last time General Ismay saw the deck during the voyage, as he was kept busy with Chiefs of Staff meetings. He found the environment good for getting some work done:

> The *Queen Mary* was a most convenient and comfortable work-shop. We were all under one roof, and each had our own offices. There were ample conference rooms, and the reproduction and circulation of papers went forward with the same methodical precision as in London. We received the usual stream of telegrams, and the Prime Minister's Map Room, in charge of the indefatigable Pim, was kept as up to date as its counterpart in Great George Street.[5]

The ship was now heading south-west, on the edge of the area 600 miles from Brest which was regarded as most dangerous from the air. The three Chiefs of Staff went up to the bridge again before lunch to watch their escorting cruiser *Scylla* ploughing through heavy seas, but a large ship like the *Queen Mary* was not bothered by the waves. At 4 o'clock the *Indomitable* was in sight twelve miles to the south, giving extra reassurance and some fond memories. She had been launched by Clementine Churchill three years previously, and Winston cherished a photograph of his wife looking ecstatically happy on that day.

In conversation with Harriman, Churchill showed his usual attitude to danger. When a U-boat was reported to be crossing their path some miles ahead, Churchill asserted, 'Pound says we are just as likely to ram the submarine as it is to see us first.' He told of his orders to have a machine gun in his lifeboat in case the ship was sunk:

> I won't be captured. The finest way to die is in the excitement of fighting the enemy. (*Then, after a moment's thought*) It might not be so nice if one were in the water and they tried to pick me up.

Harriman found this alarming.

> Prime Minister, this is all very disquieting to me. I thought you told me that the worst a torpedo could do to this ship, because of its compartments, was to knock out one engine room, leaving suffi- cient power to steam at twenty knots.

Churchill, still pessimistic about the survival ability of the *Queen Mary*, replied:

> Ah, but they might put two torpedoes in us. You must come with me in the boat and see the fun.[6]

Ismay was much more sanguine: 'Apparently the chances of a U-boat being able to get into the correct position to score a hit on a zig-zagging ship of the speed of the *Queen Mary* was infinitesimal; and in any event we were assured that she could take half a dozen torpedoes and still swim.' This was probably true. Since the loss of the *Titanic* 30 years ago, the shipping companies had been keen to reassure paying passengers that their ships were safe, both in the provision of lifeboats and by preventing or limiting severe damage to the hull. This was enforced by the standards set by the International Convention on the Safety of Life at Sea and by the British Board of Trade. A leading company such as Cunard made a point of exceeding these high standards; the underwater hull of the *Queen Mary* was divided into 18 separate watertight compartments along its length, and each was subdivided into at least three sections across its width. In all there were 160 watertight compartments below a watertight bulkhead deck, and the doors in them could be closed automatically from the bridge. But unlike the Side Protection System of the battleships, this was designed for collisions and groundings rather than torpedo hits; also, unlike the SPS, it was never tested in action, as no ship of this size came into contact with the enemy.

By midnight on 6/7 May they had passed out of the 600-mile radius from Brest, and the meridian of 20 degrees west beyond which enemy aircraft did not normally operate. The *Indomitable* parted company but the *Queen Mary* was now entering another danger area. She would pass across the track of several U-boats coming in and out of the French Bay of Biscay ports. Yet it was not as perilous as it seemed, for naval intelligence knew the routes they would use, and individual boats could be picked up either by radar or radio direction finding. Moreover, they were about 600 miles away from the bases, and by that stage the boats had begun to fan out to head for different areas, so the chance of meeting one head-on was remote.

Brooke was fatalistic and went to bed at midnight, just as the ship turned on to a more southerly course to pass through the area as quickly as possible, at right angles to the U-boat tracks. Next morning he awoke to hear that they were safely through and were 500 miles west of Cape Finisterre. At noon they altered course to head straight for New York. There was news of the attack on convoy ONS 5 many miles away between Newfoundland and Greenland, and the loss of 13 ships, in exchange for five U-boats. There was a much less ambiguous success as General Alexander reported on how the Germans and Italians in North Africa were being increasingly isolated in their remaining stronghold in Tunisia The war in North Africa which had caused Churchill so much anxiety over the last three years was almost over. The only problem was what to do next, and that would be discussed in Washington.

Sir Dudley Pound was not impressed with the conduct of the cruiser *Glasgow* during her brief appearance on the 7th. She 'could have been some use both against U-boats and aircraft had she taken station ahead of SS *Queen Mary*, instead of which she was generally out of sight on the beam or bow'. She parted company immediately on the arrival of her replacements *Uganda* and *Charybdis*, rather than waiting two more hours until noon as had been planned. The *Queen Mary* signalled her frantically by light and flag to order her to stand one mile away on the beam to receive messages for onward transmission, but she paid no attention. As a result, important dispatches were delayed for eight hours until the next cruiser left. Pound was angry enough to signal his deputy in London demanding a full report. Meanwhile the *Queen Mary* altered course to 225 degrees to go more westerly and head straight for Washington. The cruiser *Uganda* took station five miles ahead, forcing any U-boats that might be in her path to submerge and lose more than half their speed.

★ ★ ★

Churchill was as busy as ever on the journey, though he spent most of his time with the Chiefs of Staff and did not need much typing from Elizabeth Layton. She and Kinna still had to receive and send on messages to the Prime Minister, but she found time to socialise with the typists from the Cabinet Office, and was able to mix rather nervously with 'some of the most famous people in the land', who were, 'for the time being on seemingly equal terms'. This did not include the Chiefs of Staff who were too busy, but she enjoyed the jokes of bluff Admiral Somerville, and was embarrassed when an army officer she was teasing turned out to be a full general.

One problem was the disposal of secret waste material, which Royal Marine orderlies collected each day for burning. On the first night it was taken below to the boiler room, but it caused the funnels to belch 'a bright cloud of burning paper' which was a beacon to U-boats. It was decided to dispose of it by other means. Captain Pim's Map Room was more successful, as always; Joan Bright thought it was 'particularly nice, with good lighting, a soft carpet and plenty of space for maps showing the progress of the war at sea, on land and in the air'.

The passengers included Sir William Beveridge who had recently issued a report which would form the basis of the National Health Service after the war. Churchill was distinctly unenthusiastic about it and it had triggered a Parliamentary revolt earlier in the year. Beveridge was not part of the main party but was on honeymoon with his formidable new wife and former secretary. The insect life had penetrated their cabin, the outermost one in the privileged part of the ship. They had bitten Lady Beveridge but not Sir William. Churchill invited them to dinner and on seeing her ladyship's bites he asked, 'What's the matter, Beveridge – are you sleeping apart?' The party did not go well and Wilson recorded that 'The atmosphere was correct without being unduly cordial.'

Churchill was able to send almost daily reports to his wife, in the style of a postcard – 'All well. Great comfort, much love, tell all', and 'All well, most pleasant voyage, everyone working hard, love to all.' He used the rather thin disguise of 'Air Commodore Spencer to Mrs Spencer' – Air Commodore was his honorary rank in the Royal Auxiliary Air Force and Spencer was one of his middle names.

Brooke describes a typical day at sea for the high command:

8 May
Another day devoted mainly to conferences. We started the day with a discussion over my opening statement at the conference in Washington. We then had another discussion on shipping attended by Lord Leathers and Cherwell, a good conference which has gone a long way towards clearing the air. The afternoon I spent reading up a paper on our action in the event of the collapse of the Italian nation, which we then discussed at 5.30.[7]

Early in the afternoon of the 9th the lookouts sighted the USS *Augusta* which had been Roosevelt's base during the Placentia conference nearly two years before. She was accompanied by two destroyers and at two o'clock, as they crossed the 50 degree meridian which marked the edge of American responsibility, the faithful *Uganda* and *Charybdis* parted company and the US Navy took over the escort. More ships soon arrived and Churchill's notes to his wife began to sound almost complacent:

Six US Warships escorting, three more arriving tomorrow. Voyage continues to be most pleasant. Love to all.

Followed by:

Surrounded by ten US warships including eight destroyers.
Poor Lady Beveridge has been terribly bitten by bugs who are advancing resolutely. So far their spearheads have not penetrated our citadel.[8]

On the last night, 10 May, Pound held a small sherry party for the naval officers serving in the *Queen Mary*. Sir Charles Wilson was intrigued by the system of tipping, which highlighted the class system on board. A total of £150 to £200 was to be spent, and individuals would contribute according to the standard of their accommodation, and the Ministry of War Transport's 'idea of what might reasonably be expected of us having regard for our supposed worldly circumstances'. The £10 class was 'very select' and included only the Prime Minister, Harriman, Beaverbrook and Lord Leathers. Wilson was in the £6 group along with the Chiefs of Staff, Wavell, Ismay, Prof Lindemann and Air Chief Marshal Peirse. The rest of the group was divided into £2, £1 and ten shilling classes.

That night Brooke noted:

This should be our last day at sea as we are due to arrive tomorrow morning if we go on defeating submarines as we have done up to the present, but most of them are concentrated further north. There are only two reported in front of us in the approaches to New York. But as we have now picked up a Catalina flying boat in addition to our two cruisers and four destroyers we should be well protected.[9]

Keen as always to get the best out of his journeys, Brooke got up early to view the famous skyline of New York. He was unlucky, for 'There was a heavy mist and then rain which made it difficult to see even the shore or the approaches.' In any case the ship stopped at Staten Island well short of the main harbour and the party was transferred to a train for Washington. Captain Pim was impressed that it included a barber's shop and showers:

This was my first acquaintance with the American railways and I was immediately struck by the extra height and width of their carriages although the gauge is the same as in England. We sat down to a lunch of cold asparagus soup, an omelette, a 'small' (they apologised for this) steak which in turn was followed by an ice cream on the top of a slice of cherry pie and coffee … The 'small' steak was equivalent to a week's meat ration for a family of three in Great Britain.[10]

★ ★ ★

On 11 May in the President's oval study in the White House, Churchill opened the Trident conference. He began by referring to the last time he had been there and heard about the fall of Tobruk. This was unfortunate, as the Americans could never understand the British obsession with the Mediterranean, and they needed no reminding about British failures. He took the bombing offensive against Germany and the anti-U-boat campaign for granted; then he painted a dramatic picture of the effects of knocking

Italy out of the war. Her fleet would be eliminated, leaving the sea to British and American naval power. It would be possible to route shipping through the Suez Canal instead of round the Cape of Good Hope, saving a million tons. He did not believe that the Germans would remain in Italy, and from there it would be possible to support resistance movements in Greece and Yugoslavia which would harass them further. Turkey might give permission to use her airfields to bomb the Ploesti oilfields, Germany's main source of supply. Furthermore, 'The collapse of Italy would bring a chill of loneliness over the German people, and might be the beginning of their doom.' He recalled 1918, when the defection of Bulgaria led to the collapse of Germany. He outlined other objectives – to aid Russia, to plan for the cross-Channel invasion in 1944, and to support China, though he was sceptical about a campaign in Burma where the terrain was difficult and sea power was of little use. Instead he argued for operations against the northern tip of Sumatra and the waist of the Malayan peninsula.

There was little time for visits during the two weeks of hard negotiations, but on 15 May the party visited Shangri-La, later Camp David, in the hills of Maryland. Churchill impressed his hosts by quoting at length John Greenleaf Whittier's famous poem *Barbara Frietchie*, about the American Civil War – 'Shoot if you must this old grey head, But spare your country's flag, she said.' Brooke visited colonial Williamsburg and was pleased with its restoration.

Back in Washington, the members dispersed to form their separate groups. Among the Joint Chiefs of Staff, Brooke initially found that the Americans were as difficult as he had expected. They seemed unprepared, and there was a big difference between the two sides:

> What is more the Americans are now taking the attitude that we led them down the garden path by taking them to North Africa! That at Casablanca we again misled them by inducing them to attack Sicily!! [for Brooke was fond of the exclamation mark] And now they are not going to be led astray again. Added to that the swing towards the Pacific is stronger than ever and before long they will be urging us that we should defeat Japan first![11]

Brooke, like other members of the party, was suffering from illness or its after effects and became strangely depressed and occasionally bored. At one stage he memorised the collection of objects on Roosevelt's desk, but later admitted that 'I would have been better employed trying to reduce the confusion that the conference had got into.' He found that Churchill, also suffering from after effects, was often surprisingly indecisive:

> At times the war may be won by bombing and all must be sacrificed to it. At other times it becomes essential for us to bleed ourselves dry on the Continent because Russia is doing the same. At others our main effort must be in the Mediterranean, directed against Italy and the Balkans alternatively, with sporadic desires to invade Norway and 'roll up the map in the opposite direction to Hitler'! But more often than all he wants to carry out ALL operations simultaneously irrespective of shortages of shipping![12]

He found that the Chiefs of Staff tended to divide on service lines. For the RAF, Portal wanted to build up the bombing offensive against Germany, which he felt was the key to winning the war. Sir Dudley Pound of the Royal Navy was already in declining health, but 'when he wakes up wishes we would place submarine warfare above all other requirements'. Neither of these was disputed in principle, though the amount of resources allocated to each was often a matter of controversy. Meanwhile Admiral King of the US Navy wanted to put maximum effort in the Pacific, while General Marshall of the US Army wanted a large-scale invasion across the English Channel as soon as possible. Brooke himself subscribed to Churchill's policy, that an invasion of Sicily would lead to an attack on Italy, with great consequences on the war.

After much hard negotiating there was a series of compromises, but Brooke was ultimately pleased with the results. 'Looking back on the conference in the light of the results that ensued, the compromise that emerged was almost exactly what I wanted! We continued with the war in Italy with the aim of eliminating Italy.'

The party dispersed in several directions. Four Liberators were to leave on the 27th, taking the main groups from the Admiralty, War Office, Air Ministry and War Cabinet Offices across the Atlantic. Several, including Harriman and Beaverbrook and their staffs, were staying behind, while Paymaster-Captain Knott signalled back, 'Now for the night life of Washington.' The remainder were to go in the *Queen Mary* again, and Elizabeth Layton found it very different from the voyage out, as there were 16,000 American troops on the ship with them and 'fourteen young women shared one cabin, but we had plenty of fun and laughed at the catcalls and whistles which our appearance on deck evoked'. Joan Bright described their 'twice-daily walk to the dining saloon' which was, 'accompanied by cat-calls, whistles, sighs – "Look out, dames coming!", "Whew-w-w!", "Watch your talk!" Their sleep was interrupted by 'the click of the dice in their eternal crap games.'

The Prime Minister had plans of his own.

★ ★ ★

Churchill, realising that General Marshall was the greatest obstacle to an advance through Italy, resolved to take him across the Atlantic to see the situation for himself. Roosevelt eventually agreed, rather to Wilson's surprise, and Churchill decided to do it right away, rather than go home and have to convince the War Cabinet yet again. This time he took the decision to sidestep the doctors' advice and fly. Realistically there was no other way, and in any case the eastward air passage was generally easier than the westward one because of the prevailing winds. Sir Charles Wilson was ill himself by this time, and found that 'It is not easy to do my job with these bouts of high fever.'

This time the flight across the Atlantic was to be carried out by the *Bristol*, again captained by Kelly Rogers. They took off early on 26 May and Churchill studied a draft of a communication from the Russians. He found it difficult to understand the President's handwritten amendments, until he gave it to General Marshall who had it retyped. He was impressed with the clarity of Marshall's thinking as expressed in the new edition. By the time the aircraft landed at Botwood for refuelling, a final version was ready to send back to Washington. The party had dinner and then the plane took off again to follow a great circle track, the shortest route between Newfoundland and Gibraltar. Churchill went to the bridal suite and slept for several hours, until there was a sudden shock and a bump. Wilson heard a small 'pop' and Brooke heard 'two bangs followed by a flash as if something had hit the hull of the flying ship', but both went back to sleep. Ismay slept on, but Churchill woke up and put on his zip suit to go forward to the co-pilot's seat. Kelly Rogers told him, 'We were struck by lightning, but there's nothing wrong.' Churchill was relieved, and even more so when he saw a small tramp steamer in the sea 7,000 feet below – it might be useful, he implied, if they had to make a forced landing. He went back to bed and slept until dawn.

The concept of 'jet lag' was of course unknown in those days, but Churchill was aware of some of its effects as he went forward to see the sun rise ahead. 'I adhered to my rule in these flights that meals should be regulated by stomach time. When one wakes up after daylight one should breakfast; five hours after that, luncheon. Six hours after luncheon, dinner. Thus one becomes independent of the sun, which otherwise meddles too much in one's affairs and upsets the routine of work.' Brooke looked out of the window to see a perfect landfall off Cape St Vincent in the south-western corner of Portugal. They flew along the coast, then passed Cape Trafalgar to see the Rock of Gibraltar in the distance. As they approached, the promised air escort failed to materialise. Instead a Spanish aircraft took some interest, then disappeared. Brooke thought Gibraltar Bay was covered in mist, but it was only a strip outside the harbour. The aircraft alighted on the water at 5 p.m. local time after a flight of 17 hours. A launch towed it to a buoy, to be met by the Governor in another boat. It was too late to fly on that night, so the party stayed in Gibraltar until the morning. Wilson left the party and flew home. Churchill would travel without him for the first time since the Newfoundland conference.

★　★　★

Churchill made no immediate comment on the new aircraft which was waiting for him there. It was the first of a new type of transport plane, the Avro York. It was also the first that the Prime Minister could really call his own, for the Liberator was used for many purposes besides Prime Ministerial transport. There was an informal agreement that the Americans would produce transport aircraft while the war lasted, and Britain's overstretched resources would be concentrated on bombers and fighters. The York was conceived before this took effect, and development continued. It was simply an adaptation of the famous Lancaster bomber, which had been in service with the RAF since early 1942 and was now the mainstay of the bomber offensive against Germany. It was only ten days since their most famous exploit, the breaching of the Mohne and Eder dams by 617 Squadron under Wing Commander Guy Gibson. The York used the engines, wings, undercarriage and tail structure of the Lancaster, except that an extra central fin was added to increase stability. Only the fuselage was completely new, almost square in cross-section to give it twice the volume of the Lancaster's. The bomber's mid-wing layout would have been difficult for a passenger aircraft, because the wing spar would have passed through the centre of the passenger cabin. Instead the York adopted a high-wing layout, with the bulk of the fuselage below the level of the wings. The bottom of the fuselage was quite close to the ground when on land, but unlike the Lancaster there was no need to get under it to load bombs. At one stage in the planning it was suggested that it might land with its undercarriage up during an airborne assault, but that idea was shelved after the development of suitable, and more expendable, gliders.

The third York built was numbered LV633 and was the first with the triple fins. It was allocated for the Prime Minister's use and was the only one with square windows to improve the view. It was put in the charge of No. 24 Squadron, the government communication unit based at Hendon in the north London suburbs. The airfield there was quite small, and restricted by housing and radio masts. The test pilot Bill Thorn managed to land successfully when he delivered the aircraft in April, but while he was taxiing one of the main wheels of the undercarriage sank into the ground. It took a major operation to get it out, and it was decided that the York should be based at Northolt, in the western suburbs of London. This had the advantage that it was on the Prime Minister's route to Chequers and he could drop in to inspect it on the way there. Administratively it was rather less convenient. Northolt was the home of the famous Polish Spitfire Wing until April 1944. Although the fighters used the same Merlin engine, they were much less hungry for fuel than the long-range York. When a long flight was planned, a 2,000 gallon petrol bowser, or tanker, had to be driven eight miles through the suburbs of London to supply the York. There was no place for cutlery, china and bed linen in Spitfire hangars, so these were stored in the officers' mess.

★　★　★

While the York was under construction, Churchill asked Vanderkloot and his crew if they wanted to continue to fly for him, for as he wrote, 'I like flying with people I know.' This was rather indiscreet, for the RAF had other ideas. Perhaps Kimber's suggestion that future flights should be made by an all-RAF crew had struck home with Portal, and possibly the Chief of Air Staff was embarrassed by the incident on the runway at Adana, though he had not been present in person. But more generally, the RAF was becoming increasingly sensitive about having to rely on American and Canadian civilians for such a prestige job. Churchill wrote to Portal: 'I did not know that any point was being made by the Royal Air Force. I quite see the difficulty, and will give the matter further consideration.' It was decided that an RAF crew should be appointed. Vanderkloot and his men continued to fly *Commando*, but it was used less and less on VIP duties.

To crew the York, the Air Ministry did not turn to the young and hastily trained men coming out of the flying schools in large numbers. The six offi-cers nominated were steeped in aviation history, and most of them had stayed faithful to the industry during its lean years in the early 1930s. The captain and first pilot, Wing-Commander H. B. Collins, was known as 'Dad' because, at 38, he was considered ancient by wartime aircrew standards. He had already completed 7,000 hours flying in the RAF and with civil airlines, as well as serving as a navigation instructor. He flew Churchill to some of his meetings with French leaders and took command of No.24 Squadron in July 1942. He was of large build with a red face and a dark moustache, superb eyesight and a good deal of stamina for long flights. It was Collins who devised the name of *Ascalon* for the York, after the lance which St. George was said to have used to kill the dragon.

The second pilot, Squadron-Leader D. A. Cracknell, was 33 and had also flown with civil airlines, then served two operational tours in bombers, a total of 38 sorties. The reserve second pilot, 32-year-old Flight Lieutenant 'Bill' Fraser, had joined the RAF in the ranks, qualified as a sergeant-pilot in 1934 and was commissioned in 1940.

The navigator, Squadron-Leader John Mitchell, was the exception that proves the rule. He left school at 18, which was relatively rare in those days, to become a customs officer, then joined the RAF at the beginning of the war. He learned navigation from retired master mariners – they knew nothing about the problems of an aircraft that travelled at least ten times as fast as a ship, but he was given a good grounding in navigation by dead reckoning and by the stars. The status of that branch was in the course of improvement – now observers were sergeants or officers, much closer to pilots in authority. Mitchell completed an operational tour in Whitley bombers and was awarded the Distinguished Flying Cross before being posted to Canada for a six-month specialist navigation course. He spent eight rather frustrating months dealing with navigational training problems on the staff of the Air Ministry. He was 'well qualified and a good practical navigator' with 600 hours' flying behind him. He was only 24, but he was probably as experienced and flexible a man as the RAF could offer at the time.

Flying Officer William 'Jock' Gallagher was as Scottish as his nickname suggests, 'a volatile character, quick to anger, but equally quick to great friendship.' He was a Wireless Operator/Air Gunner, though he would have no chance to use the second part of his skills in the unarmed York. He too had risen from the ranks and had served in Coastal Command and with the transatlantic ferry service, where he learned much about the problems of long-distance flight.

The sixth member of the crew was the oldest and in some ways the most experienced, though the most junior in rank. The new aircrew grade of flight engineer consisted mostly of young men with a mechanical bent who did six months' training and were qualified to assist the pilot on take-off, monitor engine dials during the flight and carry out minor emergency repairs. Pilot Officer Sidney Payne was a fully qualified maintenance engineer, able to service the aircraft or supervise a local crew, while it was away from normal RAF facilities. Nicknamed 'Jack' after a well-known bandleader of the day, he was 41 and had served in the ranks as an RAF fitter, then worked for the Texas Oil Company developing fuel for internal combustion engines, and with the Bristol Aircraft Company testing proto-type engines. He returned to the RAF at the beginning of the war and was commissioned in January 1943. He had been involved in the development of the York itself, so he knew the airframe and engines backwards. His skill and resourcefulness would keep the York flying through many difficult servicing problems in faraway airfields.

★ ★ ★

The cockpit of the York owed nothing to the Lancaster, for it had two pilots side by side instead of a single pilot, as in the bomber. As with many high-wing aircraft, the engine controls were situated above and between the pilots. This shortened the route of the control levers, but it also left some space between the pilots and improved access, which was useful with Churchill's habit of taking the controls. Unlike a bomber there was no nose-gunner's position to restrict the view, and the fuselage was unpressurised as always, so it was possible to put in large windows.

One great problem with the York was noise. The Rolls-Royce Merlin engines, famous as the power plants of the Spitfire, Hurricane and Lancaster, were loud at the best of times and their open exhausts were known as 'cackle-pots' to the Americans. It was not so much of a problem for the crew, who were mostly situated well forward; but the passengers were abreast the engines, and the box-like body was 'a wonderful sound resonator', according to John Mitchell. When King George VI was returning from a visit to North Africa in June 1943, he insisted in breaching protocol by landing two hours early because he 'found the noise of the aircraft very trying, comfortable though it was for that era'.

The crew of the York had orders to meet the Prime Minister at Gibraltar on 27 May after his flight from Newfoundland, so they took off from Northolt on the evening of the 25th. They carried Group Captain Jeffs of the Air Ministry who had overseen Churchill's first Clipper flight across the Atlantic and was to arrange liaison with the various small airfields that might be visited on the way; Wing Commander Slee who had been involved in the trials of the new type of aircraft at Boscombe down; and John Peck, another of Churchill's private secretaries.

★ ★ ★

The York, making its first flight with 'the owner', left Gibraltar at 1.40 in the afternoon of 28 May for a two-and-a-half-hour flight to Algiers. They crossed the African coast east of Mellila in Spanish Morocco and had a fine flight in excellent visibility, staying ten or fifteen miles south of the coastline. The crew was unhappy with the escort of American P-38 Lightning fighters, as the pilots seemed more interested in getting close enough to see the Prime Minister through a window and hoped to get a glimpse of his famous V sign. Unused to Churchill's ways, the crew provided only a light buffet for the passengers, who included General Marshall as well as the usual travelling companions. Drinks and snacks were served by Corporal Shepherd, who was Collins's batman as CO of No. 24 Squadron. They began to use Sawyers as a conduit between them and the Prime Minister, hoping to gauge his mood. They were unaware that the valet was 'an old fuss-pot' who would 'give a confused reading, especially after he had served drinks with Lunch – he had a sip each time he returned to the galley'. They landed at Maison Blanche near Algiers at 4.30. If Churchill seemed indifferent at first, Brooke was full of praise for the new York – 'Very comfortable, with a special cabin for PM, drawing room, berths for 4 besides PM and lavatory.' According to Tommy Thompson, 'After the comfortless austerity of the Liberator it was almost luxurious.'

Churchill went to stay in Cunningham's fine villa but the admiral was not totally happy with his presence. He was 'a bit wearing after dinner never getting to bed till after one', and 'A perfect nuisance interfering with the work.' Cunningham cleared out and went to live on a ship in the harbour. Meanwhile the crew of the York, encouraged by Group Captain Jeffs, used the prestige of their distinguished passenger to get accommodation in the Aletti Hotel, normally reserved for brigadiers and upwards. They spent three 'very pleasant days' while Churchill conferred with Eisenhower and Cunningham, and visited troops. Brooke felt vindicated about his emphasis on the Mediterranean and quoted the statistics of the latest campaign. Churchill had some success in moderating Marshall's scepticism about the importance of that war sector. 'General Marshall replied that he was not arguing against the particular commitment made in Washington to aim at the fall of Italy. He only wished to emphasise that we must exercise great discretion in choosing what to do after the conquest of Sicily.' Cunningham took Churchill to visit the submarine crews in the harbour and he made a 'delightful speech' to come away with tears running down his cheeks. But Cunningham was rather concerned about the effects on morale as he talked about 'boys walking in the valley of the shadow of death'.

On 1 June the Prime Minister flew west to the American air base at Château du Rumel. After landing he attended a briefing and then saw a wing of Flying Fortresses take off to bomb the Italian island of Pantelleria. The Prime Minister's party left at 11.30 and Corporal Shepherd served lunch on board the York for the first time. The crew had not yet learned how to use local resources fully, and there were no real cooking arrangements, so the meal was cold, though the beverages were adequate. They arrived that afternoon at El Anerin aerodrome near Tunis. Churchill was taken to Carthage where he addressed the troops in the old Roman amphitheatre. The acoustics were perfect and it was a marvellous setting. Brooke mused that 'in the same spot years ago Christian girls had been thrown to the lions to tear!' At dinner that evening Churchill was in tremendous form according to Brooke, and commented. 'I am no lion and I am certainly not a virgin!'

Next day the York's crew changed their base to the airstrip at Grombalia south of Tunis, where they were joined by Churchill and the party. They expected to fly across the sites of the battles and then on to Enfidaville and perhaps towards Tripoli. They went over the Kasserine Pass where an American force had fought a fierce battle with a German Panzer division, but then the Prime Minister, perhaps lured by the attractions of Cunningham's villa, decided to return to Algiers. He came forward to sit in the pilot's seat and asked to try the controls. Collins consented but used the tail trimmer to correct some of his more violent motions. This annoyed Churchill, and Collins compromised by working the rudder himself while the Prime Minister operated the elevators. Churchill enjoyed it, but the feeling was not shared by Air Marshal Tedder in the passenger compartment. Brooke commented on the 'swaying passage' and the US fighter escort was confused by the movements. Despite this they landed safely at Maison Blanche by eight in the evening, and Collins explained matters to the escort commander.

By breakfast time on the 3rd, Churchill had decided to start for home the next day. After more meetings, they duly took off at 3.30 in the afternoon of the 4th. Churchill was less than tactful at the airfield, when he decided to take General Alexander with him to continue talks. This meant that Ismay had to be left out, and he had to retrieve his luggage and follow in another plane. His enormous patience was almost exhausted. 'Looking back on that incident, it is remarkable that neither Alexander nor I felt in the least aggrieved at Churchill's deliciously ingenious lack of consideration for our personal convenience.'

They approached Gibraltar, where the Boeing was waiting for them. Churchill was already in the cockpit as usual, and Collins let him stay in the second pilot's seat as the engine controls could be operated from a position between the two pilots' seats. He was about to touch down for a three-point landing when he found that he could not pull the control column back fully, due to the Prime Minister's girth. The landing took a little longer than expected but was carried out safely. It was agreed that in future Churchill would watch landings from the navigator's station.

Meanwhile, a rather bizarre and tragic incident had given them thought about their safety. On the morning of 1 June, a civilian KLM Dutch flight from Lisbon to Bristol had been shot down over the Bay of Biscay by German aircraft. All the crew and passengers, including the actor Leslie Howard, were killed. Why should the Germans risk bad publicity by shooting down a civil airliner, on a route which had operated peacefully for several years? It is not likely, as some have suggested, that one of Howard's fellow passengers was mistaken for Churchill. It is just possible that the Germans had a personal grudge against Leslie Howard. He had played a distinctly anti-Nazi part in *Pimpernel Smith*, the film that had impressed Howard Spring during the *Prince of Wales* voyage, and also in *The First of the Few*, in which the designer of the Spitfire is shocked by Nazi attitudes during a pre-war visit to Germany. But more likely, as Squadron-Leader Mitchell concluded, 'the Luftwaffe policy had been to shoot at all and everything crossing the Bay while Churchill was known to be abroad'.

In any case the passengers and crew of the York were undeterred. Churchill, who had not yet been informed of Howard's death, was disappointed that bad weather delayed his departure from Gibraltar, but by the evening the weather cleared, and they were able to depart in the York, rather than the Clipper, at 10.30. Mitchell and Thompson both saw this as a sign that the Prime Minister liked his new aircraft, though there is no doubt that the weather was a factor as well. They headed out to 12 degrees west, to get clear of enemy interference.

The crew now had to get used to Churchill's nocturnal habits for the first time. Corporal Shepherd was dozing on his stool in the galley when the Prime

Minister's face appeared, saying, 'I want some soup: hot, clear soup and I want it now!' Shepherd was not a cook, and he knew that the electric urn for heating water would be far too slow to satisfy Churchill. Disregarding safety, he got out a primus stove which was normally for ground use, and heated up some pea soup and mulligatawny which seemed to satisfy the Prime Minister. Churchill later went to the pilot's seat, but did not attempt to operate the controls this time. The aircraft flew up the Bristol Channel and landed at Northolt at 6 on a sunny summer morning. The flight had been highly successful, but the crew realised that there were 'many lessons to be absorbed about the needs and habits of the owner. Clearly, some domestic modifications to the aircraft's interior were needed.'

To Churchill, the trip as a whole was also successful. In addition to the agreements reached in Washington, the Mediterranean tour was highly enjoyable and he wrote: 'I have no more pleasant memories of the war than the eight days in Algiers and Tunis.' Thompson went slightly further: 'Although I accompanied the Prime Minister on many further journeys, this week in North Africa was the happiest and most successful of our missions abroad.'

XII
Poetry in the North Atlantic

At the end of the Washington conference it had been decided that the Chiefs of Staff would meet again 'in July or early August in order to examine the decisions reached at this conference in the light of the situation at the time'. By the middle of July, Field Marshal Dill in Washington was hearing rumours that the conference was to be held in Canada in September. He was 'somewhat disturbed' by this:

> Surely if the conference is to be held on this side of the Atlantic, Washington is the only place. Not only are we in Washington sitting on the best system of communications and have the best offices, but it would surely be very awkward to sit among Canadians who could not be allowed to come in. Also, isn't September – a month I have heard mentioned – far too late for the next conference?[1]

Meanwhile in London, Churchill was coming to a similar conclusion about the date at least. As he told the Chiefs of Staff:

> In view of the rapid progress in 'HUSKY' [the invasion of Sicily], it seemed that the early autumn would be too late for the conference and that we should aim at a date during the first half of August. In the meanwhile, it was of the highest importance to settle with the Americans the next step after 'HUSKY'. In his view, the only right course was to take advantage with the utmost rapidity of the signs of disintegration in Italy and to attack the mainland with the immediate object of occupying Rome.[2]

As to the venue, Dill suggested Scapa Flow for the eastern side of the Atlantic but that had no attractions. The Americans were keen on Quebec, as the heat in Washington was intolerable in August, and air conditioning was far from universal. Also, it would allow both sides to get out of their normal office environment, a view reinforced by the experience of Casablanca. But there was one difficulty with Canada, as Dill had pointed out. The Canadian government might well object to a conference held on their own soil, but excluding them.

Roosevelt was firm on this point. Inclusion of Canada would almost certainly result in demands from the more distant allies of China and Brazil for membership of an exclusive club. It might even involve Mexico, which also had a border with the United States. The President was keen on 'preventing the deterioration of our Combined Chiefs of Staff in Washington into a debating society by refusing membership to representatives of other Allied Nations'. The Canadians were not to be invited, and they took it very well in the circumstances.

The operation was given the codename of Quadrant, which Ismay knew was not very cryptic as a follow-up to Trident, and 'not likely to deceive anybody. Perhaps it was not intended to.' It was decided to use the *Queen Mary* again, although that would make security more difficult than for Trident, since they were repeating an operation, which was always risky. The staff who were not in the know would realise that preparations were very similar to those for Trident and would soon come to conclusions. The fittings in the *Queen Mary* had been taken out after the last prime ministerial voyage, and would have to be put in again. It would not be hard for 200 workmen to guess what was going on, though notices were to be put up in Dutch to spread the rumour that the exiled Queen Wilhelmina of the Netherlands was travelling to America.

The great liners were now sailing on a regular pattern based on the phases of the moon, and it would not be long before the Germans began to see that. But on the other hand, the risk at sea was less than ever. The war against the U-boats was going well and 37 of them were sunk during July alone. Only six merchant ships were lost, all well away from the North Atlantic area. There were fewer than 60 U-boats at sea in the whole Atlantic, and no sign of any reinforcements, for they were still licking their wounds after their defeats in May and June.

Nevertheless, cover stories had to be devised for the party. The Prime Minster and Chiefs of Staff were going to visit the Home Fleet at Scapa Flow and then the new port at Faslane on the Clyde, which would in fact be a convenient place to meet the *Queen Mary*. Rumours were to be spread that it was now the Americans' turn to visit the Western Hemisphere, perhaps in the Mediterranean. The Château Frontenac Hotel in Quebec was not to be commandeered until four days before the conference started. The Prime Minister was given the codename of Colonel Warden, which was not impenetrable – he was Lord Warden of the Cinque Ports, and anyone looking at the list of travellers could not help notice that Colonel, Mrs and Miss Mary Warden were ranked above everyone else, including the Foreign Secretary and the Chiefs of Staff.

★ ★ ★

The Quadrant party was the largest yet – 205 members plus 61 marines. It was stratified into three groups, telling us something about the British class system of the time, and hinting that the boundaries were becoming blurred. The 'Top Flight' included the Prime Minister with his wife and daughter, Averell Harriman from the USA, the Foreign Secretary and Lord Cadogan in the Prime Minister's party. From the army, General Brooke and Field Marshal Dill were accompanied by three more generals from COSSAC (Chief of Staff, Supreme Allied Command in Europe). Admiral Pound and Air Chief Marshal Portal were the only representatives of their services at this level, while Lord Mountbatten was to come from Combined Operations and General Ismay from the Ministry of Defence, to make a total of fifteen in all. There were to be some changes, and Eden eventually came by air, while Lord Leathers was included in the sea party.

In addition, Churchill found a pair of war heroes to show off to the Americans. Brigadier Orde Wingate had recently led a large raid behind Japanese lines in Burma, where his 'columns', or expanded infantry companies, caused havoc with the enemy. He had just returned to Britain and was still wearing his tropical uniform when he arrived at the Downing Street Annexe an hour before Churchill was due to leave for Quebec. Believing he had found a new Lawrence of Arabia, Churchill decided on the spur of the moment to take him on the ship. Wingate protested that he had no suitable clothes and Churchill brushed that off – 'Oh, don't bother about that, I'll lend you some, I've plenty.' When Wingate objected that he had not seen his wife for a long time, Churchill ordered that she be found in Scotland and brought to meet him. This was rather trying for Mrs Wingate, who was contacted by the police in Aberdeen, and did not know whether it was bad news about her husband until the two met in a station in Edinburgh. Thus according to Wilson, 'The Wingates were carried off, as you pick up a couple of books on the station bookstall to beguile the tedium of the journey.'

Churchill's other guest was clean-cut and handsome compared with the lean, bedraggled Wingate. He was Wing-Commander Guy Gibson VC, who had led the famous raid on the German dams while Churchill was on the way to Trident. His chief, Air Chief Marshal 'Bomber' Harris, was keen to give him a rest from operations after at least 73 missions over enemy territory, and agreed with Churchill that this was a good way to do it. Gibson was to tour air bases in the United States and Canada, lecturing on the raids and on Bomber Command. As it turned out, he never settled into his allotted role, either as Churchill's companion on board ship, or as a lecturer.

There were 75 people at the 'Medium' level, including Churchill's and Harriman's secretaries, Commander Thompson, Sir Charles Wilson, two newsreel cameramen and dozens of staff officers in every rank from army captain to brigadier. The 'Low Group' was just as mixed. The Scotland Yard detectives were relegated again, as were the typists and clerks. They were equivalent to Sawyers the valet, Mrs Churchill's lady's maid, Petty Officer Longbottom the steward, and Mountbatten's marine batman Coulson. Oddly enough the 27 junior WRNS cipher officers were included here, showing that rank in the women's services was still not fully recognised.

For marines, 50 newly trained recruits were selected from the barracks at Plymouth, with an average age of barely 18; but Major Buckley, in charge of the party, felt that the previous group had been too small, and decided that additional officers and NCOs should be included. He took a young lieutenant, two colour sergeants, one sergeant and six corporals. In addition four marines, aged between 18 and 19½, were promoted lance-corporal to act as orderlies to the Prime Minister. An advance party of 20 men under an officer was sent to London to pick up the baggage, to be joined by the others on three special trains to Scotland.

★ ★ ★

The party travelled north by train and boarded the great liner at Greenock after lunch on 5 August. Brooke was pleased to see that she had been repainted and looked much smarter than last time. She sailed later in the afternoon. There were not many people who knew more about the sea, and its hazards in peace and war, than her captain James Bissett, who had returned from leave to take command. Born in 1883 in Liverpool, he went to sea in a three-masted sailing barque at the age of 15. He transferred to steam seven years later and gained his master's ticket, which qualified him to command a merchant ship, in 1907, and started work with Cunard soon afterwards. In 1912 he was a junior officer in the *Carpathia* when she rescued survivors of the *Titanic*. During the First World War he commanded destroyers as an officer in the Royal Naval Reserve, but returned to Cunard where he captained some of the smaller ships. He was appointed to the command of the *Queen Mary*, the summit of any merchant seaman's ambition, in February 1942.

Bissett had a reputation for firmness with his crews and tended to enforce regulations thoroughly:

Air Raid Precautions (ARP) every day, testing the water-tight doors on D deck daily, repeated admonitions against sneaking a cigarette on deck at night, Prohibiting the hospital from using its X-ray machines because of the strong signal emitted, requiring daily lifeboat drills by key crew members and lifejackets on everyone, including medics – these were some of the standard precautions to be observed.[3]

Cunard officers were trained to be tactful with passengers, even the lowly conscripts that they now carried in their thousands. Bissett was tolerant when the GIs dropped chewing gum on his precious decks, and even when they carved their names on the ship's rails. He bit his tongue when he overheard one soldier say, 'I bet the British wish they could build a ship like this.' But he would not indulge in flattery, especially at the expense of nautical truth. Churchill came to the bridge on the first morning and said 'Ah, I see that the wind's coming from dead ahead, Captain.' If Bissett had been a reader of the novels of Evelyn Waugh he might have answered, like Lord Copper's subordinates, 'Up to a point'; but instead he said, 'No. sir, it's coming from dead astern!' Churchill grunted 'Huh!' and soon went below.

★ ★ ★

On board, the Royal Marines found plenty of work to do after the ship sailed. As Major Buckley wrote:

> During passage the R.M. Detachment provided orderlies for the Prime Minister, First Sea Lord, the Chief of Air Staff and General Ismay: messengers for the Information Bureau and Conferences and sentries at the Map Room and at all entrances to the reserved part of the ship. [Officer Commanding Royal Marines] acted as assistant at the Information Bureau. Lieutenant Hunton and myself had the honour of dining with the First Sea Lord during the passage.[4]

The other passengers worked just as hard. The ship was a 'miniature Whitehall', according to Miss Layton, as Churchill and the others settled into a regular work pattern. Two days out, Ian Jacob visited his cabin:

> I saw the Master for the first time this morning about 8.45, he was lying in bed smoking a cigar as long as a trombone and brooding over South-East Asia. He had a bedtable in front of him with two thick sorbo pads on either side of it, presumably to save his forearms when he rests them on the edge of the table when reading papers. He questioned me on various points, and then I got away to breakfast.[5]

Churchill's offer of clothes to Wingate had never been realistic, and the latter was found wandering the decks wearing a blue suit loaned by the captain. He cut a poor figure on board. Churchill soon discovered that he was merely a gifted eccentric, and lost interest in him. Jacob compared him not to Lawrence of Arabia, but to the much less successful General Gordon who had been killed at Khartoum in 1885 after disobeying orders. To Ismay his military expeditions had been expensive in men and of little strategic value, and he doubted 'whether there has ever been a man who went so far out of his way to be intolerable to the very people who wished to help him'. One of the major-generals on Brooke's staff was encouraged to befriend him, but found it very difficult. Wingate, however, was later to prove a hit with the Americans. Gibson was far more popular on board and according to Miss Bright, 'There was not one of us girls who was not dazzled by the five simple but remarkable medals for gallantry on his chest, or softened by his direct masculine approach to each of us.'

Sir Dudley Pound held his usual cocktail party on the last day of the trip, but Brooke was uneasy that the Americans would continue to press for an invasion of northern France and an advance through Burma. The CIGS watched from the bridge on the afternoon of the 9th, as the great ship manoeuvred into place in Halifax, while the passengers enjoyed 'a wonderful view of the harbour and of the pilot carrying out the difficult task of bringing the vast Queen Mary into port'. The pilot cutter could not come alongside because of the swell and the pilot got into a small boat instead. Its engine failed and he had to be rowed to the ship by two men, amid 'good natured gratuitous advice' from the soldiers on board the liner. The personnel disembarked from the square on C Deck; as the ship was able to berth alongside a pier, no tender was needed and they walked down a gangway.

Two special trains were provided by the Canadians. The first one, of ten coaches, carried the Prime Minister and his family plus the valet Sawyers in coach J, which consisted of three bedrooms, offices, a lounge and a dining room. The First Sea Lord and Lord Leathers shared similar accommodation in coach G, and Brooke and Portal were in H. Coach I, next to the Prime Minister, had his immediate staff of naval aide, secretaries, typists and detectives. Forward the train was more crowded, with coach A carrying baggage and office equipment and B carrying 20 marines in double bunks. There was a dining car followed by a rather crowded coach for middle-ranking personnel of both sexes, in which Joan Bright and Paymaster-Commander Knott were trusted in adjacent bunks – they had worked together in the War Cabinet Offices for some time. The next two coaches, E and F, had five compartments each plus a lounge and dining room and were used by the Wingates, Lord Mountbatten and various high-ranking officers. The second train carried most of the junior personnel, 153 of them squeezed into seven coaches. Brooke was delighted with his accommodation, in 'a most comfortable train, with the most wonderful compartments'. Captain Pim had to adjust to

> the Canadian and American type of sleeping car in which the day seats form the lower berth and the upper berth is lowered from a position where it has been successfully concealed during the daylight hours. This makes accommodation for 12 persons down each side of the car. Passengers either have to sit in their berths behind curtains to undress, or, alternatively, to stay in the narrow corridor between bunks while fellow passengers and car attendants move up and down causing considerable confusion and much treading on toes.[6]

Pim was more impressed with the huge engine, almost 100 ft long and weighing 330 tons. He was allowed to drive it for a time under close supervision, paralleling Churchill's exploits in the air.

★   ★   ★

Quebec was a city of 150,000 people, the capital of French Canada and characteristically French in most respects, the language being spoken by the great majority of the population. It was built at a key point where the St Lawrence River narrowed and could be defended from cliffs above. It had been taken for the British by General James Wolfe in 1759 to confirm their hold on Canada, but it also led to the American colonists becoming much more secure, enabling them to revolt against the British a decade and a half later. There was no question of the loyalty of the French Canadian population in the circumstances, and indeed the site might be said to represent four great allies – the United States, Britain, France and Canada.

The conference party was to be accommodated in two places. The Citadel was the great star-shaped fortress at the top of the heights of Cape Diamond, incorporating the original French fort but largely built by the British between 1820 and 1831 as a defence against the Americans. It included the Quebec residence of the Governor-General who represented the King in Canada, and that was to be taken over by the two principals, with the President on the upper floor and the Prime Minister on the lower. On arrival, Mrs Churchill and her daughter 'stood for quite a long time gazing at the twinkling lights below – it seemed the most marvellous sight after four years of blacked out Britain.'

The rest of the party would live and work in the vast Château Frontenac Hotel. Named after a former French Governor of the colony, it too stood on the top of the heights. The lower part had been built at the end of the nineteenth century in the style of a French Renaissance château by William Van Horne, the general manager of the Canadian Pacific Railway which still owned it. A great central tower, looking rather like an early New York skyscraper, had been added in 1924 to a total height of 16 storeys.

The hotel had been almost cleared of existing residents, except a dozen who were too difficult to move because of bad health or other factors – according to Ismay one old lady was not expected to last the week but was still alive when the party returned a year later. Brooke was given 'a most comfortable bedroom and sitting room looking right up the St Lawrence'. Dining room A on the first floor was for officers and senior personnel, B on the ground floor was for enlisted personnel and 'in addition it is expected that junior personnel will normally make use of this room'. Normal facilities such as laundry were still available. Security was tightest on the third floor where special passes were needed. There were six conference rooms, the largest reserved for the Combined Chiefs of Staff on the second floor. Royal Marines provided sentries and messengers. General Ismay felt that 'It was a great convenience to have both delegations living under the same roof. Problems which had not been fully resolved at committee meetings could be thrashed out at the luncheon or dinner table, and on the whole the work went forward more smoothly than at any previous gathering.'

★   ★   ★

Since he was a few days early, Churchill decided to go south to visit the President at Hyde Park. His wife was exhausted by the pressures of wartime living in Downing Street and by sleeplessness on the way out, and in any case she had never fallen under the spell of Roosevelt, whom she considered arrogant. She refused to go and Wilson commented, 'I wish sometimes that one member of this singular family would behave like an ordinary human being. Clemmie is the culprit this time; she is being difficult – over nothing.' Churchill went with his daughter on the private train of the President of Canadian National Railways. He stopped to show her Niagara Falls and was asked if they had changed much since he had been there in 1900. 'The principle seems the same. The water still keeps falling over.' Hyde Park was oppressively warm, and he was glad to start back for Quebec on the 14th.

The citadel was more crowded after Roosevelt arrived, and Elizabeth Layton had problems with the security:

And now the whole of the Citadel was no longer free to us, the upper floor being occupied by the President and guarded from the top of the stairs onward. We were not used to worrying about our security from this angle. Once or twice, sent up there by the Prime Minister, I forced my way past an indignant guard to deliver a paper to the President's office, inviting them to shoot me in the back if they wished.[7]

Mackenzie King, the Canadian Prime Minister, was not invited to the conference but attended many of the social events. According to Sir Charles Wilson, he was 'rather like a man who has lent his house for a party. The guests take hardly any notice of him, but just before leaving they remember he is their host and say pleasant things.'

There were only two plenary sessions of the conference, plus many staff talks. Perhaps the most significant result was Churchill's final commitment to the Second Front in 1944. As he put it himself, 'I emphasised that I strongly favoured "Overlord" in 1944, though I had not been in favour of "Sledge-hammer" in 1942, or "Roundup" in 1943. The objections which I had to the cross-Channel operation were however now removed.' As an outsider to the conference, Sir Charles Wilson heard the news from Harry Hopkins:

He told me that at yesterday's session Winston 'came clean' about a Second Front, that he 'threw in his hand.' Hopkins said this in rather an aggressive way, as if I were in the P.M.'s camp.

'Winston is no longer against Marshall's plan for landing on the coast of France. At least, so he says.'

Harry grinned.

'But he might change his mind again, at least he did last year. I don't believe he's really converted.'[8]

The other great decision concerned the commander of the operation. For political reasons it was decided to choose an American. Brooke was devastated. He had turned down the command of the Middle East army in 1942 because he felt he was needed to restrain the Prime Minister. Now, however, 'the strategy of the war had been guided to the final stage, the stage when the real triumph of victory was to be gathered, I felt no longer tied to Winston, and free to assume the Supreme Command which he had promised to me on three separate occasions. It was a crushing blow to hear from him that he was now handing over this appointment to the Americans.'

Churchill was not at his most sensitive when he wrote later that Brooke 'bore the great disappointment with soldierly dignity'.

Elizabeth Layton became privy to one of the great secrets of the war, when she was asked to type documents on 'Tube alloys', which she soon realised was the project to combine British and American resources to create the atom bomb. 'I felt ready to burst with this staggering information. For a long time after that, now I was in on the secret, I was the only one in the office to copy all TUBE ALLOY papers. It very soon became just another facet of everyday work.'

Wilson was as lonely as ever in the Château Frontenac:

> In this vast hotel full of soldiers, sailors, airmen and oddments, both British and American, I don't suppose I speak a dozen words during the day. Breakfast alone in the big restaurant at 8.30; work in my room at the book till 1 o'clock, when I lunch, again by myself. Then I go for a tramp, then tea (alone) and I dine in a solitary state.[9]

He was excessively pleased when Brooke approached him and opened up uncharacteristically about the Prime Minister's conduct, though Brooke did not tell him the underlying story, about his refusal of the supreme command. But Wilson was Churchill's doctor and had scant interest in the rest of the party. He paid little attention to the rapidly deteriorating health of another of the Chiefs of Staff. Sir Dudley Pound's health was in serious decline. On 12 August, during a fishing trip, he was caught by Mountbatten as he lost his balance and nearly fell into a ravine. Later Ismay visited him in his room and found him a changed man, unable to recognise the General. He made light of it but then he suffered a series of strokes, and a naval surgeon-commander was flown out to tend him on the voyage home.

★ ★ ★

There was a break during the weekend and the President and Prime Minister went fishing on a lake twenty miles from Quebec. According to Tommy Thompson:

> There we were given a boat and a boatman each. As usual the Secret Servicemen were much in evidence. Three of them went afloat with a

walkie-talkie radio and cruised round with Mr Roosevelt. I had Inspector Thompson with me, and we tried to show the Americans that we too were on the job, but every time we came within a hundred yards of the P.M. we were violently denounced for disturbing his fish.[10]

The conference finally ended on 24 August and Brooke felt 'the inevitable flatness and depression which swamps me after a spell of continuous work'. Then the party broke up. Brooke and Portal changed into civilian clothes to go fishing at Lac des Neiges then flew home by Clipper. Churchill toured Quebec, made a radio broadcast from the Citadel, and then went south again to stay with the President in the White House and receive an honorary degree from Harvard University. While in the White House he lunched with the newspaperwoman Helen Ogden Mills Reid, who asked him about the state of the Indian people. Churchill made his classic defence of the Empire. 'Before we proceed let me get one thing clear. Are we talking about the brown Indians in India, who have multiplied alarmingly under the benevolent British rule? Or are we speaking of the red Indians in America who, I understand, are almost extinct?'

★   ★   ★

Since Churchill's schedule was highly variable and the *Queen Mary* had to remain close to a punishing trooping schedule, other arrangements were made to get him back from the conference. Flying was still dangerous for him, none of the other transatlantic liners had suitable accommodation, so a capital ship was provided.

HMS *Renown* was truly the last of her line, the only surviving British battlecruiser. The type had been conceived by Admiral 'Jacky' Fisher in 1905, as something faster than the standard Dreadnought battleship of the age, with an equally heavy gun armament but less armour protection. For a while it was Fisher's favourite type of ship, and ten of them were completed by 1914. In the First World War they soon caught the public imagination under the glamorous Admiral Beatty, although they were not being used as Fisher had intended. He had planned them as ocean-going ships, chasing enemy raiders from the high seas. Instead they were being employed as a fast division of the battle fleet in the North Sea. There was disaster at the Battle of Jutland in 1916, when three of them blew up under heavy German gunfire, causing nearly half of the 6,000 British deaths in the battle.

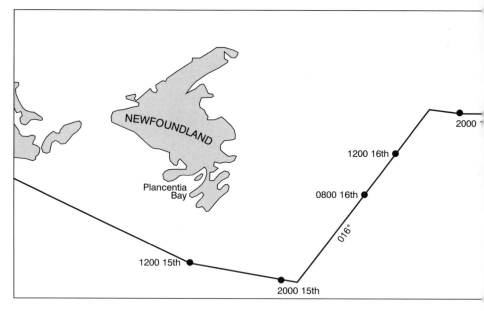

The *Renown* and her sister *Repulse* were already nearing completion by that time, the first battlecruisers to mount 15-inch guns, but still with very weak armour, like their predecessors. Three eccentric ships each carrying a small number of very large guns – the *Courageous, Glorious* and *Furious* – proved unsuccessful and were converted to aircraft carriers. The *Hood,* whose construction began on the same day as Jutland, was not completed until 1920. The surviving Jutland ships were all scrapped under the disarmament treaties between the wars, leaving the *Renown, Repulse* and *Hood* as the only battlecruisers in 1939.

Disaster struck again in May 1941 when the *Hood* was sunk by a broadside from the *Bismarck,* proving yet again that the armour was too weak. The *Repulse* accompanied the *Prince of Wales* to the Far East later in the year, only for both to be sunk by Japanese air attack. When one young gunner was drafted to the *Renown* late in 1942, he could not help having misgivings. He was not helped by the drafting officer of the Plymouth barracks, who told him, 'Bugger your luck. Everything happens in threes, laddie, and she's the third, having lost her two sisters, *Repulse* and *Hood*.' That was not strictly true as the *Hood* was not a sister ship, but it was no comfort.

The *Renown* was 794 ft long, 40 ft more than the *King George V* class. She was rather narrower and displaced only 32,000 tons, compared with nearly 37,000 for the *KGVs*. Her 15-inch guns were carried in three twin turrets, two forward and one aft. She still had the old-fashioned ram bow, unlike the *Hood*

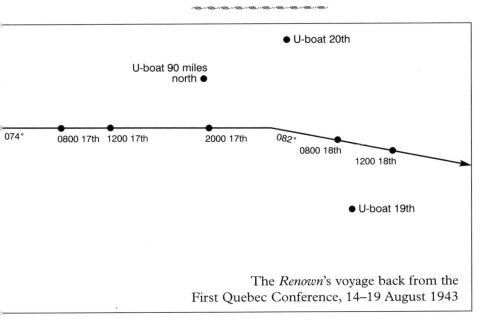

● U-boat 20th

U-boat 90 miles
north ●

074°   0800 17th 1200 17th   2000 17th   082°
                                          0800 18th
                                                 1200 18th

● U-boat 19th

The *Renown*'s voyage back from the
First Quebec Conference, 14–19 August 1943

and the more modern ships, but the battlecruisers had been designed for the open ocean and it was more efficient at ploughing through rough seas than those of the *King George V*s. She was the last of the old ships to be modernised before the war started, so she had one of the best anti-aircraft armaments – though probably not good enough, as British design was rather backward in this area. She also had new engines and boilers which were rated at 120,000 hp but could actually develop more, making her the fastest capital ship in the fleet with a speed of nearly 31 knots. Her aircraft had recently been removed, and their hangars provided much needed extra accommodation, and a cinema. The armour had been strengthened, but it was still very weak by modern standards and was never really tested, although she distinguished herself in action against the German battlecruisers *Scharnhorst* and *Gneisenau* during the Norwegian campaign of 1940, and fought the Italians at Cape Spartivento later that year. On joining, one young engineer officer thought, 'She was indeed a lovely ship to look at; her lines were quite classical.'

There were positive and negative reasons for sending her to meet Churchill. Positively, she was the fastest ship of her size, especially since her nearest rivals the *Hood* and *Repulse* had been eliminated, and the *KGV*s could only make 28 knots. Negatively, she was less useful with the Home Fleet, for her armour was too weak to stand up against the *Bismarck*'s sister ship, the *Tirpitz*.

Despite the misfortunes of the others of her type, the *Renown* seems to have been a happy and well-disciplined ship. Her captain, W. E. Parry, had distinguished himself in command of the cruiser *Achilles* at the Battle of the River Plate in 1939. The second-in-command, who was mainly responsible for the administration and discipline of the ship, was the fearsome Commander Condor. She had a stable ship's company which had built up a team spirit over several years. John Roche joined as an able seaman in March 1941, was promoted to leading seaman in October 1942 and stayed on to become a petty officer. The young seaman who joined in the spring of 1943 found that she was 'really a smart and efficient ship in most departments and reasonably happy but cheesed off at the thought of the continued cold and rain in Northern Waters'. The chaplain, Rev. Henry Lloyd, had already won the Distinguished Service Order in the carrier *Illustrious* and was a popular figure who spent a good deal of time organising concerts. Music played an important part in the life of the ship. There was a large Welsh contingent who formed a choir, while the Royal Marine band included a former dance band leader who set up a group for entertainment, and amateur bands flourished.

Renown had settled into a routine at Scapa Flow and in the Russian convoys, until it was broken on 24 August when the ship sailed west into the Atlantic. According to the young seaman mentioned above:

Then it happened ... 'Commander Speaking – We are leaving harbour at such and such a time and also leaving the Home Fleet, destination later.' Buzz, buzz, buzz. Everyone knew better than the skipper where we were going – Far East, back to the Mediterranean, Russia – you name it. Only the lads on watch knew that we were heading south and west, the Atlantic and America.[11]

The voyage out provided no relief, for the ship was hit by a severe storm on the 27th. The surgeon found that his sick berth, situated well forward on the starboard side, had been flooded to a depth of one or two inches. The marines' messdeck was also deluged, as were the after cabins which were to be used for the accommodation of the passengers. Hours were spent mopping up, but meanwhile Commander Condor gave the crew a huge clue about who was coming on board, when he announced that 'we are to make extra large ashtrays for our future guest and will be met shortly by units of the Canadian Navy'.

The crew hoped to see the bright lights, the bars and the well-stocked shops of New York, so their arrival at Halifax, Nova Scotia, was a slight disappointment. Pubs were not allowed in the province, and beer and liquor had to be bought in special shops for consumption at home – a problem for sailors who had nowhere to go. Many drank in the parks and public spaces, which caused some friction with the local police. But a few days of rest in the great natural harbour were welcome, and the shops were not empty. One seaman bought 'a huge dressed doll for my daughter and real moccasins for my wife with lots of goodies'. On the 9th, the day after Italy capitulated, a company of seamen and the ship's Royal Marine detachment marched through the city accompanied by the band. The band also played in the park, and there was a shooting competition with the Royal Canadian Mounted Police. Unlike the army, the marines retained their pre-war blue ceremonial uniforms for parades, though there were complaints that their ordinary warm-weather khaki drill uniforms were of a 'very poor standard of material and cut' compared with other services.

Meanwhile a party of one officer, one sergeant, two corporals and 20 marines trained intensively to get the passengers' baggage on board as quickly and efficiently as possible, for 'it was understood that on some previous occasion there had been disorganisation in the Baggage arrangements'. The surgeon and the ship's medical team took the chance to view a large hospital run by the Royal Canadian Navy, and the sick bay of a modern American battleship. Surgeon-Commander Ommanney-Davis concluded that their arrangements, though obviously lavish, were not much better than the Royal Navy's. Seamen watched in wonder as the great liner *Queen Elizabeth* got ready for sea at a nearby jetty, and seemingly endless streams of American soldiers went on board over four or five gangways. On 11 September an advance party arrived at the *Renown* with much of the baggage, and it was sorted out and stowed in the cabins by the Royal Marines.

The *Renown*'s idyll ended after 16 days on 14 September, when the Prime Minister and his party arrived, just hours after the *Queen Elizabeth* sailed. Churchill was pleased to see the *Renown*, a 'splendid ship'. He came on board with his party and the marine guard of honour saluted him as the band played, while the others took the rest of the baggage on board. At three in the afternoon the ship cast off from the dock and sailed out as the band of the Royal Canadian Mounted Police played *Rule Britannia, O Canada* and *Will Ye No' Come Back Again?*

★ ★ ★

The *Renown* was not the only Royal Navy ship waiting in North America, for the Admiralty had decided on a strong escort. The destroyer *Matchless*, with the *Orwell* under her wing, was ordered to Newfoundland and encountered the same storm as the *Renown* on the way over. Arriving there, her men were quite happy to live a day-to-day existence and await further orders. Commander Mowlam called on the Governor and renewed his acquaintance with his naval aide-de-camp, Lieutenant Ludovic Kennedy RNVR. He was enchanted with the beautiful countryside. Meanwhile the *Orwell* was ordered to take on board the man of letters A. P. Herbert, whose position was ambiguous to say the least. He was a Member of Parliament and part of a group looking into the constitutional future of Newfoundland, but at the same time he was a petty officer in a London river patrol. He and Kennedy both called each other 'Sir'. At last, according to Mowlam, the 'halcyon days' at St John's came to an abrupt end with a signal ordering the ship to meet HMS *Renown* in the ocean.

The crew of the cruiser *Norfolk* were not sorry to get away from Iceland, where they had been stationed for ten weeks. The climate was cold, the people were unfriendly. It was just a few days since the admiral in command had walked through the streets of Reykjavik to find that five out of six sailors had their collars turned up, contrary to orders, and at least ten ratings had looked straight at him and failed to salute. He ordered that the crews were to be paraded on deck that Saturday morning and told that all shore leave was cancelled.

The *Norfolk* was a proud ship that had distinguished herself in the *Bismarck* action, but the crew was weary after spending 49 weeks north of Scapa Flow in the last two years. They sailed on 12 September and the captain informed them that they were to meet HMS *Renown* 1,500 miles to the south, in an operation involving great secrecy. Orders were quickly changed, and on the 14th a notice was pinned up telling them that they were to meet her 300 miles east of Newfoundland and they would not go south of 50 degrees, about level with the south coast of England. There was no further news on the 15th as the *Norfolk* passed through the area in the middle of the Atlantic where many of the U-boat actions had been fought in the last three years.

Finally, on the 16th they made contact, and were grateful that they had radar as they manoeuvred in a thick Newfoundland fog. The *Renown* used her own radar to pick up the *Norfolk* at a range of six and a half miles, while the cruiser used hers to approach her sister ship *Kent* on a converging course. All this was done in safety though the ships were on opposite courses and carrying out unknown zigzags. Now Captain Bain was able to reveal the purpose of the mission to the crew, and the reasons for secrecy: 'We have made contact and now form a unit of the Force which is taking the Prime Minister across the Atlantic after the Quebec Conference ... The utmost secrecy has been ordered regarding the Prime Minister's crossing of the Atlantic, and the size of the Force employed shows the importance which is attached to it while he is in the care of the Navy.' *Norfolk* was stationed three and a half miles ahead of the port bow of the *Renown*, with *Kent* on the other side. There were two destroyers, but they would not be able to use their asdic to detect submarines at these speeds. Captain Bain believed that 'Their main function is to pick up Mr Winston Churchill (and others), should he have to swim for it.'

The *Matchless* and *Orwell* joined that afternoon, while the *Obdurate* and *Opportune* parted to send dispatches. Commander Mowlam of the *Matchless* could not help contrasting conditions with the storms on the way out: the weather was as good as in the Mediterranean. He admired the *Renown*, which he thought was one of the most beautiful capital ships ever built.

Petty Officer A. P. Herbert MP, now a passenger in the *Orwell*, had many talents, including poetry. He composed a verse to flash by signal lamp to the *Renown*, avoiding the use of the name Churchill for security reasons but dipping into Greek mythology instead, on the return of Ulysses, with Mrs Churchill as his wife Penelope.

> Return Ulysses soon to show
> The secret of your splendid bow.
> Return to make all riddles plain
> To anxious Ithica again.
> And you Penelope the true
> Who have begun to wander too,
> We're glad to greet you on the foam
> And hope to see you safely home.

Churchill set his staff to work on a reply, and his daughter Mary provided the best one, beginning:

> Ulysses, and Pempy too,
> Return their compliments to you.
> They too, are glad to wend their way
> Homewards to Ithica after a stay
> With friend from where the land is bright
> And spangled stars gleam all the night.

It was Churchill himself who wrote the last two lines

> To chide these simple lines be chary!
> They are the first attempts of Mary.

227

That was not the end. Before parting on the 18th, the *Orwell* sent another verse with a contribution by Herbert's travelling companion, Major Sir Derrick Gunston MP. With no classical reference books to hand they could not check if Ulysses had a daughter, so they used a feminine version of his son's name.

Telemacha, the sailors send
Their greetings to a fighting friend.
The Major adds a smart salute
To any lady who can shoot!
And I, poor scribbler, must give place,
To one who writes with such grace.
Why not (when Masefield's passed)
A lady laureate at last?[12]

★ ★ ★

Before the Prime Minster's party joined there had been an undercurrent of criticism among the ratings of the *Renown*. There was a certain amount of hero-worship of 'Uncle Joe', and his reportedly simple lifestyle was contrasted with that of Churchill. This was dispelled after the party came on board. The Prime Minister did not monopolise the ship's cinema, as had been claimed, and his wife and daughter moved freely among the ship's company.

The *Renown*'s destination was marked as 'X' in the ship's log, but she soon set a course of 83 degrees, just north of due east, which would have taken her straight to the English Channel. British naval intelligence now knew that the German High Command had decided that a renewed attack on the Atlantic shipping routes was the only way in which the U-boats could decisively affect the war. The submarines were about to return to the offensive, retrained and armed with new weapons. They were also being more circumspect with their radio signals. The British had decoded messages for five out of the first nine days of September, but they were not very revealing. Most worrying of all, about 20 U-boats had recently left bases in the Bay of Biscay and were unaccounted for, having been told that their main object for the moment was to remain unobserved. They were to refuel from a tanker U-boat, and naval intelligence believed that it was either close to the Portuguese Azores Islands, or about 600 miles north of them. This was in the *Renown*'s path if she continued on her original course of 83 degrees. At nine in the evening of the 15th she altered course to 16 degrees, which would take her more than a thousand miles north of the islands.

The admiral's quarters in the stern of the *Renown* were far more habitable than those on the *King George V* class, for they suffered much less from vibration. They provided enough space for the Prime Minister and his wife and daughter, Brendan Bracken, General Ismay, Wilson, the secretaries Martin and Rowan, and Commander Thompson. Sir Dudley Pound would live in the captain's quarters, tended by Surgeon-Commander Miller who had flown out specially to treat him. He often sat on the deck with Captain Pim, who had just had an operation on his leg in America.

Cabin accommodation for the senior officers, including Pim, was provided by senior officers of the ship moving into junior officers' cabins, while the junior officers lived in temporary bunks behind canvas screens in the torpedo space. The three civilian typists and ten WRNS cipher officers provided a different kind of problem. They were accommodated two by two in cabins, but to reach them they had to pass under the hammocks of one of the fire parties sleeping, in traditional seaman's night clothes of singlet and underpants, in the wardroom area. This caused a certain amount of excitement among men who were often starved of female company for weeks on end. The officers welcomed the women into their wardroom mess, even the typists who had been classed with servants in the *Queen Mary*. On Saturday night the traditional toast of 'Sweethearts and wives' was extended to include 'Husbands and boy friends'. It is not recorded if anyone replied with the traditional *sotto voce*, 'May they never meet.' But romance did flourish during the voyage. Leslie Rowan, the 35-year-old bachelor private secretary, became engaged to Third Officer Judy Love, 'the prettiest of the Cypher officers', according to Elizabeth Layton. This was no fleeting shipboard romance, for they were married four months later and were to have two sons and two daughters.

If Churchill used the admiral's quarters for sleeping, dining and recreation, he still retained the admiral's sea cabin under the bridge for working. There he found the main instability of the *Renown* – her tendency to roll. Her high speed was bought at a price, for her maximum breadth was only 90 ft, 13 ft less than the *King George V*s. The roll tended to be accentuated high up, as in Churchill's cabin, and Elizabeth Layton found it difficult to work there:

> The roll of the ship made it impossible to sit still, and his matches and pens were continually sliding about. He decided he would prefer to light his cigar with a candle, and it was my job to light this every half hour or so and then take it into the adjoining bathroom to blow it out,

so that the waxy smell did not reach him. I thought, like Alice, 'Curiouser and curiouser.'[13]

Churchill had done a good deal of post-conference work on the train to Halifax, and during the voyage he was mainly concerned about the landings at Salerno in Italy, which he followed in Captain Pim's Map Room, set up in the ship's chapel. The landings did not go well at first. Churchill found it difficult to settle down to write his speech for a forthcoming debate in the House of Commons, and according to Wilson he stayed brooding in his cabin for most of the time. On the third day at sea, as the telegrams seemed a little more hopeful, he said over dinner, 'My feeling is that we are going to win.' After that his spirits improved.

The 15th was Mary Churchill's 21st birthday and on the previous night she bested her father for once. He pointed out that he had come under fire for the first time in Cuba on his own 21st birthday, to which Mary replied that she had beaten him by just over a year, in her anti-aircraft battery. Next day the *Renown's* shipwrights presented her with a joke birthday cake made of wood. She walked on deck, and went towards the stern with the ship's instructor officer. The wind was slight that day, and hardly exceeded Force 2 on the Beaufort Scale, but heavy seas can be whipped up by distant winds in the Atlantic, and the ship's constant turning and zigzagging caused her to roll. Lieutenant David Williams noticed what was about to happen when the ship altered course, but he was too late to intervene and Mary Churchill was hit with what she called 'a pale emerald-green wall'. She was swept to one side and came upright against a stanchion, which prevented her from falling overboard. Commander Condor saw what was happening and was about to order 'man overboard' and the dropping of a lifebuoy, when she recovered. Condor took her below and gave her a stiff brandy followed by a Scotch, while the offending instructor officer was given a severe dressing down. The whole affair was concealed from Churchill, but Mary had only one uniform and it was wet. When she appeared at dinner that evening wearing a bright cocktail dress, the Prime Minister reprimanded his *aide-de-camp*. 'I did not give you permission to wear plain clothes.'

Not that Churchill avoided danger himself. The next day he fell off a gun platform and sustained a four-inch contusion on his left thigh. The ship's doctor, Surgeon-Commander Ommanney-Davis, conscientiously treated him and recorded the incident in the Minor Injury List in his official log in red ink. Churchill's rank was given as 'Prime Minister' and he was discharged 'to Duty' on the 18th.

★ ★ ★

Gunnery was one of the main distractions during the voyage. On the morning of Wednesday the 16th, a 'throw-off' shoot was carried out against the cruiser *Kent*. This meant that the 15-inch guns were aimed at her, but 6 degrees off so that they would miss by a fixed distance. After eleven minutes and six rounds per gun the favour was returned and *Kent* exercised her own 8-inch guns for six minutes. Elizabeth Layton was one of the party watching from a platform above the bridge. She did not understand what was going on but the noise was deafening and she was glad when it finished. On Friday morning there was a much quieter exercise when the air plotting department had some training, but in the afternoon it was as noisy as ever as the Oerlikon anti-aircraft gunners fired their 20mm weapons and the Prime Minister himself was allowed to take a hand, aiming at the wake of the destroyer *Matchless*.

The crew and passengers of the *Renown* were aware of the much more effective air cover now given by Coastal Command, as Liberators, Sunderlands and Catalinas were sighted at regular intervals, forcing any U-boat in the area to stay down. There were occasional reminders of the dangers and horrors of the Atlantic war. As the *Renown* passed south of Newfoundland on the 15th, a body was seen floating face downwards in the water, but there was no time to stop. In the following evening there was a strong smell of fuel oil from the sea, suggesting that a ship of one side or the other had been sunk. And on the afternoon of the 17th, the Oerlikons were used to destroy a floating mine.

At ten in the evening of Saturday 18 September, the water under the *Renown* shallowed to 100 fathoms, showing that she was approaching the continental shelf near the British Isles. A small convoy was sighted just after midnight, and at 3.30 in the morning the lookouts saw Oversay light, to the south of the Scottish island of Islay, four miles away to port. By dawn they were well inside the safe waters of the Firth of Clyde, and they were secured to a buoy off Greenock before 10 o'clock.

As the *Renown* arrived in the Clyde, the long anticipated convoy battle took place 450 miles west of Rockall, not far from the waters the *Renown* had passed through two days earlier. The frigate *Lagan* was severely damaged by a new type of acoustic torpedo which homed in on a ship's propeller noise. The westbound convoys ON 202 and ONS 18 were attacked, and their escorts combined together, creating a very strong force. Five merchant ships were sunk, but in return naval intelligence estimated that three out of 20 attacking U-boats were destroyed, and six more were severely damaged. This was maximum effort from the Germans, and their attack had fizzled out. The new acoustic torpedo was quickly identified. It was only effective against ships making speeds of between 10 and 18 knots, so it would have been no threat to the *Renown* on her passage at a speed of 25 knots. But the northern area that *Renown* had passed through was not entirely free of enemy activity. The day after *Renown* reached port, *U-338* was sunk by British aircraft 90 miles north of where she had passed three days earlier, and *U-346* was sunk by accident 120 miles to the south.

Safely in the Firth of Clyde, Churchill addressed the crew of the *Renown*. Leslie Rowan wrote a letter of thanks to Captain Parry, who replied in similar vein:

> We are all very grateful to you for giving us a welcome break from our normal routine. It has all been great fun and we should love to do it again. My only moan is that I had to stay perched in Olympian grandeur on my bridge and see so little of the distinguished passengers ...
>
> It is more than flattering to hear your opinion of my ship, and you are right in saying one does get fond of ships in some incredible way, although they remove one from one's family and most of the things one cares about.[14]

XIII
The Big Three at Tehran

As they held their summer of 1943 discussions in Quebec, Roosevelt and Churchill were aware of the need to include Stalin in the next meeting and telegraphed him on 18 August. 'We fully understand strong reasons which lead you to remain on battle-fronts where your presence has been so fruitful of victory. Nevertheless we wish to emphasize once more importance of a meeting between all 3 of us.' They suggested Fairbanks in Alaska, which was less than 600 miles from Soviet territory in the east, though more than 4,000 miles from the war front against Germany. Stalin replied to Roosevelt alone: 'I consider that a meeting of the responsible representatives of the two countries would positively be expedient', though he conceded that 'I do not have any objections to presence of Mr Churchill at this meeting.' He suggested Archangel in the north of Russia, which could only be reached by a long flight in the Arctic Circle, or Astrakhan in the south, which would be slightly easier than a flight to Moscow for the western allies. On the 25th Churchill telegraphed the War Cabinet mentioning the 'bearishness of Soviet Russia' and the fact that Stalin had 'studiously ignored our offer to make a long and hazardous journey in order to bring about a tripartite meeting'.

By mid-September the idea of Tehran had been raised – it was outside the Soviet Union, but close enough for Stalin to get back quickly if he was needed. As always, Churchill was willing to travel almost anywhere but Roosevelt claimed that the US Constitution placed serious restrictions on him. It demanded that he deal with bills and other matters within ten days, and it would be difficult to be certain of getting the relevant documents to him and then back to Congress in time. He could not act by cable or radio; a physical signature on the actual document was required:

> The difficulty with Tehran is this simple fact. The over-the-mountain approach to that city often make flying impossible for some days at a time. This risk of delay is double, both for the plane delivering the documents from Washington, and for the one returning these documents to Congress. ... I must carry on a constitutional government more than one hundred and fifty years old. Were it not for that fact I would gladly go ten times the distance to meet you.[1]

Averell Harriman, now Roosevelt's ambassador to Moscow, worked on Stalin to no avail. He was a notoriously paranoid dictator who was always reluctant to leave the centre of power, but he had the more legitimate excuse that his was the only country under invasion, with the enemy not quite cleared from his territory. After all, even Churchill had not left Britain when it was under threat. As a compromise, Basra in Iraq was suggested. Roosevelt would not have to cross the mountains, and secure links could be set up between there and Russia. But Stalin insisted that the telegraph line between Tehran and Moscow, guarded by Soviet troops, was essential to his conduct of the war. Eventually the Americans came round. It was discovered that fears about Tehran were exaggerated, that only two flights between Cairo and Tehran had been delayed in November in the past two years. If any urgent legislation had to be signed, Roosevelt would fly to Tunis to meet it. Tehran was therefore agreed as the site for the conference. It was also agreed that Churchill and Roosevelt would have a preliminary meeting in Cairo, to discuss matters of common interest that did not affect the Soviets.

★ ★ ★

In view of Churchill's delicate health, it was decided to use the *Renown* again for the first part of the trip out, across the Bay of Biscay where autumn flying conditions were most difficult. Of course the ship's company was used to the VIPs by now, but this time they were to carry a party of 60, instead of 20 last time. One-third of these were women, including five typists and 14 WRNS signal officers. Churchill could no longer spend days at a time with very little contact with home, and he demanded constant information on the domestic situation and the progress of the war.

This time it was Churchill's daughter Sarah's turn to go as her father's aide. She had joined the Women's Auxiliary Air Force in 1941 when her marriage to the entertainer Vic Oliver had collapsed, and became a Section Officer in photographic interpretation at Medmenham on the banks of the Thames west of London. She was summoned by her commanding officer early in November 1943 and told of the mission, to her delight. Her duties were

> mainly to see, along with others, to my father's comfort and wishes, to relay messages, and to drape myself silently along with the coat racks in the ante-chambers of the conference rooms with the other ADCs assigned to similar duties. I did not have any ideas above my station.[2]

Third Officer Doreen Drax had already sailed in the *Renown* on the trip back from Halifax and she was delighted to be chosen again. Elizabeth Layton was also pleased to be going on her second trip – while it had been thrilling to sail west, it was doubly so to be going east, sailing into the unknown under blue sky and hot sun. The typing staff was supplemented and Olive Christopher was recruited through the Mayfair Secretarial Agency to work in General Ismay's office.

The ship was moored to a buoy in Plymouth Sound when the party of Wren officers arrived on board in two motor boats on the afternoon of 11 November. Miss Drax felt very superior to most of the others, having been on board before. They were shown to their cabins, even more crowded than last time. Most of the male officers had moved out again, and each cabin was fitted with an extra bunk so that two women could live in it – there was hardly room to turn round, according to Miss Drax. Each cabin was tended by a marine, always very eager and efficient. The two women had not yet agreed who was to have which bunk and the marine left a coin behind for them to toss, hinting that the lower one was better. At 6 o'clock they went for drinks with Captain Parry, then were received by Commander Condor in the wardroom ante-room. After dinner a few of them went to join the midshipmen in the gunroom as the marine band played outside. They slept well and were woken next morning by the marines knocking on the door. During the day they familiarised themselves with the cipher office, watched various dignitaries arriving and helped to set up the Map Room, until Churchill arrived late at six in the evening, his train having been delayed.

The *Renown* prepared to sail right away and was out of the harbour by seven that evening. The battlecruiser proceeded along the Cornish coast and passed the Scilly Isles by midnight. Course was altered to almost due west, to take them clear of enemy aircraft in France. The wind was up to a force 8 or 9 on the Beaufort scale, a strong gale, and it was coming from the west-north-west, almost ahead of the ship, so conditions were not comfortable.

It was not a good beginning for Sir Charles Wilson, who had recently been raised to the peerage as Lord Moran. He had a fall getting into the tender taking the Prime Minister's party out to the ship, and Churchill enjoyed himself even more when he suffered from seasickness during the first 24 hours of the voyage. When he got up from lunch looking distinctly uncomfortable, Churchill delayed him for another ten minutes giving him advice, and was fond of remarking: 'Charles when ill refuses his own drugs with a sad air of inside knowledge.' He was not the only one with problems. During the night the Wren officers in the Cipher Room found that the documents began to swim before their eyes, and they disappeared one by one. Doreen Drax had to go frequently to the side of the ship, where she stood shivering with cold in the spray and pitch darkness. They had a chance to watch the escorting cruiser *London,* pitching and heaving even more because of her smaller size. Surgeon-Commander Ommanney-Davis wrote: 'Sea Sick Tablets were issued liberally and apparently cut down the incidence.' In the afternoon of the 15th there was some improvement and Wilson noted, 'I can go about without a hat and sit on a deck chair.'

By that time they had sailed south to the latitude of Gibraltar, and then turned east to enter the Mediterranean. The original plan was for Churchill to join his aircraft at Gibraltar, but the York was delayed for two days by bad weather at Northolt, and only took off just after midnight on the 17th, by which time the battlecruiser had left. The *Renown* entered Gibraltar harbour just long enough to pick up the Foreign Secretary, Anthony Eden, then headed into the Mediterranean towards Algiers, to the delight of the Wren officers who wanted to see more of the world. Winds were much lighter as they proceeded along the coast of neutral Spain, and there was plenty of shelter, so it became a pleasure cruise for some. Admiral Cunningham, who had succeeded Pound as First Sea Lord, had never been at sea in the old ship before. He was impressed with her sailing qualities at speed.

Signals traffic was heavy during the voyage, and Captain Pim was on board in the Map Room as usual. Each day he was sent a signal describing major ship movements and the position of convoys at 0800 that morning. The Wren officers were arranged in watches to be available for decoding at all times, but these soon began to collapse in practice because of the constant peaks and troughs in the volume of messages. Work was very hard for the four officers on duty in the first four hours of the 14th, as many corrupt signals were received and they had to rack their brains to understand unfamiliar place names. There was very little to do in the afternoon, until the Prime Minister arrived and asked if there was any news for him. They told him there was nothing, then began to worry if there was anything they had missed. That evening things were so slack that some of the watch was allowed to go to the cinema in the old aircraft hangar. Churchill had selected most of the films, but he was not present that night to see *My Sister Eileen* starring Rosalind Russell, a light comedy based on a Broadway hit. Doreen Drax and her colleagues were able to recline in style in the front row. The peace did not last long and there was another 'flap' for half an hour next morning. Meanwhile Elizabeth Layton found romance on board. 'He was a lieutenant with a beard, tall and rather artistic, named Michael ... I thought he was wonderful.'

Churchill was not well, in 'the doldrums', according to Lord Moran, who hoped that a long sea voyage would improve his health and 'get him into good fettle for the strenuous days that lie ahead'. His cabin was kept at a constant temperature of 73 degrees Fahrenheit (25 centigrade) which some found uncomfortable when they visited him. Moran wanted the Prime Minister to take it easy for a while, but he refused to co-operate. On the night of the 15th to 16th, for example, he sat up in his cabin until till five in the morning playing cards with Randolph. At other times he read a book on William Pitt given to him by his wife, and as usual there were resonances – Pitt was the last great prime minister to face the threat of foreign invasion, until his death in 1806.

Meanwhile, Gil Winant, the US Ambassador to Britain, charmed almost everyone who met him. According to Moran, 'Gil Winant breaks pleasantly our ordered lives. Other men have to win the confidence of those they meet; Winant is allowed to skip that stage. Before he utters a syllable people want to see more of him.' To Brooke he was 'a man who had made a deep study of life and had not arrived at his convictions easily'. Cunningham admired his 'sincere and forthright nature'. One exception was Sir Alexander Cadogan, who joined the party later and failed to penetrate the ambassador's shyness. He found Winant 'clings like ivy, and is a great bore'.

Algiers came into view early in the afternoon of the 16th, and the women passengers were shepherded below to avoid giving away the nature of the trip, though the Prime Minister undermined this by walking up and down the quarterdeck with his son. Sir John Cunningham, who had succeeded his namesake as Commander-in-Chief of the Mediterranean Fleet, came on board while some members of the party transferred to the cruiser *London*, which was to go ahead and set things up in Cairo, and was not due to call at Malta. The *Renown* also picked up the latest charts showing enemy mining activity in the region. She sailed after less than seven hours in port.

Again there was intensive signals traffic as Doreen Drax and her 13 colleagues worked in the overcrowded signals room amid scenes of increasing chaos. There was a great deal of noise and it was almost impossible to concentrate as signals poured in. Worse, it was close to the Map Room and the dignitaries insisted on passing through to visit it. Fortunately they did not end up with a large number of corrupt signals.

There was some attention from the enemy as the ship passed the island of Pantelleria on the 17th and they were sighted by a German aircraft, but there was complete air cover and no attack followed. Otherwise the voyage to Malta was a triumphal procession. Sixteen months ago, in August 1942, Operation Pedestal had brought a convoy to Malta, with the loss of nine out of fourteen merchant ships, an aircraft carrier and two cruisers. Now a battlecruiser could travel through the Mediterranean virtually unmolested. Captain Pim had followed the great Mediterranean battles from his Map Room and remarked, 'Even more strange was it that this great ship carrying the Prime Minister should be moving in waters which a few short months before were almost impassable to Allied ships and which had been the scene of historic and gallant attempts to bring much-needed food and fuel to the garrison and people of Malta.'

★ ★ ★

There was a security scare around Cairo on the 17th, when the Americans found out that several journalists were alerting their papers by cable about a big story on the way. British censorship had cleared a dispatch from one in telegraphese stating, 'Possibly fore-shadowing international developments Mena House Hotel sub-shadow Pyramids favourite ex diplomaticers ministers will be closed publicward soon profumigation in anticipating visits conversations great portent to held Cairo.' Other journalists wanted to stay on longer for reasons they did not clarify, or predicted heavy scheduling later in the week. The Americans were furious and wanted to change the venue. The British apologised but it had to be accepted that 'possibilities of complete security are not nearly so great as in territory directly administered by His Majesty's Government or American Government'.

Eisenhower telegraphed to suggest Malta instead. The island, he thought, had good communication and accommodation which could be supplemented by ships in harbour. It was a fortress with high standards of defence, it was on the route of both Roosevelt and Churchill towards Cairo, and a large amount of air cover could be provided. But it was out of the question for the British, who had much more detailed knowledge of what enemy bombing had done to the island. Hundreds of buildings had been destroyed and their rubble harboured millions of sand flies, food was still short, and troops stationed on the island often lived under canvas in muddy fields. Ismay commented:

> The majority of both delegations would have to be housed in bomb-shattered barrack-rooms without any modern conveniences, and subsist almost exclusively on army rations. This might be a salutary change after the lush comforts of the Anfa Hotel at Casablanca, the Statler in Washington and the Château Frontenac at Quebec, but it would not be conducive to good work or good tempers.[3]

This was largely confirmed by the passengers in *Renown*, which arrived in Grand Harbour, Valetta, on the evening of the 17th. Like many Royal Navy captains, Parry had some difficulty with the tight spaces and sharp turns in the harbour, and it could be highly embarrassing. The harbour was like a giant amphitheatre and the population of the city might turn out to watch the arrival of a fleet. More than one celebrated naval feud had begun over attempts to moor in Grand Harbour. Admiral Cunningham and Commander Thompson, with their seamen's eyes, tried to keep the Prime Minister below while 'Chaos reigned on deck; everywhere ropes lay in tangled confusion.' When Churchill insisted on going up, the Admiral told him, 'I wouldn't go out there if I was you, Prime Minister … it's like a snake's honeymoon!' Eventually after an hour and 22 minutes the ship was secured to C Buoy.

Malta was a long-established British possession in the Mediterranean, having been taken in 1800. Most regular sailors had happy memories of the island as a peacetime base for the Mediterranean Fleet, though army personnel tended to become bored with their confinement to the island. Since the war with Italy began in 1940, the island had gained almost legendary status among the British, for its dogged resistance to German and Italian bombing. The main island was 17 miles long and no more than 8½ miles wide, while the smaller one of Gozo measured 26 square miles. Between them they supported a population of nearly 300,000. There were good harbours at Marsaxlokk to the east and St Paul's Bay to the north-west, but Valetta, near the middle of the north coast of the island, was one of the finest natural harbours in the world. Marsamexett harbour was to the west of the tongue of land on which the city of Valetta had been built by the Knights of St John against Moslem incursions in the Mediterranean, and now it was used for destroyers and submarines. To the east of the city was Grand Harbour, overlooked by the great fortifications of the city on one side, with several inlets to the east which contained the main dockyard facilities. Despite the bombing there was practically everything a fleet could require – dry docks, cranes and stores for the ships, sports grounds, clubs, bars and brothels for the men.

Security was tight at Malta and Churchill's visit was not publicised, so he was driven to the Governor's Palace near Valetta by a devious route. According to his daughter 'It was a lovely place. The gardens were magical – five of them, all walled – lovely paved courtyards, wonderful flowers, and fine red earth.' It was a busy city, however, and Churchill was disturbed by the noise of the crowds outside. At one stage he opened his window and shouted out, 'Go away, will you? Please go away and do not make so much noise.' His cold was dragging on, and Moran took much of the blame. 'He expects me, when summoned, to appear with a magic cure.' Churchill was not happy with Lord Gort's Spartan regime in the Palace. Ismay visited him in bed and he wailed plaintively, 'Do you think you could bring me a little of butter from the nice ship?' He was unable to get a decent bath, but despite his illness he insisted in meeting with the Chiefs of Staff who had arrived in Malta separately. The war news was not good – the island of Leros had been attacked by British forces in September, but despite strong naval support it was retaken by the Germans on 16 November.

Lord Moran had little to do for most of the time during Churchill's trips, and he did not fit easily into the social milieu. Instead he worked on his book, an analysis of the reaction of soldiers to combat during the First World War, in which he had been an army surgeon. It was Churchill himself who suggested changing the title, from the negative *The Anatomy of Fear* to *The Anatomy of Courage*. Even then, the Prime Minister had no truck with 'all this psychological nonsense'. Moran saw courage as a bank account, which could become depleted or overdrawn if too much was taken out of it. For Churchill, a soldier who showed cowardice should be shot, and that was that. There was bad news waiting for Moran at Malta. A letter from his wife told him that the publishers Macmillan, headed by the brother of the Minister of State for the Middle East, had turned the book down. It was even worse when Churchill seemed to agree with them, and Moran rethought the idea of having him write the preface. He found comfort with the more diplomatic Gil Winant.

The *Renown*'s crew were given welcome leave, even though the delights of Valetta were much curtailed by the after-effects of bombing. On the full days in harbour, two out of three watches were allowed ashore between 12.30 and 10.30 in the evening. The WRNS officers also found time for sightseeing among the rubble and were horrified by the extent of the damage. Sarah Churchill was given a flight in a photo reconnaissance Mosquito, seeing in real life the places she had interpreted in photographs back at Medmenham.

The weather was still bad at Malta and Churchill's health was not improving, so it was decided to continue by ship. The *Renown* slipped her buoy just before midnight on Friday the 19th. She headed close to the North African coast where she could be given air cover, and she carried out zigzags. For most of the voyage she was at the second state of anti-aircraft readiness, which meant that the crew were on standby for an attack which could come at any moment – action stations were fully manned but men could fall out in turns to get some rest. As they approached Alexandria late in the morning of the 21st, Sarah Churchill was invited to speak to the fighter pilots overhead by radio. Overcome by the occasion, and feeling that she had to live up to her RAF uniform, she said, 'Hello, would you like to come and beat us up?'

The air crackled with static or something: 'Would we like to what?' – 'Come and beat us up.' – 'Who's that speaking?' – 'Sarah,' I replied, my eyes gazing up at their orderly circle above our heads.[4]

As the planes began to swoop on the ship, a naval officer realised that the ship's gunners were trained to respond instantly to any threat, and rushed for the intercom. 'Gun control, the following beat-up is official, for God's sake hold your fire.' Churchill and Cunningham were on the bridge as the Spitfires 'shot by them, dipping to almost sea level, when with an enormous roar, they soared back into the sky. It was magnificent, but I was never so glad as when it was over, and I kept out of sight until we docked'. The *Renown* moored to B2 buoy in eight fathoms of water and the principals in the party were put into aircraft for the 40-minute flight to Cairo.

★   ★   ★

The American journalist was right in that the main conference was to be held in the Mena House Hotel, less than half a mile north of the Great Pyramid and about seven miles from the centre of Cairo. According to a pre-war Baedeker Guide it was at the terminus of the tramway from Cairo and had 200 beds, a post office, gardens, baths, swimming pool, golf course and tennis courts. A hundred and twelve rooms were cleared to make way for office facilities and there were several conference rooms with a total seating of 120. The largest had a special 40 ft table installed for the Joint Chiefs of Staff. There was a post office, catering tent, eight typing pools, a security tent and a signal office. Several hundred desks and chairs were assembled from the British army's resources, or the supplies in the hotel, or were purchased locally. The conference used 30,000 sheets of typing paper and 55,000 sheets of duplicating paper as well as 500 stencils. They needed 30 boxes of paper clips, 35 packets of pins, eight pints of ink and 60 sticks of sealing wax. There were difficulties with the hotel staff as 'the civilian manager of the hotel was absolutely bewildered by the organisation which was going on around him and in the early stages was of little or no use to the catering branch'. Few of the porters and waiters could read and write and army personnel were drafted in, as well as storekeepers and clerks.

The members of the delegations lived in more than 30 villas and other accommodation strung out along the road between there and Cairo. The

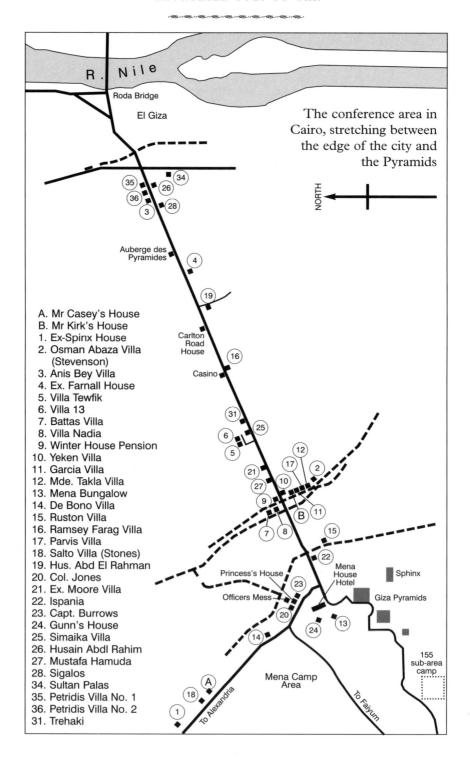

R. Nile

Roda Bridge

El Giza

The conference area in
Cairo, stretching between
the edge of the city and
the Pyramids

NORTH

35
34
26
36
28
3

Auberge des
Pyramides
4

19

Carlton
Road
House
16

Casino

31
25
6
5

12
17
2
21
27
10
9
B
11

7
8
15

22

Princess's House
Mena
House
Hotel

Sphinx

23
Officers Mess

Giza Pyramids

20

14
24
13

155
sub-area
camp

A
18
Mena Camp
Area

To Alexandria

To Faiyum

1

A. Mr Casey's House
B. Mr Kirk's House
1. Ex-Spinx House
2. Osman Abaza Villa
   (Stevenson)
3. Anis Bey Villa
4. Ex. Farnall House
5. Villa Tewfik
6. Villa 13
7. Battas Villa
8. Villa Nadia
9. Winter House Pension
10. Yeken Villa
11. Garcia Villa
12. Mde. Takla Villa
13. Mena Bungalow
14. De Bono Villa
15. Ruston Villa
16. Ramsey Farag Villa
17. Parvis Villa
18. Salto Villa (Stones)
19. Hus. Abd El Rahman
20. Col. Jones
21. Ex. Moore Villa
22. Ispania
23. Capt. Burrows
24. Gunn's House
25. Simaika Villa
26. Husain Abdl Rahim
27. Mustafa Hamuda
28. Sigalos
34. Sultan Palas
35. Petridis Villa No. 1
36. Petridis Villa No. 2
31. Trehaki

domestic arrangements of each villa was in the charge of a British woman NCO, and a bus service was run to the Mena Hotel. They were given the privilege of free drinks. 'All delegates are the guests of His Britannic Majesty's Government and they are requested to make no payment for any meals, drinks or services provided or to tip the hotel or villa staffs.' Each day the conference consumed 80 bottles of whisky (half of them Scotch), 12 of brandy and 34 of gin, as well as more than 500 bottles of beer. It also needed 20,000 cigarettes, 20 ounces of tobacco and 75 cigars.

The Prime Minister's party numbered fourteen, for it had been joined by Randolph Churchill as well as the usual private secretaries, doctor, typists, detectives and valet. It was to stay in the Casey Villa, also known as the Beit el Azrak, which lost something in translation to Blue House. It was about 2½ miles north-west of the Mena Hotel, while Roosevelt was in the Kirk House about two miles to the east of the Hotel. The Casey Villa had been let from a prominent British resident for the Minister of State in the Middle East, who moved out for the occasion. According to Elizabeth Layton, 'The place had been carefully fitted out to suit the Prime Minister. Everywhere there were bells, buzzers, telephone extensions, mosquito nets, fly swats and the like.' He liked to sit next to a fountain in the garden and had a marine orderly to control its flow to his satisfaction. The house was managed with great efficiency by Captain Francis Stonor, one of 'these delicate young men, some even with peroxided hair, who seemed rather numerous in these parts as personal assistant to generals, and so forth'. The rest of the entourage lived in the Agent's House about 150 yards away, where the cooking of the army corporal in charge of the kitchen proved very popular and attracted visitors. The Blue House was fitted as a headquarters. According to Stonor:

> The Secretariat was organised in four rooms on the ground floor of the Villa. Two of these rooms had to be built, this was done by enclosing the loggia giving onto the central courtyard. One of these temporary rooms was then fitted up as the Map Room. It was panelled from floor to ceiling with Essex boarding for maps, and flood-lit by lights fitted to adjustable brackets. This room proved most successful, in particular as regards the lighting arrangements.[5]

The marine guards were much less comfortable in tents in an army transit camp three miles away. Washing and cleaning facilities were poor, there was only limited transport between the camp and the site of the conference and the last meal of the day was at 4.30, which was often missed by guards coming off duty. Their major explained that 'although Royal Marines were quite capable of roughing it on service, the requirements of our duties on this operation were such that a high standard of smartness was essential'. Churchill demanded that they wear their blue uniforms instead of the more normal khaki, but that needed extra cleaning, which could not be done easily in a tent in the desert. After consultation with Hollis, they were moved to a US Army camp much nearer to the hotel. In gratitude, they took part in a Thanksgiving Day parade on 25 November.

Overall, the area was patrolled by three squadrons of Spitfires, three of Hurricanes and one of night fighters. A radar chain covered the whole coast and there were 82 anti-aircraft guns in the immediate area, with observer posts to spot enemy aircraft. The conference area was guarded by five battalions of infantry and an armoured car squadron. The British presence was resented by nationalists, and delegates to the conference were warned that the city had 'a large cosmopolitan population, some of whom are not sympathetic to the allied cause'. They were told not to leave any papers exposed in their rooms, and to burn them personally when they were finished with them.

★ ★ ★

Chiang Kai Chek, the Chinese leader, had arrived early with his wife, the only woman to feature at high level in wartime conferences. Brooke thought the Chinese president looked like 'a cross between a pine marten and a ferret' and had 'no grasp of war in its larger aspects', like almost everyone Brooke met, except Stalin. His wife made a lasting if not always favourable impression – 'a queer character in which sex and politics seemed to predominate'. Brooke thought she was 'not good looking, but she had certainly made the best of herself and was well turned out'. Thompson the detective was more impressed with 'a smart, well-dressed and attractive woman' who was 'the moving force in the relationship'. When she appeared with her husband at the first meeting on the 23rd, Brooke was not sure whether she had gatecrashed. 'It makes little difference, for I feel certain she would have turned up whether she was invited or not.' Roosevelt wanted to expand the 'big three' of himself, Stalin and Churchill to a big four including China. But Stalin flatly vetoed this, using the excuse that the Soviet Union was not at war with Japan.

The Americans were concerned that the Soviets might fear that they and the British were getting together against them. The British had no such scruples, believing that the two western powers had to discuss plenty of operations where they would fight side by side, and there was no need for such detailed co-operation with the Soviets. Anglo-American discussion was mainly centred on South-east Asia, where Mountbatten had a plan for an advance through Burma; and on the Greek island of Rhodes which Churchill wanted to capture. As a result of these complications, scruples and diversions of aims, the Americans and the British left Cairo without any clear agreement on how to deal with Stalin. On the morning of 27 November Churchill was driven out to the airport to join his Avro York aircraft at last.

★ ★ ★

After the experience of the North African trip in May and June, some modifications had been made to *Ascalon*'s interior. A heavy wooden table in the saloon was replaced by one made in aluminium. The 'hay-box' in the galley was only suitable for keeping food warm, but pre-cooked meals were not likely to be available on isolated staging posts, so a grill, fast heaters for drinks and a toaster were installed. Bunks had been fitted for the crew on the starboard side forward, but these had to be removed to make space for the navigator's charts and instruments, and the flight engineer's tools. The forward cabin would now be used for the crew, though sometimes it might have to be given up to the detectives. Meanwhile Corporal Shepherd returned to his normal duties on the ground. His place was taken by Sergeant Jock Duncan, a chef from the officers' mess at Hendon, who could provide a much better cuisine, while Sawyers served it.

Meanwhile, two more Yorks were allocated, for use by the Chiefs of Staff and others, and fitted 'with due regard to the age and dignity of the passengers'. A permanent flight was set up at Northolt under John Mitchell, and the crew was kept on 24 hours standby for operations. Rolls-Royce, the makers of the Merlin engines, were keen to prove their value in transport aircraft with a view to post-war sales, and sent a permanent representative to Northolt.

The crew of the York had gained a good deal of VVIP experience while Churchill was occupied elsewhere. The Prime Minister had decreed that the plane was not to be used for other purposes without his permission, but in practice he was quite generous with this. In June the aircraft took the King to visit the troops in North Africa, though he did not like flying in the noisy York. Early in October they took Mountbatten part of the way to take up his new post as Supreme Commander in South-east Asia, though he had to transfer to another aircraft at Tunis, as the York was diverted to carry one of their favourite passengers, the South African Prime Minister Jan Smuts, to Britain. Almost immediately they were alerted to fly the Foreign Secretary, Anthony

Eden, to Moscow, but again they were diverted, to take a friend of the Prime Minister's, 'a less than V-VIP', as Mitchell put it, to Cairo for treatment.

During this time Jack Payne proved his resourcefulness as a flight engineer. In Cairo West airport he was able to locate a spare Merlin engine to replace one that had caught fire in flight, and install it with the help of local engineering staff. On the way back home they carried the Secretary of State for the Colonies and his secretary, a retired admiral. Payne heard rattling noises during the night and traced them to a tooth mug in one of the toilets. He threw the contents into the Elsan toilet, but later found that they included the admiral's dentures, so he had to search the chemical fluid and then wash them down. Another new engine was needed by this time. Payne declined the offer of a reconditioned Bomber Command one, and used his contacts in Downing Street to get a brand new one from Rolls-Royce. It was installed by 4 November, by which time there were orders to get ready for another flight.

Churchill had already begun his voyage in the *Renown* when the York took off from Northolt just after midnight on 17 November, carrying Brooke, Portal, General Laycock, who had taken over from Mountbatten as head of Combined Operations, and Brooke's staff officer Lt-Col Brian Boyle. Brooke enjoyed the comfort of Churchill's private cabin as they landed briefly at Gibraltar, then went on to Malta and Cairo. There, the crew were accommodated in insect-infested tents like many others, so Dad Collins showed his bites to the senior medical officer and got a certificate saying he and the crew were unfit to fly. This resulted in a quick transfer to a hotel.

★   ★   ★

For the flight to Tehran, the group was divided between five aircraft. *Ascalon* took a normal Prime Minister's party, including Churchill and his daughter, Anthony Eden, Moran, Martin, the Thompsons, Kinna and Sawyers. York No. MW100 carried the Chiefs of Staff and their aides, with General Ismay from the Ministry of Defence. Liberator No. 545 carried Cadogan and Hollis, several other officials and two women typists. Dakota 900 took various junior officers and officials and two more women typists, while No. 905 carried a dozen typists and orderlies. Many of the planning staff were left behind in Cairo, including Elizabeth Layton who was happy to visit the Pyramids and go dancing with some of the Map Room officers, notwithstanding her affair with the young naval officer.

The five aircraft began to leave at 6.30 in the morning of 28 November, and *Ascalon* was last to take off at 8.30. The early flights were delayed slightly due to fog, and Portal was annoyed that he was not informed and was got out of bed early. Churchill's voice was failing due to his cold as he came on board, but he said to his daughter, 'Now for the high jump.' Sitting down, he continued, 'We shall be crossing four great rivers, the Tigris, the Euphrates, Jordan, and Nile, and the wilderness and the mountains. There will be nowhere, should we feel tired, that we could put our feet down to rest.' Sarah tingled with excitement and enjoyed 'a wonderful flight over the rocky desert, then over the desolate range of the Persian mountains, for the most part sepia coloured, but every now and then slashed with a red or aquamarine seam of colour'. Lord Moran was on his first flight in the York, having missed the trip to Algiers last time, and he was impressed:

> This plane has a starboard curtained off part with a little table like a disc on left so that he can sit and read and look out. And a light at his bed and at starboard a WC. There is a long narrow fixed table, say 2 ft wide with 3 chairs … on each side and at each end, 8 in all. When we fed the PM sat at the head of the table and we sit round table. When table is cleared we swing round chairs to face where we are going.[6]

Churchill occupied the co-pilot's seat for a time as usual and looked out over the Gaza Strip, the Dead Sea and an oil pipeline linking Haifa and Kirkuk. With the much improved cooking facilities, the crew typed out a menu and served a lunch of turtle soup, with a choice of hot roast chicken or cold ox tongue and salad, with sauté potatoes and peas, followed by jelly, cheese and biscuits. Churchill's daughter was enthralled with the flight and wrote to her mother:

> I think flying is probably the best way to see this type of country. Miles and miles of sand desert – thorn rock desert – all of which might be alternatively monotonous or forbidding by horse, camel or motor car, but is magnificent when seen as a panorama. Particularly the wilderness just south of Jerusalem (How could they ever have called it the land flowing with milk and honey?) and then, of course, the great range of Persian mountains we had to cross. That was absolutely thrilling – we flew at about 12,000. Mountains came up to meet us – then slipped away (never of course – to reassure you – very close; 12,000 clears most, and the one or two higher ranges were given a wide berth!)[7]

As they descended through the mountains into Tehran, Churchill confided his misgivings to Moran. The Americans still wanted a quick invasion of France and might throw away what Churchill thought were 'shining, gleaming opportunities in the Mediterranean'. Meanwhile, the campaign in Italy was flagging and allowing the Germans to draw breath. He foresaw a difficult conference, and he was not in his best health to conduct it. They landed at Meherabad airport after five and a half hours in the air, to encounter another bizarre situation.

★ ★ ★

The security problems at Tehran were different from those in Cairo, and they turned out to be more serious. Persia, now more accurately known as Iran, had never formally been a European colony, but it had seen rivalry between three great powers over the last decades. The Russians were the main trading partners, the British largely controlled the oil industry and the Germans supplied numerous technicians and had large numbers of people on the ground. After the war between Germany and the Soviet Union began, Russia and Britain invaded. There was little resistance, but the modernising ruler Riza Shah was replaced by his son and the government was much weaker. Iran declared war on Germany in September 1943 and was now technically an independent Allied power, though she was not expected to do any fighting. Allied control was less effective than in Egypt, with far fewer troops stationed there, and there were numerous German supporters, including paratroops recently dropped into the country.

The British military authorities were not experienced in this type of situation, for Churchill had spent little time there on his last visit. They had to decide between keeping quiet and risking a lack of co-ordination, or telling everyone, including the local authorities, whose discretion and competence they did not trust. In practice they fell between two stools, and carried out an operation which Inspector Thompson condemned as 'inadequate and ill-conceived'. They decided not to take the Persian government into their confidence and have the route closed to normal traffic, so instead they devised a cover plan. One of the Chiefs of Staff's cars arrived at the main gate of the British Legation flying prominent flags to give the impression that they were the main party, while Churchill travelled much more quietly by another route. As a result the speed of the Prime Minister's car was governed by the other traffic on the route, although a few side streets were closed by the military police, and a small number of them attempted to clear the way as far as possible. Churchill's car was preceded by a jeep carrying soldiers, but they kept the hood up and had a very poor view of the crowds in the street. There was no co-ordination between the two vehicles. 'Whilst the driver of the P.M.'s car was very reliable and experienced, he had of necessity to keep behind the leading jeep. The driver of the jeep obviously worried more about the possibility of outstripping the P.M.'s car than reaching his objective swiftly.' Consequently the convoy travelled very slowly through the city streets, which were crowded because the people expected the Shah to pass that way on his own business. Plain-clothes military police mingled in the crowds, and uniformed policemen stood at intervals along the route, but to Thompson's alarm they faced the road rather than the crowd, and saluted as the convoy passed.

Sarah Churchill thought the ride to the Legation was 'spine-chilling', that 'anyone could have shot my father at point blank range or just dropped a nice little grenade into our laps'. Churchill was aware of the problems but admitted that he did not see what the troops in the jeep could have done in any case. At one point they were held up for three minutes, and Sarah and her father held hands. Churchill grinned at the crowd which 'for the most part grinned back', according to his account.

The Legation itself was, according to Ismay, 'a ramshackle house built by the Indian Public Works Department in the days when our Minister required a small escort of Indian cavalry for his personal protection'. Now it was guarded by 350 soldiers of the East Kent Regiment, popularly known as the Buffs. To Sarah it was 'cold and cheerless' and the change in temperature from Cairo was very noticeable. Brooke thought, 'They have had an awful job to fit us all in but have made good business of it.'

The administrative staff had to work hard during the conference. Miss Olive Christopher was delighted to be allowed to continue on to Tehran. She found it was three days and three nights of hard work, from nine in the morning till three the following morning, and wrote: 'I have never worked so consistently hard in all my life.' She was accommodated in the local American YWCA, where food was 'very indifferent' and there were few amenities. 'They had done their best to make it comfortable but if any privacy for washing was required, it could be had only in a little stone outhouse which was very, very cold. There were baths, but there was no hot water. When one let the taps run there was a most appalling stench.' The city offered no relief. 'Teheran itself we all thought was the most filthy place. All the drains are open and run through the streets. The inhabitants carry out their ablutions, do their washing ... and wash their dishes, in public, usually seated on the street kerb.' As she wrote later: 'In fact, it took a week to get the smell of Teheran out of our clothes.'

Meanwhile, Stalin had invited Roosevelt to stay with him in the Soviet Legation which was just across the road from the British, while the American one was a mile away. The two leaders met for the first time in the afternoon of the 28th, and got on well together. Neither of these points boded well for Churchill.

★ ★ ★

Churchill met Harriman and facetiously suggested

> that he had a right to be chairman of the meeting because of his age; because his name began with C and because of the historic importance of the British Empire which he represented. He waived all these claims but would insist on one thing, which was that he should be allowed to give a dinner party on the 30th, which was his 69th birthday.[8]

Even a joking reference to the British Empire had its dangers, for Churchill was likely to become isolated. Stalin and Roosevelt each represented very different political and economic traditions, but they discovered a certain amount in common. Roosevelt, having used economic intervention and welfare policies to deal with the Great Depression of the 1930s, was about as far to the left as any American President was likely to be. Although Stalin had for the moment abandoned any revolutionary aims, both men represented states which had been founded by revolution, and which were opposed to imperialism (though some would doubt the sincerity of either claim in view of subsequent history).

Churchill, on the other hand, was a strong advocate of imperialism, and it was only a year since he had told a distinguished audience, 'I have not become the King's First Minister in order to preside over the liquidation of the British Empire.' That empire had expanded with every successful war in the preceding three centuries, although after the most recent one imperial growth came in the form of League of Nations Mandates. Churchill was obsessed with the Mediterranean, and it might be assumed that he expected to make some gains there, perhaps in North Africa or the Balkans. Roosevelt and Stalin, despite Churchill's persuasiveness when he met them individually, saw the Mediterranean as a diversion from the real task in the west, the invasion of France. The composition of Churchill's party did not help here. As always, it was composed of senior officers and civil servants and gave the impression of a very conservative, class-ridden Britain.

In fact, Churchill's views of the empire were purely defensive, and he had no plans to take on new territory. His hesitation in invading northern Europe was based on genuine fears, partly caused by his experiences of the Western Front in the last war. He preferred to explore the alternatives – a mass rising in occupied Europe led by resistance movements; bombing of cities which would weaken the enemy will; starvation blockades, as in the last war; an advance through Italy, the 'under-belly of the Axis' that would leave Germany isolated. None of these was really working as bombing tended to stiffen rather than weaken national determination; the Germans remained adequately fed, and they mounted a dogged defence of Italy, which was not too difficult in the narrow and mountainous peninsula. As for resistance movements, they were mostly kept in order by Nazi ruthlessness, and next year the disastrous Warsaw Uprising would remove any hope there. British and American forces had won control of the seas and of much of the air over Europe, but that was not enough, and mass armies were the only way to conclude the war.

The first plenary session of the Tehran conference began in the Russian Embassy at 4 p.m. on 28 November. Brooke wrote:

This was the first occasion during the war when Stalin, Roosevelt and Winston sat round a table to discuss the war we were waging together. I found it quite enthralling looking at their faces and trying to estimate what lay behind.[9]

He found that Stalin, unlike most people, had 'a military brain of the very highest calibre'. The Soviet dictator, however, continued to insist on a second front as soon as possible and the session brought no concrete results.

In the second session on the 29th, Brooke and Marshall reported on the preparations for the invasion of northern Europe. Stalin immediately spotted the weak point when he asked who the commander-in-chief was and was told that none had been appointed. Stalin asked frankly if the British really believed in it, or were just trying to placate the Russians. Churchill had actually set up the Combined Operations organisation before the final French collapse in 1940 to plan such ventures, and replied, quite sincerely, that if conditions were right, 'it was the duty of the British Government to hurl every scrap of strength across the Channel'. Stalin also made what Churchill called the 'momentous declaration' that the Soviet Union would enter the war against Japan as soon as Germany was defeated, supplying the vast human resources that would be needed for an invasion of the Japanese islands.

One of Churchill's duties was to present the Sword of Stalingrad to Stalin. This had been made in honour of the Soviet resistance to Hitler's armies, and was a hugely popular icon in Britain. Evelyn Waugh, a close friend of Randolph Churchill, was no lover of communism, but his description of its display in Westminster Abbey in the novel *Unconditional Surrender*, is jaundiced but not fictional:

> The sword they had come to see stood upright between two candles, on a table counterfeiting an altar. Policemen guarded it on either side. It had been made by the King's personal command as a gift 'to the steel-hearted people of Stalingrad.' An octogenarian, who had made ceremonial swords for five sovereigns, rose from his bed to forge it; silver, gold, rock-crystal and enamel had gone into its embellishment. In the year of the Sten gun it was a notable weapon ... Every day the wireless announced great Russian victories while the British advance in Italy was coming to a halt. The people were suffused with gratitude to their remote allies and they venerated the sword as a symbol of their own generous and spontaneous emotion.[10]

Brooke describes its handover to the Soviet dictator:

> At 3.30 we went over to the Russian embassy to see Winston present the Stalingrad Sword to Stalin. Bands, Guards of Honour, national anthems etc. Speech by Winston after which he handed sword over in the name of King to Stalin. Stalin kissed sword and handed it over to Voroshilov, who promptly dropped sword out of its scabbard! However it was finally handed over to commander of Russian Guard of Honour and marched off securely.[11]

That evening over dinner Stalin suggested that 50,000 German officers would have to be shot when the war was over. Churchill, despite his remarks to the dinner party back in July 1941 and later comments in Cabinet, was shocked and was not placated when Roosevelt tried to ease the tension by joking that only 49,000 needed to be shot.

Next day, 30 November, was Churchill's 69th birthday and his daughter remembered the party vividly: 'It was the high spot; not only because of all the "great" that were gathered, but because of why they were gathered, and most of all how they really get along.' Roosevelt proposed the first toast to her, and she was moved. She noticed that in Churchill's presence the President almost forgot that he could not walk, and tried to rise from his chair. She thought that Stalin, known popularly and in signals as 'Uncle Joe', was a great man, with a sense of humour as quick as her father's. When Churchill said during one of his toasts that 'England is getting pinker', Stalin replied, 'It is a sign of good health', followed by 'a great roar of laughter that is only heard among friends'. Even brother Randolph was unusually well behaved, as she told their mother: 'The old restraint kept me seated, and a new restraint kept Randolph seated too – and I couldn't help thinking how a few years ago he would never been off his feet! He is trying you know – there is a big change in him.'

The post-war settlement began to dominate on the last day of the conference, and there were clear differences here. Poland was a particular issue with Churchill, as Britain had ostensibly gone to war in 1939 to defend the nation while Stalin had stabbed it in the back with the Machiavellian Nazi-Soviet pact. But Roosevelt, facing an election the next year, was not keen to get involved and Harriman saw the flaw, that the Soviets might be in physical possession of the country before any decision was made. They agreed on a declaration which left many issues vague but heralded the setting-up of the United Nations to solve disputes. The leaders declared themselves committed to 'the elimination of tyranny and slavery, oppression and intolerance', though Stalin's definition of these evils was not the same as that of the others.

Ascalon took off from Tehran at 8.00 in the morning of 2 December, carrying Churchill and his usual party plus Clark Kerr, the British Ambassador in Moscow. It climbed initially to 11,500 feet to clear the mountains, then went down to 10,000 feet. Duncan served lunch of quail accompanied by white wine. The Prime Minister was in good from, sitting in the co-pilot's seat again wearing his siren suit and RAF greatcoat as the aircraft flew in circles to give him a good view. The sun was in his eyes as they headed south-west. He ordered Sawyers to produce his sunglasses and Panama hat but they had gone in one of the other aircraft and the unfortunate valet was blamed again. The aircraft landed at Cairo West airport in mid-afternoon.

XIV

Convalescing at Marrakech

Churchill had still not given up hope of help from Turkey, and on 3 December the York was sent to fetch President Inonu from Adana. The authorities had learned nothing about the need for civilian clothes on missions to neutral countries, so that the bazaars of Cairo had to be searched for ill-fitting sports jackets for the crew to wear above RAF trousers. The York made its landing in Turkey on 3 December and was joined by Randolph Churchill. Next morning the Turkish presidential train arrived, but the Americans had also sent the Skymaster *Sacred Cow*, a far more comfortable aircraft, on a similar mission. Randolph appeared at the door of the York to announce that 'they' had got the President on board. Jock Gallagher explained that it was not possible to send a message ahead to Cairo with the news, as they could not transmit at that range until after they had taken off, and in any case it would take too long to code and decode.

Since the York was slightly faster than the Skymaster, it was decided to take off and cut directly across the eastern Mediterranean instead of following the coast as they usually did. Carrying the Turkish Vice-President and some diplomats, they landed at Cairo West just ahead of the Americans. Air traffic control had ascertained that they had VIPs on board, so they were directed to the place of honour where the Prime Minister and other dignitaries were waiting. The Turkish national anthem was played but Randolph came out of the door to explain the situation to his father. The Skymaster was sent to a distant corner of the airfield to be met by a jeep, and the President disembarked by ladder as there were no suitable steps.

It was not an auspicious start, and the Turks were no more inclined to enter the war than before, especially since the British had recently suffered a reverse at Leros. For the return flight, Churchill personally guided President Inonu to the door of the York with no Americans in sight. The President kissed him but Eden later commented ungraciously that it was 'the only gain from fifteen hours of hard argument'. On the flight the large Turkish party was hosted by Randolph, who did not abstain from drinking himself. Champagne and 'delicate sandwiches' were served. On landing Randolph was presented with a gold wrist watch while the aircrew got 100

Turkish cigarettes each and Jock Duncan the chef was tipped with £20 in notes.

★ ★ ★

Preparations were made to fly out of Cairo on 10 December, after Churchill had met Fitzroy Maclean, head of the British mission to Yugoslavia, to discuss the Yugoslav partisans, as well as King Farouk of Egypt, the exiled King of Greece, and various British ministers, diplomats and officials. Harold Macmillan thought that he was 'in great form and holding forth to a circle of these young men'. In fact, Churchill was still unwell with a cold and the crew of the York were ordered to warm up the interior with an electric fire well before the flight. He was in a difficult mood even by his standards, though his daughter acted as mediator with the crew. In her RAF uniform and with her natural charm, she was to prove very successful in this role, replacing the panicky Sawyers.

As they approached El Aouina airport near Tunis on the road to Carthage, the present-day Tunis airport, the crew of the York contacted local air traffic control and were told to their surprise that the airfield was closed to traffic. They were diverted to 'Whipsnade', a small strip ten minutes' flying time away. They questioned these instructions but were not able to disclose full details of their mission over voice radio, so they flew over El Aouina with their undercarriage down, indicating a desire to land. Still air traffic control ordered them on, and they found Whipsnade among the many landing strips in the area. Assuming that the diversion had been caused by some last-minute accident or obstruction to the runway, they landed on a bleak airstrip inhabited by a Beaufighter squadron.

Unloading of luggage began, while the Prime Minister insisted on coming out of the hot aircraft into the frigid morning air. He 'looked around blankly and then, in spite of our protests, took off his hat and gloomily surveyed the sandy ground. The wind blew a wisp of his hair this way and that, his face shone with perspiration.' He sat there for about ten minutes on a packing case as a scruffy jeep arrived with a bewildered officer. Ground crews peered through the distance and were amazed to see the solitary and disconsolate Prime Minister looking forlorn a few hundred yards away. The sudden transition to the cold airfield, in which 'a mean little breeze whipped around', did nothing for the Prime Minister's declining health. Following on from his isolation at Tehran and the slowing up of the war effort, it was the lowest point of his foreign travels. Telephone calls were made to El Aouina, and it was soon established that the field had been closed to allow the touch-down of Churchill's flight. Passengers and luggage were re-embarked and they arrived at the correct field ten minutes after take-off, to meet a group of embarrassed VIPs.

The damage had been done. That afternoon Churchill was too exhausted even to read his usual telegrams. Staying at Eisenhower's villa that night, he complained of a pain in his throat and later he was found to have a temperature of 101. Moran was used to balancing the needs of politics with those of medicine but he was unsure what to do. 'We have had alarms like this before that have come to nothing, and in his position you cannot prepare for an illness without letting it be known everywhere. On the other hand, if he is going to be ill we have nothing here in the God-forsaken spot – no nurses, no milk, not even a chemist.' It was Brooke who forced a decision. He asked what Moran would need if it was pneumonia and he replied, 'a pathologist, 2 nurses and a portable X-ray set'. The doctor and nurses would have to come from Cairo and the X-ray set from Algiers. Brooke wanted to wire for them straight away but Moran begged him to wait in case it was a false diagnosis: 'I told him that it did not matter if it was a false diagnosis. In that case, thank heaven, they would not be required and could be flown back. On the other hand if it was pneumonia we should never forgive ourselves for having wasted 24 hours. It is fortunate that those wires were sent to Cairo.'

Doctor Pulvertaft, a pathologist, was flown in from Cairo with two nurses, followed later by Dr Bedford – Colville remarked of Moran, 'He seldom treated Churchill's ailment himself but always knew the right specialist to summon.' Less kindly, Colville is quoted as saying that if Churchill was indeed ill Moran 'would send for a real doctor'. In any case an X-ray specialist arrived from Tunis with his machine and Churchill and Moran examined the pictures together.

'Well, what does that signify?' the P.M. asked.

'You've got a small patch of congestion.'

'Do you mean I've got pneumonia again?' He demanded impatiently.[1]

Moran dosed him with his favourite remedy of M and B, produced by the firm of May and Baker, and settled down to treat a long illness.

Chief Petty Officer Pinfield, who had cooked for Churchill on several previous voyages beginning with the trip to Argentia, was still in the *Renown* at Gibraltar and he was flown out to run the kitchen. According to Captain Pim, 'Pinfield was a great asset to us all – and even under the most alarming difficulties he would contrive to produce the most acceptable meals and keep the P.M. and everybody else on his staff contented.' Security was a problem at the White House, which was close to an exposed beach only 150 miles from enemy territory in Sardinia. There was a severe risk of landing, or shelling from a submarine, or air attack, so a battalion of Coldstream Guards was brought in and motor gunboats patrolled offshore. The York was ostentatiously flown to Cairo and a villa in the area was heavily guarded as a decoy.

As he recovered slowly, his daughter read him Jane Austen's *Pride and Prejudice*. For once his reading material did not have resonance with the war effort, almost the reverse. According to the critic John Bayley, Jane Austen was 'really happiest working on two or three inches of ivory and turning to art the daily lives of three or four families in a locality' – something of a contrast to Churchill's world travelling and global outlook. It was also a very different age in which the Napoleonic Wars and the threat of foreign invasion barely affected people's daily lives. As Churchill commented, 'What calm lives they had, those people! No worries about the French Revolution, or the crashing struggle of the Napoleonic Wars. Only manners controlling natural passion so far as they could, together with cultured explanations of any mischances.'

Mrs Churchill was told about the illness by her husband's telegram of 12 December:

Colonel Warden to Mrs Warden
I am laid up here at Carthage with a temperature of 101 and rather violent neuralgic sore throat, due, I think, to a draught in the aeroplane. I shall therefore stay in bed and recover for two or three days.[2]

On the 15th another telegram confirmed that he had pneumonia again and Clementine was anxious to come out to join him. She took Jock Colville, now released from the air force but still wearing his flying officer's uniform, and Mrs Grace Hamblin, who had managed her affairs for many years. They took off from Lyneham in a Liberator after a long drive through the blackout, and tried to sleep on mattresses on the floor. The weather was perfect, according to Colville, and they did not go above 5,000 feet, but Mrs Churchill was anxious and could not sleep, so they stayed awake for most of the night. They landed at Gibraltar before daylight and took off again at 9.30. Colville tried the controls with more competence than Churchill, and they too looked over the battle site at the Kasserine Pass. They landed at three in the afternoon, to be met by a large party including Sarah Churchill, Tommy Thompson, John Martin and Air Chief Marshal Tedder, commanding the air force in the region. Churchill was delighted when his wife was brought to the house, but Clementine was sceptical. As she told Wilson, 'Oh yes, he's very glad I've come, but in five minutes he'll forget I'm here.' She was apparently not satisfied with Chief Petty Officer Pinfield and an American team was put in charge. This caused an improvement at first, but soon she was complaining that the food was 'vurry' American. Sawyers was shocked to discover that they cooked partridges for an hour and a half, whereas the cook back home did it for 15 minutes.

As the Prime Minister began to recover, Elizabeth Layton recorded: 'Mr Churchill was still in complete control of the British Cabinet and war affairs, and all documents and directives had to pass through the narrow bottleneck of Peter and myself. It kept us extremely busy – in fact it was a most peculiar Christmas.' The festivities were squeezed in between Churchill's need to rest because of his illness, and his desire to carry on business. It was attended by 'what Americans call "high ranking Generals and other notabilities"', according to Mrs Churchill. They arrived for a series of conferences in the morning, then Churchill made a speech and lunched with them, his first meal outside his bedroom. Clementine and Sarah went to church in a corrugated iron shed full of ammunition and a dove flew out, causing a Guardsman to whisper, 'Look now, that means peace.' Even General Alexander was inspired enough to hurry to the house to check if there had been a sudden change in the war, but there was nothing. In the evening there was a cocktail party followed by a cold buffet and Lord Moran took the chance to question Harold Macmillan about his company's refusal of his book. Churchill appeared, apparently in good health. According to Colville, 'everyone finished the day feeling the merrier for Christmas'.

Churchill had planned to fly to Marrakech on Boxing Day, but his wife persuaded him not to interrupt whatever Christmas festivities were possible in the circumstances.

My Darling One,

May I plead with you to make the 27th our *first* flying day? – *Not* on the grounds of your health for I believe that is being well taken care of, but on the grounds of kindness of heart ... this is a question only of personal wishes & Christmas means so much to the great mass of humanity & those who are not fortunate in being together like ourselves value their little celebrations with their comrades while they think of their wives and children at home.[3]

Churchill agreed to the postponement.

★　★　★

The main problem in getting to Marrakech was the flight over the Atlas Mountains, which were over 13,000 feet in places. The York's crew was called to a conference on 26 December, with Air Marshal Tedder, the doctors and the Meteorological Officer. The doctors did not want the Prime Minister to go above 6,000 feet, and one possibility was to take the long route, along the Mediterranean coast, through the Straits of Gibraltar and out into the Atlantic, to fly south to Marrakech. Tedder disliked this, because the numerous convoys in the Mediterranean might mistake the York for a Focke-Wulf Condor and fire on it. Another possibility was to 'fly inland south of the Algerian coastal mountains over the relatively low desert hills, over the Shatt el Hodna'. After that they would go through the Taza Pass which was no higher than 3,000–4,000 feet, hoping that it was clear of clouds, although passage through it would be very bumpy even in the best conditions. A BOAC York carrying other members of the party would fly ahead and send weather reports. If conditions deteriorated it would be necessary to change the route, or to use oxygen masks which the doctors did not like. 'Dad' Collins decided to opt for the inland route and Tedder agreed, but he was determined to be safe. He suggested they should take the principal medical officer of his command, Air Commodore Thomas Kelly, who arrived at the villa on midday on Boxing Day with a portable oxygen apparatus to instruct the Prime Minister in its use:

He was lying propped up in bed, surrounded by his documents. He looked at the oxygen apparatus and asked me to explain how it worked. This I did. Then he said, 'Will you do a trial run on me now?' I turned the oxygen on to 3,000 feet. And after a minute or so I asked him could he taste it? He removed the mask from his face and said, 'I'll have you know, my boy, that I took oxygen before you were born. Do you think oxygen will be necessary?'[4]

Kelly replied that no weather forecast could be relied on for a flight over the mountains. 'As a measure of prudence it ought to be available. If it is not available there may be an unpleasant incident.'

Early next morning the party, including Winston, Clementine and Sarah Churchill, Lord Moran and Sawyers, got ready for the flight. Just as they were about to leave, there was good news for most of the party at least. Churchill was beaming as he heard that the *Scharnhorst*, one of the last of the large German warships, had been sunk on Boxing Day by the covering force of an Arctic convoy including the *Duke of York*. Moran was more concerned, for he discovered that one of three cruisers present had been hit, and his son was serving as an ordinary seaman in the *Belfast*. He remained in suspense until news of his son's safety was received.

Churchill was in his RAF uniform as he left the villa and gave the impression that he was fully active, though Moran knew better. He walked slowly past the guard of honour formed by the Coldstreams. The party was airborne in the York by 8.15, and they flew at a safe height of 6,000 feet. All went well for the first few hours, as Churchill took breakfast, then worked on his papers. Kelly was not welcomed by the regular York crew. They considered his voluminous oxygen kit 'quite unnecessary' as the aircraft already had its oxygen supply with outlets at all the passenger seats, and Kelly was in the way, 'both from the crew's point of view as well as Lord Moran's'. His lordship made no mention of his rival's presence in his memoirs.

The weather began to deteriorate, as shown by the crew's own observations and radio weather reports. Already visibility was very poor; it was clear that the Taza Pass was filled with cloud, and it was a bumpy ride near the high ground on either side of the track. Collins now had to choose whether to turn northwards towards Melilla and go the long route via the Straits of Gibraltar, or to climb for 15 minutes to 11,500 feet to pass over the top. According to Air Commodore Kelly:

The Prime Minister got anxious and began sending up frequent messages to the captain of the aircraft as to our height, position, and what weather reports we were getting from the pilot of the Liberator flying ahead. The messages were going up so frequently that at one time there were three or four of us waiting to talk to the captain of the aircraft to get information for the Prime Minister. A message came back that the weather was very bad and bumpy. The Prime Minister said: 'If I were not on this aircraft it would be flying at 19,000 ft. It is ridiculous keeping it low, it will crash into the mountains.' He told Mrs Oliver to go and tell the captain to go higher, but as he was leaving the cabin he said to her, 'It is my wish but do not give an order.'

Collins was happy to follow this, though according to John Mitchell it was Kelly who was the main source of panic, and he 'nearly passed out with fright'.

Churchill lay on the bed in his cabin as oxygen masks were put on and the climb began. The aircraft broke out into glorious sunshine, as the Air Commodore 'darted breathlessly up and down with questions of all and sundry'. Kelly held the mask to the Prime Minister's face, then on request he attached the strap to hold it round his neck. Churchill pushed it aside occasionally to send messages to Collins. As the plane climbed, Kelly raised the pressure from 1,000 to 10,000 feet, and Churchill's colour became more normal. The aircraft stayed level at 11,500 feet for about 20 minutes, then began to reduce height slowly towards Marrakech. Kelly advised staying in bed for a while with the oxygen on, as a sudden withdrawal might have a bad effect on his heart. Lunch was served just after one and Churchill was 'happy playing with his oxygen apparatus' while drinking brandy and soda. They landed at Marrakech after a flight of six hours.

Hollis, Colville and some of the WAAF cipher officers went out in a Liberator, and had a much more eventful flight. One of the engines cut out, and then a side panel blew out, letting a blast of icy air into the fuselage. According to Colville the WAAFs shrieked while he and Hollis held it in place with all their strength until the flight engineer arrived to make temporary repairs.

★ ★ ★

The Villa Taylor was taken over as before, and Colville found it 'spacious and luxurious, if slightly vulgar'. To Mrs Churchill it was 'a mixture of Arabian Nights and Hollywood'. A chef from the French embassy in Moscow was employed. Churchill had a small Map Room organisation flown out to Marrakech, consisting of Captain Pim and two others. The captain was asked to help reduce cipher staff by accepting the signals in a less neat form, not divided into columns which took up time. It was set up next to Churchill's bedroom, and on 6 January he delighted a local chieftain by showing him the strategic situation. That day, the daily signal had reported on bombing raids on Berlin, Kiel and Munster in Germany, on 'military objectives' in northern France, while fighters had taken part in sweeps over Holland. British and Indian battalions were advancing in Italy, although far too slowly for Churchill's liking. There were reports on Russia and Burma, and American infantry had landed at Saidor in New Guinea. The press reported that Cossack units had crossed the border into German-occupied Poland, while the Germans were mobilising ten- to sixteen-year-old boys for war work, even inside school hours, and one of their radio commentators admitted that 'the year 1943 has without doubt watered the wine of our hopes. The Russian Command have learnt much. In many respects they have left us behind.' The victors of the *Scharnhorst* action were awarded honours, and there was an eerie echo of Churchill's distant past. 'Peter the Painter', an anarchist who had caused Churchill a great deal of trouble when he was Home Secretary in 1911, was said to be living in the Soviet Union and holding an important job.

That was not of much significance to the Map Room, but the distribution of Allied shipping was. Signals reported the positions of two dozen Allied vessels in the North Atlantic, including convoy support groups and landing craft on delivery trips. Eight more were reported in the Mediterranean, on patrol or heading for Algiers, Port Said and the Suez Canal. There were close on 30 convoys in the Atlantic, such as ONS 26 of 31 merchant ships, which was 700 miles south-west of Ireland, heading for North America on a course of 245 degrees at a speed of 7 knots, escorted by the frigate *Chelmer,* two destroyers, three corvettes and a merchant aircraft carrier. The great liners *Queen Mary, Queen Elizabeth* and *Aquitania* were all at sea, known as convoys TA 82, AT 84 and AT 85 respectively. Churchill was very satisfied with the work of his WAAF cipherers, and later he congratulated their leader, Squadron-Officer Williamson, that he 'had never had better service in the handling of his signals'. He cited the example of a signal given to them at 1.30 in the afternoon which was in the hands of the War Cabinet four hours later.

Churchill had many visitors during his two and a half weeks at the Villa Taylor. Beaverbrook flew in on the 28th at Clementine's request. Before the war she had resented his influence with her husband, but now she valued it. On New Year's Eve Eisenhower and Montgomery arrived. Mrs Churchill had the reputation as one of the few people who could keep General Montgomery under control. When one of the general's aides was invited to dinner, he commented, 'My A.D.C.s don't dine with the Prime Minister.' Mrs Churchill looked at him witheringly and said, 'In my house, General Montgomery, I invite those who I wish and I don't require your advice.' There was a party, during which clerks, typists and servants joined to sing *Auld Lang Syne.* General de Gaulle arrived on 12 January, but the meeting was not cordial. Churchill was living in former French territory without any acknowledgment to the French Governor, and appeared to treat North Africa as if it was his own.

The crew of *Ascalon* was employed ferrying in VIPs. Randolph Churchill turned up with his superior officer Fitzroy Maclean. During the flight they were served a fine meal, for 'they wouldn't be getting this sort of menu in Yugoslavia'. Despite Randolph's reputation as someone 'who always seemed to turn up when there was free drinks and food to be had', the bar was not opened before the aircraft took off. This rule was broken for Alfred Duff Cooper, the British Minister to the Free French in North Africa and his wife Lady Diana. They showed 'jangled nerves before the flight', which could only be cured by champagne.

As Churchill slowly recovered, the party adopted the habit of picnicking in the Atlas Mountains. On 30 December, for example, as Colville noted:

We picnicked near a river in the Atlas foothills against a background of prickly pear. All of us except the P.M. and Lord B. walked up the valley, through a ramshackle Jewish village, and Mrs C. and I forded a stream on a donkey while the others, led by Lord Moran, preferred wading to the risk of verminous contact. But neither Mrs C. nor I suffered for our rashness.[5]

Churchill's painting kit had been sent out, and one evening he ordered Inspector Thompson and his assistant Sergeant Davies to carry him up the tower of the villa. They fitted some poles to a chair and got him there with some difficulty. His easel was set up, but he was unable to start. He sat there looking over the blue mountains for some time and then said, 'Take me down, Thompson.'

The others went on separate visits. On the 4th, Clementine and Sarah visited el Glaoui, the Pasha of Marrakech, but were disappointed not to be allowed to see his harem, which was bolted securely. Instead they were fed mint tea and 'all sorts of oriental sweetmeats', and waited on by 'a terrific great giant who looked like Othello', and 'two lovely black slave girls'. Mrs Churchill asked the British Consul's wife if they were really slaves and was told, 'No, but they think they are, and probably like to think they are, so it comes out to the same thing.'

There was a dinner party each evening. On 4 January, for example, Churchill sat opposite Dr Benes, the head of the Free Czech government, who according to Colville was 'agreeable but specious and, perhaps, unduly optimistic'. On his right was Lebedev, Soviet ambassador to the Czechs, who 'spoke no word of English, French or German and had hair like a virtuoso'. On the Prime Minster's other side was Smutny, a Czech minister-in-exile, and the secretaries Colville and Martin filled one end of the table. Sarah was on the corner next to Benes, and on the other side, opposite her husband, was Mrs Churchill. General Hollis was next, while Tommy Thompson had the other end of the table to himself, with Moran on the corner next to Lebedev. Three nights later there was a larger though less polyglot group of 16, including Randolph Churchill on the opposite corner of the table from his sister, Lord Moran, half a dozen British generals and brigadiers, and General Bedell Smith from Eisenhower's staff. Colville went to eat at a hotel with the general's aides.

Lord Moran now knew that his son's ship had not been damaged in the *Scharnhorst* action. He agonised about asking for special permission for him to come to North Africa, until the Admiralty gave the young man two weeks' leave before his officer training course. He arrived in civilian clothes and the Prime Minister was enthralled by his account of the sinking of the German ship.

★   ★   ★

On 14 January the Prime Minister boarded the York again, with his wife and daughter, Lords Beaverbrook and Moran, the Thompsons and Sawyers. At 12.45 they left Marrakech for an enjoyable two-hour flight, passing over Casablanca and the straits to land at North Front aerodrome, Gibraltar, at three in the afternoon. There was the possibility of going on with the York, in an eight-and-a-half-hour flight to Lyneham, and Churchill had told the crew that he would rather do that than go home in 'a draughty battleship'. But the *King George V*, sister to the *Prince of Wales* and *Duke of York*, was standing by and the doctors felt that a long sea voyage might be better for him. Churchill was to be told that the York was unserviceable – one of the engines was covered by a tarpaulin and step ladders were placed against it. Collins was to be given strict instructions not to take off empty that night, and was to be forcibly restrained if he did so. Churchill, according to Squadron-Leader Mitchell, was 'shanghaied' to the battleship.

He was familiar with the layout and was accommodated in the admiral's sea cabin yet again. Colville also found his own cabin very comfortable. The ship sailed at three in the morning of the 15th, and according to Colville there was 'sunshine and gentle breezes' as they headed out into the Atlantic. He explored the ship and found it to be 'exceedingly overheated'. He approved of the arrangements for the passengers: 'Nothing was left undone – even Marines to precede and escort us down the passages.' The practice with the 14-inch guns, however, was 'ear-splitting'. There was divine service on Sunday the 16th, though neither the Prime Minister nor Lord Beaverbrook attended. On Monday, as they came near to the English coast, Churchill went down to the gunroom to talk to the midshipmen, as described by Tony Barter. He took questions for an hour and tried to answer every one, 'talking of Russia, Italy, France, the Beveridge Report, U-boats and hosts of other subjects'. He had apparently recovered his health and seemed 'amazingly well' with 'a terrific personality which seems to radiate from him'. He took the young men to Pim's Map Room and 'described everything for about half an hour, taking each front in turn, including the Atlantic. On talking of the U-boats his eyes lit up and he waxed most enthusiastic.'

The *King George V* arrived at Plymouth late that evening and the party was taken ashore where the King's own train was waiting. After an overnight trip,

Churchill reached Paddington Station to be greeted by the other members of his family. He went straight to the House of Commons and entered the Chamber in the afternoon. In the past he had come home from a highly successful conference to a frosty reception or even a vote of no confidence. Now after a relative failure, the feeling was very different. Most members were unaware that he was back and reacted with surprise, as described by Harold Nicolson:

> Suddenly they jumped to their feet and started shouting, waving their papers in the air. We also jumped up and the whole House broke into cheer after cheer while Winston, very pink, rather shy, beaming with mischief, crept along the front bench and flung himself into his accustomed seat. He was flushed with pleasure and emotion, and hardly had he sat down when two huge tears began to trickle down his cheeks. He mopped at them clumsily with a huge white handkerchief.[6]

XV
'Just a Little Bit of Wishful Thinking ...'

Churchill did not leave the country for nearly five months after his return from Marrakech in January. He was exhausted but devoted most of his remaining energy to the invasion of France, as he had promised Stalin. He presided over the Overlord Committee of the War Cabinet where, according to Ismay, his 'fiery energy and undisputed authority dominated the proceedings'. There were no international conferences on his level, for the general course of the war had now been set, and the principals were not yet ready to settle the terms of the peace – particularly Roosevelt, who had to face an election in November.

On 6 June 1944 the nature of the war changed completely when troops of the western Allies stormed ashore on the beaches of Normandy and the long-awaited second front began. This attack on well-entrenched Nazi forces was an immensely complex operation involving unprecedented levels of co-operation between different armies, navies and air forces. It followed a huge build-up of troops and supplies in Britain, which relied on victory against the U-boat. It deployed 4,126 landing ships and craft, nearly all of which had been designed and built since 1940. Many thousands of men had to be trained to operate them on the British sector alone. It was preceded by large-scale heavy bombing of the area, followed by fighter-bomber attacks which relied on total air superiority. It used amphibious vehicles such as DUKWs and swimming tanks, with various degrees of success. It needed special tanks to clear mines on the beaches, and most dramatically of all it deployed two great floating harbours that were towed across and assembled in Normandy. It needed a level of sophistication of which Stalin, for one, had no conception.

The timing was largely dictated by tides and weather, but also by American and Russian pressure for an early result. The final plan was for 5 June, but the weather was clearly unsuitable. It was launched the following day during a brief and uncertain weather window, but even then sea conditions were worse than had been planned for. Despite that, it was highly successful on four out of five beaches, with casualties far fewer than had been expected. This might be taken to mean that Churchill was over-cautious, except that heavy casualties on the American Omaha Beach suggest the contrary. In any case the foothold in northern Europe was established and within a month the armies were advancing out of the beachheads. Meanwhile, on 20 July, a group of German officers failed to assassinate Hitler. In effect this ended another of Churchill's dreams, that the regime would be overthrown by forces within Germany itself.

★   ★   ★

Churchill's improving health and the progressive liberation of Europe offered more opportunities for short-range travel, which form a story of their own. He wanted to land in Normandy on D-Day, 6 June itself, but the King threatened to go with him, which stopped that project. He did land there on the 12th in the destroyer HMS *Kelvin* and toured the area by jeep and DUKW. He was back again in July, when he flew in by US Army Air Force DC-3 and visited the newly liberated towns of Cherbourg and Caen and the artificial harbour, partly created out of his imagination, at Arromanches. A few days later he flew to Naples again in his York, and watched the Allied landings in the south of France from the destroyer *Kimberley*, before travelling to many places in Italy. Again he was exhausted, and arrived back at Northolt on 29 August with a temperature of 103.

This illness did not last long and he was about to resume his long-distance travels. He wanted to discuss the war in Italy, the role that British forces were to play in the Pacific, and the settlement of Germany after the war. His idea for another three-power conference fell through when Stalin refused to leave the Soviet Union, and Roosevelt declined an invitation to Britain in the absence of Stalin; and in any case he had to face his own re-election that November. Churchill suggested Quebec again and on 12 August, while the Prime Minister was in Italy, the President accepted.

Roosevelt was keen to keep the size of the party down, partly because hiring the Château Frontenac Hotel again during the tourist season would give a clear indication of what was happening. Also perhaps, he appreciated how much advantage a large and experienced travelling party had given to the British at Casablanca. Churchill, as always, was in favour of the larger group. He would be away from home for about three weeks and had to take an adequate cipher staff and office organisation with him. The Chiefs of Staff would also require their own advisers, particularly as a large part of the conference would be about the Far East, with which they were less familiar. He proposed seven for his own party and private secretaries plus an administrative staff of six. He needed 42 clerical and 30 cipher staff, with a marine guard of 36. These were 'the machinery with which I carry on my work and without which I could not leave the country'.

By mid-August, as Churchill travelled in Italy, there was no decision about the means of travel. The *Queen Mary* was the most likely, but it would involve a delay and the Air Ministry was to be warned to get a Clipper ready, while the Liberator AL 504 was a possibility. At that stage, however, Churchill was still considered to be 'very well in spite of his yellow pills', according to Thompson.

September began in an optimistic mood, with Churchill looking back to the last war. 'The glorious events in France and in the Balkans have completely altered the whole outlook of the war and with people like the Germans anything might happen. Last time Bulgaria proved the lynch pin which when pulled brought everything crashing down.' On 4 September the port of Antwerp was captured almost intact, much shortening the Allied supply lines towards Germany. Operation Market Garden, a plan to capture the Rhine bridges by paratroop landings, was scheduled for the 17th.

There was a feeling that the long war with Germany, which had begun almost exactly five years ago, was almost over. But during all this, Churchill had lost sight of another point. He was now aware of the full horror of the Nazi death camps and on 11 July he had minuted the Foreign Secretary about 'the greatest and most horrible crime ever committed in the whole history of the world'. Yet plans to publicise this, or to bomb the railway lines carrying the prisoners to extermination, were never brought forward as he became more absorbed in his travels.

Churchill's health seemed to improve quickly after his return from Italy, but Moran was naturally cautious about more travelling, even in the luxury of the *Queen Mary*, in which he would be away from specialist medical help. He arranged for a leading bacteriologist, Sir Lionel Whitby, to come on the trip, as well as a nurse, Mrs Pugh. Their role was to be kept secret to avoid fears about Churchill's health leaking out.

There was no specific cover plan this time. It was obviously a repeat of Quadrant, and getting the *Queen Mary* ready would give a clear signal to anyone who knew about it. Instead, the British side relied on the strictest security arrangements to prevent a leak.

★　★　★

Administrative arrangements in Quebec were to be handled by Miss Joan Bright, a 33-year-old temporary civil servant who normally ran the Secret Intelligence Centre in the War Cabinet Office. Born in Argentina to much-travelled British parents, she lived in Spain for some time before doing a secretarial course in London. She developed a great affection for what most people considered a rather menial trade, only fit to occupy a young woman until she found a suitable husband: 'With a shorthand pad and a typewriter I could be a valuable and mobile interpreter of others' thoughts, a human machine with the power to give and receive confidence.' Even typing could be compared with playing the piano, interpreting words rather than music. She worked for the British Embassy in Mexico before being sent home because of an unsuitable romance. Just before the war she began typing for a Territorial Army Unit and gravitated towards more secret work. By 1940 she was in the War Cabinet Offices under General Ismay, setting up an information system to be consulted by visiting commanders. She created an elaborate filing system for war information.

Joan Bright had great organising ability combined with charm, with an eye for detail but never losing sight of the broader picture. She needed great tact, for example when allocating hotel rooms or ship's cabins to dignitaries. She rose through the ranks but never lost touch with her roots. She was still flexible enough to do shorthand and typing for General Ismay as required, and she lamented the condition of her former colleagues during voyages: 'How actually would these men in their comfortable quarters get on if they had no shorthand typists? Does it ever occur to them that the girls are not working less hard but that they are certainly less well provided for?'

Miss Bright was flown out by Clipper with her clerk on 31 August. She travelled in unaccustomed luxury in the 'honeymoon suite' but was used to wartime austerity and did not know to unfold her blankets during the night, so that she was far colder than she needed to be. Of her organisation, Colonel Cornwall-Jones of the Ministry of Defence thought that 'no one could do it better' but he wanted an even stronger party. The Americans would probably send three full colonels who would 'take charge to our disadvantage'. He had underestimated her ability.

There had been some complaints about excessive privilege last time, particularly in the free drinks which were paid for by the Canadian Government, even though members of the party had an additional allowance of 3 dollars a day. The question had come to a head in Cairo, and some thought that it was 'approaching a scandal'. This time drink, apart from wine, would be served free at meals but on other occasions they would have to sign a chit behind the bar, and pay for them out of their allowance. At least they would be duty free.

★　★　★

Meanwhile the first train left London for the conference, carrying Lords Leathers and Cherwell, General Ismay and most members of the planning staff. The Prime Minster's Special Train left Addison Road Station in London at 9.40 in the morning of 5 September and Colville found it luxurious. He lunched with the Prime Minister and his wife, the three Chiefs of Staff, Lord Moran and his wife and younger son who were travelling to Scotland, John Martin and Tommy Thompson. There was a setback after 20 minutes when it was found that the Prime Minister had forgotten his glasses, and a message had to be sent back to get them. They stopped briefly at Carlisle, where they received a report that Hitler was about to sue for peace. Churchill phoned Eden and someone suggested that they might have to turn back before sailing, but nothing came of it. They arrived at Greenock at 7 in the evening and Churchill inspected a guard of honour. As the party was transferred by tender to the *Mary*, Moran watched his wife and son standing on the quay, until 'the Admiral's Flag Lieutenant, splendid in his golden ropes, appeared and took charge of them and their rather inadequate luggage and the two disreputable bicycles'.

Most of his travelling party were used to the *Queen Mary* and this time took the trip in their stride. To Elizabeth Layton, the second Quebec Conference 'did not have the glitter and magnitude of the first, nevertheless it was a most welcome break and also an opportunity to stock up one's system with food – food of which one sometimes dreamed'. John Colville was an exception to the general indifference, for it was his first transatlantic voyage, and his first overseas trip as the Prime Minister's secretary, apart from the return from Marrakech.

Colville was particularly impressed with the accommodation. Two years ago he had travelled to South Africa in the squalor of a troopship, and returned in slightly more comfort as a sergeant-pilot, but this was very different: 'I found a spacious cabin and devoured an even larger and more spacious quantity of dinner (oysters, champagne, etc.).' Admiral Cunningham was another new traveller, and he found it rather different from his usual standards on a battleship. 'It was difficult to realise one was in a ship and not a hotel. I had a suite with sleeping cabin, two sitting rooms and three bathrooms, and on leaving my palatial quarters, I was always in doubt whether to turn right or left to go forward or aft.' Brooke occupied the same cabin as on the last two trips, but he was not looking forward to the conference, as Churchill was becoming increasingly difficult to work with, and was obsessed with his idea of an invasion of Sumatra as an alternative to the campaign in Burma. Brooke himself was 'frightfully mentally tired and disinclined for a difficult conference'.

The *Queen Mary* had been due to sail on 3 September, as part of a tight schedule, and it was noted that 'any postponement ... would definitely prejudice trooping programme of this and another big ship'. It was held up by Churchill's illness, even though several thousand American wounded were already on board. When he later heard that the waiting time would come off their leave, he asked the American authorities to extend their time at home.

The *Queen Mary* was again commanded by James Bissett, now promoted to commodore, or senior captain, of the Cunard Line. He was sent north to Glasgow wearing the single broad strip of his new rank and told to expect a Very Important Person with his Special Party. He was on board before he was told officially that it was the Prime Minister with his 195-strong group. The ship sailed at 8.30 p.m. on the 5th, under cover of darkness, carrying a total of 3,594 passengers and 1,107 crew. The ship was now fitted with radar which could detect U-boats on the surface and help prevent collisions. In any case the Admiralty was much more confident about dealing with the U-boat threat, since the invasion of France had forced them to abandon their bases in the Bay of Biscay. However they had developed the schnorkel, the retractable tube which allowed them to stay underwater for much longer periods, and they were mounting an inshore campaign in British waters, which for the moment was mostly taking place in the north of Scotland. The southern route through the Irish Sea was much safer now, and the *Queen Mary* was routed that way for the first time since the war began.

The main party was headed as usual by Churchill and his group of 13 – two secretaries, both Thompsons, four typists led by Mrs Hill, Lord Moran and Sawyers. Mrs Churchill came too, but Sarah was to busy to get away. In addition there was an extra detective sergeant and two marines as orderlies. The Ministry of War Transport brought seven civil servants, while the First Sea Lord had 12 officers, three typists and a petty officer steward. The CIGS's group was even larger, with 15 officers and seven warrant officers and NCOs, while the Air Ministry contented itself with a total of 13, and the Combined Operations Organisation had only five. The War Cabinet Offices provided the conference secretariat from the British side, so it had officers, officials, clerks and typists. Lord Cherwell needed only two staff of his own. There were 17 WRNS cipher officers, though not Miss Drax this time. A party of six WAAF cipherers had already gone ahead to set things up in Quebec. There was a party of marines under a major, as well as six naval communications ratings and an RAF corporal to repair office equipment. The group overflowed from the sealed-off area on the main deck and filled a huge dining room. The marine guard took over the library on the Promenade Deck above.

Churchill found a certain amount of time to relax and read Anthony Trollope's novel *Phineas Finn*, about a young man with no strong party allegiances who made an impression on the House of Commons at a very early age. The war news was good and there was a mood of optimism. He went down to the Map Room regularly to watch the advance through Italy and according to Captain Pim:

> It was always a source of pleasure to the Prime Minister to mark in chinagraph pencil in very considerable detail advances made by the various Divisions and Brigades, and if just a little bit of wishful thinking was included and the advance portrayed somewhat opti-mistically, at least no harm resulted.[1]

On the morning of the 7th Mrs Churchill listened to the ship's radio and sent a note to her husband a few cabins away:

> Darling – How are you this morning?
> What a rousing news Bulletin this Morning! Calais, Boulogne. Dunkirk, Le Havre, more and more closely invested – 19,000 Pris-oners to the poor unnoticed British! Is the Moselle the frontier between France & Germany? Because if so we are in the Reich.[2]

Unfortunately it was not, and there was still much fighting to do. However, Mrs Churchill was equally pleased to hear that the Home Guard was being disbanded, recognising at last that there was no threat of invasion.

Colville read numerous political and economic files that had been brought with the party, but found time to walk on deck where he got into conversation with an American Liberator pilot, one of the few who had returned safely after a full tour of duty bombing Germany. The American thought it was appro-priate that his countrymen had named this great ship after a British queen. Colville pointed out that it was a British ship, and showed him the ensign at the stern:

> He gasped. 'You mean this really is British? And the *Queen Elizabeth* too?'
> 'Yes, I do.'
> 'But they're the biggest in the world. How could our Government have let themselves be out-smarted like that?'[3]

Cunningham used his seaman's eye to keep a watch on the escorting cruisers, and he was more satisfied than Pound had been. 'It said a lot for the

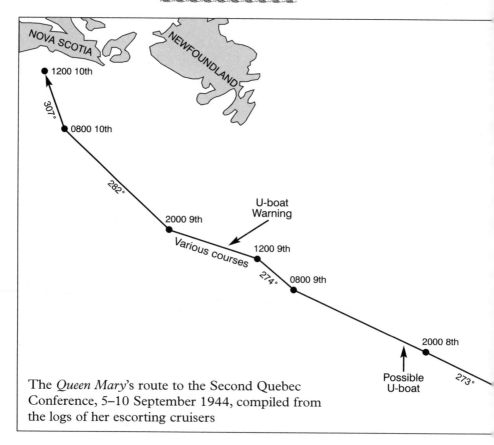

NOVA SCOTIA

NEWFOUNDLAND

● 1200 10th

307°

● 0800 10th

282°

U-boat
Warning

2000 9th

Various courses

1200 9th

274°

0800 9th

2000 8th

Possible
U-boat

273°

The *Queen Mary*'s route to the Second Quebec
Conference, 5–10 September 1944, compiled from
the logs of her escorting cruisers

steaming qualities of the sixteen-year old cruisers *Kent*, *Berwick* and *Devon-shire* which in turn escorted us out and home, that they were able to keep station on the *Queen Mary* at 29 knots and sometimes more.' The *Kent* was the escort when the ship left the south coast of Ireland in the afternoon of the 6th, and headed south-west. For a time that evening she was joined by two destroyers, the Tribal class *Tartar* and *Iroquois,* though the area off the Bay of Biscay was not as dangerous as it had been, since the U-boat bases there had been almost abandoned.

Soon after dawn on the 8th the *Kent* came abeam of the *Queen Mary* and began to take signals for onwards despatch, though it was another hour before the new escort, the *Berwick*, joined company. The *Kent* left just after midday. At 8.41 that evening, the *Berwick*'s radar detected an object six miles away, bearing 305 degrees and not far off the ship's course of 274 degrees. It was quickly assessed as a possible U-boat and signalled by light to the *Queen Mary*. Course was altered to port, and it was soon left behind.

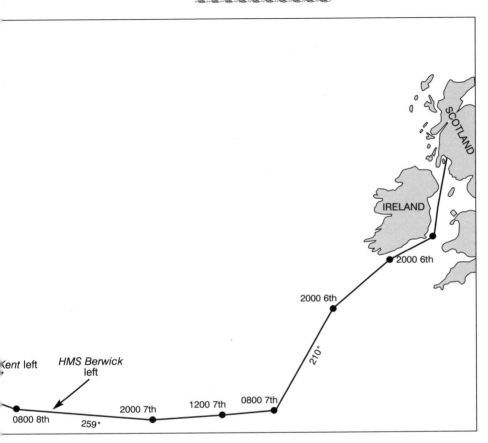

By that time they were in the Gulf Stream, to which, according to Colville, 'our national debt has never been sufficiently acknowledged'. Churchill went on to read another Trollope novel, *The Duke's Children*, as recommended by Colville, but the oppressive heat was beginning to affect him. At a Chiefs of Staff meeting, Brooke noticed that he 'looked old, unwell and depressed. Evidently he found it hard to concentrate and kept holding his head between his hands. He was quite impossible to work with, began by accusing us of framing up against him and of opposing him in his wishes.' Churchill wanted to alter course to get out of the Gulf Stream faster, and sent for Captain Bissett to discuss it, but he and Cunningham were adamant that they could not deviate from the route laid down by the Admiralty except to avoid dangers. At midday on the 9th John Colville noticed a drop in temperature of 20 degrees as they left the Gulf Stream, and there was a diversion to the south as a U-boat, which had been operating in the Cabot Straits between Newfoundland and mainland Canada, was believed to be in the vicinity. Still the Prime Minister's mood did not improve. That evening they watched a film starring Greer Garson and Walter Pidgeon on the life of the radium scientist Marie Curie, which even Brooke enjoyed. But the events of the next day inspired the CIGS to produce one of his most savage criticisms of his chief in his private diary:

> He knows no details, has only got half the picture in his mind, talks absurdities and makes my blood boil to listen to his nonsense. I find it hard to remain civil. And the wonderful thing is that ¾ of the population of the world imagine that Winston Churchill is one of the Strategists of History, a second Marlborough, and the other ¼ have no conception of what a public menace he is and has been throughout this war!

Brooke later admitted that these criticisms were 'unnecessarily hard' and 'written in a moment of exasperation', but the voyage continued to be a difficult one for the Chief of Imperial General Staff.

At 8.18 on the morning of the 10th the ships crossed the 100 fathom line which showed they were approaching land, and at midday they sighted Chebucto Light almost dead ahead. An hour later they were inside the great harbour at Halifax and the *Queen Mary* began to disembark her distinguished passengers before proceeding to New York, while the *Berwick* moored alongside a jetty to await the return trip.

The party was greeted by Malcolm Macdonald the High Commissioner (the equivalent of an ambassador for a Commonwealth country), and the Prime Minister of Nova Scotia, a province of Canada. A special train was waiting and Olive Christopher, a typist, and one of her friends were impressed with conditions on board; 'Sylvia and I were thrilled with Canadian trains and gurgled happily when confronted with the splendid array in the "Ladies'-Room" (as compared with our own scruffy trains!) Pale green marble washbasins, pale green pile carpet and curtains to match. All the towels, glasses, etc., were sterilised.' The journey took 21 hours, during which the people of various towns turned out to see the Prime Minister, especially where there was a stop to change the engines or take on water.

★　★　★

The train arrived in Quebec at 10 a.m. on the 11th, to find that the President and his wife had arrived by train shortly before them. They were greeted by the Governor-General, the Earl of Athlone and his wife Princess Alice, a granddaughter of Queen Victoria. The principals were taken to the Citadel, while the others went to the Château Frontenac Hotel. That evening there was a large dinner party hosted by Princess Alice, including generals and admirals from Britain, the USA and Canada, the Archbishop of Quebec, the Canadian Prime Minister and many others.

There were several disappointments awaiting Churchill in Quebec. The first was that Harry Hopkins was in poor health and was no longer in the President's inner circle, so he did not attend the conference. Roosevelt too was in decline. Colville met him for the first time and was not impressed as he greeted him 'for several minutes in flowery language as if I was a public meeting'. He relaxed later but said 'nothing impressive or even memorable and his eyes seemed glazed'. To Moran's more expert eye, 'He seemed to me to have lost a couple of stone in weight – you could have put your fist between his neck and his collar.'

The city of Quebec was disappointing to some of the entourage, for its shops had still not recovered from their spree last year. Elizabeth Layton found that 'our demands in the stocking line could not be fulfilled'. Olive Christopher had not been there before, and was much more excited after blacked-out London. She looked out of her hotel bedroom to see 'all the lights winking at us. Lighted trains sliding like glowworms across the sky, the lights of cars winding their way down the hills opposite'.

> Quebec, however, was quite the noisiest city I know. Guns fire, river boats boom, taxis squeak impertinently, bicycle bells tinkle incessantly, church bells ring, motor klaxons shriek, trains whistle, pneumatic drills brrr-brrr, and three tines a day the band plays 'God save the King', 'O Canada' and 'Star Spangled Banner' in quick succession.[4]

Miss Bright had already taken a good deal of trouble over the allocation of rooms:

> In the peace of the interim wait Tony Bishop and I spent three and a half hours walking round the vast hotel looking at each bedroom to see whether our allocations fitted in with the size of the room and the rank of the occupant, whether there were twin beds or double beds in rooms destined to be shared. We found out two which we had to change: the first, into which we had put a brigadier alone, was an inside box with no basin or cupboard; the other, which we had given to two Royal Marine orderlies, turned out to be one of the finest and most luxurious rooms on the upper floor of the hotel.[5]

To Miss Christopher food was 'marvellous' after British rationing. 'I used to have sliced fresh peaches, lashings of cream and sugar and coffee every morning for my breakfast.' Work in the office, however, was 'pretty hellish'. There were 28 meetings in five days and typists were nominally on duty from 8 in the morning until 3.30 or 4 the next morning, though Miss Christopher managed to get two hours shopping in the middle of the day by foregoing her lunch, and she was usually relieved by 6 or 10 in the evening. There was dancing every evening in the hotel, but she was only able to go twice. She bought a dress, a 'hyacinth blue moss crepe suit, superbly cut, with three quarter length sleeves' and wore it to a reception held by the Canadian Prime Minister Mackenzie King.

The first plenary session was held in the morning of 13 September, when Churchill noted how everything had 'turned to gold' since their last meeting in Cairo ten months ago. The British got their way on a reinvigoration of the Italian campaign quite quickly. That evening over dinner, Churchill disputed the future of Germany with Henry Morgenthau, the US Secretary of the Treasury. Morgenthau wanted to 'pastoralise' Germany, to destroy her industry and eliminate her war potential. Churchill felt that it was wrong to punish a whole people and quoted the eighteenth-century Tory philosopher Edmund Burke: 'You cannot indict a whole nation.' He said repeatedly, 'What is to be done should be done quickly. Kill the criminals, but don't carry on the business for years.' A few years later he would put on the front of his war history, 'In victory: magnanimity.'

On the 14th the British plan for their intervention in the Pacific was accepted. With the Italian and German surface fleets almost out of the picture, it was now possible to send a force to the Far East, with a large number of aircraft carriers and their support vessels. Despite the support of Roosevelt, this was strongly resisted by the anglophobe Admiral King. In practice the British Pacific Fleet would find it very difficult to make an impact on the war, as its resources were stretched and it was much less practised than the Americans in long-distance operations and in techniques such as refuelling at sea.

Relations between Churchill and his military advisers remained strained throughout the conference. Ismay, 'dear old patient Pug' as Brooke called him, reached the end of his tether and offered his resignation, which was ignored by Churchill. Brooke himself resented the fact that Churchill kept sending for them, although 'it entailed collecting cars and driving up and back to the Citadel, which wasted precious time'.

The final plenary session was held at noon on the 16th, and after lunch the President and Prime Minister were conferred honorary degrees by McGill

University. There was a press conference before the President left at 5 p.m. Churchill provided a justification for his insistence on such meetings:

What an ineffectual method of conveying human thought correspondence is – (laughter) – telegraphed with all its rapidity, all the facilities of our – of modern intercommunication. They are simply dead, blank walls compared to personal – personal contacts. And that applies not only to the President and the Prime Minister of Great Britain, it applies to the principal officers who at every stage enter the closest association, and have established friendships which have greatly aided the tasks and toil of the fighting troops.[6]

Churchill and some of the most senior people went to a dinner party hosted by Lord Athlone. Next morning Mrs Churchill attended a service in the cathedral, and the party began to disperse.

The Chiefs of Staff flew north for a fishing trip in Oriskany, looking like peasants in their civilian clothes. Cunningham had to leave early to rejoin Churchill, but the others had great success. Churchill sent them a very official-looking telegram which asked, 'Please let me know how many captives were taken by land and air forces respectively in the Battle of Snow Lake.' Portal replied that 'Enemy forces were aggressive throughout' but 'Casualties inflicted by our land and air forces were approximately equal' and that 'our air forces accounted for the largest submarine yet seen in these waters' – a trout caught by Portal. The Boeing Clipper was reserved to take the CIGS and the Chief of Air Staff home on the 21st, and Brooke enjoyed 'a comfortable journey over the clouds' after a take-off from the St Lawrence River.

★ ★ ★

Olive Christopher enjoyed the 14-hour train journey south to New York with Churchill's party:

The country from Quebec until we crossed the border was relatively dull – rather flat and uninteresting. Montreal is very attractive but we were only there about an hour. Immediately we crossed the border the country became magnificent – vast fir forests sweeping away into the distance, tree-covered mountains, terrific waterfalls, lakes – Oh! It was all so lovely. We slid round the shore of Lake Champlain, which is 131 miles long. It took us 2½ hours. We arrived at Grand Central Station, New York at 9.30 p.m.[7]

She visited the city and walked down Broadway. She was not impressed by the 'dim-out', the American answer to the British black-out. 'The lights were brighter there than anything we have ever had in London.'

Churchill went on to visit Roosevelt at Hyde Park again. Harry Hopkins was there but had obviously lost much of his influence and Mrs Churchill found his presence 'sad and rather embarrassing'. The two statesmen discussed plans for the settlement of Italy and heard news that the first ballistic rockets, the V2s, were causing destruction in London. The Duke of Windsor, formerly King Edward VIII before his abdication in 1936, came to lunch. Although Churchill had backed him in the past, the Duke had been less than faithful in his support of the Allied cause and relations were now strained. Mrs Churchill wrote: 'He ... still has a boyish appearance which is rudely dispelled when one sees him close to.' Churchill worked in bed on the morning of the 19th, then he and Clementine had a picnic lunch in the woods with the President and his wife. After that they left by train.

★   ★   ★

John Colville and other members of the party joined the *Queen Mary* at Pier 90 in New York Harbour and she sailed at 7.30 on 19 September. Colville was disappointed that 'The New York skyline only just emerged from the mist through which a very sallow sun was struggling.' For security reasons Churchill did not embark at the pier, but he and the rest of the Hyde Park party were picked up by a tender from Staten Island and Colville thought he was 'looking far better'. The ship was more crowded than on the way out though not operating to full capacity as the build-up of troops in Europe was slowing down. This time she carried 9,084 passengers and 1,110 crew.

As soon as they arrived in Canada, Tommy Thompson had begun to investigate the possibility of a slightly faster route home without disrupting the *Queen Mary*'s schedule. He suggested that the Prime Minister might be taken off by tender farther south in the Irish Sea, and then to his train in a Welsh port, Milford Haven for example. This would allow him to get to London on the evening of 24 September. It had been hoped to route the ship farther to the north this time, across the Grand Banks and avoiding the Gulf Stream, but because a U-boat was still active in the area despite being hunted by USS *Bogue*, the ship went farther south, though still slightly north of the track used last time.

Ismay found the voyage home a 'delightful relaxation'. For the first time he had little work to do and he was able to find time every day for a 'delightful promenade on deck'. As the only one of the Chiefs of Staff on board, Cunningham enjoyed unusual influence with Churchill. 'I was asked to look over the military portions of his speech for the reopening of Parliament. He had a habit of making out that the army was doing nearly all the fighting, so I put in a few amendments.' Olive Christopher had a cabin to herself as most of the party had gone back by other means, and she felt guilty that it might have cost £170 or £200 in peacetime, and that the 9,000 troops were herded together below decks. Life was much easier than on the voyage out, with a 'round of deck tennis, lazing in the sun on the sports deck, and, in the evenings, a round of cocktail parties, dinner parties, etc.'. The highlight was Mrs Churchill's cocktail party on the night of the 24th, though the Prime Minister himself did not attend.

Churchill did a certain amount of work during the voyage, and often played bezique late into the night. He saw far fewer films than in the past. In the afternoon of the 21st he watched newsreels about the war, but that could not be considered something that 'takes the mind away from other things', as on earlier voyages. On the following afternoon he watched the first half of a little-known film about the life of President Wilson, who had tried to bring America out of isolation during and after the First World War, but had been hampered by fatal illness – he did not know how prescient that last part was. It struck some resonances, for it contained a diatribe about German perfidy, and a reminder of the U-boat campaigns in the last war. Wilson was played by the Canadian actor Alexander Knox who was nominated for an Oscar but lost out to Bing Crosby. However, this was not Churchill's usual time of day for films, and he left to go on the bridge for half an hour, and completed the viewing the following afternoon. He lunched with the American generals commanding the troops on board, and showed them around the Map Room. On the bridge that day, he made a point of talking to the ship's engineer officers as well as the commodore.

By midday on the 24th the ships were 400 miles south-west of Ireland and level with La Rochelle in France, when they were joined by the destroyers *Serapis* and *Nubian*. The four ships turned to the north-east for the Bristol Channel. Meanwhile there was news of setbacks in the war effort. It was becoming increasingly clear that the parachute offensive had failed, that Arnhem was 'a bridge too far', in the phrase which became a classic. The fight was not over until the 25th, as Churchill was almost home, and Montgomery withdrew the surviving quarter of the First Airborne Division across the

Rhine. It was seen as a British rather than an Allied defeat, for Montgomery had been its main advocate and British paratroops had formed the spearhead which had failed. Apart from the heavy losses, it was a blow to hopes that the war would end soon. It meant a long fight in which British resources would become increasingly depleted, her economy would suffer and her prestige and influence would decline.

The Prime Minister's train was waiting at Milford Haven, but the plan to take him off by tender in the Irish Sea proved difficult. It needed almost perfect weather and in fact there was a force 4 wind and a moderate swell, so they had to go up the Irish Sea to the Clyde, which they reached around 5 p.m. on the 25th. From Downing Street, John Rowan had organised another special train which was not far inferior to the usual one. It had two saloons of the semi-royal type, each with two beds, two first-class sleepers with twelve berths each, a composite sleeper with first- and third-class berths, an ordinary carriage with 42 seats and a dining car. It left Greenock at 7.50 that evening and was in Euston Station in London by 10 next morning, where it was met by members of the Cabinet. Churchill was able to take questions in the House that afternoon. He was not to stay inactive for long.

XVI
Percentages in Moscow

Churchill had already conceived the idea of a second visit to Moscow by the time he was back from Quebec in September 1944, and on the 27th, the day after he arrived in London, he asked Portal for a plan to get there. It was Churchill's idea alone. Roosevelt was not prepared to travel any great distance with an election in hand. Stalin was not prepared to travel at all; he told Harriman his doctors had told him 'any change in climate would have a bad effect'. He hinted at admiration for Churchill, 'that desperate fellow' who was always flying around the world. To the British Ambassador he 'grumbled about his own health' – he was never well except in Moscow, and the visit to Tehran had made him ill for a fortnight.

Churchill was convinced that there were advantages in his going to see Stalin. On one level, he told John Colville, he wanted to discourage any idea that might be inspired by the Quebec conference, that the USA and Britain were becoming closer and excluding the USSR. At another, he felt that Stalin was in a sympathetic mood now that the second front had been launched at last. This was encouraged on 30 September when Stalin replied to his suggestions for a visit: 'I wholeheartedly welcome your desire to come to Moscow in October. Military and other problems of great importance need to be discussed.' Churchill regarded this as very positive in tone. He telegraphed General Smuts a week later:

> Eden and I are off to see Ursus Major [the Great Bear] and will soon
> be on the wing. I think it vital to get there now and certainly Uncle Joe
> has shown himself more forthcoming than ever before. We must strike
> while the iron is hot.[1]

Churchill had two main issues he wanted to discuss with Stalin. One was Soviet participation in the war against Japan, though Roosevelt was very doubtful about putting this on the agenda, as he did not want a major discussion on it in his own absence. Harriman attended some, but not all, of the meetings to represent the American point of view, but with reservations. Roosevelt wrote to Stalin: 'Mr Harriman would naturally not be in a position to commit this Government in respect of very important matters which very naturally will be discussed by you and Mr Churchill.' To Harriman he wrote: 'My hope is that this bilateral conference should be nothing more than a preliminary exploration by the British and Russians, leading to a full-dress meeting between the three of us.'

The other issue was the settlement of various countries in Europe after the war, of which Poland was still the most important to Churchill. As the Soviet armies approached, the resistance movements in Warsaw revolted against German rule on 1 August. They were savagely repressed, and the Soviet Army refused to push forward to help them. They were defeated by 2 October after more than two months of fighting. It was the end of another of Churchill's hopes. Mass risings of resistance movements were not going to shorten the war. It also meant that Poland was not going to liberate herself without help from the Red Army, and it made the future settlement of the country all the more urgent. One possible reason for Soviet hesitancy was that the resistance leaders supported the exiled Polish Government in London. Stalin had set up his own Polish group based in Lublin, in territory that the Soviet Army had recently occupied. The two groups of Poles had great differences, and Churchill wanted to reconcile them. As always, he believed that the personal touch would make a difference.

Brooke, now promoted to field marshal, was the only Chief of Staff to go with the party. As Churchill told them, he was to 'explain on the map the situation on the Western Front' and also to 'set forth the plans and intentions that we and the Americans have'. He would also describe the situation in Burma and the plans against Japan.

★　★　★

Meanwhile, 'Dad' Collins had fallen out of favour at the Air Ministry. In November 1943, while taking the Chiefs of Staff to Cairo, he had used the device of reporting sick to get better accommodation for his crew in Malta. This had not found favour with the authorities. Later that month at Cairo, Portal was annoyed at being called out of bed for an early take-off when he should have been informed that there was a delay due to fog. The Chief of Air Staff was losing confidence in Collins, and agreed with the C-in-C of Transport Command that he was 'past his prime as a pilot'. Collins was not happy about this and wanted to leave the RAF to seek private work as a VIP pilot, but he was transferred to the staff in the Air Ministry. Bill Fraser was given the job of first pilot and at Churchill's request he was eventually promoted to wing commander. He had been carefully vetted by the secret service, and a Scotsman posing as a friend of his father's had called at his house to make discreet enquiries about him.

Churchill's route to Moscow was discussed at the highest level. Clearly it was going to be far easier than last time, with France, Italy and North Africa now in Allied hands and Turkey sympathetically neutral. SHAEF, or Supreme Head-quarters Allied Expeditionary Forces Europe, was consulted and confirmed that it was safe to fly over France. It was decided to land at Naples to refuel and confer with military leaders in Italy. Next they would make for Egypt, avoiding enemy territory in Greece and Crete. From there they would fly among the Greek and Turkish islands, after getting the latest intelligence about the progress of the war there, and discovering which islands to avoid. They would then fly over the Dardanelles, where Churchill's career had foundered nearly three decades ago. Because relations with Turkey were still uncertain, the authorities would not be told about the flight until it was past the danger points. They would then cross the Black Sea, reaching Soviet territory in the Crimea between Yalta and Sevastopol.

The last part of the flight needed the most detailed negotiation. On 4 October Churchill telegraphed Stalin to outline his needs:

It is not good for me to go much above 8,000 feet, though I can if necessary do so for an hour or so. We think it less of a risk to fly across the Aegean and Black Sea ... So long as we can get down safely to refuel if necessary at Simferopol or at any other operational landing ground on the coast which you may prefer, I shall be quite content with the facilities available. I have everything I want in my plane. The only vital thing is that we may send an aircraft on ahead to establish with you a joint signal regulating our homing and landing.[2]

Stalin agreed that they could land at Sarabuz airfield near Simferopol, and that a signal aircraft could be sent there. The Soviets were sent detailed descriptions of the aircraft to issue to fighters and anti-aircraft gunners – the fuselage of *Ascalon* was described as 'fish-shaped', which might be true in profile, but no fish ever had such a square cross-section.

Two C-87 passenger Liberators left Northolt at nine in the evening of 5 October carrying the advance party for the conference. The first carried the redoubtable Miss Bright, and included six female civil servants and typists, two army sergeants, a wing-commander, a police inspector and two RAF aircraftmen for maintenance duties. Passengers in the second plane comprised four cipher officers, three female and one male, six women typists and another two RAF mechanics. The Russians were fussy about details and had to be provided with each traveller's date of birth and passport number.

★ ★ ★

The main party flew out in the early hours of 8 October, in three aircraft – two from Northolt and one from Lyneham. *Ascalon* was lightly loaded for this trip – only the Prime Minister, Lord Moran, John Martin as secretary, Sawyers and a detective. Walter Thompson, who was ill from the stress of looking after Churchill and the death of his son in a bomber over Germany, was resting in the police convalescent home at Hove. His place was taken by Inspector W. L. Hughes, a quiet Scotsman from Fife who had once been a merchant seaman. He had been with Churchill's Downing Street guard since 1940, so he was not a stranger. According to Mitchell, they were in a jolly frame of mind as they took off from Northolt at 12.10 in the morning of 8 October. 'Everybody gay and in optimistic mood – though we could not know the problems the Old Man had to face with Stalin as a result of the Tehran Conference.' Churchill, however, had had one of his frequent rows with his wife over lunch the day before, and it was preying on his mind. As soon as he could he telegraphed her; 'Anyway forgive me for anything that seemed disrespectful to you, & let your morning thoughts dwell kindly on, yr penitent, apologetic & ever loving W.'

To Mitchell, 'It was a wonderful feeling to leave England Southwards instead of Westwards. We roamed out over Selsey Bill and entered France at Barfleur.' They had checked with Allied headquarters that it was safe to fly over France, and the whole route was a contrast to last time, when the power of the Axis was at its height. It was still a long trip round Germany and Greece, but only 11,000 miles instead of 17,000.

Jack Payne was sent to stay with Churchill as he slept and take his pulse regularly, though as an engineer his 'medical knowledge was at best rudimentary'. He asked Sawyers what Churchill's normal pulse rate was and quoted that. 'Not bad for an old man,' said Churchill. Moran, however, found the York very cold and woke up early on the morning of the 8th. He discovered that Churchill had been taking oxygen throughout the night, though they were not flying above 3,000 feet. As he arrived the Prime Minister was dozing and the mask had fallen off his face on to the bed with oxygen still hissing out of it, while he had a lighted cigar in his hand. 'One day', wrote Moran, 'we shall all go up in flames.' He was about to turn the cylinder off when it emptied and stopped. For once Moran asserted himself and lectured Churchill. 'When the P.M. teaches his soldiers and sailors how to do their job it's their affair, but when he sets up as an apothecary it's time to take a stand. He accepted it meekly.'

They arrived at Pomigliano airport, Naples, after a seven-hour flight, to be met by Generals Wilson and Alexander, Harold Macmillan and Admiral John Cunningham. Brooke's plane landed soon afterwards, and they were driven to a villa in Naples for baths, shaves and breakfast.

General Alexander informed Churchill about the state of the war in Italy, and was not optimistic. When members of the 90th Panzer Division were eventually captured, they were asked why they had continued fighting when it was obvious they were defeated. They answered, 'We belong to the 90th Division. As long as it is in the field we fight.' Churchill and Alexander could not help admiring their spirit, but it did not bode well for the British war effort. There was not going to be a quick victory in Italy, leading to advances in the Balkans. Yet again, Churchill had to accept that it was a fight to the death. He telegraphed Roosevelt saying that he was 'much distressed by their tale' and asking for two or three American divisions to be diverted to Italy where the Allied forces were exhausted.

★　★　★

For the onward flight, Eden transferred to *Ascalon* to talk with the Prime Minister, but Brooke declined the offer with the excuse that he wanted to draft a telegram to London on the results of the conference in Naples. They took off at 11.15 to fly to Cairo. Moran was not entirely happy with the York, and found it very noisy. 'The P.M. addressed half a dozen observations to me during lunch, and I did not hear one of them.' But through Eden he did pick up that there was increasing criticism of him in the Cabinet and medical profession, for allowing the Prime Minister to make these dangerous journeys. Churchill had said, 'A good many people are abusing Charles, but I feel very well.' Eden added that 'more will abuse you when the news comes out at noon', suggesting that the War Cabinet was discussing the matter. However ominous this might have sounded, nothing was reflected in the War Cabinet minutes, and no signal followed.

They flew across the Straits of Messina dividing Italy from Sicily, then went well south as the Germans were still in possession of Greece and Crete. The reached Benghazi in Libya and flew across the desert for the last thousand miles. Approaching Cairo at 8.15 local time, *Ascalon* was directed towards the little used north–south runway in Cairo West. It had 'a nasty crest or bank at the point of touchdown', according to John Mitchell, and it was difficult to see in the dark. For once Bill Fraser misjudged a landing to hit it and bounce into the air. There was no time to use a burst of engine power to break the impact of the next touchdown and the aircraft 'landed, or stalled, with a bang and a rattle!' There were no injuries but Fraser was embarrassed that this should happen on his first trip as captain with the Prime Minister on board, and apologised profusely.

Churchill and his party went for dinner with Lord Moyne, his new minister for the Middle East, now living in the Casey Villa. It was interrupted as the lights went out for a time. They left at midnight to drive to the airport, where there was bad news. *Ascalon's* crew found that one of the oleo legs which supported the undercarriage was seriously damaged. It could be patched up, but that could not be relied on to last and in Moscow there were few facilities for British aircraft such as the York. The only alternative was to fit a new one using the skills of Jack Payne and local help. Although a spare part was available, the repair was a time-consuming process that would not be complete until two in the morning. This would have interrupted the Prime Minister's schedule, so he had to transfer to another York, MW 100, flown by Squadron-Leader Tony Watson. It was less comfortable than *Ascalon,* but it did have bunks. The party now included Churchill, Eden, Brooke, Ismay, Moran, Martin, Thompson and Corporal Lockwood, Brooke's batman. It took off at one in the morning of the 9th.

★ ★ ★

During the flight across the Aegean they avoided islands such as Lemnos, Leros, Kos, Rhodes and the western half of Crete, which were still in enemy hands and had partially manned anti-aircraft guns. They were less worried about enemy aircraft, for there were no enemy fighters left in Greece, only reconnaissance and transport aircraft. They crossed into neutral Turkey near the Greek border at Alexandropolis and flew parallel to the Dardanelles to avoid the mountains and major towns. They were not worried about intervention from the Turks, whose air force was British trained and largely pro-Allied, unlike their army and navy. English-speaking liaison officers were placed in selected airfields by the Turkish government, in case of any possible misunderstanding.

They crossed the Black Sea where the Soviet Navy provided air-sea rescue facilities, and reached Soviet territory at the Crimea, but Brooke could see nothing as it was still dark and the cloud base was low. There was no need to land at Simferopol to refuel. After breakfast of shredded wheat, boiled egg and ham, Brooke looked out of the aircraft window to see signs of war such as 'derelict trenches, gun emplacements, demolished houses, anti-tank ditches etc'. But he felt that the country had not been so heavily fought over as some

Right: Churchill wears earguards during firing practice in the *Renown*. (IWM H 32941)

Below: An aerial view over the Pyramids, showing the site of the Cairo conference with Mena House on the centre right. (IWM TC 10778)

Above: Stalin raises a toast to Churchill for his 69th birthday. (IWM A 20731)

Below: The Stalingrad Sword after it was handed over. Portal, Churchill and Eden look on. (IWM NYF 12902)

Above: Churchill meets local Arab chieftains during his convalescence. (IWM K 6610)

Below: Brendan Bracken, General Ismay and Mary Churchill on Churchill's train. (IWM H 32957)

Below: Quebec – Mackenzie King, Smuts, Roosevelt, Pricncess Alice and Churchill on the roof of the Citadel, with the Château Frontenac behind. (IWM H 32139)

Right: The Vorontsov Palace at Yalta. (Coward-McCann)

Below right: With Roosevelt during the Yalta conference. (IWM EA 52857)

Left: The control room at Gatow airfield. (IWM CL 3161)

Below left: Churchill tours the ruins of Hitler's Chancellery in Berlin. (IWM BU 8962)

Right: Churchill meets Truman at Potsdam. (IWM BU 8944)

Below: The Potsdam conference in session. Churchill has Eden to his right, with Attlee two places to his left. (IWM BU 8985)

Churchill after his return from Potsdam in the Skymaster. (IWM BU CL 3159)

of the more devastated parts of France, where the conflict was much more intense over a small area.

The flight to Moscow was much more carefully controlled than last time, with detailed directions from the Soviets and numerous radio beacons to take fixes on. They were to proceed directly, while avoiding large towns. They were not to fly above thick cloud, or at more than 5,000 feet. Various emergency airfields were listed in case of need. Despite all the planning, they could not find the airfield, perhaps because John Mitchell was not there to navigate them. According to Brooke: 'It became evident that the pilot was not quite clear where he was, and he started hawking around and finally found an aerodrome.' They put down safely but it was the wrong place. They were told to head for another aerodrome 30 kilometres farther on, so they took off again. As they approached, this aircraft too had difficulty with its undercarriage. It would not come down properly and had to be lowered by means of the emergency compressed air. They finally landed at Moscow Central Airfield just before noon.

The delayed *Ascalon* had eventually taken off at 2.15 in the morning after Jack Payne and his helpers had 'worked like demons' to repair the undercarriage. Because it had only four passengers, it followed a different route, flying over Jordan, Turkey and the Caucasus Mountains. John Mitchell thought the flight over Russia was 'a navigator's nightmare. We had to report our precise position every sixty minutes and always fly in contact with the ground – with blithe Slavonic disregard of the cloud base. This led to some pretty hair-raising moments, especially over Moscow!' It proved difficult to use radio bearings because only a Soviet operator was allowed to turn the tuning key in ground headquarters, while a British operator made the transmission. According to Mitchell, 'To all intents and purposes, we had either to map-read or Bradshaw our way across tens of thousands of acres of flat, featureless landscape.'

★ ★ ★

The welcome in Moscow was far more effusive than ever before, now that the second front had been launched. According to Brooke, when they finally found the right airport they were met by 'Molotov, Maisky, a bevy of Russian Generals, Clark Kerr, Brocas Burrows, etc, etc. A guard of honour to be inspected and marched past, the whole of God Save the King and the Russian national anthem. Finally a broadcast speech by Winston.'

Churchill had hoped to stay in the same house as the previous time, but instead he was offered a dacha 20 miles from the city centre. Elizabeth Layton found it unimpressive from the outside, and surrounded by a palisade and a wooden gate. It was comfortable inside, but the service was unconventional, even in the wing allocated to the junior members of the entourage:

> We were much impressed by the service of the Russian maids, one of whom was always in attendance to scrub one's back when bathing. They made our beds in such a queer way, too, folding the sheets and blankets together with the corners underneath, so that when once beneath them one had to keep still or everything fell off – one couldn't get *into* bed. We were told that the reason for this was that the Russian people have a trapped feeling if tucked into bed.[3]

According to Thompson, the house was run by a 'very pleasant middle-aged woman in the black alpaca garb of a Victorian English housekeeper; round her waist was a chain bearing an enormous bunch of keys'.

Churchill too was pleased with the house when he arrived earlier than Miss Bright and her staff had expected, but not for the first time he had trouble with his bath. Sawyers was still dealing with the luggage and Churchill tried to run the bath himself. He turned on one tap that was marked 'hot' with sticking plaster, but because it was not hot straight away he turned it off. He called for Sawyers but Moran came instead, to turn on another tap which emitted a blast of icy water over Churchill. Inspector Hughes ran down the stairs calling out, 'The Prime Minister doesn't know which is the hot tap and the bath is filling with cold water!'

Churchill also had the use of a smaller house in Ostrovkaya Street near the city centre. There was only room enough for him, Martin, Moran and Sawyers, and he found it very noisy. Miss Layton managed to persuade the guards to stop chattering, but it was impossible to turn off the street public-address system, which broadcast a 'howling' soprano. Telephone lines were poor, and the Prime Minister objected to John Martin trying to make himself heard over a bad line. The last straw came when hammering was heard inside the house, and had to be stopped.

The instructions for the travellers offered a sample of Russian culture to those who wanted it. Sights included the Historical Museum, where they could usually find an interpreter, St Basil's Cathedral, and the Park of Rest and Culture with a display of captured German weapons. Unfortunately Lenin's tomb was closed due to the war. Shopping was possible, though goods were not plentiful. Small bowls and Russian dolls could be bought quite cheaply as souvenirs, and parties were organised by Miss Bright. There was a symphony concert on the 11th, including Tchaikovsky's Fifth, and a performance of *The*

Bachschiserai Fountains – 'a spectacular ballet'. The following evening the opera offered *Prince Igor,* 'The most spectacular if not the most musically perfect show in Moscow.' The following night there was 'Eugen O'Negin' [sic], Russia's No. 1 classic'.

Brooke sampled most of these delights during his visit, and had his own opinions. The exhibition in the Park of Culture included 'captured German weapons of all types, from veterinary equipment to aeroplanes' and was 'A very well run show.' At what he called 'the Moscow equivalent of Selfridges', the counters were crammed with goods at 'frightful prices', for example an eider-down for £10. However, there were many articles that could not be found in Britain, and children's toys which were 'far better than you could raise in Hamley's'.

Stalin and Churchill were locked in talks on the night of the 13th, so four-teen seats at the ballet were allocated to other members of the party, a dozen in a box and two more in the stalls. The stalls tickets were given to two sergeant clerks but it turned out that despite Soviet ideology, 'other ranks' were not allowed there. Instead they were given places in the box, and two brigadiers of the staff took their place. Brooke found that 'the scenery was again uncannily good, the duel scene was by half light in the snow amongst snow covered birch trees, with a cold mist rising up from the valley and a changing sky of pearl grey with a few occasional breaks of light. The singing was also quite beautiful.'

The night of the 14th was set aside for a special command performance in the Bolshoi Theatre attended by the principals. Churchill, Harriman and Stalin sat together in the Royal Box (if such a name was appropriate in revolutionary Russia). It was a great compliment to the visitors, as Stalin rarely appeared in public. Churchill stood up during the first interval and was cheered by the audi-ence, and the roar was even louder when the Russian dictator stood up beside him. The performance of the first act of *Giselle* was not exactly to Churchill's taste, but he became more animated when Russian military marches were played in the second part of the entertainment.

The crew of *Ascalon* knew how to make the best of the situation in any foreign city. Despite their exhaustion, they enjoyed a party organised by Brigadier 'Pop' Hill of 30 Mission, the British military mission in Moscow. They sang *John Peel* and *Auld Lang Syne* until well into the night, after which they retired to the National Hotel, where Brooke and many of his staff were also staying. This was a 'shabby but comfortable hotel of late Victorian – or rather Tsarist – style with plush and dusty chandeliers'. They were tended to by women receptionists, telephone operators and guides whom they suspected were in the pay of the secret service, the NKVD – apparently their silk stockings had to be returned to the store after the visit. There, according to Mitchell, 'every meal was the same. We started with caviar and vodka and went on to all sorts of smoked fish and then a vast assortment of cold meats. There were bottles and bottles of wine with every course. Passers-by would stare at us through the windows of the Hotel restaurant, squashing their noses against the glass and licking their lips. This made us ashamed of our appetites.'

The crew, the '*Equipage Churchill*', was wildly popular with the Red Air Force and with the citizens of Moscow. They sat in the next box to Churchill at the Bolshoi Theatre, and were given a special tour of the Kremlin arranged by Tommy Thompson. They had easy access to the airport, which was normally denied even to the British air attaché. They were allowed a squad of Russian 'Mrs Mops' to clean out the aircraft until it was spotless. But they went too far when they dressed a stuffed bear in their hotel in a RAF greatcoat. The manager told them severely that a Russian bear needed only one greatcoat, of fur.

★ ★ ★

Life in Moscow settled into a routine during the ten days the party was there. Churchill worked on his papers in bed every morning, had lunch, then a nap, and was ready for a meeting in the late afternoon. Most evenings there was entertainment and a late finish, even by Churchill standards. On the 13th, for example, he telegraphed Clementine:

> Everything is going well here and there is great cordiality. Life is however the same, I did not get to bed till 4 am this morning. I have a house in Moscow as well as in the country, both splendidly served. I am just off to the country house, 45 minutes away, as we are going to have a quiet night tonight.[4]

On the question of Japan, it was agreed that Harriman and Major-General John R. Deane would put forward the American view as the British military representative, General Brocas Burrows, was out of favour after hidden Soviet microphones had apparently revealed his contempt for the Red Army. General Deane decided to take the bull by the horns and ask Stalin directly – How soon after the defeat of Germany would the Soviet Union declare war on Japan? How long would it take them to build up forces for an offensive in the Far East? Could the Trans-Siberian Railway be used to support an American air offensive against Japan? Churchill was impressed: 'Young man, I admired your nerve in asking Stalin those last three questions. I have no idea that you will get an answer, but there was certainly no harm in asking.' To everyone's surprise, Stalin told them next evening that the Soviets would take the offensive three months after the German surrender. The Americans would be allowed air bases, but would have to bring their supplies across the Pacific.

The main issue of the talks was the post-war settlement of Europe. Churchill said to Stalin, 'Your armies are in Rumania and Bulgaria. We have interests, missions, and agents there. Don't let us get at cross-purposes in small ways.' Churchill then suggested the percentage interest of each state in all the countries concerned, and wrote it down on a piece of paper, which he later called his 'naughty' document. There was to be a 50–50 split on Yugoslavia and Hungary, with 90 per cent Soviet predominance in Rumania, 75 per cent in Bulgaria and 90 per cent British and American influence in Greece. Churchill passed it to Stalin, who put a tick on the top right-hand corner. Churchill soon had cold feet about this way of doing business, as it might be thought a very casual way to settle the fate of millions of people, and it had overtones of the old imperial idea of 'spheres of influence' which was anathema to the Americans. He suggested burning the paper, but Stalin told him to keep it. Eventually, after much hesitation, he reproduced it in his history of the war.

Churchill worried about the impact of 'proselytising Communism' on the world, but perhaps that was not the real issue. Arguably that idea had been abandoned with the policy of 'Socialism in one country' when Stalin came to power in the 1920s. Communist parties and sympathisers in other countries were useful to him as political weapons or occasionally for espionage, but they did not actively foment revolution. Moscow tended to react to events rather than initiate them, as with Spain in the 1930s or later, for example, with Greece and Cuba. But none of this undermined Stalin's desire to maintain a strong buffer zone under his control between the Soviet Union and Germany.

The 13th was set aside as 'all Poles day', as Churchill described it to the King. An aircraft of 24 Squadron had been standing by to fly out the leaders of the 'London Poles' who had taken refuge there when their country was conquered by German and Soviet forces in 1939. On the evening of the 12th Prime Minister Mikolajczyk, Foreign Minister Romer and Professor Grabski of the Polish National Council arrived in Moscow. Discussions began the next day, but it soon became apparent that Stalin's protégés, the 'Lublin Poles', were 'mere pawns of Russia' and Eden called them 'the rat and the weasel'. In order to get the two sides together and produce some kind of coalition government, Churchill was prepared to make concessions on Poland's eastern border, which had been set by the Germans after the Russian defeat in 1918 and included territory where many Ukrainians lived. But the London Poles refused to accept this, despite the offer of much German territory and the port of Danzig in compensation. Churchill had no respect for them either and called them 'a feeble lot of fools', while the delegates from Lublin were 'the greatest villains imaginable'. There was no possibility of agreement, and soon the occupation by the Red Army would settle the question for many decades.

★   ★   ★

The British Embassy in Moscow already had a staff of six to deal with coded messages, but two male and three female cipher officers were summoned from Britain, and another from Baghdad. Six typists were also sent out, plus Mr Jones, the head of the Foreign Office communication department. The traffic was expected to be as erratic as ever, and the Foreign Office sent a request to the Embassy:

> We expect that during traffic peaks (especially immediately after any periods during which wireless communication has been suspended because of atmospherics) that the whole of the staff will have to be on duty simultaneously. Can you arrange that sufficient tables and chairs are available?[5]

A courier service was set up between the Embassy and Churchill's dacha. It was generally agreed that the accuracy of coding and decoding was high, with very few corrupt words. But despite all the efforts, there were complaints about the length of time that it sometimes took to get copies typed, duplicated and distributed. The volume of signals was heavy – the outward series of Drastic telegrams reached its first hundred between the 9th and the 14th. They included a seven-page report by General Wilson on the conduct of the war on land, and one on the passage of the Town and Country Planning Bill which had caused much difficulty to the government at home, but had very little to do with the talks with Stalin.

The usual signal arrangements were supplemented by high-flying Mosquito aircraft, which carried papers directly to Moscow over enemy territory. One left every 24 hours for the seven-hour flight, and a bag containing the papers was handed over to the navigator. Senders were warned: 'These machines will be flying over enemy-occupied territory. No paper should therefore be sent in these bags which would compromise secret sources or military plans if it fell into the hands of the enemy.' But it did allow a greatly increased volume of routine material, and Churchill was to be found in bed most mornings dealing with it. He apologised to Stalin that he had little time to see Moscow because he had 'received an air courier every day entailing decisions about our own affairs'.

★ ★ ★

On the afternoon of 15 October, Churchill's temperature rose to above 100 degrees and Moran was sent for. Churchill was in despair and feared another attack of pneumonia. He buried his head in his hands, while exercising his frustration on Sawyers. Moran remained calm and refused to call specialists out from Cairo. 'If, on our journeys, I were to send for specialists and nurses every time the P.M. runs a temperature we might as well add them to our travelling establishment.' A telegram to Cairo had already been prepared, but the names of Bedford and Pulvertaft were crossed out. Some junior doctors and nurses were to be sent out and the 'most extraordinary measures' were to be taken to get them in Moscow by air next day.

Churchill asked Miss Layton to read to him, though his appetite for books was much reduced by this time. She was given a heavy tome called *Primer of the Coming World* by Leopold Schwarzchild, 'all about finance capitalists, the influence of capitalism on wars, the prospects of preventing Germany starting another war, and so forth'. Miss Layton enunciated carefully and Churchill, wearing a black bandage over his eyes, interrupted her occasionally to show that he was still awake. To her it was 'quite a strain'. The temperature was soon down and all was well. But Brooke was aware of the nightmare situation that might arise if Churchill were to be stuck for several weeks in the Moscow winter instead of the Moroccan sun, with Soviet spies and microphones all around.

Brooke finished his discussions with his Soviet opposite numbers by the 15th and spent some time sightseeing in the Kremlin. Birdwatching was poor, although he saw three great tits in the garden, far more interesting than a vast cannon. He heard that the return had been put off for another 24 hours as no progress had been made over Poland, so next day he visited the offices of the British newspaper in Moscow, *British Ally*. There was further delay on the 18th so that a grand Kremlin banquet could be held. The dinner turned out to be

good and less oriental than last time, consisting of caviare, hors d'oeuvres, soup, fish, chicken or beef, partridge and ice cream. The usual toasts and speeches went on continuously. To start with they were proposed by Molotov and later by Stalin himself. Molotov proposed my health with some very nice words to which I had to reply. We rose at about 11.30 pm and went into the next room for coffee and fruit, and remained there till about midnight. We were then taken off to see two films which lasted till 2.15 but they were very good. After that we broke up and went home.[6]

★   ★   ★

At last, on the morning of the 19th, it was time to go back. The voyage across Russia was to follow the same principles as the one out. The aircraft had been refuelled slowly, as the Soviets insisted on filtering every drop through chamois leather. The captains and navigators went to the Hydro-met office every morning to receive weather forecasts. Churchill would have preferred to leave early, but Thompson suggested that the crews should be allowed to get the latest forecast at 10.30.

The main party assembled at the airport, and were greatly honoured to be seen off by Stalin himself, despite the rain. Churchill arrived only slightly late, national anthems were played and a guard of honour was inspected. After speeches and handshaking, *Ascalon* took off just before midday, closely followed by the York MW 100 and the faithful *Commando*. The clouds cleared and Brooke looked out to see the Kremlin receding into the distance. They flew south at 4,000 feet, maintaining visual contact with the ground through the broken cloud. The weather improved slowly, and Mitchell found map reading easy. They flew over Kharkov and crossed the River Dnieper west of Dniepropetrovsk and then passed over the salt marshes of the Crimea to land at Sarabus at 3.30.

An hour-long car drive took them to a house at Simferopol where they would rest overnight. Churchill stayed there to sleep while Eden, Brooke and Ismay were driven out into the mountains. There was no time to go as far as Sevastopol, where British forces had engaged the Russians 90 years earlier; but it was their first detailed look at the Crimea, which had suffered terribly in the war. Despite that, Brooke judged it to be 'far more prosperous than the rest of Russia that we saw. Houses better, clothes better, and general impression of more amenities of life.' Thompson was struck by gangs of chained prisoners working on the roads, 'Dressed in rags, filthy and obviously near starvation.' His embarrassed interpreter told him that they were Soviet criminals, but he remained convinced that they were German prisoners.

That evening there was a dinner at the house, 'of Moscow lavishness'. As there was only one table, Elizabeth Layton, Inspector Hughes and Sawyers were invited to sit with the rest of the party:

It was an amazing scene, like something out of Hans Christian Andersen. The room was lit only by candles, and we were served by fresh-faced Russian girls, obviously hastily thrust into waitress uniform, wearing unaccustomed high heels on which they tottered awkwardly around. Course succeeded course, the air became wavy with cigar smoke, the candles glittered, the vodka flowed. Soon toasts and speeches began.[7]

Eventually Churchill rose to his feet with a wicked twinkle to propose the health of Miss Layton, the only woman present. General Yermetchenko, who had clearly taken a fancy to the young lady, dropped a dripping bouquet of flowers in her lap as she answered, 'Thank you very much, I feel greatly honoured.' Later the general took her into an ante-room to drink red wine, after which John Martin rescued her by calling her to leave for the aircraft.

The crew of *Ascalon* had gone to relax in a primitive local mess, leaving Soviet sailors on guard. Churchill was furious to find that his plane was guarded by foreigners and raged against Bill Fraser. 'The Cossacks are our friends – now. But I insist that one of the crew always stays in *Ascalon*. She must never be left unattended. Never.' They took off at one in the morning. The possibility of a trip to Cyprus had been considered, with perhaps the chance to negotiate with the Turks again. But if that were revealed, there would be a strong risk of demonstrations by Greek nationalists on the island, which would not be helpful, and the idea was eventually dropped. Instead, *Ascalon* flew the usual devious route to Cairo. They went south-west over the Black Sea, then rose to 8,000 feet to pass the Dardanelles with a fine view of Istanbul, and past the northern Greek island of Samothrace. They flew south towards Khios, Ikaria and Kos, then turned south-east and dropped gradually to 5,000 feet, heading towards Egypt.

They landed safely at Cairo West after a flight of seven hours. Churchill had not slept well this time, and was 'somewhat sour', while Brooke was suffering from a heavy cold. They were met by Lord Mountbatten, who conferred with the military representatives on possible offensives against the Japanese from India. Brooke decided to stay in the Mena Hotel rather than with General Paget in Cairo. Churchill was likely to summon him to the Casey Villa for conferences, and he needed to be on the spot. There was a dinner that evening during which the Prime Minister showed much better form. He produced 'several gems', and informed the travellers that they were to start back at 11 next morning, rather than waiting until midnight. Brooke was delighted that he would be getting home 12 hours sooner.

Brooke travelled in *Ascalon* for the next part of the journey, along with Moran, Martin, Thompson and a typist. They flew over Benghazi again and were served 'an excellent lunch with hors d'oeuvres, soup, hot roast beef, beans, cheese, coffee and with it whisky soda, port and brandy!' Brooke found it difficult to believe that he was flying at 8,000 feet and 200 miles an hour as he read the decoded German signals that Churchill had passed on to him – though in fact the aircraft was mostly at 6,500 feet where it was clear of any turbulence. They landed at Naples after exactly seven hours, where Harold Macmillan carried Elizabeth Layton's suitcase down the steps. They had tea and held a conference until 8.15 in the evening about possible seaborne operations in the area. Brooke found it 'very weary work running conferences after a long flight, even though it is carried out in the greatest of comfort'. After dinner he was kept up until one in the morning, or 3 a.m. Cairo time.

That morning a question arose over the departure as bad weather threatened. There was a possibility of heading for Malta and using their superior night-flying facilities for a later start, but for the moment Brooke settled down in bed until 8.30, when he was suddenly told that the weather had improved and he was to leave the house in half an hour. With only a short time to breakfast, shave and dress, they were in the air by 10.10. Flying along the Italian coast, they passed over Corsica at Bastia with 'a grand view of North Corsica silhouetted against a stormy sky'. They crossed the French coast at Narbonne, but Brooke was disappointed not to glimpse the medieval walled city of Carcassonne. After that the weather was bad and no more was seen until they were over the Cherbourg peninsula. *Ascalon* eventually crossed the English coast at the Isle of Wight, passed over Andover and turned east to land at Northolt at 5 p.m. where Clementine Churchill and various dignitaries were waiting.

There was one further embarrassment. The party had been given large quantities of caviar and vodka before leaving Moscow and on arrival they distributed it among members of the party. But there was a misunderstanding, for much of it had been intended for the Soviet Embassy to celebrate Red Army Day. Eden had to apologise. Apart from that the trip was considered a success. The press was favourable about more co-operation with the Soviets, although the lack of any agreement on Poland was to signal the start of troubles that would last for nearly half a century. It proved to be Churchill's last flight in *Ascalon*. Except for the mishap on landing at Cairo West, John Mitchell felt that it had gone very well.

XVII
Christmas in the Skymaster

The American delegates to the Casablanca conference had arrived in the new Douglas airliner, the C-54 Skymaster. The British were still in the squalid Liberators, and Portal was mortified.

> When I was at Casablanca and saw the aircraft in which the American delegation arrived and compared them with those in which we flew to the scene I experienced a feeling of humiliation which was if possible intensified on my return by a frontal attack delivered by my colleagues on the Chiefs of Staff Committee.[1]

Portal realised that the new York was on the way for the Prime Minister himself, but he wanted better conditions for his colleagues as well, with a view to 'maintaining the dignity and prestige (to say nothing of the health and tidiness) of the Chiefs of Staff '.

Roosevelt arrived at Tehran in his new plane the *Sacred Cow,* another Skymaster, and Churchill's crew soon noticed it:

> We were already decidedly envious of the 'Sacred Cow'. It had all sorts of refinements, an electric lift was built in to the floor of the Owner's Stateroom so that the handicapped Roosevelt could be raised and lowered to ground level in his wheel chair. There was a large picture window on one side of the aircraft so that he could have a comfortable view out from the position where his wheel chair was clamped to. It had the main folding steps electrically operated from within the aircraft and they stowed neatly when retracted. Above all, the aircraft had a long operating range with its air cooled engines, a bonus (however worthy our own Rolls Royce Merlins) in the hot ground temperatures encountered.[2]

The DC-4 was designed by the Douglas Aircraft Company of Santa Monica, California and based on the experience of the most prolific of all transport aircraft, the DC-3 Dakota which equipped both the American and British air forces – in all, more than 10,000 were built. The DC-4 had four engines instead of two, which did much to increase safety, and it was designed for possible pressurisation, though in practice that was never fitted during the war. This gave it a long cylindrical section in its fuselage, familiar to the modern traveller but much rarer then. The first aircraft (there was no proto-type in the usual sense) flew three months after America entered the war and it was quickly adopted for military use, with the designation C-54. Its standard range of 2,000 miles made it suitable for the Pacific war, and for transatlantic travel on the shorter routes. Unlike other aircraft, none were available for Britain.

There were many other reasons, besides comfort and prestige, for getting a C-54 for the Prime Minister. The war in Europe was expected to end in 1944, and after that his attention would be focused on the Pacific, where distances were much greater. The range of the York was too short for this, even if extra fuel tanks were added. An improved Skymaster, on the other hand, could fly 4,600 miles without refuelling compared with 3,100 for an upgraded York. In December 1943 the Ministry of Aircraft Production looked at the possibility of using an 'austerity Lancaster', another variant of the bomber which could be given a range of 4,000 miles, with 'rather hard' accommoda-tion for seven people. This sounded rather like the bad old days of the Liber-ator, but over even longer distances.

Meanwhile Churchill used his friends in high places and negotiated with General 'Hap' Arnold, head of the US Army Air Force. The general made a special case for one Skymaster, on condition that it was used 'primarily for the personal use of Mr. Churchill and other V.V.I.Ps.' – for already the term 'VIP'

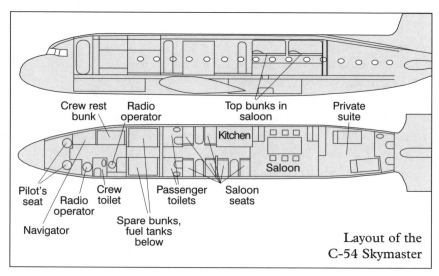

Layout of the C-54 Skymaster

was being overused and an alternative was needed for the highest in the land. By April 1944 Arnold had allocated Churchill an aircraft from the production line, and on 27 May he telegraphed him that 'It gives me great pleasure to announce that your Skymaster C-54B aeroplane is ready for delivery to you.' Churchill was sensitive about using an American-built plane as his personal transport. Any enquiries about this were to be fobbed off with the story that by agreement, the Americans were to concentrate on transport aircraft, the British on bombers and fighters. In compensation, Churchill ordered the interior designers to 'make it look British'.

There were still many delays after the plane's arrival. The aircraft was now in the hands of the Ministry of Aircraft Production, a much more bureaucratic animal than in the days of Beaverbrook. He had used the slogan 'Meetings take the punch out of war', but civil-service style reasserted itself after he left. On 19 June 1943, for example, there was a meeting of 17 people, including Collins and Fraser from 24 Squadron, to plan the conversion of the aircraft to Churchill's standards – there were five such meetings in July alone. The current minister, Sir Stafford Cripps, was also very different from Beaverbrook, who disliked him intensely. He was a lean, austere left-wing socialist and Beaverbrook's own *Daily Express* was not unbiased when it described him. 'His figure is tall and spare, his complexion grey, his features generally unsmiling. His health keeps him permanently on a vegetarian diet.' It was unlikely that such a man would give high priority to a luxury conversion. In any case the aircraft industry was now geared to mass production rather than special jobs like this.

During the summer Churchill was distracted by his trips to Normandy and Italy, which mostly used smaller aircraft. But the matter returned to his attention on 1 September as he prepared for the second trip to Quebec and realised that the Skymaster would not be available to fly him home. He wrote a blistering letter to Cripps. He had been told that a whole month had passed before the ministry did anything at all. Work had been 'rendered impossible by the complete lack of interest and energy shown by your Department'. He wished he had taken up General Arnold's suggestion to fly the plane back to America for fitting out. He concluded, 'Altogether, I do not feel that I have been well treated in a matter which I asked you so specially about'.

Cripps had the affair looked into. The charge of a month's delay was not answered, but there were reasons for the current difficulties. A huge amount of effort had been put in, including the services of up to 31 draughtsmen. Design alone had taken up 14,700 man-hours and construction required 35,000 more. Only a limited number of men could work on the aircraft at a time, and there were 20 of them working round the clock already, including holidays and weekends. In the wartime economy it was difficult to find supplies of the standard required. 'We could have been quicker if we had been prepared to use any shoddy material that was to hand, but I had given instructions that it was to be made a first class job.'

Meanwhile the question of a pressure capsule for the Prime Minister surfaced again. Air Ministry experts calculated that 'if the Owner wishes to experience no height above 8,000 feet' then the capsule would need ½ lb per square inch at 9,500 feet, rising to 5½ lbs per square inch at 25,000 feet. It could be dangerous if pressure within the capsule was suddenly lost at, say, 18,000 feet, but Churchill discounted this. He would only fly at heights of up to 12,000 feet when crossing a mountain range and did not propose to go any higher than that. The capsule would also take up a great deal of space in a C-54. It could only be entered by opening a door in the top, which needed space for the lid. If fitted in the Owner's cabin, it would replace the main bed and a new door would be required. In the saloon, it would displace the conference table and four chairs, 'destroying all effective use of the Saloon for dining or for conferences'. In the forward passengers' accommodation it would necessitate the removal of eight seats or four bunks, almost half the space available. Anyway, who was going to wake the Prime Minister in the middle of the night, or tear him away from a meeting or the study of his papers, to insist that he alone go into the chamber? Moran disposed of the issue finally in 1945 when he wrote that 'the real advantages of such a chamber cannot be safely obtained, and that the mechanism was not sufficiently accurate and reliable to make its adoption advisable'.

Parachutes were another possible safety feature. They were not normally given to passengers on RAF aircraft, as they needed special training in their use, which was quite risky in itself. Nevertheless one was provided for Churchill personally, stowed under the mattress, which had to be removed to get at it. Churchill asserted that he would not go without Sawyers to attend to his needs, which conjured up an image of the valet clinging to the Prime Minster's legs during the descent.

When finished, the Skymaster was something to see. In the nose, the crew's compartment was finished to the austerity standards. The pilot and co-pilot sat side by side, as usual. On the starboard side behind them, Mitchell was allowed a large chart table taking up a third of the aircraft's width. On the other side the radio operator had a more modest space. Aft of him was the crew's lavatory and behind that was a small compartment for Jack Payne, the flight engineer. On the other side were two sleeping bunks for the crew, and this time they were not taken over by luggage, for there was plenty of room in the cabin. Aft of the crew's quarters were two fuel tanks, one on each side. They were totally enclosed to prevent fumes from entering the cabin. There was a bunk above each, to be used when the others were full.

The passenger area proper began with a lavatory on each side. The area aft of that, above the wings, was divided into four compartments, two on either side. Three of these contained two facing double seats, enabling four people to sit there and converse. The back of one of these could be taken down to bridge the gap between the two and form a single bunk in each compartment. There was another bunk above, to be lowered when used for sleeping, and two more bunks in the saloon aft. The fourth compartment in the centre section was the kitchen, fitted out from long and hard experience of Churchill's needs. The new galley had a lightweight kettle specifically for heating soup in the middle of the night. It also had an electric stove, grill, hot plates, refrigerator, hot cupboard, cocktail cabinet and a control panel for summoning the staff.

Next came the conference room, the *pièce de résistance* of the plane. A 7 ft by 3 ft table was offset to one side to allow passage. The mistakes of the early York were not repeated and it was made of walnut veneer on a very light metal frame. There was one chair at the head and one at the foot. The three chairs on the starboard side were close against the side of the fuselage, but were on rails to let people in and out. Three more chairs on the starboard side were on swivels, as was the chairman's seat at the aft end facing forward. All were upholstered with blue leather. But it was the décor of the inner fuselage sides that attracted most attention – walnut woodwork with brown curtains and a light beige roof. To one American reporter it was 'decorated like the drawing-room of an English castle', the centrepiece of a 'flying palace worth more than a king's ransom'.

The Skymaster could carry eight passengers in addition to the Prime Minister on long flights where sleeping accommodation might be required. Two more could be added if the bunks above the fuel tanks were used. This was an ideal number for the Prime Minister's party, which usually included a visitor or two relevant to the work in hand, Moran, Commander Thompson, a detective, one or two private secretaries, a pair of typists and the valet Sawyers. It could carry 20 people, besides the Owner, on short flights when sleeping accommodation was not required.

Then came a small lobby used for storing steps and leading to the Owner's cabin. The cabin itself was furnished in pale beige with sycamore woodwork, a grey Wilton carpet, leather upholstery and leather wall covering. It was fitted with a fixed bed on the starboard side, a desk and two chairs. At

Churchill's insistence a second berth could be fitted on demand, to accommodate his wife if she went with him. Aft of that, the last compartment in the interior of the plane, was the Owner's toilet and dressing room. Extra windows were fitted in the Prime Minister's compartment, including one on each side in the toilet.

★ ★ ★

As the Skymaster neared completion, Fraser and Cliff, the new second pilot, were sent across the Atlantic for a conversion course in the C-54 in Delaware. As Charles E. Cannon of Douglas Aircraft had told them in April, 'This aircraft has characteristics which can be compared with no other flying today.' The tricycle undercarriage was not familiar to British pilots, and the York crew had never flown the Liberator. The aircraft was steered by the nose wheel when on the ground, but during take-off the transition to normal control was difficult:

> During the early part of the take-off run, the aircraft must be controlled directionally by the nose wheel only, this is done by the first pilot while the co-pilot holds the control column central. As soon as the weight is off the nose wheel the aircraft is controlled in the orthodox manner by either pilot.[3]

One fault of the Skymaster, unrecognised at the time, was that the fuel selector controls were difficult to see and this could lead to accidents, though these were far less likely with a skilled flight engineer on board. Apart from that, RAF pilots were generally pleased with the handling of the C-54 as a type. The controls were well balanced and light in operation, directional stability was good and it had no bad habits.

It occurred to Commander Thompson that there might be time for a training and proving flight with the full crew while Churchill was more preoccupied with affairs in Moscow, and this was agreed. They set off late in November to fly between the Azores, Montreal and back to Northolt, in order to test the aircraft, its long-distance performance, its cockpit lighting, the catering facilities on long flights and the functioning of all the equipment. The aluminium tubes in the cold-water system split as the crew had predicted, and were later replaced with copper. Everything else worked 'like a charm'. They stopped over in Maine for a final check by a US Army Air Force Skymaster unit, who were impressed but thought the interior 'a bit cissy'. On the flight across the Atlantic, John Mitchell enjoyed the chance to practise his celestial navigation. 'At cruising levels in a beautifully clear polar air stream the view of the night heavens was magnificent – all the stars one's eyes could see available for navigation.' The crew reported 'a clean bill of health' to Thompson and it was ready for service. Mitchell thought optimistically that 'we were back to base with the prospect of Christmas at home … and the birth of our first-born expected at the end of the year'.

★   ★   ★

On 4 December Churchill had lunch in Downing Street with Harold Balfour, who had bought the Boeings and was now minister resident in West Africa; Harold Macmillan, his minister for the Mediterranean; and Paul Boncour of the Free French. Colville found the Frenchman 'a crashing bore' who knew no English and 'spat while talking to an extent unusual even in France'. Reports from across the Channel were optimistic as the army advanced, but Churchill was becoming increasingly obsessed with a country at the other end of Europe. The Germans had retreated from large parts of Greece and there was a substantial British force there, though not enough to prevent the country from descending into civil war between nationalists and the communist group ELAS. Churchill was less concerned about growing Communist power in Italy and Yugoslavia, for example, but Stalin had promised in Moscow that Greece would be 90 per cent under western influence. That night Churchill sat up till 4 in the morning dictating telegrams and urging his ambassador to 'treat Athens as a conquered city'. Over the next three weeks the issue dominated discussions in the entourage, and it was mentioned in John Colville's diary as a main item almost every day. On 8 December there was a vote on the issue in the House of Commons. The government won comfortably as always, but a large proportion of the Labour Party abstained, threatening the coalition. Anthony Eden wanted to appoint Archbishop Damaskinos of Athens as regent. The exiled King of Greece did not agree, and neither did Churchill, who thought he was too left-wing.

By the 12th, Colville was bored with the subject. 'The isles of Greece, indeed. I shall never feel any sentiment towards them again.' Public opinion in Britain was not in favour of intervention and thought of ELAS as 'a heroic left-wing resistance movement', according to Colville. Meanwhile, on the 16th the Germans began their great counter-attack in the Ardennes, threatening the Allied advance into Germany. The Cabinet was concerned about Churchill's obsession with Greece, and his failure to read his papers on anything else.

There was danger of a real rift with Eden over the appointment of the Arch-bishop. The press was against intervention, as were the Americans. On Friday the 22nd Churchill spent so long in the Map Room that it was too late to go to Chequers. That night he formed an intention to visit Greece to settle matters there himself. Eden offered to go in his place, but it was finally agreed that both should travel together.

For once Clementine Churchill cracked under the strain. She had planned Christmas at home with her husband and family after the traumas of a year ago. She had invited a large group of relatives and friends, including her three daughters, for the weekend at Chequers. According to Mary:

> This Christmas seemed to have a special atmosphere; the dark, war years were drawing to their end; even the least optimistic could reasonably feel that this, the sixth, was the last wartime Christmas. Everywhere families were making their arrangements, despite gaps in the family, despite the black-out, and despite rationing. Among them, Clementine had taken infinite pains to prepare a glowing Christmas-tide. Nellie Romilly arrived at Chequers at about tea-time on Saturday the 23rd; she found Winston sitting in the Great Hall. He welcomed her, and then, under the seal of secrecy, told her that he was off the next day to Athens; he begged her to go and find Clementine, who was upstairs and 'very upset'. Nellie went to her sister's bedroom and found her in floods of tears.[4]

Still there was indecision at the top. By the end of lunch at Chequers on the 24th, it seemed that Churchill had been talked out of this rash venture. By 5.30 he had spoken with Eden on the telephone, and it was on again. According to Colville, 'A chaotic evening ensued, with the P.M. telling the King, Attlee, Bevin, Beaverbrook on one telephone, with me warning the C.A.S., Admiralty, Tommy, etc., etc. on the other. Mrs C. was greatly distressed but resigned herself to the inevitable.'

Colville sent for his RAF uniform, while Churchill lay on a sofa reading and annotating telegrams, 'and carrying on a conversation with Mrs Romilly (who was most outrageously reading the telegrams too) all at the same time'. It was difficult to disengage him from this, but at 11.30 in the evening the party set off for Northolt. There were ten in the group – Churchill, Eden, Moran, Commander Thompson, Colville and Pierson Dixon, Eden's secretary, the typists Misses Layton and Holmes, a detective and Sawyers. It soon transpired that the two women were going to a war zone, a great change in attitude from the days when they had not even been allowed to travel by warship.

★ ★ ★

At Northolt there was a feverish rush to get the Skymaster fully equipped. Sergeant Davis of the WAAF produced the table linen, knives and forks and lightweight chinaware with the outline of the Skymaster on every piece. The crew worked hard to stow 'bedding and sheets, table linen, knives and forks, towels; all the new lightweight china, not to mention glassware and corkscrews'.

The call to the maiden flight came suddenly on 3 December and it was a surprise to the crew, as John Mitchell recounted:

> Bill Fraser and I were summoned to the Cabinet Office to hear from Tommy Thompson, the ADC, what was required. The destination, Athens via Naples, came right out of the blue. A trip to France seemed more likely from what we knew. So much for Christmas leave and being present for the arrival of our first child.[5]

Lord Moran was at home on the evening of Boxing Day 1944, wondering rather belatedly how to produce a good Christmas for his wife, who had had 'a dusty war'. The phone rang and Churchill told him, 'I'm off to G. …' Lady Moran thought this might mean Gibraltar and the couple drove though the darkness to Chequers, happy at least that the blackout restrictions on headlights had been removed and they were able to 'sweep along a road thrown up by a searchlight instead of groping our way anxiously along the dark lanes around Harefield'. When they got there they found out that 'G. is Greece.'

Everyone was impressed on boarding the Skymaster – to Colville it was 'remarkably comfortable and very quiet', to Miss Layton it was 'firm, powerful and secure'. With his usual lack of modesty among his entourage, Churchill stood in the lobby of his cabin wearing his combination underwear, directing the passengers to their places – for these routines were not yet established as they had been in the York. Sawyers was fussing with the baggage, for now there was room to stow everything in the cabins and he did not have to worry about what was 'not wanted on voyage'. Mitchell was sent for by Portal for a last-minute consultation on the route, and stepped on a nail in the hangar. He had it quickly bandaged but was in pain for the trip out. When told to see Lord Moran about it, he exclaimed 'Good Lord, is he a real doctor?'

307

Modern safety rules were not in place, and Churchill summoned the steward to his cabin while the aircraft was taxiing, so that he had to use the handholds as the plane moved down the runway. 'With the luxury of a level cabin floor of the Skymaster ... and the relative quietness after the York, the Owner had been lulled into believing that a take-off was no longer a matter of thrust and aerodynamic lift defeating the forces of gravity!'

According to Mitchell, the flight took off at five past midnight on Christmas Day, though this does not tally with Colville's timings. They ascended to a height of 8,000 feet which was safe for the Prime Minister, and left the English coast over Selsey Bill. The party was served with drinks and the Prime Minister came into the cockpit as they crossed the coast of France. The forward and sideways view was better than in the York and 'His access to the cockpit seat could be accomplished without putting his hand or feet on some lever or switch,' as John Mitchell commented tartly. The flight continued towards Toulouse, using a standard route that had already been established over France in the few months since the Liberation. There was room for all the passengers to sleep on the bunks while the aircraft headed south-east to cross the Mediterranean coast at Sete.

The plane climbed to 13,500 feet to get over the mountains and it was considered wise to wake Churchill to get him to put on his oxygen mask. The others were not disturbed, but woke with splitting headaches next morning, even John Colville with his RAF experience. Over the Mediterranean it was decided to climb above 10,000 feet again to get above the clouds, and the sudden change in engine note woke Churchill. Mitchell was summoned and had to explain what was happening. Churchill remembered that they had flown over the Ligurian mountains at 7,000 feet, and Mitchell pointed out that that had been done in clear weather. At 9 o'clock in the morning they landed for a short stop at Pomigliano airfield near Naples.

The passengers were taken to breakfast less than 100 yards from the aircraft, to a 'rather bare building which had only slightly recovered from the many bombardments it had had to withstand'. They were met by Admiral Sir John Cunningham of the Mediterranean Fleet, and Air Marshal Sir John Slessor of the air force. There had been doubts as to whether an aircraft as large as the Skymaster could land at Athens, but these were settled and it was not necessary to change aircraft. They took off after less than two hours and flew over Taranto in the heel of Italy where the Fleet Air Arm had seriously damaged the Italian Fleet in the darkest days of 1940. Colville, still in his RAF uniform, took over the controls for a while 'without in any way endangering the passengers', implying a contrast to Churchill. The plane continued towards Cape Otranto and Cephalonia where the classically educated Colville was pleased to see that the islands of Cythera and Ithaca were 'cloud-capped' in the Homeric tradition. Finally, they flew along the Gulf of Corinth and landed at Athens.

★ ★ ★

The flight had been pleasant and reasonably safe, but things were very different on the ground as civil war raged. Field-Marshal Alexander, the Commander-in-Chief in the Mediterranean, Harold Macmillan and Reginald Leeper, the ambassador, came on board the aircraft. The plush conference room of the Skymaster began to earn its keep, as they sat down with Churchill and Eden to decide what to do next. But expensive décor could not keep out the cold, and there was no heating once the engines were turned off. The light was poor, and the aircraft rocked in the wind. At 4 o'clock Elizabeth Layton was called in, to see Churchill wrapped in an overcoat and scarf. The Inspector had a red nose and cheeks and Sawyers 'looked half dead'. She began to type a communiqué but her hands were cold and she was distracted by gunfire outside.

Following some amendments and retyping it was agreed that the party should be accommodated in the cruiser *Ajax* which was anchored in the harbour. They got into armoured vehicles provided by the British Army for the rough journey. The Prime Minister and his associates got into the first one, manned by half-frozen soldiers who had been standing around the airfield for two hours. The two ladies got into the second vehicle:

> We were cold and hungry, Marian had a rotten cough and Sawyers was just starting a cold. We sat on swivel chairs fitted onto the iron floor, piled around with luggage and our Secret Boxes, Mr. Churchill's coat over our knees, and every time the truck swung around a corner or crashed over a bump, boxes and bags fell onto our heads. Suddenly tension snapped and we began to laugh.[6]

After 45 minutes of this they reached the Naval College, where officers were waiting to embark them. They were put into the admiral's barge, 'not, of course, a barge in the usual sense, but a very super speed boat with a small cabin to seat about four'.

★ ★ ★

HMS *Ajax* was one of the best-known ships in the navy in the early part of the war, when Churchill was First Lord of the Admiralty. Built in 1933–5, she was one of three cruisers which cornered the German pocket battleship *Graf Spee* in Montevideo and forced her to scuttle herself. Since then she had served with great distinction in the Mediterranean, fighting at the Battle of Cape Matapan in 1941 and escorting Malta convoys. She was in Piraeus harbour on 6 April 1941 when the Germans launched a surprise attack. Later she bombarded enemy positions in North Africa and on Rhodes, and supported the D-Day landings on Gold Beach. The *Ajax* was small even by cruiser standards and at 7,270 tons she was about a fifth of the size of a *King George V* class battleship. As flagship of the Fifth Cruiser Squadron, she was already overcrowded with Rear-Admiral J. M. Mansfield and his staff. The ship had received the first intimation of a high-level party at three that morning, when a signal arrived, 'only to be deciphered by the Admiral's Secretary'. It stated that two VVIPs were to be found accommodation with a party of fourteen, including 'one female'. An hour later this was amended. 'For one female, read two.'

Speculating on the identity of the guests, the officers and crew made the ship ready, vacating cabins as necessary. The admiral's barge was sent to collect the party from the quayside and it was only on its arrival back that Captain J. W. Cuthbert of the *Ajax* realised that his guest was the Prime Minister himself. He said to him, 'I hope, sir, that while you are with us we shan't have to open fire, but as you know our purpose here is to assist the Army. If we are asked to give supporting fire I must do so.' Churchill, always attracted by the prospect of battle, was delighted: 'Pray remember, Captain, that I come here as a cooing dove of peace, bearing a sprig of mistletoe in my beak – but far be it from me to stand in the way of military necessity.'

Colville found the hospitality on the ship 'astonishing':

> *Ajax* is temporarily the Flagship of Admiral Mansfield, who is a man of great charm. The Captain, Cuthbert, was in the Cabinet Office early in the war and greeted me as an old friend. One or two of the complement of the K.G.V., who brought us home last January, are also on board.[7]

It was decided to invite the Greek Prime Minister, Papandreou, on board the cruiser with the Archbishop. Unlike Churchill, Captain Cuthbert was not prepared to interrupt the crew's Christmas for affairs of state but Jock Colville considered it quite appropriate that the ship's choir was singing *The First Noel* just as the Greeks arrived. Unfortunately the crew were also having a 'funny party' to celebrate Christmas:

A group of sailors, garbed in extravagant fancy dress, go their rounds of the ship clowning and generally making fun at everyone's expense … somehow or other they had succeeded in getting into the Captain's Lobby, and there they stood – a hula-hula 'girl' with a grass skirt and a brassiere with winking red and green lights on either side; the clown Coco; Charlie Chaplin; and three other equally grotesque figures with equally blackened faces.[8]

They caught sight of Damaskinos, a magnificent figure in his black robes, and concluded that he was with another party organised by the commander. They howled with laughter, while Commander Thompson made frantic signs to stop, and muttered to the Archbishop, 'You know, sir … Christmas Day, sir … very funny sir!' as the Archbishop brushed past. Fortunately he had a good sense of humour and was not put off by the incident. Mess-deck parties continued well into the night as the sailors enjoyed their annual saturnalia, when the authority of the officers was in abeyance. Churchill was quickly captivated by Archbishop Damaskinos, just as Eden began to cool towards him.

Next morning Colville went on deck to hear the noise of gunfire from the city, and smell the smoke of battle. He watched as RAF Beaufighters fired rockets at rebel positions. As the party left the ship by barge they were straddled by shells. They went to the British Embassy, then to the Ministry of Foreign Affairs to conduct 'what must surely be the strangest conference which a British Prime Minister and Foreign Secretary have ever attended'. The building was gloomy at best, and the room was lighted with hurricane lamps. The ELAS representatives entered 'dressed shabbily in khaki battle-dress and glancing furtively around as if they expected a trap'. After some wrangling and irrelevant speeches from both sides, the British party eventually left the Greeks to sort it out. Churchill declared, 'We have begun the work. See that you finish it.'

Colville and Marian Holmes went back to the ship via the British Embassy but had trouble with Greek irregulars who treated Colville's blue RAF uniform with great suspicion. There was no boat to take them back to the ship, until they managed to get a lift from a Greek destroyer's launch. 'This was a precarious undertaking and I began to regret it when for the fifth time we failed to come alongside the ship properly and appeared in imminent danger of capsizing.' After getting on board they were kept awake all night by the explosions of depth charges, used to deter the rebels from attacking the *Ajax*.

It was even colder next morning as Eden and his secretary went ashore to learn the result of the discussions among the Greeks. The rest went to the embassy in armoured cars, and a burst of long-range machine-gun fire hit a wall 30 feet above the Prime Minster's head. Colville was amused that the British army's first reaction was to fix bayonets. He met the American ambassador and then held a press conference 'speaking to the dirtiest and most unreliable collection of "news-hawks" ever assembled'. They returned to the ship, which was far more hospitable than the embassy. Next morning they decided that further meetings were unnecessary and they would fly home.

★ ★ ★

The crew of the Skymaster had troubles of their own. The RAF staging post at Hassani was 'a bleak spot to spend Christmas'. Morale was low among the local RAF personnel, and not helped by an incompetent and puritanical commanding officer. The Skymaster crew had brought a firkin of beer for their own enjoyment, but their aircraft was better equipped for opening champagne bottles than wooden casks. They had to find a tool to remove the bung, so they used the skills of a local RAF engineer to fit a tap to it. The CO did not join in the fun.

They did not feel secure on the airfield. Some of the local population, they believed, worked for them during the day and ELAS by night. It was said that women carried hand grenades under their skirts or in shopping baskets. During the night there was a burst of gunfire near by, but it was discovered that an airman in the Guard Room had fired his sub-machine gun by accident – 'Moral: never let the RAF have their hands on loaded small arms.'

On the second day the captain and navigator were summoned to the embassy:

> There was no question of an armoured car for us; we were driven into town on the back of an open RAF truck, 'guarded' by an evil-looking local desperado with a sten gun on his lap. These weapons are notoriously light on the trigger. The vehicle bounced horribly. I was much more afraid of being shot by the guard than by ELAS.[9]

The return route was arranged without any difficulty, but it was not easy to get provisions for use on the voyage, as neither the embassy nor the airfield had much to spare. However, Jock Duncan and his assistant were loading up with emergency supplies of meat, tins of soup and vegetables when a party of

RAF police arrived to check the aircraft for bombs, although 'Jack Payne had already declared that we were ready for take off with everything clean and polished and our carpets spotless from our privately acquired Hoover Dustette.' An officious policeman was ordered to take his boots off the clean carpet. 'Would the Corporal like the floor-boards up? Would he like the tanks emptied of fuel? And how about these tins of soup? Should they not be emptied one by one? And there could be bombs in the bully beef.' This was interrupted by the arrival of the Prime Minister and his party, and the RAF police departed 'at some speed'.

★ ★ ★

They took off from Athens at 1 p.m. local time, with Macmillan and Alexander joining the passengers to Naples. 'Soon, we were circling high above the Piraeus in our beautiful bird; looking down, we could see the *Ajax* in the blue water.' They took the same route back, and landed in Italy just before sunset, where the RAF crew was pleased to escape the discomfort of Hassani. They left again early next morning for the seven-and-a-half-hour flight, which Colville enjoyed even more than the journey out.

> The weather, as throughout the expedition, was glorious. We saw Rome and Ostia below us to starboard, with the Tiber winding its way inland, and then it was Corsica, crowned with snow, the Mediterranean, deep blue, Toulon, Narbonne, and the Pyrenees on our left. There was no cloud, as we flew northwards at between six and eight thousand feet, until we had crossed the Loire.[10]

Colville dictated a description of the conference to one of the typists, while Moran schemed 'shamelessly' to have himself appointed Provost of Eton College, the famous boys' public school. The party had lunch, presumably picked up at Naples, as they passed over Mont St Michel off the Brittany coast, and Colville 'started a hare' by pointing out that the nearby Channel Islands were still in German hands. Apart from that they were 'very comfortable and soporific … in the relative quietness of the new accommodation'. The weather was still unseasonably bright as they arrived over England, but the ground was white with frost. There was fog in the London area, and they had to land on an American airfield at Bovington near Watford. It had the advantage of being close to Chequers and a large party including Mrs Churchill was diverted to meet them there. The RAF crew went off to a splendid New Year's

Eve party at Northolt, and Mitchell was able to go home to see his son who had been born while he was away. Colville had a long and undisturbed sleep, then went to church with his family.

★ ★ ★

Churchill found only two criticisms of his new aircraft. The clock ticked too loudly, which was a tribute to the soundproofing; and his private toilet had been provided with a 'hot seat' to take off the chill at high altitudes. Despite the assurances of Elsan, the manufacturers, its switching-off mechanism did not work, and 'Jack [Payne] was told in no uncertain terms to disconnect it.' These were minor faults and Churchill was delighted. He wrote to Cripps at the Ministry of Aircraft Production:

> After completing my first flight in the C.54 I would like to say how well satisfied I am with the general lay out and the comfort and convenience of the arrangements. The sound proofing seemed to be notably efficient … The results appear to be a credit to British crafts-manship and augur well for the future when British firms will once again be turning out the highest class of air liner. I trust the experience gained and the lessons learned in surmounting the various difficulties which arose during the fitting out of the aircraft have, as was hoped, been of profit to all concerned with the future of civil aircraft production in this country.[11]

The success of his trip to Greece was unexpected by almost everyone except the Prime Minister himself. Some kind of peace had been arranged among the Greeks and the danger of a Communist takeover had been removed for the moment. The press, which had been critical of Churchill, was now largely favourable. Meanwhile, the tide had turned in the 'Battle of the Bulge' in the Ardennes and the advance into Germany could be resumed.

XVIII
The Ways to Yalta

Clearly there was still need for a three-power conference, to plan the defeat of what was left of German power, to settle the fate of Europe after the Nazi occupation, and to organise the final assault on Japan. On 23 October 1944, the day after his return from Moscow, Churchill telegraphed Roosevelt that 'UJ' or Uncle Joe was not willing to travel by air because of medical advice. Northern Russia was out of the question because of the severe winter climate and the risk of German attack by sea or air. It would be difficult to take warships out of the Black Sea through the Dardanelles unless Turkey declared war, but the Soviets were keen on that solution. Another possibility was for the three to meet in the Crimea. Churchill commented:

> From what I saw of the Crimea, it seems much shattered and I expect all the other Black Sea ports are in a similar state. We should therefore in all probability have to live on board our ships. I am enquiring about Athens from Eden who will be there in a day or two. Personally I think it is a splendid setting and here again we should have our ships handy. Cyprus is of course available where absolute secrecy, silence and security can be guaranteed together with plain, comfortable accommodations for all the principals.[1]

Roosevelt, whose health was actually far worse than Stalin's or even Churchill's, was almost equally reluctant to travel by air and his advisers did not like Stalin's idea: 'My Navy people recommend strongly against the Black Sea. They do not want to risk a capital ship through the Aegean or the Dardanelles as it would involve a very large escort needed elsewhere.' He was lukewarm about Churchill's ideas for Jerusalem, Alexandria or Athens but suggested another plan to Stalin: 'I should hope that by that time you will have rail travel to some port on the Adriatic and that we should meet you there or you should come across in a few hours in one of our ships to Bari and then motor to Rome, or that you should take the same ship a little further and that we should meet in a place like Taormina in Eastern Sicily, which should provide fairly good climate at that time.' But Stalin had no tourist's instinct, as Churchill was aware. 'There is, in my opinion, much doubt whether U.J. would be willing or able to come to an Adriatic port by January 30th, or that he would be willing to come on a non-Russian vessel through this heavily mined sea.' Stalin replied to Roosevelt late in November:

> It is too bad that your naval authorities question the advisability of your original idea that the three of us should meet on the Soviet Black Sea coast. There is no objection, as far as I am concerned, to the time of meeting suggested by you – late January or early February; I expect, however, that we shall be able to select one of the Soviet sea ports. I still have to pay heed to my doctor's warning of the risk involved in long journeys.[2]

Roosevelt was constrained by his fourth inauguration, which was to take place on 20 January. He was reluctant to give way to Stalin but agreed with Churchill that he could get to the Black Sea 'even at great difficulty on account of Congress'. The two could meet at Malta and fly there. He believed that 'Yalta is almost intact, though the roadstead [i.e. anchorage] is open and we should probably have to live ashore.' This had hardened by 23 December when he told the Prime Minister:

> If Stalin cannot manage to meet us in the Mediterranean I am prepared to go to the Crimea and have the meeting at Yalta, which appears to be the best place available in the Black Sea, having the best accommodations ashore and the most promising flying conditions. We would arrive by plane from some Mediterranean port and would send in advance a naval vessel to Sevastapol to provide necessary service and living accommodations if it should be necessary for me to live aboard ship.
>
> I would plan to leave America very soon after the inauguration on a naval vessel. You will be informed later of as date of arrival that will be satisfactory to Churchill and me.[3]

Although Roosevelt still hoped that Stalin still might be persuaded to travel farther, Churchill had no dislike of travel and responded positively to this. He even proposed the code name Argonaut, a repetition of the one used for his far more dangerous Moscow trip in 1942. He was implying that he and Roosevelt were intrepid travellers, and hinting that Stalin was not. The meeting was confirmed by Stalin's telegram to Churchill on the 3rd day of 1945. 'I look forward very much to this momentous meeting and I am glad that the President of the United States has been willing to make this long journey.'

Churchill still felt the need to settle some of the details with Roosevelt and telegraphed him:

In none of your telegrams about ARGONAUT have you mentioned whether U.J. likes this place and agrees to it and what kind of accommodation he can provide. I am looking forward to this. It has occurred to some of us that he might come back and say "Why don't you come on for the additional four hours and let me entertain you in Moscow?" However I am preparing for Yalta and am sending a large liner which will cover all our troubles. Would it not be possible for you to spend two or three nights at Malta and let the staffs have a talk together unostentatiously?[4]

But Roosevelt had no taste for such a meeting which might be seen as going behind the Soviets' backs. Quebec was rather different; that had been largely about strategy against Japan, which the Soviets were not involved in so far. So although Churchill remained persistent, Roosevelt replied:

With favourable weather at sea I can arrive Malta February second and it is necessary to proceed by air the same day in order to keep the date with U.J. That is why I regret that in view of the time available to me for this journey it will not be possible for us to meet your suggestion.[5]

★ ★ ★

Unlike Churchill's comparatively casual visits to Moscow and Washington in the past, this was to be a major international conference involving three nations and hundreds of people. The British end was planned by a committee of 18, chaired by General Ismay. Other representatives from the War Cabinet Offices and the Ministry of Defence included Ian Jacob and Joan Bright, while the Prime Minister's office sent Tommy Thompson and one of the private secretaries. There were three officers from the Admiralty, Brooke's aide Boyle from the War Office and a civil servant from the Air Ministry. Combined Operations Headquarters, the Ministry of War Transport, the Foreign Office and MI5 were also represented.

The British had become rather blasé about cover stories for international conferences over the years, as no serious leaks seemed to have taken place. At first it was decided that no particular story was needed for Yalta, as it was 'highly unlikely that the enemy would be in a position to undertake deliberate attacks on shipping or aircraft proceeding to or leaving ARGONAUT, even if there was a genuine leakage regarding time and place'. But the Americans objected to this and it was decided to give the impression that the conference was taking place at Habbinaya Aerodrome 55 miles west of Baghdad. Housing was to be procured for 100 delegates, radio circuits were to be set up, and teams were to be sent out to prepare the airport for flying in important delegations.

One priority, as Churchill had suggested, was to find a ship to act as headquarters. The *Franconia* was another Cunard liner, although at 20,175 tons she was only about a quarter of the size of the *Queen Mary*. She had been launched in 1923 from the same shipyard, John Brown's of Clydebank and was designed mainly for the Liverpool to New York service. Since transatlantic emigration was declining at that time, she was also planned to serve as a cruise ship, and her round-the-world trips became famous. The last one was in 1938, when she travelled more that 41,000 miles and visited 37 ports. Converted to a troopship at the beginning of the war, she took men to Malta, evacuated forces from Norway in 1940 and rescued 8,000 troops and civilians from Quiberon Bay in France, during which time she was bombed by the *Luftwaffe*. She participated in the invasion of Diego Suarez in Madagascar in 1942 and the assault on Sicily in July 1943.

Franconia's new captain was Harry Grattridge, who had started as an apprentice in a four-masted barque in 1906. He joined Cunard in 1914 and during World War I he was an officer in the Royal Naval Reserve, spending nearly a year in a minesweeper in the Dardanelles. Between the wars he took part in many world cruises during which he got to know dignitaries such as Lord Beaverbrook. He was chief officer of the troopship *Lancastria* and was one of the few survivors when she was sunk by German bombers at St Nazaire in June 1940 with the loss of several thousand lives, the greatest disaster in British maritime history. He was summoned to the Admiralty on 11 January to meet Admiral Sir Andrew Cunningham himself and was told of the latest mission. No British ship had sailed through the Dardanelles since the war began, but by treaty Turkey had to allow civilian vessels, and it was clear that they would turn a blind eye to the presence of service personnel on board. The greatest danger was mines, many of which had drifted from established German and Soviet fields. Ideally, the *Franconia* should moor or anchor at Yalta itself, but that was thickly mined and their positions were not well plotted.

There were just eight days left to convert *Franconia* into a headquarters ship for perhaps the most important international conference in history, and she berthed at Liverpool at 1.30 in the afternoon of 8 January. Comfortable accommodation replaced her fittings as a troopship, and staff were imported from the *Queen Mary*, including her chef and hairdresser. A special cabin was fitted out for Churchill, forward on A deck, with 'deep armchairs upholstered in dark green, and apple-green silk bedstead, tall vases gay with daffodils'. There was a stool in the bathroom so that he could shave sitting down. Previous experience in the Crimea showed how short the Soviets were of land transport, so she was to carry a total of 46 vehicles. Cranes were fitted to lift them in and out. Six boats were carried to transport the VIPs, along with two amphibious DUKWs. A thousand tons of diesel oil was carried to power generators for the extensive radio and electronic equipment that was being fitted. To mislead the enemy, she was equipped with heaters on the bridge, anti-freeze oil was used and the ship's whistle was lagged to give the impression that they were sailing to the north of Russia. The ship was ready by midday on the 16th, except for the adjustment of the compasses and the calibration of the direction-finding equipment, which could only be done afloat.

A special 13-coach train was to take the passengers to the *Franconia* in Liverpool. Twenty-four of them were allocated first-class accommodation with sleeping berths, 56 more (mostly Wrens officers) had third-class seats with sleeping accommodation and 50 more, mostly Royal Marine other ranks, would also have to spend the night in third-class seats. The train left Addison Road at 20 past midnight on the 17th, but spent five hours in a siding near Liverpool to arrive at ten in the morning.

After taking on the passengers, the *Franconia* left Liverpool at one in the afternoon of the 17th. Captain Grattridge took the ship round the north of Ireland, as the U-boats were now fitted with schnorkels which allowed them to breathe underwater and they had begun a new campaign in British waters. By the afternoon of the 18th there was 'a great smoky sea piling up from the north-west', and he was obliged to reduce speed to three knots to avoid damage to the vehicles and DUKWs on deck. According to Captain Pim, 'The glass had been falling all day and by night-fall a full gale was blowing from the north. This reached such a velocity, gusts of 115 miles an hour being recorded, that the ship was hove to for some 20 hours. In spite of this it was almost impossible to keep one's seat in the saloon although, as may be gathered, this did not really affect many people as there was a great number of vacant chairs.'

Ilene Hutchison, one of the typists sent on the voyage, was seasick, but not so bad that she wanted to die. She felt much better after a walk on deck. Grattridge spent the next ten days 'pacing the bridge, duffle-coated, conferring with John Wood, the best staff-captain I could have had for the job'. But the weather improved by the time the ship was off the coast of Spain and Ilene Hutchison began to enjoy herself with sun bathing and deck tennis. She was allowed to look round the ship's wireless room and was impressed with its range of Morse transmitters and teleprinters. They passed Gibraltar in the middle of the night and could see little, but were recompensed by a fine view of the stars. After that the voyage became a pleasure cruise. The Mediterranean was calm with a beautiful moon, and just as romantic as fiction had led her to expect. They approached Malta on the 25th. Miss Hutchison found it a large, flat island. In the afternoon they anchored some distance away from the quay in Grand Harbour, Valetta, and were disappointed not to be allowed ashore.

Joan Bright, arrived on board 'dark and vivacious', according to Captain Grattridge and 'the organising genius of the War Cabinet Secretariat'. She announced a complete change of plans. It was now accepted that the Soviet conference and living facilities were adequate, so the meetings would be held ashore, though *Franconia* still had a role to play: 'The powerful wireless station on board would be the receiving and transmitting station for the conference, the one link with the outside world. I still had to bring this intact through the minefields.'

★ ★ ★

Originally Churchill planned to leave Northolt in his Skymaster at midnight on the 29th, to arrive at Malta around daybreak. Tommy Thompson received a call from the Air Ministry to say that snow was on the way, and they would have to leave by 9.30 that evening to miss it. All members of the party were summoned, including Lord Moran who was at home in Uxbridge, close to Northolt. The crew were pleased to see that Sarah Churchill was with them for her first flight in the Skymaster, and they showed her around proudly.

Because of the change in plan, the aircraft arrived in Malta at 4.30 in the morning of the 30th. Churchill had no wish to have his sleep interrupted, so he was to be allowed to stay in bed, and there was to be no reception committee. This led to what Ian Jacob would have called a 'Tommy muck-up'. In the commander's own words:

As the Skymaster approached the island I got up and put on a monkey jacket over my pyjamas as I wanted to leave the aircraft on arrival and explain to Air Commodore Whitney Straight, who was in charge of the R.A.F. arrangements there, that Mr Churchill would need transport to the dockyard at eight o'clock. When we stopped on the tarmac and I left the plane I was blinded by floodlighting. As my eyes became accustomed to the glare I saw to my horror that every high-ranking officer and civilian from the Governor downwards was standing to attention in front of me. Our message from Downing Street had not been received. To make matters worse at least three other signals had come in during the night, all giving different times of arrival; the final one had announced that the P.M. would land at 3.30 AM., but this was Greenwich Mean Time. As a result General Sir Edmund Schreiber, the Governor; John Cunningham, the Commander-in-Chief, Mediterranean; Pug Ismay, and many others had all been waiting on the airfield for over an hour, cursing our lack of consideration. Surrounded by this bunch of nearly explosive V.I.Ps, I felt I was lucky to regain the Skymaster without being torn limb from limb.[6]

Worse was to follow when Churchill woke an hour later. Sawyers pulled back the curtain on Moran's bunk to tell him that the Prime Minister had a high temperature. Churchill blamed the tablets Moran had been giving him, but the doctor denied that these could have been responsible: 'The P.M. has views on everything, and his views on medicine are not wanting in assurance.' Churchill wanted to send for specialists again, but Moran was sceptical – it was 'the Moscow performance all over again'. Churchill, he noted, had developed a habit of running a temperature during his journeys. However, he did acknowledge a real mental decline in his patient. 'It is not only the flesh that is weaker. Martin tells me that his work has deteriorated a lot in the last few months; and that he has become very wordy, irritating his colleagues in the Cabinet by his verbosity. One subject will get to his mind to the exclusion of all others – Greece, for example.'

Churchill rested in the aircraft until noon, then he was taken to the cruiser *Orion* which had been made ready for him in the harbour. In peacetime she had served in the West Indies and the Mediterranean, where in war she saw action in the Battle of Matapan against the Italian Fleet and the defence of Crete against the Germans. After repair in California she supported Malta convoys and the invasions of Sicily and Italy. She gave gunfire support on D-Day but was back in the Mediterranean in time to support the landings in the south of France which Churchill had witnessed. The Prime Minister was given the captain's cabin in the stern, and the rest of his party was to be kept together. Churchill's daughter Sarah had the next best cabin, from which the ship's commander was evicted, while Tommy Thompson was to displace the chief engineer officer. The other members, ranging in status from Sir Edward Bridges and Lord Moran to Inspector Thompson and Frank Sawyers, were allocated lieutenants' cabins.

The Prime Minister's illness was another false alarm, but Moran was becoming increasingly tired of his difficult patient. 'Surely this bout of fever should put sense into his head. But Winston is a gambler, and gamblers do not count the coins in their pockets. He will not give a thought to nursing his waning powers.' Instead he stayed up half the night playing bezique with Harriman, who had flown in from Moscow to await Roosevelt.

Other ships were available in Malta to accommodate members of the party. HMS *Largs* was a headquarters ship with much in common with the *Bulolo* as used at Casablanca. She had space for many middle-ranking officers, from captain to brigadier, and some of the Foreign Office party. The 10,000-ton passenger and cargo liner *Eastern Prince* of 1929 was taken over, appropriately enough, by Lord Leathers and some of the staff of the Ministry of Shipping. Ashore, the travellers lived among several layers of Malta's rich history. Brooke and Eisenhower lodged in the San Anton Palace, built in 1620 for one of the leaders of the Knights of Malta and now used by the Governor. Cunningham stayed at Admiralty House in Valetta, and held a dinner there on the night of 31 January when Brooke was impressed. 'Nelson's old headquarters, I must say that I felt swept off into the old ages imagining him here with his romance and his wars!'

★　★　★

Brooke was driven through the snows of London in the morning of the 29th, dreading another journey in 'cold space'. However, after taking off at nine, he had 'a wonderful trip mostly at 12,000 ft height over the clouds in brilliant sunshine'. He and his fellow chiefs had landed in Malta by 3 p.m, to begin a round of talks with their American counterparts. But there was terrible news for him on 2 February, as Brian Boyle entered his office. His *aide-de-camp* and dear friend Captain Barney Charlesworth was missing after his flight had crash-landed.

Two Yorks were ready at Northolt in the morning of the 31st, to take passengers to Malta. EW 623 took off on time, but EW 617 had engine trouble and could not go. However, there was another aircraft, MW 116, which was getting ready at Lyneham to begin a scheduled, 60-hour trip to Colombo in Ceylon. Its crew was hurriedly rebriefed for a very different flight, and the passengers, including Captain Charlesworth, were driven the 65 miles into the Wiltshire countryside.

The crew of MW 116 was not short of experience. The captain, Flight-Lieutenant Alfred Eaton-Clarke, had served in the elite Pathfinders of Bomber Command and completed his tour of duty before passing out proficient as a York pilot. The co-pilot, Anselne Vernifuwe, had joined the Belgian Air Force as an observer in 1936 and then retrained as a pilot. When his country was invaded he spent nearly three years in hiding with the French Resistance, then escaped to join the RAF, where he completed a six-month tour of duty as captain of a Lancaster. The navigator, Flight-Lieutenant James Holdaway, had joined the RAF Volunteer Reserve as an observer in 1938 and had an above-average assessment on completing 35 missions with Bomber Command in 1941. He served as an instructor and then completed another tour of 35 missions before converting to Yorks.

The crew had trained together for three weeks on a largely ground-based course at Nutts Corner in Northern Ireland, but bad weather had prevented any cross-country flying. Squadron-Leader Graham Midpath, the training officer of 511 Squadron, had doubts about their readiness for a 'special' flight as they had never completed a scheduled flight in a York. The acting commanding officer of the squadron wanted Midpath to take over, but this would consume an hour or more of extra preparation and the situation was urgent. None of the passengers was rated as a VIP, so Eaton-Clarke and his crew were allowed to go.

They took off and flew across France by way of established corridors well away from pockets of enemy resistance. Flying down the coast of Italy, the aircraft found itself in ten-tenths cloud at 5,000 feet and the crew believed they were off Naples. They flew out to sea intending to turn round and make an approach. As they dropped through layers of cloud they saw two islands, which they believed were in the Bay of Naples. The could get no radio contact with the Italian airfield, but the wireless operator, Warrant Officer Wright, reported that he could hear Malta very clearly and they decided to proceed there – it would be difficult to get back to the south of France against the winds. By the time they reached the western end of Sicily, the cloud had reduced to three-tenths, though it was now dark and there was no moon. They took radio bearings to establish their position and got a favourable weather forecast from Malta. By this time fuel was running low and Eaton-Clarke was concerned enough to send out an SOS message. They sighted some lights to starboard and saw an island, which they circled several times. There was an airfield on what turned out to be the tiny Italian island of Lampedusa, but it was clearly too small for a York. Unsure of his position and with only ten minutes' fuel left, Eaton-Clarke climbed to 8,000 feet to see if he could find Malta. Around 7 p.m. he decided to ditch near the island he could see.

All the crew except the captain and navigator were sent aft to open the hatches, get the dinghies ready and look after the passengers. They landed on the water at a speed of a little over 100 miles per hour and all seemed to go well at first. Then the aircraft sank rather quickly and there was a noise like an explosion after which it sank more rapidly. Some reports suggested it had hit a submerged wreck, but this was not confirmed at the court of inquiry. Most of the crew got out and made it to shore by dinghy or local boat, though the fishermen removed some of their watches and clothing. However, one of the passengers, Air Commodore Anderson, was found floating in the water still strapped to his seat and more bodies were found later.

The court of inquiry later made specific comments. The crew was too inexperienced in transport flying, and in future none should be allowed to go on such a flight without training in ditching drill. More care should be used in calculating fuel endurance, and the navigators and wireless operators should use their equipment more regularly. But it concluded: 'Flight-Lieutenant Eaton-Clarke cannot be criticised for his behaviour as Captain as throughout the flight he gave primary consideration to the safety of his passengers, and it was not his fault that he was deceived in his observation of weather conditions at POMIGLIANO.' Flying, it implied, was still a dangerous business.

News filtered through slowly to Malta and at first there was some hope for Charlesworth as it was believed that seven out of twenty passengers had been saved. The news of his death was confirmed at 8 in the evening of the 2nd, 24 hours after the accident. Brooke was devastated. Charlesworth had been with him since Dunkirk, the two had shared many travels together and he even lived in Brooke's flat in the War Office. 'It is a frightful blow as Barney had grown to be a most intimate companion. I always knew I could discuss anybody or anything with him without fear of him ever repeating anything. He was always cheerful and in good humour no matter how unpleasant situations were.' Grief would cast a shadow over the whole of Brooke's trip.

★ ★ ★

The *Franconia* sailed from Malta at midday on the 26th, escorted by the destroyer *Kelvin*. She headed for the Dardanelles where she would pass into the Black Sea. Pim described this part of the trip:

The passage through the Dardanelles was one of great interest. After passing Cape Helles we were abreast of the Anzac beaches and could clearly see the War Memorial to those who died in the Gallipoli landings. Chocolate Hill and other places often mentioned by my brother in letters while serving with the Gunners in the Dardanelles during the Great War were pointed out to me. At Chanak where the Dardanelles became really narrow we picked up a Turkish pilot who took us through the Sea of Marmora.[7]

The British had still not come to terms with the difficulties of equipping service personnel with civilian clothes for a visit to Turkey. They were used to wearing uniform on and off duty in wartime, and clothing was strictly rationed, so it came as a shock to some to be ordered to change as they approached the Dardanelles. Double-breasted suits with broad chalk-striping had been bought from a British multiple tailor and Captain Grattridge issued the order 'Suits this morning, please, gentlemen.' The ship's guns were hidden under tarpaulins, and the solders began to appear in unaccustomed 'plain clothes'. 'One general's suit was so tight that his elbows jutted sharply through the cloth. Another, whose trousers flapped about his thighs like an empty potato sack, had rolled up his turn-ups as if ready for a paddle. The British naval attaché remarked on 'A fine body of civilians.' Ilene Hutchison was amused as the service personnel had to change into civilian clothes to pass through a neutral country. They were badly fitting as usual: most of the men were only used to uniform after years of war, and it was strange to see privates and generals in apparent equality. Most were glad to get back into uniform.

Out in the Black Sea, the difficulties became more serious. Miss Hutchison thought it uninteresting and cold, looking pale blue rather than black as she had expected. Captain Grattridge and his crew only had eyes for the dangers as they passed through a channel swept of mines, led by two Soviet destroyers and two minesweepers. As they arrived off Sevastopol at 11 in the morning of the 31st, they were hit by a blinding blizzard, to the dismay of Captain Grattridge:

From then on I knew I was on my own. I had no interpreter on board, no knowledge of wrecks or minefields. As we approached Sevastopol at noon it seemed that I had no pilot either. For the Russian Rear-Admiral who had boarded for the job stared at me bleakly and offered no suggestions. Staring at that blinding white curtain of snow, I knew that for the first time in my life I must take a ship into an unknown harbour without any recent local knowledge and moor her myself.[8]

It was completed after an anxious three-quarters of an hour, after which the second officer asked from the after end of the bridge, 'Did you see the wreck, Sir?' Grattridge went aft to look. 'I saw it then, a faintly rippling shadow, like the turning fin of a shark, just below the surface of the water, about eighty yards from the stern. There was no marker buoy or any kind of indication.' He tried to radiate a captain's confidence, but ordered the chief engineer to keep steam ready in case they drifted towards it.

To Captain Pim, Sevastopol was 'undoubtedly the most terrible sight I had ever seen. There was not a single building in the whole town with a roof and very few with glass in their windows. After two sieges one expected a great deal of damage but hardly such complete devastation. The majority of the inhabitants were living outside the town in huts.'

Grattridge now had to 'navigate the chilly waters of Soviet diplomacy', as he put it. The most urgent task was to get the 46 motor vehicles unloaded before the main party arrived in two days' time. The harbour was desolate and littered with ice and there was no crane on shore. He considered the rather desperate possibility of lashing lifeboats together to carry the cars, but that seemed too dangerous. A Soviet water lighter and some barges could be seen, but the Russian admiral refused to let them be used. Grattridge tried a bluff. He had Captain Peter Dawnay, the naval signals officer, take a message, in the presence of an interpreter:

> I began to dictate slowly. 'To the Admiralty. Owing to poor water transport facilities – got that? – impossible land cars … that's right … land cars … then – urgently suggest Prime Minister's visit be delayed two days.[9]

This was enough to frighten the admiral, who put a flotilla of barges at the *Franconia*'s disposal.

★ ★ ★

Roosevelt had sailed from Newport News in the cruiser *Quincy* on 23 January, for he had to avoid a long trip by air. He too needed to be kept in touch with affairs during this, his first long wartime sea voyage as President, and he devised a very different system from Churchill. Important papers were put in a bag and dropped by long-range aircraft, to be picked up by a destroyer. He had a party of almost 150, much more than the 35 he had originally suggested. He rested, slept late and watched movies, as Churchill had done on his first voyage.

The *Quincy* arrived in Malta around 10 a.m. on 2 February and passed slowly by the *Orion* with Churchill on board. According to Moran, 'The President, in a cloth cap, sat scanning our ship for Winston, who was on the quarterdeck raising his hat in salutation.' Roosevelt held meetings with his Chiefs of Staff and his new Secretary of State Edward Stettinius, and took a tour of the island while Churchill had his afternoon nap. That evening Churchill came on board the *Quincy* for a meeting and dinner. He left by 10 p.m. and both parties went out to the aerodrome for the flight to the Crimea.

For the Prime Minister's flight across Turkey, Portal recommended giving President Inonu 24 hours' notice to ensure that the correct orders were received by all fighters and anti-aircraft guns. He felt there was no real risk of the Germans gaining any advantage if it should leak out, as they had no fighters within range. The Soviets offered the airfield at Saki. It was farther from Yalta than Sarabuz, which Churchill had used before, but it had better runways.

The route from Malta to Turkey was suggested by Portal, in consultation with General Ira Eaker commanding the Allied air forces in the region and his deputy Air Marshal Sir John Slessor of the RAF. The main constraints were the need to arrive at Saki in daylight hours, and the necessity to keep the President's aircraft below 6,000 feet, which made a flight over the mountainous Greek mainland out of the question. It was equally important to keep away from Greek islands still in enemy hands. They suggested leaving Malta around midnight for the seven-hour, 1,300 mile flight, and flying almost due east from Malta for 400 miles to pass south of the island of Kithira just south of the

The flight from Malta
to the Black Sea, 3 February 1945

Greek mainland. They would turn north-east, still skirting the mainland, and would stay east of the islands of Skiros, Limnos and Samothrace. Then they could reach Turkey west of the Dardanelles, and leave the country over Midya on the Black Sea coast to head for the Crimea. The highest point near the route was on Samothrace, which rose to 5,000 feet and would require flying at 7,000 feet in poor visibility to give a margin of safety. Portal felt that the aircraft would have to fly singly which might complicate the navigational arrangements, and that there was a slight risk in travelling the last part in daylight.

Churchill remembered that he had flown as high as 8,000–9,000 feet to avoid peaks on his previous time on that route, and wanted to know if that was a problem for the President. He suggested leaving Malta in daylight, which would allow them light to pass the Aegean peaks and then cross Turkey by dark, but this would mean a dangerous night landing at Saki. He wrote to Roosevelt proposing the route, and remarked on his own experience of it. If the President was worried about Samothrace, another alternative would be to leave Malta at 3 a.m. and pass it at dawn, and that was agreed.

Air traffic control was a relatively new field for the Royal Air Force in 1945. Until 1937 there was only a duty pilot provided by each squadron, mainly to keep a record of take-offs and landings. After that each command, home and overseas, developed its own system with little co-ordination. Malta, however, was well equipped for mass flights. It had several airfields, including the largest one at Luqa, which was being developed as a control centre for the central Mediterranean, so facilities were good. The American Colonel Ray Ireland was in charge of the runway and take-offs began before midnight. Churchill and Roosevelt both joined their aircraft before that and slept in their cabins, until the Prime Minister's aircraft took off at 3 a.m., followed by the President half an hour later.

Escort was provided by the 27th, 71st and 94th Squadrons of the First Fighter Wing of the United States Army Air Force, which had been shadowing Roosevelt ever since the *Quincy* arrived off North Africa. They flew twin-engine P-38 Lightnings, which had a range of 1,100 miles and an endurance of six hours. Four aircraft took off from Malta at ten-second intervals to escort Roosevelt, and four more for Churchill. They formed up, two on each side of the VIP aircraft. Off Andros to the south-east of Greece, they were replaced by a similar escort of planes from Athens, and Churchill's was led by Lieutenant John Hurst of the 27th Squadron. They would fly all the way to the Crimea and land at Sarabuz to save space at Saki.

★ ★ ★

If the difficulties at Malta were challenging enough, the Crimea presented a different level of problems, where facilities had to be improvised out of almost nothing. To prepare the airfield facilities at Saki, a party of about 20 RAF officers and 85 other ranks was sent out and known prosaically as Staging Post 150. Although the RAF was responsible for the facilities of both the western allies, they were slightly embarrassed when an American colonel arrived first, and their officers on the spot tended to have higher rank, so the Russians deferred to them. There were many difficulties in setting up air traffic control and maintenance systems. The Soviets had very different attitudes on most matters, which caused confusion. Their system was rigid and there was no delegation of authority. All kinds of commodities were in very short supply, and communications were unreliable. Despite their revolutionary history the Soviets were extremely rank-conscious. They also preferred careful and detailed preparation. 'It cannot be stressed too much that nothing pleases the Russians more and is more helpful to all concerned than a concrete plan down to the last detail, which can be given to the Russians at the earliest possible moment.'

The core of the airfield party was gathered at Lyneham on 20 January for the flight out to the Crimea. There were two control officers, Wing-Commander Bulstrode and Flight-Lieutenant Crickmay. Each carried a full set of maps and equipment, including Admiralty charts of the Black Sea in case any air-sea rescue work was needed. The controllers flew out in separate aircraft in the event one was lost, and many more personnel arrived in the *Franconia*. There were doctors, meteorologists, administrative and technical officers, all headed by Group-Captain W. J. Pickard.

Saki airfield was a few miles from Sevastopol. It had an east–west runway 1,500 yards long and 100 yards wide which was into the prevailing wind and quite satisfactory. The other runway was only 1,000 yards long and was not needed for landing so it was used to hold aircraft, dispersed against any possible enemy attack, as was usual in wartime. Apart from that there were very few facilities. Large marquees were erected for radio and meteorological services. The Met Officer was quite happy with the size of his, which was 30 ft by 17 ft, even though he shared it with the camp switchboard. A slightly larger tent was used for operations, briefing and debriefing. 'Several forms and tables were supplied by the Russians, but had to be added to by packing cases and boxes to give the necessary writing and seating accommodation.' The Soviets built a small wooden control tower with an open top, which was never comfortable:

The top half of the Control Tower was a wicked place to work in bad weather. It measured some six feet square and was walled with single thickness boards, the sky showing through the cracks between them. In snowy weather the snow drifted in through the cracks and lay on the radio sets, the cross beams overhead, and the floor. The floor became covered with a hard pack of beaten snow which had to be chopped away with a spade.[10]

Sometimes the runways were covered in snow up to two feet deep in the drifts, in which case the Soviets would provide a thousand men and women labourers to clear it, starting perversely with the unused short runway. When the snow melted it was waterlogged and conditions for the personnel were almost intolerable. According to Wing-Commander Bulstrode, 'Those who have not tried walking about on the Crimean soil in a thaw can have no idea what a labour it was to get to or from the aircraft in use with messages – one carried the message and half the Crimea every time!'

There was no living accommodation in the airfield, so personnel were transported five miles every day to and from a sanatorium. Transport was always difficult, especially when the Soviets 'borrowed' two jeeps and damaged them beyond repair, after which they were looted for spare parts. At the sanatorium, each man had an iron bedstead with linen supplied by the Canadian Red Cross, but as all the travellers were to find out, 'The washing and lavatory facilities were of a very low standard.' At first there were difficulties with the food. Squadron-Leader Sheehan found that the Russians started breakfast with cheese and bread and finished lunch with apple juice, which seemed wrong to the British. He met the Russian officials and offered to supplement the rations from British supplies, but that offended them and they claimed they had ample food. Next day there was a definite improvement, with three eggs for each man. Sheehan thought that the management of the British camp was poor, as the senior officers had to work all the time on their control duties. The men were ill-disciplined, which made a poor impression on the Soviets. Morale remained high, but that was only because of the shortness of the stay.

Control of the airfield was divided. The Soviets were in charge of airfield services, including runway conditions and the provision of fuel, and of messing, provisioning and security. The US Army Air Force would provide much of the transport, leaving the British to take charge of meteorology, communication and aerodrome operation, including clearance of aircraft, briefing, and operating the control tower. There were a few cultural differences that caused friction. For example, the Americans distributed gifts freely, such as wrist watches, radios and cigarette lighters, which made the British look mean. The British were issued with arms, which made it appear as if they did not trust the Russians to defend them, so they were locked away. But on the whole co-operation was surprisingly good.

The British considered the Crimean facilities primitive:

The Russians operated a visual system of airfield control from the down-wind end of the runway. Prohibition signals were given with red flags and red cartridges which emitted varying numbers of stars. Permissive signals were given with white flags and green or white cartridges. There was no significance in either the number of stars – varying from one to five – or the colour – green or white. The cartridges were captured German stock, and it is doubtful whether the new owners were always sure what would come out of the spout when they pulled the trigger. Simultaneous firing of green and red cartridges was seen at once! The wind 'T' was normally white, but red when on snow. The wind sock was too small to be seen easily from the air, but the Russian controllers had an effective type of smoke generator, which was not often used.[11]

Elaborate air-sea rescue facilities were set up for the aircraft as they passed over the Black Sea. Two of the RAF's Vickers Warwicks and a US Navy Catalina flying-boat left Athens on 30 January but the Catalina crashed on the way, while the second Warwick had great difficulty landing at Saki in continuous snow and ten-tenths cloud. Another Warwick was sent out to replace the Catalina but in an accident-prone operation, it had to force land and was unable to get there in time. One Warwick would be on patrol and the other on standby during flying operations. The Soviets provided two Catalinas, a minesweeper and a surfaced submarine.

For the signal section, 2 February was 'the blackest day in the unit's history' as conflict with the Soviets came to the boil. Since the start of the mission there had been conflict between the British and the Soviets about whose equipment was superior. The Soviets used higher power, the British believed that theirs was better set up. Marshal Dhavoronkov called a meeting to express 'extreme dissatisfaction' with the signal arrangements and demanded that they all go over to the Soviet system. The British, aided by 'Pop' Hill, eventually persuaded him that it was impossible at such short notice. But in general the British were very satisfied with the Russians' co-operation.

Naturally, 3 February was by far the busiest day at Saki. The weather began fair to cloudy with stratocumulus clouds varying between three-tenths and ten-tenths density and a base of 3,000 feet. There was a good visibility eight to ten miles, a light south-easterly wind and temperatures rising slowly from 19 degrees Fahrenheit to just below freezing point. By the afternoon, when the VIP planes were arriving, the wind had dropped to nothing and the cloud was no more than five-tenths. It was still cold in the improvised control tower, which was filled with people for the occasion:

> Flying control that day established what is likely to remain an 'all time high' for rank! Upstairs, on the balcony of the top storey, was a Russian one-star General, Kornariov, on the telephone to the runway controller and the local observer network. Downstairs in the W/T cabin was another one-star General, Alexiev – a Signals General – and outside there prowled a Marshal who from time to time barked orders at the Generals! The Generals were, as usual, accompanied by their indispensable followers. The crowd on the top storey did not get too great, consisting normally of F/Lt Crickmay, the airfield controller, General Konariov, and his interpreter. But downstairs the population problem was acute. There was the Russian W/T operator – a very efficient man – the British operator, a Russian Signals captain, General Alexiev and W/Cdr Bulstrode.[12]

Aircraft soon began to converge on the field from Malta, Naples and Athens. For security reasons each had to fly over the control tower, make a 90 degree turn to identify himself to the nervous Soviet anti-aircraft gunners, then land. Twenty four-engine planes landed in the space of five hours, all within seconds of their estimated time of arrival. Over the course of the day there were 13 British transport aircraft carrying 139 passengers and 70 crew, and ten American with 120 passengers and 80 crew. Among them was Churchill's Skymaster EW999. Jack Payne struggled with the block and tackle arrangement used to lower the aircraft's steps, and the party disembarked.

XIX

'We Could Not Have Found a Worse Place'

The Crimea's only advantage was its location, the easiest part of the Soviet Union for the western leaders to get to, and with the best climate. It had been captured and recaptured three times by each side, and suffered from the usual German destruction as they withdrew for the last time. Churchill later told Harriman that 'if we had spent ten years on research we could not have found a worse place in the world than MAGNETO.' Miss Bright had already discovered the difficulties as she led the advance party. She telegraphed Ismay:

> Destruction in Crimea almost complete. Russians in two weeks have rebuilt and furnished only possible accommodation left standing for British and American delegations. This accommodation will stretch people's tempers to the limits but it is the best possible and the Russians have done wonders ... Everyone except V.I.Ps will have to share two and four, some six to nine, in room. Bathrooms few and far between. In Vorontzov three will have to cover up to thirty people.[1]

Yalta, according to a document issued to the British delegation, was 'situated in an amphitheatre rising from a large bay of the Black Sea. Under the Tsars it had been the most fashionable and most expensive of the Crimean bathing resorts. In the background are the steep slopes of the Yaila mountains (about 4,000 feet)' It had been used by the Tsars and their richest aristocrats, and had associations with Chekhov, the nineteenth-century playwright – his sister was still the curator of a museum dedicated to his life. Not much of the grandeur had survived the Revolution and the German occupation and withdrawal. The British delegates were given a very short leaflet on local attractions. As well as the Chekhov Museum, it mentioned the Swallow's Nest, a beauty spot three or four miles away; the Nijitsky Botanical Gardens ten miles away – a park used by the Soviet equivalent of the Boy Scouts – and Massandra, another beauty spot where some of the local wine was produced.

★ ★ ★

The Soviets had put up a tent at the end of the runway at Saki for the reception of the visitors, which undercut a similar one which the British had worked all night to erect. After that, the party was put into cars for the drive to Yalta. Churchill had always had misgivings about the road journey, and as early as 21 January he had asked Portal, 'What is the story of four to five hours or more, even in daylight, motoring from ALBATROSS [Saki] to MAGNETO [Yalta]?' If true, he wanted to draft a telegram to Roosevelt 'mentioning this new fact of the ALBATROSS–MAGNETO motor ride as additional proof of the charm of the place he has chosen'. Portal confirmed that the route was 70 to 80 miles long over very poor roads and would be over 100 miles if they were blocked by snow and they had to use the coast road via Sevastopol. The journey would take at least four hours.

Moran travelled with Churchill and was aware of the Russian guards – 'All the way I caught glimpses of sturdy girls, dressed like Russian soldiers, and carrying tommy-guns, who stood rigidly to attention as each car passed.' Elizabeth Layton stayed awake during the five-hour drive, unlike Moran, and she saw 'a picturesque country – dark green cypresses and terra-cotta earth. We passed some magnificent country villas, now looking shattered and uncared for.' Inspector Thompson was now back with the party, and his policeman's eye could not help admiring the skill of the women traffic controllers along the route. 'They were exceedingly smart at this work. They worked with a red flag in the right hand and a yellow one in the left. After signalling drivers to proceed, the red flag was passed to the left hand and a salute given in one movement.' Churchill found the trip no more pleasant than he had predicted and turned to his daughter. 'After what seemed an eternity, Papa asked how long we had been going and I replied "about an hour". "Christ" said Papa "five more hours of this" and gloom and muttered bad language set in.' But the road began to improve when they reached the mountains after 2½ hours. They passed Roosevelt's convoy which had stopped for refreshments and 'the call of nature was pretty desperate' by the time they reached a rest house where Molotov was waiting with lunch. After that they set off and reached their villa in Yalta in the evening. Churchill went to bed after 14 hours of travelling.

Stalin travelled down in an armoured train protected by flatbed trucks carrying anti-aircraft guns. He and his party were to live in the Yusopov Palace, once owned by the man who had assassinated Rasputin. Roosevelt was in the famous Livadia Palace, built for the Tsar in the early twentieth century but used only four times by the Imperial family. General Marshall slept in the Imperial bedroom and Admiral King was in the Tsarina's boudoir, with a private staircase that was said to have been used by Rasputin. The Palace had been used as a tuberculosis hospital after the revolution, then as the German headquarters and they 'did a thorough job of looting'. The only surviving furnishings were two paintings in the President's bedroom – all the rest had been brought in specially for the conference.

The British were in the Vorontsov Palace, built in 1837 by a Russian prince, diplomat and courtier. It was a strange combination of Gothic castle and Moorish palace. It was in a better state than most, for it had served as the residence of Field Marshal von Manstein. He had hoped that he would be given it after the war, so efforts to destroy it were tardy and ineffective. Moran was impressed with the entrance:

> Passing through a great Moorish archway, I descended a wide flight of steps, flanked by six marble lions, to the garden, which falls in terraces to the Black Sea. There are two fine cypresses in the court-yard, and rare subtropical plants are scattered through the garden. The house is sheltered by mountains, which are clothed with vine-yards on their lower slopes, and higher up there are dark pine trees. When I returned to the house I found that the reception rooms are what might be expected from the gentleman who was responsible for the lions, but the plumbing and sanitary arrangements are elemen-tary.[2]

Cadogan for one was happy with it:

> We are really quite comfortable here. The Russians had 1,500 men working on this house for a fortnight before we came. Every pane of glass had to be put in and, I suspect, all the electric light. The latter works well, but there is a system of 'remote control' of lighting which is somewhat embarrassing. The lights in Anthony's room, his bath-room, and in all the offices turn on and off from a switchboard at the end of the passage! So that a Russian housemaid or heavy-fingered Marine either plunge one into darkness or switch on the light at 6 a.m.! However, I think I'm curing them of that. Otherwise, everything is done for our comfort – bowls of fruit and bottles of mineral water in every bedroom. Also a decanter of vodka![3]

According to Miss Layton, 'The Vorontsov Villa boasted several banqueting halls, various reception rooms, a conservatory containing lemon trees and many ferns, and so on.' But as Miss Bright had predicted, washing facilities had been neglected. It was also overcrowded and Moran found what had once been the servants' quarters full of air marshals, generals and admirals, frantically looking for tins to wash in. Churchill telegraphed to Clementine that '16 American colonels are to be quartered in one room'. She replied, 'I hope that neither Miss Layton nor Miss Sturdee will have to share rooms with 16 American colonels!'

Another problem was the prevalence of bed bugs, which Squadron-Leader Sheehan came to regard as 'part of the normal flora [sic] of the Russian bedroom'. He and the surgeon of the *Franconia* discussed it with Moran, but the promised DDT powder never turned up and local army supplies had to be used. Nevertheless Sheehan was impressed with the Vorontsov Palace:

> Life at Yalta is a pleasant change from Saki. All the waiters and staff have been imported from the Metropole Hotel in Moscow, lots of glamorous interpreters and champagne, cocktails merely for the asking. Feel I would not mind 'roughing it' at Yalta for another few days but have to go back to the mud of Saki tomorrow.[4]

Captain Pim had issued specifications for the site of his Map Room. He needed a space at least 16 ft long, 12 ft wide and 11 ft high. It had to be close to a smaller room to be used as an office and map store, and adjacent to the Prime Minister's quarters, with wheeled access for the President. Four ft by 8 ft Essex boards would be used to hold the maps. Special lamps would be brought to light it, but fittings were needed at 4 ft 6 intervals at the top of the boarding.

Vorontsov had been a man of wide interests who had once been ambassador to Britain. This was reflected in his library, which was now used as an office by the Chiefs of Staff. Cunningham was surprised to find a book on the old palace at Bishop's Waltham, the ruins of which were in his own garden. Churchill recognised one of the pictures on the wall as a member of the Herbert family, with whom the Vorontsovs had married.

★ ★ ★

In these strange surroundings, the three leaders would make some of the key decisions about the future of the world. They would also leave many matters undecided, so that the post-war world would continue to have many problems.

There were sixteen topics on the Foreign Ministers' list of items for discussion, most of them contentious and with far-reaching effects.

Churchill rested for the first day and was visited by Stalin in the evening, when he conferred the order of a Commander of the British Empire on his interpreter Pavlov. Churchill showed Stalin to the Map Room and Stalin suggested moving troops from Italy to go through the Balkans towards Vienna. After that, life in Yalta settled into a regular routine, as it had done in Moscow. The schedule was less demanding than earlier conferences, and Churchill was able to rest and carry on his paperwork until 4 in the afternoon when the plenary session started. The 'big three' spent four or five hours together, then on most nights Churchill dined quietly with his daughter and Eden, much to Sarah's relief. Then the papers arrived at midnight, having been flown in by the Mosquito service, and he worked on them for perhaps two hours. He was sleeping well, even without the use of his usual pills. His eyes were giving him trouble, however, and he had to have the curtains in his bedroom adjusted to stop the sun shining in his eyes.

He was in much better health than President Roosevelt, whose decline was far more marked than in Quebec five months earlier. The President's family and his own doctors seemed confident, but Moran saw it differently. 'To a doctor's eye, the President appears a very sick man. He has all the symptoms of hardening of the arteries of the brain in an advanced stage, so that I give him only a few months to live.' It had a serious effect on his performance:

> He intervened very little in the discussions, sitting with his mouth open. If he has sometimes been short of facts about the subject under discussion, his shrewdness has covered this up. Now, they say, the shrewdness has gone, and there is nothing left. I doubt from what I have seen if he is fit for the job here.[5]

★   ★   ★

For some time the conferences had been moving away from discussing the war to planning the peace, and Yalta was to prove the most crucial one for the future. None of the participants seems to have recognised this when they made up their delegations to attend, and large numbers of generals, admirals and air marshals came as usual. This mattered less with the Soviet and American groups, as their generals were more political. The distinction between civil and military life was blurred in the USSR, while American generals such as Marshall and Eisenhower were political figures, and Eisenhower later became

President. But British generals had far less of a political tradition. At the San Francisco conference in the spring of 1945 (not attended by Churchill), Ian Jacob wrote: 'There was little of real military interest, and the general atmosphere was so different from the vital war conferences when something concrete was being done ... I could not derive great satisfaction from all the political haggling and the welter of words.'

Ismay thought that the Yalta conference was unnecessary from a military point of view. When the vital issue of the boundaries of Poland was under discussion, no suitable maps could be found, for Pim's Map Room was concerned with military operations, not ethnic divisions. Churchill could have found experienced economists, geographers, ethnographers and historians who would have helped his arguments on the Polish question, but as always he liked travelling with people he knew, and he had settled into a routine with his usual party. Sir Edward Bridges, Secretary to the War Cabinet and head of the civil service, was conscious of the growing problem and wrote to Churchill:

> Will the next stage be that at some future Conference the affairs of several Civil Departments may be concerned and that the British Secretariat, instead of being run by the military side of this office plus the Foreign Office, might require to be organised on a wider basis? If and when that happens, shall we be at a disadvantage that none of the Senior Civil staff of this office have had any experience of these conferences?[6]

He hesitated to propose himself, but Churchill scrawled on his letter, 'Come with me', and Bridges found himself in the snows and mud of the Crimea.

★   ★   ★

Because of the President's poor health, the meetings were held in the Livadia Palace where he lived. Churchill managed to deflect the idea of dismembering Germany permanently. Stalin demanded huge reparations from Germany but that issue was shelved – Churchill knew that reparations had been disastrous after the last war. A plan for a United Nations was agreed, and Soviet demands that each of her constituent republics be allowed a place was watered down, and it was agreed that the five main victors – the USSR, the USA, Britain, France and China – should form the Security Council on which each had a veto. Churchill wanted France to be restored to European status and to have both a zone of occupation in Germany and a seat on the Control Commission; he was worried that America might withdraw from Europe in a few years and leave Britain alone to face the Soviets. To most people's surprise, he got his way on that. Stalin agreed in principle that German war criminals would be tried and not summarily executed. The biggest issue, nevertheless, was Poland.

Churchill had severe doubts about the Soviet plan to extend the country westward, giving more territory to the Soviet Union and taking if from the eastern part of Germany – the idea of forced movement of population was anathema to him, even at the expense of the defeated Germans. Roosevelt failed to back him on this, and also on the question of the recognition of the 'Lublin Poles' who now formed the basis of Stalin's puppet government of the country. The best he could get was a reassurance that free elections would be held as soon as possible, and that British and American ambassadors would be there to supervise them. In this case Churchill felt that he suffered from the lack of information about what was really happening in Poland, while Stalin had armies and agents in the country.

Rather casually over a private meeting with Stalin before the final plenary session, Churchill agreed to continue repatriating Soviet prisoners who were being liberated from prison camps taken by the allies, or in some cases had been fighting for the Germans. Stalin remarked that 'Those who had agreed to fight for the Germans could be dealt with on their return to Russia' and Churchill failed to pick up how sinister that was from the lips of Stalin. In fact a majority of the returnees, including innocent prisoners of war, were executed or sentenced to labour camps.

For all the disagreements, there was some room for social events. Stalin hosted a dinner on the evening of the 8th after the fourth plenary session. Speeches 'mostly consisted of insincere, slimy sort of slush'. Churchill's was the exception, for he was on superb form. He began by saying that Stalin's life was 'most precious to all the hopes and hearts of all of us'. He hoped that he would 'be spared to the people of the Soviet Union and help us all to move forward to a less unhappy time than that through which we have recently come'. He concluded, 'My hope is in the illustrious President of the United States and in Marshal Stalin, in whom we shall find the champions of peace, who after smiting the foe will lead us to carry on the task against poverty, confusion, chaos, and oppression.' It was a fine evening and after his return to the Vorontsov Palace late that night, Marian Holmes overheard him singing *The Glory Song.*

The British were the hosts on the night of the 10th, when Churchill was equally fulsome in his praise. There had been misunderstandings and differences in the past, but now, 'We feel we have a friend whom we can trust, and I hope he will continue to feel the same about us. I pray he may live to see his beloved Russia not only glorious in war, but also happy in peace.' He mentioned that an election was due in Britain soon, and that he might have to say harsh things about the communists during it. 'You know we have two parties in England.' 'One party is much better,' said Stalin. Churchill took his guests to his Map Room again and he discounted any suggestion that he might make a separate armistice with Germany by singing, 'Keep right on to the end of the road.' The President commented that Churchill's singing was 'Britain's secret weapon'.

Ismay summarised the results of the conference succinctly. 'From a gastronomical point of view, it was enjoyable: from the social point of view, successful: from the military point of view, unnecessary: and from the political point of view, depressing.'

★   ★   ★

To a military man like Brooke or a historian like Churchill, the Crimea was best known as the site of Britain's largely pointless and mismanaged war with Russia in 1854–6. To the general public the war was best known for Tennyson's poem *The Charge of the Light Brigade* which celebrated the discipline of the British soldier in the face of his leaders' stupidity. It also gave the army one of its most famous expressions, 'The Thin Red Line', in which a reduced force of the 93rd Regiment, later part of the Argyll and Sutherland Highlanders, had held out against the Russian advance. It led eventually to army reforms that helped create the force which Churchill had joined in 1893, and which Brooke now led. The military staffs had finished their discussions by the 7th, and Churchill gave them permission to visit the battlefields, provided one officer was trained to take him around later. The Soviets provided an excellent guide and good cars. They drove up the winding Vorontsov Road, named after the former owner of the house they were in, and had superb views over the land and sea. They saw fat, healthy children and felt that the Soviets were beginning to put wartime famine behind them. They saw the site of the Battle of Balaclava and the place where the Light Brigade had charged. They also saw mementoes of much later battles and found a skeleton, which Moran was unable to identify as Soviet or German.

★   ★   ★

After a joint statement was issued on the 11th, Churchill was driven back to his quarters and had a sudden urge to leave the Vorontsov Villa and move on. 'Why do we stay here? Why don't we go tonight – I see no reason to stay here a minute longer – We're off!' He sprang out of the car into the private office and gave the orders that he wanted to be away in 50 minutes:

> After a second's stunned silence, everyone was galvanised into activity. Trunks and large mysterious paper parcels given to us by the Russians – whoopee – filled the hall. Laundry arrived back clean but damp. Naturally 50 minutes gave us the time to change our minds six times more. 'We will spend the night here after all and leave tomorrow lunchtime – We will fly – We will leave tonight and go by sea – We will go to Athens – Cairo – Constantinople – We will not go to any of them – We will stay on board and read the newspapers.[7]

Sawyers was close to nervous collapse as he packed and unpacked, saying, 'They can't do this to me.' But after an hour and 20 minutes, at about 5.30 in the evening, the cars left the villa for Sevastopol. The mountain road was no less frightening in the dark, as Sarah wrote to her mother 'We crept right up to the base of the granite peaks. Once, near the top, we got out and looked. 400 to 500 feet sheer precipice of rock rose above us – so straight, it seemed to lean over like the beetling brows of a giant.'

Churchill arrived on board the *Franconia* at midnight to be greeted by Captain Grattridge – the rest of the crew had been ordered to stay out of the way, but a cheer arose from the ship and heads could be seen at every porthole as he arrived. He was pleased and gave his famous V sign. He soon got down to work, amid the dispatches which had recently arrived and using the *Franconia*'s sophisticated signal facilities. 'Churchill's transformation of the *Franconia* was the most break-neck change in the atmosphere of a ship that I have ever seen. Day and night you passed secretaries speeding to and fro along the corridors like abstracted White Rabbits whose timepieces had betrayed them.' The ship's card room had to be closed after Churchill complained about the noise from it. Grattridge wrote about Churchill's entourage: 'I think all of them felt as I did that no matter how trying he could be or how often he changed his mind, it was a small enough price to pay for living close to greatness.'

Churchill was ready for a battlefield tour by the 13th but at first Tommy Thompson had difficulty in making clear what was wanted. 'The P.M. said he would like to see the battlefield of Balaclava nearby. I explained this to the interpreter, and off we went to the little fishing village after which the battle is named. We were shown where German submarines had been moored, but no reference was made to the battle of 90 years before, and it turned out that none of the Russians present had ever heard of it.' But Brooke had trained Brigadier Peake and they went round with the Soviet admiral commanding the Black Sea Fleet. It soon became clear that two war sites overlapped:

> As Peake pointed to the line which the Light Brigade had been drawn up, the Russian admiral pointed in almost the same direction and exclaimed, 'The German tanks came at us from over there.' A little later Peake explained the Russian dispositions, and pointed to the hills where their infantry had stood, whereupon the Russian admiral intervened with obvious pride: 'That is where a Russian battery fought and died to the last man.' I thought it right at this juncture to explain that we were studying a different war, 'a war of dynasties, not of peoples'. Our host gave no sign of comprehension, but seemed perfectly satisfied.[8]

There was time for relaxation in the usual Churchill style. He enjoyed the *Franconia* and telegraphed his wife, 'We are taking another day's rest here on this most comfortable ship with its *Queen Mary* staff.' Moran found it 'comfortable to the point of luxury' as the *Mary*'s chef provided them with 'perfect food' among which 'white rolls take one back to times of peace'. Early one morning Churchill enjoyed a dinner of partridge coquette – 'a dish made up of roast partridge, bacon, diced artichokes, mushrooms and sherry'. He commented 'That was excellent – really first class', and asked that the remains of a bottle of Liebfraumilch should be kept for breakfast. But his taste for films was not so strong as in the past. He began to watch *The Uninvited* at six on his last night on board. It was a much-praised film, a ghost story set among Cornish cliff tops starring Ray Milland, but Churchill did not see much of it. After five minutes he decided it was too cold and sent for a dressing gown. Five minutes later his eyes were giving him trouble again and he left for his cabin.

Churchill addressed the crew through the public address system before leaving. He had difficulty with the captain's name, but he went on to tell the crew of their importance of the ship's role in accommodation and signalling and providing land transport. He apologised for not having stayed for the whole conference, but 'Our Russian friends made such extraordinary exertions that they were able to get their house in good order and we were able to get to our work much quicker on the spot than if we had to pass from one place to another.' He concluded by asking the captain to 'splice the mainbrace' and issue extra rum – a custom which belonged to the Royal rather than the Merchant Navy, but no one objected. He left the ship at nine that morning to 'a resounding volley of cheers'.

It was suggested that the party might go from Yalta to Sevastopol by sea to avoid travel over the snowy roads, but this was rejected by Admiral Archer, the British naval representative. He was confident that the Russians would clear the roads on time as they always did, 'A typical piece of Russian improvisation which seems to work well.'

This was true, and the party reached Saki after 'bumping for three and a half hours on a bad road'.

★   ★   ★

House-proud as always, the Skymaster's crew were concerned about the effect of the climate on their aircraft. Jack Payne 'quickly assessed that the wet and dirt of our surroundings would soon make a mess of our interior, even just unloading the baggage etc. The damp would soon turn our bed linen, etc., mouldy. It would be most unlikely that several fan heaters could be provided to keep going day and night for the next ten days or so, which we expected that the conference would last.' They found out that the *Sacred Cow* was going to the US base at Cairo until called for, and asked Tommy Thompson if they could do the same. It was agreed, and they flew out after three hours in Saki. They landed at Cairo at half past eight that evening, where the new Skymaster caused 'quite a stir', according to John Mitchell. They also carried Brigadier 'Pop' Hill, who smoked a cigar and looked a little like Churchill from a distance. Accidentally they had provided a cover story, and Berlin radio was soon reporting that the conference was in Cairo. Unfortunately it was wasted, as the true location was announced to the press shortly afterwards.

They took the chance to survey local airfields for possible future visits and were given the use of a small 6-seater Beechcraft Expeditor with a pilot, visiting Gianaclis near Alexandria. It had a good runway but poor road access. They flew on to the flying-boat base at Aboukir Bay, where Nelson had defeated the French in 1798. The single runway there was short and it was cut by a light railway line, so the local officers felt that the Skymaster would find it very difficult in a cross-wind. The crew knew better; it would not be a problem with a steerable nose-wheel.

The crew spent ten enjoyable days in the Cairo area, but the RAF authorities were sceptical about the arrangements made with Thompson and added an extra 48 hours to the safety margin, so they had to fly back on 8 February. It was agreed that Jack Payne and the two stewards would remain on board, but it was found that they had the best of the deal. The others

> were driven over to our accommodation in a Russian truck, through a sea of mud and slush. Once off the taxi-way on the airstrip there was no such thing as a paved road. We were billeted in bungalow-type accommodation that might well have once been part of a hospital or sanatorium ... Our collection of huts housed most of the RAF crews and ground staff. The Americans were similarly situated. There were no streets as such but only rows of cottages and huts in the mud ... We ate our own tinned rations and drink had also been imported specially for us, whisky and beer.[9]

When the crew learned that Churchill's party was spending some time on the *Franconia* from the 12th onwards, they decided to do a test flight 'to blow out the damp and the cobwebs'. One of the engines began to belch smoke and they had to land on three. Jack Payne soon identified the problem but there were no spare parts to hand. However, the *Sacred Cow* had had one of its engines changed a few days earlier, and Payne realised that the old one could be cannibalised:

> He worked all through the night, with the aid of a small Russian flood-light – removing the ruined cylinder and taking the good one off the USAF engine and fitting it to ours. Jack was a master craftsman. The rest of us could offer nothing but unskilled manual help and the delivery of hot drinks and food. It rained on the open air operation and was bitterly cold but Jack had finished by midday the following day and we tested the aircraft that afternoon.[10]

Bill Fraser was ill with severe coryza on the 12th and he had difficulty in clearing his ears, which was essential in an unpressurised aircraft. Sheehan considered giving him some very scarce penicillin. He was quite relieved when the Prime Minister's departure was delayed for another 24 hours, and Fraser began to recover. 'Will not use the Penicillin nose drops as it is an inopportune time for experiments.'

By these means *Ascalon* was made ready by the 14th, when the Prime Minister's party arrived from Sevastopol after its trip over the snow. According to Sheehan:

Everything went with a bang. The Prime Minister was in great form and looked very fit. He shook hands with all of us and chatted with all and sundry as he wandered about with a glass of Vodka and his cigar. The Russians are obviously amazed as ordinary mortals are not allowed within a mile of any of their Cabinet Ministers. The N.K.V.D. see to that. To my surprise, Mr Eden remembered me. I had briefed him at Montreal. He has my vote in the next election. There were several toasts and I noticed that Lord Moran had seen to it that the Prime Minister had one of the small glasses.[11]

Churchill inspected a large guard of honour of 200 NKVD troops, using his usual method of looking each man straight in the eye. At midday they were in the air, heading for Athens.

With the departure of EW 999, Staging Post 150 could begin to wind up its operations, even though there were still a dozen American Dakotas and Skymasters waiting to leave. They calculated that in all they handled 120 British and 152 American aircraft movements, including 26 dispatch-carrying Mosquitoes, three dozen Skymasters, 52 Dakotas and 20 Yorks. They had hoped to fly home, but there was no space for them and they went in the *Franconia*.

★　★　★

Freed from the worries and discomforts of the Crimea, the party members were cheerful as they headed for Athens, and this was reinforced by Jock Duncan's lunch. Churchill came forward to the co-pilot's seat as usual and looked down over the Gallipoli beaches where his reputation had foundered 30 years ago. They landed at Athens where Churchill had a very different reception from six weeks previously; he was met at the airport by Macmillan, Randolph and other dignitaries and driven into the city. He addressed a crowd of about 40,000 and was given tremendous applause, which he enjoyed very much and saw as a vindication of his Christmas visit.

By this time all the party except Churchill were very tired. After dinner that night, according to Moran:

The P.M. was in terrific form ... and we had a long sitting. But people are no longer accustomed to these drawn out sessions. Ismay was practically asleep from 11 onwards. Martin's face for the last hour gave no sign that he was listening. The Air Force ADC confessed at the end that he could hardly keep awake. And so forth. Yet here was the big man of the conflict talking (practically a monologue) for nearly four hours on every subject without any reserve, an entertainment and an experience which millions in GB would give their right hand to add to their memories and nearly everyone wanted to go to bed and wondered how much longer he would go on and whether they could decently break up the party.[12]

Churchill slept on board the Skymaster and they were off again at 5.30 next morning, for Cairo. Bill Fraser astonished the local VIPs by landing on half the length of the runway at Aboukir, so his reconnaissance there had not been a waste of time. Churchill was taken straight to a ship waiting for him in Alexandria harbour.

★ ★ ★

The cruiser HMS *Aurora* was one of the smallest of her type in the fleet, belonging to a class built in the early 1930s to fill gaps in the tonnage allowed by the disarmament treaties. She had taken part in the disastrous expedition to Narvik in Norway in 1940 and on a more successful raid on Spitzbergen. In the Mediterranean in 1941, her crew became immensely proud of the nickname The Silver Phantom which the Italian press bestowed on the ship. She supported the landings in North Africa and at Salerno, and was visited by King George VI. On 12 February 1945 she returned from exercises and berthed at 39 Quay in Alexandria, to receive orders to prepare to accommodate the Prime Minister, though according to the cover story it was to be the commander-in-chief and his staff. Next day,

> The executive order to clear officers' cabins, post sentries and establish boat patrols was given at 0630. Since it was uncertain how long the Prime Minister would stay on board, preparations were made to accommodate him and a staff of 10, including 2 ladies, for 36 hours. Military Police and guards cordoned 24 shed which was kept clear of all extraneous personnel throughout the day.[13]

Churchill arrived at 11.40 in the admiral's barge, escorted by a harbour defence motor launch. It was soon decided that he would not spend long in Alexandria and would quickly move on to Cairo, so the cabins would not be needed. He went over to lunch with Roosevelt in the *Quincy,* while seven members of his staff remained to eat in the British cruiser. The exhausted and ill President only wanted some time to himself, but had been plagued by visitors all day. Churchill monopolised the conversation until he left around 4 p.m. The *Quincy* sailed off, escorted by destroyers. It was the last time the two would meet.

That afternoon Churchill addressed the ship's company for five minutes from the after capstan, telling them quietly about the success of the Yalta conference, his relations with Stalin and the need to be friends with Russia after the war. He concluded by remarking on the *Aurora*'s fine war record. Captain Barnard was pleased. 'This act made a very great impression on us all, because the most we had hoped for was to be allowed just to see him smoking a cigar and holding up two fingers at us.' But Commander Thompson's equally experienced naval eye saw that it did not go down very well. The sailors seemed bored and showed little enthusiasm. 'Well, he did his stuff all right, but the war's virtually over now, and it's no use him ramming speeches like this down our throats … we're just not interested.'

Having seen Churchill on his way, the Skymaster's crew had lunch in the RAF mess beautifully situated over Aboukir Bay and planned a swim in the Mediterranean. News arrived that Churchill had completed his lunch with Roosevelt, and wanted to get on the way. A disgruntled Sawyers reloaded the baggage and they made the 40-minute flight to Cairo West.

★ ★ ★

Churchill had decided to meet King Ibn Saud of Saudi Arabia, whose oil reserves were already beginning to attract international attention. His Majesty had recently met Roosevelt and impressed him for the first time with how strongly Arabs felt about the Palestine question. Ibn Saud arrived at the rather louche Grand Hotel du Lac, 50 miles south of Cairo. He had a retinue that Churchill might have compared with his own. As well as the King himself, the party included his brother and two of his many sons. The Ministers of Finance and Foreign Affairs were there, along with the ambassador to Great Britain and the King's physician. In addition to recognisable officials such as his communications and radio officers and the commander of his guards, he also brought along his astrologer and fortune teller, his food-taster, the chief server of ceremonial coffee and the second server of coffee. The party was completed by ten 'Guards with sabres and daggers (chosen from principal tribes), a valet for each royal prince and nine Miscellaneous slaves, cooks, porters and scullions.'

Churchill liked the King, a true warrior prince and a great contrast to the fat, lazy and urban King Farouk of Egypt. 'He was now over seventy, but had lost none of his warrior vigour. He still lived the existence of a patriarchal king of the Arabian desert, with his forty living sons and the seventy ladies of his harem, and three of the four official wives, as prescribed by the Prophet, one vacancy being kept.'

But Churchill got off on the wrong foot by insisting on continuing his normal habits over lunch. 'I said to the interpreter that if it was the religion of His Majesty to deprive himself of smoking and alcohol I must point out that my rule of life prescribed as an absolutely sacred rite smoking cigars before, after, and if need be during all meals and in the intervals between them.' There was further embarrassment over the matter of gifts. His Majesty produced diamond-hilted swords and many other wonders of great value, while in return Tommy Thompson had spent about £100 of government money buying a selection of choice perfumes in Cairo. Churchill had to explain that these were only token presents, that a car would follow later and indeed an armoured Rolls-Royce was sent out.

According to American sources, the King was fully aware of Britain's declining position in the world and the rise of America. Churchill allowed him the *Aurora* to take him home, hoping it would be more impressive than the American destroyer he had been in earlier, but he complained: 'The food was tasteless; there were no demonstrations of armament; no tent was pitched on the deck [that was not quite true, but it had to be improvised at the King's request]; the crew did not fraternise with the Arabs; and altogether he preferred the smaller and more friendly U.S. destroyer.'

Churchill also took the opportunity to meet other national leaders – King Farouk of Egypt and President Shukri Quwatli of Syria. He advised the former to 'concentrate on good works and in particular, on improving the condition of the Fellaheen'. To the latter, he denied that the British had any ambition to replace the French as the dominant power in his country. Churchill had a quiet day in the embassy on the 18th and then at last it was time to go home.

Taking off from Cairo in the Skymaster, Jack Payne asked for two passengers to go forward to help the balance. He caught Churchill in the middle of his usual chaffing of Kinna about his size, just as he was remarking ungallantly that they would be all right for a meal in the desert this time, 'as we have Miss Layton, and she will keep us going for at least ten days'. Amid giggles, Churchill sent her and the detective forward – 'Miss Layton must act as ballast.' Despite this, she was glad to be close to the cockpit and to get to know the crew.

They went up to 8,000 feet to avoid the bumps, then flew over Malta and up the coast of Italy to enter France near Marseilles. They flew up to Toulouse and then headed towards Cherbourg, as reports were received of fog over the London area making landing impossible at Northolt. They crossed the Channel and were diverted to Lyneham where cars were waiting to take the Prime Minister to a special train waiting at Swindon. He did not know it yet, but it was the end of his last trip outside Europe as a wartime Prime Minister.

★ ★ ★

Others made their way home by different routes. General Ismay was allowed to use the cabin in the *Franconia* which had been prepared for Churchill, and travelled in great luxury. Ilene Hutchison was looking forward to another sea voyage and was disappointed to hear that she was to be flown home as she was needed to deal with a heavy workload. She and her colleagues were driven to Saki, but too fast to see more than the occasional groups of peasant women in shawls and dark skirts. They boarded a York after midday. She was nervous on her first flight, but concluded it was no worse than getting into a car. They taxied to the end of the runway and she noticed the great rush as the plane accelerated for take-off. After a stopover in Malta they took off again at 6 a.m. next day and the pilot allowed her to sit in the cockpit for a time. She was impressed with the accommodation, including a small kitchen with cooker and refrigerator. They had to put on oxygen masks to climb to 18,000 feet due to bad weather but they breathed normally as they would on land. They crossed the Channel at great speed to land at an aerodrome near Portsmouth. The journey to London was far less happy as she had to sit around the officers' mess for some time in slacks and boots, which were not considered respectable for women even in the stress of war. She had to sit in the hard back seat of a car for the trip, which was the worst part of all.

As the Chiefs of Staff's York flew home early in the morning of the 11th, the passengers were called at 7 a.m. and told that they would be at Northolt in an hour. They shaved and dressed, and began to see patches of ground through the clouds. Brooke was puzzled, for the river was clearly not the Thames, and the town was certainly not Reading. Portal appeared and exclaimed, 'Do you know where we are? Over Paris!!' They had got lost in the mist, and radio signals could not be used because of the atmospherics. Eventually the pilot found Fécamp on the north coast of France through the clouds and was able to make a passage over the English Channel, where conditions were slightly better. They landed at 9.30 at Northolt, an hour and a half overdue. Brooke went briefly to his flat, but could not bear its memories of Barney Charlesworth, and returned home.

Another party had an even less happy trip. A group of army and naval officers and male and female civil servants, mostly from the Foreign Office, left Saki by Liberator on Tuesday 13th. The aircraft had mechanical problems at Malta and they were delayed further by bad weather. They were eventually transferred to a Dakota, but it had trouble with its hydraulic system and was forced to land at Istries near Marseilles. Facilities there were primitive, and the passengers were obliged to sleep in rooms with no furniture except beds, which had filthy sheets. There was no drinking water, and hot water was not available overnight. Food, however, was provided by the French and was reasonably good. Space was found on a flight for three passengers, but once on board they were told that it would not go beyond Paris. All aircraft were grounded by bad weather after they arrived there, and eventually they found their way back to England by motor gunboat from Dieppe. The rest eventually found spaces in various passing aircraft and were home after five or six days' journey. They complained about poor organisation and the lack of reliable information.

XX
Amid the Ruins

Churchill was highly active during March 1945, when he used the Skymaster to visit Belgium, Holland and Germany, and he made a point of urinating on the Siegfried Line, once the main defence of the Reich. Later in the month he used an RAF Dakota to visit Montgomery's headquarters on the Rhine and watched his armies crossing the great river. He stayed in Britain during the next two months, but the Skymaster was not unemployed. In April it took Mrs Churchill on a long visit to the Soviet Union, for she had spent much of the last few years organising the Red Cross Aid to Russia Fund. It left her there to travel by rail, and returned for her five weeks later.

Great events followed thick and fast. In Western Europe, the crossing of the Rhine ended any real German hopes of defending their homeland. The front was now out of range of Britain and no more of the devastating V2 rockets fell on London after 28 March. The Soviets had liberated the monstrous concentration camp at Auschwitz on 27 January and took photographs which might have revealed the full, unbelievable horror of the Nazi regime, but they chose not to release them until after the war. The Americans saw the whole truth at Ohrdruf early in April, followed by the British liberation of Belsen on the 15th and the Americans of Dachau on the 29th. In the east, the Soviets captured Danzig on 30 March.

In the war against Japan, General MacArthur's troops took Manila in the Philippines, Iwo Jima was captured to provide a base within bombing range of Japan, and the island of Okinawa was assaulted on 1 April. On the 12th came shattering but not unexpected news, that President Roosevelt had died of a cerebral haemorrhage. Churchill had lost a close friend and devoted ally, even if he had felt him moving closer to Stalin since Tehran. The new President, Harry S. Truman, was an unknown quantity. Until his recent election as Vice-President, he had been the junior senator for inland Missouri and had little experience of foreign affairs.

This did not stop the advance into Germany from both sides. The Soviets were on the outskirts of Berlin by 20 April and fierce fighting began. In his underground bunker, Hitler committed suicide at the end of the month, two days after his former ally Mussolini was killed by Italian partisans and his body hung up for public display. Hitler transferred his power to Admiral Doenitz, who spent a week trying unsuccessfully to split the western allies from the Soviet Union. The German forces surrendered and 8 May was proclaimed as Victory in Europe or VE Day in the west, although the Soviets celebrated the following day. In London, Churchill lunched with the King then broadcast to the nation. He went to the House of Commons through vast crowds and Inspector Thompson was fearful that he might be trampled on. Later he addressed the people from the balcony of the Ministry of Health. When he told them, 'This is your victory', he was answered, 'No – it is yours.'

Despite his exhaustion, Churchill was soon back at work and told the House of Commons, 'Our brief rejoicings are over.' Already there were cracks in the Grand Alliance. On 12 May Churchill telegraphed Truman referring to an 'iron curtain' that was descending across the Russian Front and preventing access to information. He was not using the term in the much broader sense in which it was taken after his public speech nearly a year later, but it was a symptom of the decline in relations.

The war with Japan continued and there was no reason to believe it would end soon. Europe was in chaos, with millions of refugees, slave workers, concentration camp victims and ex-prisoners of war fleeing from one horror or trying to regain their homeland, or a new life elsewhere. The idea for another three-power meeting first surfaced at the San Francisco conference of United Nations Foreign Ministers in May. On the 9th, Eden telegraphed Churchill to say that the new president might attend in the later stages and that he would be ready for a 'big three' meeting in June. Truman sent his representatives to negotiate with Stalin, who wanted to hold the meeting in newly conquered Berlin.

By the end of May Churchill was beginning to have doubts about the meeting and drafted a telegram. He was disappointed that London had not been selected as a venue. He had paid many visits to Washington and Moscow and it seemed only fair that his colleagues should come to visit him now that there was no danger from enemy action. 'London, the greatest city in the world, the capital of the nation which first entered the war against Germany and very heavily battered during the conflict, is the natural appropriate place for the Victory meeting of the three Great Powers. It is also midway.' However, he conceded that he would go to Berlin if necessary. He was also disturbed by another issue. It was reported that there would be a meeting between Truman and Stalin and that Churchill would join them a few days later. He drafted a telegram saying that 'representatives of His Majesty's Government would not be able to attend any meeting held at this juncture except as equal partners from its opening'. He understood that Truman wanted to meet Stalin for the first time, but he was equally keen to meet Truman. He soon detected a softening of the American attitude on holding a pre-meeting, and the telegram was not sent.

Churchill remained concerned that all three governments should be equally represented. His organisers were instructed that there should be three separate accommodation sites for the nations, for he had no intention of repeating the situation of Tehran, where the Americans and Soviets had lodged together. Nor did he want the meetings to be held in the home of one of them, as Roosevelt's health had necessitated at Yalta. There was to be a separate place for the plenary sessions, independent of the living quarters. Furthermore, he insisted that the British delegation should be entirely self-supporting within its quarters.

Potsdam was chosen as a site, being one of the few areas around Berlin that had not been devastated by bombing, shellfire or sabotage. It was not part of the city as such, and it was in the Soviet sector of Germany. It had strong symbolic associations, not so much with the Nazis as with their monarchic predecessors. It was close to the Sans Souci Palace, built by Frederick the Great who was commonly regarded as the founder of German militarism. It was closely associated with the old Prussian army and the area included military schools, armouries and the former barracks of Frederick's famous guard of giant grenadiers.

British planning was delegated to a committee chaired by Ismay, and including Hollis, John Rowan, Tommy Thompson and Joan Bright. There were three officers from 21st Army Group which occupied Berlin, including Brigadier Wales who would be in charge of the administrative arrangements for the British delegation.

⋆   ⋆   ⋆

Meanwhile, Churchill had to fight a general election. The normal life of a parliament was five years, but this one had been extended since it was elected in 1935, due to war conditions. With the victory in Europe, the Labour Party decided to leave the coalition government and the Conservatives governed alone for a few months until an election could be arranged. That task was far more difficult than usual, with an out-of-date register and millions of service men and women overseas. There would be a gap of three weeks between polling day on 5 July and the announcement of the results, during which the ballot papers were flown home, verified and counted.

Almost everyone believed that the Conservatives would win, including most of the Labour Party. Conservative tactics placed a large amount of emphasis on Churchill himself. There was little of a coherent programme, in contrast with the Labour Party which offered a definite scheme of social reform. Everything depended on the personality of Churchill, and he was booked into meetings all over the country, whereas his senior colleagues rarely appeared outside their own constituencies.

He did not begin his campaign well. He started by treating his Labour opponents as if he was still fighting Nazi Germany, even though they had worked tirelessly with him to run the country over five long years, and had often supported him while his fellow Conservatives were doubtful. On his first radio broadcast during the campaign, he launched a wildly misjudged attack on them. Their creed of Socialism was un-British, it was 'inseparably interwoven with totalitarianism and the abject worship of the state'. Their programme could not be implemented, he said, without some kind of political police or Gestapo. Attlee replied mildly and effectively. He had feared that 'those who had accepted his leadership in war might be tempted out of gratitude to follow him further. I thank him for having disillusioned them so thoroughly.'

Churchill was allowed to use his official train for electioneering, but not government cars. Tommy Thompson followed him around the country wearing civilian clothes for once. He knew to the second how long such events were likely to take but his travel advice was ignored. The Conservative Party organisers had no experience of such programmes and tried to cram too much in. Churchill was often hours late for meetings. He was received by rapturous crowds everywhere he went during a five-day tour. The strain on him was immense, especially after five years as a wartime prime minister.

The possibility of a new government had to be recognised, and Churchill decided to take Clement Attlee to Potsdam with him to ensure continuity. He told the House of Commons:

> I shall proceed to join the others at the place which has been agreed, but considering that our fortunes hang in the balance on both sides, that anyone may claim the future, and the great importance which is attached to the voice of Britain being united, I have invited my right hon. Friend the Leader of the Opposition.

Attlee was in a unique position for he was not just a potential prime minister, but had served until recently as Churchill's deputy and there was a good deal of understanding between them. Apparently in this case he was not considered as an alien influence, or the founder of a British Gestapo. He was, Churchill said, his 'right hon. Friend for this purpose as well as others, except purely Parliamentary purposes'. This caused a certain amount of controversy within the Labour Party, and it became an election issue in itself. Professor Harold Laski, the left-wing party chairman, claimed that Attlee was only going as an observer, but this was denied by Churchill and Attlee.

After the gruelling campaign Churchill flew to Hendaye near Bordeaux on the French Atlantic coast for a much-needed holiday. He took up painting again with the help of the wife of the British consul, formerly a professional artist. He bathed in the mornings, surrounded by French policemen in bathing suits. He enjoyed the company of his wife and Mary, but he could not shake off his worries about the future.

★ ★ ★

The 400 officers and men of RAF Staging Post No. 19 had to get up early in the morning of 30 June, in their base near Hamburg. They had breakfast from 5.30 onwards and were issued with rations before getting into their vehicles for the long journey to Berlin. They were formed into three convoys. The first included 22 vehicles, mostly petrol tankers, and left at 6.30. The next one, of 43 miscellaneous cars, fire trucks, coaches, lorries and ambulances, left fifteen minutes later. The final one consisted mostly of 3-ton trucks carrying personnel and left at 7.15. There were strict instructions as to how the convoys were to be conducted, what to do in the event of breakdown, and on the security passes needed to get through the Soviet sector to Berlin.

The RAF team was at Gatow airfield on 1 July, joining 284 Field Squadron of the RAF Regiment which had already taken possession of it. It had been built for the *Luftwaffe* on its revival in 1935, as a staff college. Unlike the majority of wartime airbases, it had grand architecture by Ernst Sagebeil, with a carved bust of a famous German World War I airman above the door of each accommodation block. A few weeks ago it had been a battlefield, when *Luftwaffe* cadets used 88mm guns to resist the Soviet advance. The RAF party soon found that the previous Russian occupants had 'before departure, taken away nearly all the easily moveable equipment, etc., and left litter and confusion behind them'.

The airfield was surveyed by 6 July and it was reported that the site was level with good approaches, that the topsoil was of silty clay or loam of highly sandy nature, that the vegetation consisted of grass and abundant weeds, that the topsoil gave good drainage, but that 'it was unsuitable in present condition as all weather airfield for transport aircraft owing poor bearing value and friable nature of top soil'. Civilian labour was recruited to get the airfield ready, and they had the services of a detachment of the army's Pioneer Corps, with three steamrollers. Three landing strips were prepared in an east–west direction, so that one or two could be in use if another had to be serviced. They were 50 yards wide and 1,600 yards long, marked out by pieces of American cloth 20 ft long every 180 yards. Two further runways were laid out in a north–south direction, 1,800 yards long. The numbers of the runways were marked by concrete slabs sunk in the ground at the start of each. Small transport aircraft began arriving on the 5th, and on the 9th ten more landed, carrying freight for the conference. One was full of whisky, another carried plate and glass for dinners. More personnel were flown in, including Field Marshal Montgomery in his own Dakota, and the party from 30 Mission in Moscow with five cases of vodka.

Meanwhile, the British and Americans were still trying to establish their own zones in the city which had already been occupied by the Soviets. The first reconnaissance party left on 1 July but was hindered by Soviet troops and the main body was not in Berlin until the 5th. Then there was stalemate as negotiations continued and it was the 12th before the British and Americans formally took control of their sectors.

★ ★ ★

The area chosen by the Soviets for the conference was not the town of Potsdam itself, which had been devastated, but an area to the north-east, full of very large houses – 'an oasis of material comfort in a desert of devastation', according to Joan Bright. It was a kind of 'German Hollywood', close to the Bablesberg film studios which had produced classics such as *The Blue Angel* before the war, as well as Nazi propaganda. The Soviets gave the inhabitants as little as half an hour's notice to leave, and half-eaten meals, children's toys and books were still strewn around. The houses were carefully searched for booby traps before the important visitors arrived. Each nation had a self-contained and well-guarded enclave, which undermined the practice in Anglo-American conferences of allowing the staffs to mingle and get to know one another.

Brigadier Wales telegraphed Joan Bright in London:

> Accommodation situation extremely difficult. Living accommodation for delegation consists fifty private houses in pleasant surroundings. No accommodation available at present for my enlarged headquarters or for any administrative units under my command ... Wish to emphasise whole situation extremely difficult and therefore recom-

mend most strongly that you consider very drastic reduction in numbers.[1]

Joan Bright thought differently when she arrived. There was plenty of space with so many houses for the British delegation and 'there was no need to worry about dormitory sleeping or overcrowding'. The British headquarters

was at 43 Ringstrasse, on the main tree-lined street, and for the first time [we] had a proper administrative headquarters. It was a nice big house, with a garden overlooking the lake, a big dining room where most of the juniors of the delegation would feed, bedrooms and – most valuable of all – enough rooms on the ground floor for our offices. We could spread out.[2]

Dining accommodation within the British delegation was carefully graded. The Prime Minister, Eden, Attlee, Leathers, Cherwell and the Chiefs of Staff would each have their own establishments in their houses, and CPO Pinfield was flown out again to cater for Churchill. There was a high-grade mess at No. 43 Ringstrasse with tables reserved for high-ranking generals such as Alexander and Wilson, diplomats such as Cadogan and the British Ambassador, and officials such as Sir Edward Bridges. The rest, from the other houses, were allocated to messes at 11 and 15 Ringstrasse.

The task of preparing the British site for VIP accommodation was carried out by about 3,000 members of the Fourth Line of Communication Sub Area, including troops from the Royal Engineers, Pioneers who did heavy manual labour, Royal Corps of Signals, Scots Guards, Royal Army Service Corps for transport, and the Royal Army Ordnance Corps. To begin with there was a certain amount of friction between them and the administrative staffs, 'a cold-shouldering and "keep off our preserve attitude"', which was sorted out by adopting a 'deferential, agreeable, but firm' attitude. Later Ismay sang their praises to Churchill:

These troops came here about ten days before the conference started. Their task, stated in simplest terms, was the *rehabilitation* of the Delegation area. The water supply had to be put in order, communications installed, lighting and cooking seen to, transportation arranged, security ensured, etc., etc.

Considerable foresight, powers of improvisation and very long hours of work have been involved. All units have met every demand made upon them with unfailing cheerfulness and signal efficiency. The arrangements have been well nigh perfect.[3]

Members of the ATS, the women's section of the army, worked hard to get the interiors ready. Irene Marston, formerly a private secretary and now a junior officer, found a great muddle. Newspapers speculated where the next 'Big Three' meeting would take place, but she claimed it could not happen until they had got the kitchen range working in Churchill's residence. She found the work was not without interest, as she picked up details of cabinet ministers' private habits – Eden needed fresh milk to be flown in daily for his stomach complaint, for example. But she was confident they would get through the work eventually.

The conference itself was to be held in the Cecilienhof Palace outside Potsdam. It had been built for the Crown Prince and heir to the throne in 1914, just before the German Empire entered its disastrous war. It was in the style of a mock-Tudor English country house. In the grounds, headstones of cherished royal pets stood alongside the much rougher graves of soldiers who had died in recent hand-to-hand fighting. 'Inside it was elegant and luxurious. The Russians had collected together all they could find of the original furnishings and had made good from German houses anything lacking.' Rooms upstairs were allocated to each of the principals. Churchill's had been designed for the Crown Prince himself and was decorated in blue and grey, while President Truman's was in pink and silver. Miss Bright was not able to report on Stalin's, which was guarded by sentries with fixed bayonets. The main conference chamber was to be entered by three doors of equal size, one for each of the principals. Miss Bright asked if a larger one could be opened to allow Churchill a quicker route from his room, but that was refused on the grounds of a spurious equality.

★ ★ ★

The crew of the Skymaster were warned about Churchill's impending flight in the middle of June, when Tommy Thompson told them that the Prime Minister would take a holiday before going on to Berlin. Bill Fraser suggested a reconnaissance of Gatow and they flew to Bordeaux as passengers in a 24 Squadron Dakota, accompanied by Thompson who would inspect the facilities for the Prime Minister at Potsdam. They found the airfield at Bordeaux, once used by the Focke-Wulf Condors that had caused much concern during Churchill's sea voyages, was in a sorry state but had good runways. They flew on to Brussels on 1 July but the Dakota 'gave up the ghost' there. After some time they were able to get a flight to Gatow in an aircraft of the Tactical Air Force Communications Squadron. They spent the night in the old *Luftwaffe* station where the grand architecture had suffered heavily from the vandalism of the occupying Russians. The Dakota caught up with them and they flew home on the 2nd. John Mitchell was sick throughout the four-and-a-half-hour flight and was diagnosed with yellow jaundice when he got back. He had had his last flight with the Prime Minister and he was replaced by Flight-Lieutenant Ray Bruce of the Royal Australian Air Force.

The advance party flew out in two aircraft on 7 and 9 July. Nineteen more were to take the main delegation, including Skymasters, Yorks, Dakotas and a Liberator. Eden's new Skymaster left Northolt on 14 July and landed at Tangmere on the south coast to pick up the Foreign Secretary himself. Most of the others, carrying the main body and the baggage, took off from Northolt between the 12th and the 15th, with the five VIP aircraft flying on the 25th. They flew to Essen along Air Traffic Control Corridor 14, then to Helmstedt, Magdeburg and Gatow. They were under the executive control of No. 46 Group, though the Air Officer Commanding had the right to overrule any decisions on the take-off of the Prime Minister's and the Foreign Secretary's aircraft. Mosquitoes, Tempests and Spitfires were to escort them in stages along the way. Each group was ordered to fly no closer than 1,000 feet to EW 999 and to abandon the task if poor visibility made that impossible. EW 999 picked Churchill up at Bordeaux in the morning of the 15th and they flew north to Düsseldorf, then Essen, from where they followed the same route as the others. Churchill had a 'bumpy journey', as he told Clementine.

On the ground, the crews of 19 Staging Post were ready for their 'great day', which began quietly. It was already hot at 9 a.m. when the security troops arrived, and Montgomery and Air Marshal Sir Sholto Douglas, who was about to take command of the British Air Forces of Occupation, arrived before noon. At 1445 the Chiefs of Staff landed and inspected a guard of honour. The tarmac, almost empty in the morning, was 'now filled with distinguished personages: British, American and Russian, the latter being the most colourful'. Lord Leathers arrived soon afterwards, followed by Anthony Eden and Field Marshal Wilson, and the Americans headed by Truman and Generals Arnold, Eisenhower and Marshall: 'At 1800 came the great moment for which the spectators had most eagerly awaited. The Prime Minister's Skymaster drew up on the tarmac, and excitement ran high when the steps, specially made for the occasion, were set in position and the familiar figure of the Prime Minister, with cigar appeared.' After the usual greeting Churchill

359

was whisked off to his house, and in the evening the RAF party watched a performance of *Stars in Battledress*. They were allowed into Berlin, and a ban on fraternising with the Germans was partly lifted.

★ ★ ★

There was nothing to prepare the troops or delegates for the devastation, both physical and moral, that was to be found in Berlin. The city had had a population of nearly 4½ million in 1943, but that had been reduced by bombing and flight to 2.8 million by the end of the war. The SS had hanged or shot perhaps 10,000 Germans who had even suggested surrender or otherwise shown signs of weakness. The advancing Soviet troops were given free rein to pillage and to rape about 100,000 women in Berlin alone. The city had been the venue for the death and destruction of an almost god-like leader, whose real evil was only just being revealed to the mass of the population. The Soviets were unmoved by the destruction, and saw it as just revenge for what the Germans had wreaked on their own towns and villages. The British and Americans were much more troubled. Captain Pim wrote: 'I had seen Sevastopol at one end of Russia completely destroyed by the Germans and, in the same year, Berlin and the other German cities laid low by the Nazis.'

The Germans were surprisingly cowed after their defeat. They had no tradition of irregular warfare, and the security risk from them was less than it might have been. But there was also a huge public health hazard in the devastated city. Only a quarter of the 80 fire stations were operational. There were nearly 3,000 breaks in the water mains; and there were still many dead bodies under the rubble and in rivers and canals. Nearly three-quarters of pumping stations were out of operation, and raw sewage had entered the canals. The enclave near Potsdam was immune from most but not all of these troubles.

On the 16th some members of Churchill's party were shown the ruins of Berlin. They went into Hitler's Chancellery and found the smashed top of his marble desk. Captain Pim and even the upright Cadogan felt it was legitimate to take away fragments and have them made into paperweights, but General Ismay did not gloat over the iron crosses and medal ribbons that he found strewed over one of the rooms. 'Decorations that would have brought pride to brave men seemed in that setting to be a symbol of utter defeat and degradation.' He went back to his quarters to have a hot bath with disinfectant and took a strong drink to take the taste of it out of his mouth.

As the party assembled, Irene Marston shared the lament of organisers everywhere, that the principals had no idea how much work had been done to get the place ready. Apart from General Ismay, who appreciated how much they had slaved, the rest of the delegates assumed the Russians had done it all.

The buildings mostly overlooked a lake, the Griebnitz See, one of many that extended the waters of the River Havel. The fishing in the area was restricted, which must have disappointed the Chiefs of Staff. Bodies still polluted the water, and with their typical finesse the *Waffen SS* had reportedly used explosives to kill the fish. One of Miss Bright's memos requested, 'Could you tell the Chiefs of Staff military assistants that no fly-fishing here. Chiefs of Staff can fish from garden edge with bent pin and worms. No boating or we are liable to be shot by Russians on the other side of the lake.' However, Brooke made the best of the situation and got up at 5 one morning to catch a few small fish. In a new democratic age, 'the river was spoiled by countless American soldiers fishing in every pool'. There was no bathing in the lake but there was a small swimming pool available at certain times, with changing facilities in a tent. Dances were to be held on the 18th and the 21st, and any gentlemen who wanted to look smart could visit the soldier-barber at No 43 Ringstrasse. They were warned that 'the style of haircut, however, may be rather a military one'. The British area had been controlled for the breeding of mosquitoes – the insects this time, not the aircraft that brought the messages from London – but delegates were warned that this had not been done outside the zone and some of the problem was bound to persist. The insects were not, however, malarial and they carried no danger.

★   ★   ★

Churchill met the new President for the first time on 16 July, and was more impressed than he had expected with the successor to his old friend Roosevelt. He told his daughter that 'he liked the President immensely – they talk the same language'. In the early hours of that day, or early afternoon in German time, there was another event, more literally earth-shattering this time, but secret to all but a few. An atom bomb was successfully exploded at Alamogordo in the New Mexican desert. Over lunch with the US Secretary of War Henry Stimson, Churchill was told of a telegram saying 'Babies satisfactorily born.' This meant that 'the experiment in the Mexican desert has come off. The atomic bomb is a reality.'

The conference began that afternoon and in the first plenary session the statesmen discussed the composition of the new United Nations, while Churchill tried unsuccessfully to raise his concerns about Poland. All accounts agree that he was not on his best form – not ill this time, but clearly tired. His holiday in Hendaye was not long enough after a gruelling election campaign, and perhaps made it more difficult to restart work afterwards. Moreover, he had not used it as a chance to prepare himself for the conference. On top of that, his doubts about his success in the election hung over him all the time. On the night of the 24/25th he had a nightmare, which he described to Lord Moran:

> I dreamed that life was over. I saw – it was very vivid – my dead body under a white sheet on a table in an empty room. I recognised my bare feet projecting from under the sheet. It was very life-like … Perhaps this is the end.'[4]

Stalin's methods of preparation are less well known, but they were not so difficult – his armies were in possession of all the areas he wanted in Eastern Europe, and he only had to say no to any proposals he did not like. Truman had used his voyage across the Atlantic in the cruiser *Augusta* to study the papers in some detail, as Churchill would have done in earlier conferences. For once, the British went into the meeting less well prepared than on previous occasions.

Churchill had Truman to lunch on the 18th, and took careful note of the conversation. They discussed the new Soviet demand for a third of the captured German fleet, and Churchill, still unaware of a general Soviet threat, said that he would 'welcome the Russians on to the broad waters'. More presciently he wondered, 'Were all these States which had passed into Russian control to be free and independent, or not?' He mentioned the 'melancholy position of Great Britain', saddled with £3,000 million of debt after the war. The President agreed that immense gratitude was due to Britain for having held the fort at the beginning. 'If you had gone down like France, we might well be fighting the Germans on the American coast at the present time.' Churchill returned to the theme of his first voyage and worried about the interpretation of the Atlantic Charter, and whether it would prohibit agreements within the empire.

The two statesmen agreed that the Japanese war might end much sooner than the 18 months that had been planned for, and Churchill suggested a softening of the term 'unconditional surrender'. Truman turned to the question of American-built airfields in British territory, about which public opinion at home was concerned. Churchill suggested a common use of all facilities and wanted a rather extreme form of it: 'A man might make a proposal of marriage to a young lady, but it is not much use if he were told that she would always be a sister to him. I wanted, under whatever cloak or form, a continuation of the present war-time system of reciprocal facilities between Britain and the United States.' Truman agreed, but it had to be presented in a suitable fashion for American susceptibilities. They concluded the meal and Truman was kind enough to say that it had been 'the most enjoyable luncheon he had had for many years'.

At the second plenary session that afternoon, the issue of the press dominated a relatively short meeting. Unlike wartime conferences, it was not possible for the western governments to ban them entirely, and they were to be found in Berlin rather than the delegation areas. In the absence of real information, they tended to make up stories to fill the gap. Meanwhile, the conference failed to resolve the main issues of the government of Germany and Poland. At least the meeting was well organised and Cadogan commented: 'It went so efficiently that we got through the agenda by about 6 – much to the P.M.'s annoyance, as he wanted to go on talking at random.' The following day they discussed Spain, while Britain denied any provocative acts in Greece and they tried to find a solution to the problems of Yugoslavia. Next day Stalin agreed to British, American and French troops moving into their agreed zones of occupation in Austria.

On 21 July the British held a victory parade through the city. Churchill was driven out from Ringstrasse at 9.30, in a car with Montgomery and Inspector Hughes. Tommy Thompson and Mary Churchill followed in the next car, then Eden and Rowan, then Attlee and Ismay, Fleet Admiral King of the US Navy with Cunningham, Marshall with Brooke, General Arnold of the US Army Air Force and Portal. They watched a march-past in which elements of the Desert Rats, the 7th Armoured Division, which had fought all the way from North Africa, were the star attraction. The navy was represented by HMS *Pembroke*, the gunnery school at Chatham, and the RAF by members of No. 19 Staging Post and the RAF Regiment which had the duty of guarding it. There were five bands, two from the army, one marine and two Canadian. After that Churchill went to open the Winston Club for British troops. Some thought that his reception there and at the parade was less enthusiastic than it might have been.

The conference continued, as the discussion turned to Japan. Meanwhile Stimson told Churchill more about the detail of the Alamogordo atom bomb test, which had created absolute destruction within a one-mile radius. On the 23rd Churchill had lunch with the three Chiefs of Staff, Lord Leathers, Ismay and Eden, who joined later. To this select group, he broke the momentous news about the atom bomb. Brooke was sceptical, for he was used to Churchill's enthusiasms:

He had absorbed all the minor American exaggerations, and as a result was completely carried away! It was no longer necessary for the Russians to come into the Japanese war, the new explosive alone was sufficient to settle the matter. Furthermore we now had something in our hands which would redress the balance with the Russians! The secret of this explosive, and the power to use it, would completely alter the diplomatic equilibrium which was adrift since the defeat of Germany![5]

Brooke later had to admit that he had been wrong this time, that 'Winston's appreciation of its value in the future international balance of power was certainly far more accurate than mine'.

That evening there was a grand dinner in Churchill's quarters. Sixty-three members of the orchestral section of the RAF band were sent out to Berlin with their instruments in two Dakotas. The party included 'many of the finest instrumentalists in the United Kingdom', and Portal was sure that they would 'give a very fine performance'. He thought it important that they should play to the three leaders. It was agreed that the dinner on the night of the 23rd was the most appropriate for this. Music was not Churchill's first love, and he tried without success to cut down the length of the three national anthems. The band played a selection of light music including *Carry Me Back to Green Pastures*, *The Skye Boat Song* and *Sons of the Soviets,* as well as string serenades by Elgar, Tchaikovsky and Mozart.

Back at the conference, the eighth and ninth plenary sessions were dominated by the settlement of Europe, the return of prisoners of war, the perpetual issue of Poland and the question of Soviet entry into the war against Japan. At the end of the eighth session on the 24th, Truman pulled Stalin aside and told him about the atom bomb. The Soviet dictator appeared surprisingly unimpressed, and at the time this was put down to his failure to understand the concept. In fact he understood it all too well, for his spies had informed him. At the end of the ninth session on the following day, it was necessary to suspend the conference so that Churchill could go home for the election results.

★   ★   ★

Opinion polls were rare in 1945 and were not taken very seriously, except by the *News Chronicle* which published fairly accurate Gallup Polls. The idea of the 'swing of the pendulum' was only known to experts and it was usually printed in inverted commas. Election broadcasting consisted solely of BBC radio news broadcasts every hour after 12 noon on the 26th, as the results began to come in. To fill the gap, Churchill asked Captain Pim to use the resources of the Map Room in No. 10 Downing Street. 'The Prime Minister told me he wanted to have a room in which to sit with one or two friends in privacy to see the results coming through, with a Score Board, and the Map Room seemed ideal for this.' Again Churchill was seeing the election as an extension of the war.

Pim had a replacement officer sent out and flew home from Potsdam in an almost empty Dakota. He had a few days to arrange to receive the results by ticker tape from the news agencies, and convert the Map Room:

> Every constituency in the British Isles was shown including the name
> of the existing member and the party to which he belonged, and as the
> results came in the new position was indicated in a space left opposite
> the constituency. I also had a score board on another wall, on the lines
> of an American tennis tournament court, and this showed from
> minute to minute the gains and losses of each respective party.[6]

Churchill flew home in the Skymaster on the 25th, arriving back at Northolt at 2.45 in the afternoon to be met by his wife and brother. The votes from overseas servicemen were verified that day and counted on the following day. The first results began to appear around 10 in the morning, when Churchill was in his bath. Already they began to show Labour gains and he seemed rather shocked when Pim told him about them. He dressed in his siren suit and went to the Map Room to hear of more Conservative defeats. He was joined by close colleagues and members of his family, including his wife and his daughter. Lord Beaverbrook also joined the party. Like other newspaper owners, he believed he had a special empathy with public opinion, and had predicted a Tory victory.

Pim and his assistants continued to work hard, even if it was not a conventional job for a naval captain:

> We had a staff of eight on duty all day, and there was not one moment
> for several hours when they could relax. It fell to me to read each elec-
> tion result as it came in over the Tape Machine which I had installed
> in the Map Room. With the exception of half an hour for lunch, the
> Prime Minister never left us all day, and even during the luncheon
> interval I was continually running into the dining room to read the
> latest figures. By lunchtime many members of the government had

fallen, but the Prime Minister was regaining his cheerful composure, and explained time and again that the country was fully entitled to vote in whatever direction it liked, and that, after ten years without an election, there was no reason to be alarmed. This, indeed, was democracy for which we had been fighting for six long years.[7]

In the final results, the Conservatives and their allies had 213 Members of Parliament. The Liberals had 12, and other parties had 22. Labour had 393 and a majority over all parties of 146 – by far its best result in its history so far.

The British electoral system is particularly cruel to an unsuccessful prime minister. Literally overnight, he can find himself deprived of his staff, his houses and his power. It would have been constitutionally possible for Churchill to continue in office for a few days until Parliament assembled and formally voted him out. That, among other problems, would have left a serious gap at the Potsdam conference. It would have been virtually impossible for Churchill to go back there defeated, and any agreement he reached would have no validity. If he did not attend but remained in office, it was quite possible that the remaining 'big two' would continue their meetings without Britain, and that was something Churchill had dreaded for some time.

By 5 in the afternoon he had decided to leave office immediately, and two hours later he was in Buckingham Palace tendering his resignation to the King. Attlee was appointed in his place, and as Foreign Secretary he chose Ernest Bevin, the former Minister of Labour, partly on the advice of the King. On the 28th the two flew out to Potsdam to resume the talks. This gave the Churchills a few days' grace in Downing Street. They moved first into the Annexe, then into a flat owned by their son-in-law Duncan Sandys, until their own houses at Chartwell and Hyde Park Gate were ready.

Elizabeth Layton thought that it was a great betrayal by the British people. But all the evidence suggests that Churchill, though personally popular, was not enough on his own to carry the Conservative Party to power. Labour had a concrete programme of social reform and mild socialism, the Conservatives relied almost entirely on a single man and his personality. In a presidential election Churchill might well have won a large majority of the popular vote, but in the British system only the voters of his own constituency, Woodford in Essex near London, had a chance to vote for him personally. Even that was restricted in this case, for the major parties had decided not to stand against him. His only opponent was an eccentric farmer, who thought that clericalism and wealth were the root of all evil and wanted a one-day working week. Even so, he polled 10,000 votes against Churchill's 27,000.

It was all very different from Roosevelt's triumphant re-election the previous November. In the first place, that actually was a presidential system and the public voted for the man rather than the party – in such circumstances, Churchill might have won. Secondly, Roosevelt had done as much as anyone to solve the great depression of the 1930s. Churchill had been out of office at the time but it was well down his list of priorities, while the Conservative Party in power had done nothing. Nationally, British voters had memories of the depression of the 1930s, the lack of any progress in social reform, and the drift to war. They voted against the Conservatives in large numbers, and ministerial casualties included Brendan Bracken, Harold Macmillan and Churchill's son-in-law Duncan Sandys, who all lost their seats. Clementine had never liked the Conservative Party, for she had married Winston when he was a Liberal. After the 1945 defeat she remarked, 'It may well be a blessing in disguise.' Churchill growled, 'At the moment it seems quite effectively disguised.'

Churchill said goodbye to his immediate entourage, those who had shared most of his travels with him. They had become a community, and like any other community it had its divisions and its differences, but they had gone through a common experience. None of them had been present on all of the voyages, but Tommy Thompson came closest and had only missed the flight back from Bermuda in 1942. Sawyers came next, followed by Moran. The secretaries had alternated on each voyage, and the shorthand-typists had seen the replacement of men by women at the war progressed, so they had less consistent travelling experiences. Between them they had shared in unique dangers, hardship, luxury and political intrigue. They had seen the world, from the 'dim-out' of New York to the devastation of the Crimea and Berlin. They had served one of history's great leaders and seen him in some of his most unguarded moments. All of them knew just how difficult he was to work with, but without exception they cherished the experience and felt great regret when it ended. Brooke wrote:

> The thought that my days with Winston had come to an end was a shattering one. There had been very difficult times, and times when I felt I could not stand a single more day with him, but running through all our difficulties a bond of steel had been formed uniting us together.[8]

367

Conclusion

In one respect, Staging Post 19 in Berlin had a very different role from Staging Post 150 in February. The Crimean party had thankfully packed up and gone home after the job was done, but Gatow was to become the main British airport in Berlin over the next five decades, until it closed in 1994.

Despite Churchill's doubts and its undoubted inconveniences, Berlin was to prove a strangely fitting place for the last wartime meeting and the last of Churchill's wartime voyages. It showed the western leaders what a defeated people looked like, and educated them in the effects of heavy bombing in a city. In the longer term, the city would prove to be the focal point of the Cold War that was to follow. It first stirred at Potsdam, when Soviet unfriendliness became apparent, and Churchill conceived of the 'iron curtain' that he would later make famous. The Cold War really started with the Soviet blockade of Berlin in 1948, when the Douglas Skymaster and Avro York came into their own by helping to provision the city by air, and Gatow handled more than half the supplies. It accelerated with the building of the Berlin Wall in 1961, followed by President John F. Kennedy's 'Ich bin ein Berliner' speech two years later. It came to an end with the destruction of the Berlin Wall in 1989.

★   ★   ★

The Churchill entourage dispersed quite quickly after the war and the election defeat. Many were to write their memoirs or publish their diaries. This is fortunate for historians, but proved the most divisive factor between them. Frank Sawyers belied his Christian name and published nothing, unlike modern servants to the famous. Churchill himself was given great privileges by the then government to write his own account, *The Second World War*, in six volumes. Walter Thompson, on the other hand, was denied permission to publish his full story, only a much-reduced version called *I Was Churchill's Shadow*.

Brooke, meanwhile, now ennobled as Lord Alanbrooke, had financial difficulties and had to sell his house and even his collection of bird-watching books. He found Churchill's memoirs grossly egocentric and unbalanced. The popular historian Sir Arthur Bryant published a very different account based on Alanbrooke's diaries – they were serialised in the press and naturally they highlighted his outspoken and contemporary criticisms of his great leader. Tommy Thompson also fell out of favour with the inner circle. Colville claimed that he 'unscrupulously purloined the official diary of the Prime Minister's activities'. As a result Gerald Pawle's book *The War and Colonel Warden*, which told the story from Thompson's point of view, did not have the Churchill seal of approval. Even worse was Lord Moran, who published his (largely retrospective) diary in 1966, the year after Churchill's death and who was subsequently shunned by the family.

By this time there was a definite Churchill set, consisting of the family, the former private secretaries and the Defence Secretariat including Ismay, Hollis and Jacob. Most of them remained in government service or in other high office after the war, and Jacob became Director-General of the BBC. Their diaries and memoirs are slightly less revealing than the others, though Colville's is one of the most interesting; and the unpublished parts of Jacob's give much personal and technical detail of the travels. Joan Bright, as always, is difficult to classify. She was never close to Churchill and only met him for the first time quite late on, but her memoirs give a witty and detailed account of how conferences were run once women were trusted to do it. At a more junior level, Elizabeth Layton's *Mr Churchill's Secretary* was regarded as 'excellent' by the family, even though it reveals much personal detail.

Elizabeth Layton married a South African ex-prisoner of war, for her romance with the young lieutenant in the *Renown* did not last after he shaved off his beard and she discovered how young he looked. Of Churchill's former aircrew, John Kelly Rogers went back to his native Ireland to work for Aer Lingus and, as we have seen, he was not happy about the story of nearly flying over Brest in 1942. Bill Vanderkloot returned to civil aviation in the United States and died in 2000 as 'the old, safe pilot he always wanted to be'. Dad Collins left the air force to work for Jersey Airlines, while Jock Gallagher stayed on in staff and administrative posts. John Mitchell served in several air attaché posts and rose to the rank of air commodore. Jock Duncan took up a senior position in flight catering with BOAC.

Of Churchill's ships, the *Renown* and the *King George V* class battleships were all scrapped after the war, as were all the cruisers and destroyers associated with his trips. The only surviving cruiser is the *Belfast*, in which Lord Moran's son was serving during the sinking of the *Scharnhorst*. The *Queen Mary* is intact in Long Beach, California, as perhaps the most striking memorial to Churchill's travels. No examples of the Boeing 314 clipper survive, but an Avro York can be seen in the Imperial War Museum at Duxford, with a

Liberator in the American section, and another in the RAF Museum at Hendon. *Ascalon* herself disappeared over the Atlantic in May 1945, though not with Vanderkloot's crew. Churchill's Skymaster was returned to the US after lend-lease expired, and is said to have ended up in a scrapyard in China.

★ ★ ★

Government carried on without Churchill in 1945, and many historians regard Attlee's Labour administration as one of the most important in history. Ernest Bevin proved a very effective Foreign Secretary despite his lack of involvement in foreign affairs during the war. He set the pattern for what was to follow, with the drift towards the Cold War with the Soviet Union and her allies. The North Atlantic Treaty Organisation united most North American and West European countries against the perceived Soviet threat, while Britain obtained her own nuclear deterrent. The division of Europe and the Soviet domination of Poland were grudgingly accepted, and enforced by the Berlin Wall in 1961.

At home, Churchill's old critic Aneurin Bevan set up the National Health Service, which Britons still regard with passionate affection despite its faults. His colleagues nationalised parts of industry, which proved far less successful in the medium term. But the government's courses of action were restricted in a dire financial situation, rationing and controls became increasingly unpopular, and Churchill returned to power as Prime Minister in 1951. Even so, his party was not popular with the electorate. It had narrowly lost another election in 1950, and even in 1951 it actually attracted fewer votes than the Labour Party. The great revival of Tory popularity was only in evidence after Churchill retired in 1955. His second administration was dogged by his increasingly bad health. He tried to bring a reconciliation between the western allies and the Soviets by a great 'summit' meeting, but he resented being junior to President Eisenhower, once a mere general in wartime.

Churchill's British Empire was perhaps the greatest casualty of the war. Prestige was lost with the surrender of Singapore in 1942, and the rise of nationalist movements made it difficult to sustain the colonies, except those which are too small to be viable on their own, or those, such as Gibraltar, which have another complication. Churchill's wartime travels did very little to support his idea of Empire and Commonwealth. The only parts of it he visited were Bermuda, Newfoundland and Canada, where he kept the respective governments at arm's length. Clearly visits to India, Australia or the African colonies were not essential to the war effort and one can excuse his failure to include them. But his travelling patterns reflected the new reality of the world, in which America, Europe and the Cold War with the Soviet Union would loom large in British foreign policy and the Commonwealth and the remnants of the Empire became less important except as sources of immigration.

Of the countries he did visit, Egypt and Iran would overthrow pro-western regimes in years to come, and Churchill's lack of concern for local peoples and governments, and his casual use of their territory for his own purposes, contributed to ill feeling. Cairo, Suez and Tehran would come to mean very different things to the British and their allies in the 1950s, the 1980s and the 2000s.

Despite his risk-taking and his fragile health, Churchill outlived his principal wartime colleagues, for Stalin died in 1953, Churchill in 1965 at the age of 90. Born in an age when the sailing ship was still predominant on the oceans, he lived to see world travel become cheap and easy (if not always comfortable) by means of the jet airliner. He was a pioneer of air transport, as of many other things.

★ ★ ★

It has become fashionable for writers to claim that the subject of their book 'changed the world'. This is not difficult to justify in the case of Churchill's wartime voyages. It had effects on his health, which deteriorated throughout the war. It made air travel more acceptable afterwards. He alone, of all the main world leaders, was keen to travel despite the risks, time and discomfort involved. This gave him extra leverage in world affairs, at least until November 1943 when Roosevelt and Stalin got together for the first time and began to exclude him. It strengthened Roosevelt's resolve to treat the war against Germany as the main priority. It meant that Churchill's strategy for a Mediterranean campaign was accepted despite the doubts of the others. Whether that was correct or not is another question, and some historians suggest that the second front could have opened sooner.

The other effect was on world affairs in general. From the 1950s onwards it was quite accepted that statesmen should journey between continents, even those, like George W. Bush, who had not made a habit of travel before coming to office. Of course it was done in far easier circumstances. By the early 1950s, airliners had pressurised cabins which removed most of the problems that Churchill faced on his journeys. The jet engine became standard during the same decade, making travel about three times as fast. Most important of all, modern travel was carried out almost exclusively in peacetime conditions, with none of the risks that Churchill (alone among the great leaders) faced in his voyages during the most difficult year of 1942. It was Churchill himself who coined the expression 'summit meeting', though not until 1950. But he certainly understood the concept as early as 1941, and the phrase has been used retrospectively to describe his Placentia visit. In later years, Henry Kissinger and Pope John Paul II gained reputations as men who would travel the world in pursuit of their aims, but Winston Churchill was ahead of them in this.

Just how dangerous were Churchill's voyages? In his biography Roy Jenkins writes, 'The cumulative risk to which Churchill's manifold journeys exposed him, even with the closest protection, can hardly, taking the war as a whole, have been less than 30 per cent.' This seems rather high, though it does include his western European trips which are not considered here. There was little risk from his sea trips. He was always in powerful and fast ships, well-escorted for most of the time and with good warning of enemy activity. Even if a U-boat had got within range, which was highly unlikely in the circumstances, it would always have been possible to save Churchill, unless he himself proved difficult. Almost all the danger came when he was on the ground or in the air. The Tehran visit turned out to be excessively hazardous on the ground, and there was a real possibility of assassination on the drive from the airport. But the air was more consistently dangerous.

Air travel in itself was risky during that age, even without the additional hazards of war, and a surprisingly large number of important people died on non-combatant flights. General Gott, Leslie Howard, Brigadier 'Dumbie' Dykes and Barney Charlesworth were killed on flights which were on or close to the routes followed by Churchill. Other notable casualties, all in different circumstances, included Admiral Ramsay who was Eisenhower's deputy on D-Day; General Sikorski, the Free Polish leader; the King's brother the Duke of Kent, Orde Wingate, Glenn Miller the bandleader, and the famous pre-war aviator Amy Johnson on a delivery trip. On the other side, Admiral Yamamoto of Japan was shot down and killed by American aircraft using intelligence sources – the kind of operation that the British dreaded might be used against them.

Churchill himself accepted that there was an element of risk, as when he wrote to the King before flying to America in the Clipper in 1942, recommending Eden as his successor 'in the event of my death on this journey I am about to undertake', or when he returned from Turkey and Egypt in 1943 and remarked, 'It wouldn't be a bad moment to leave.'

As well as the general risks, there were specific moments of danger – when it proved very difficult to find a safe fog-free landing place after the first transatlantic flight, or when he crossed enemy territory in a Liberator with a crew whose members were barely on speaking terms. At a rough guess, one might say that there was a ten per cent chance of Churchill's loss during his long-distance voyages. It is difficult to imagine what public grief would have ensued if it had happened, what effect it would have had on world history with the far less capable Eden in charge, and what conspiracy theories would still be circulating – if indeed we had a free society in which such things were permitted.

Notes

Introduction, 7–10
1 Quoted in Celia Sandys, *Chasing Churchill*, London, 2003, p. 43
2 Lord Moran, *Winston Churchill, The Struggle for Survival*, London, 1966, p. 10
3 Randolph Churchill, *Winston S. Churchill*, vol. 1, *Youth, 1874–1900*, London, 1966, pp. 154, 169, 241
4 Ibid, p. 267
5 Quoted in Martin Gilbert, *Winston S. Churchill*, vol. VII, *Road to Victory, 1941–1945*, London, 1986, p. 968
6 *Winston Churchill, The Struggle for Survival*, p. 560

I. A Lavish Lunch and a Good Train, pages 11–28
1 From Charles Eade's account in Martin Gilbert, *The Churchill War Papers*, Volume 3, 1941, London, 2000, pp. 972–7
2 *War Papers*, pp. 992–1018
3 Ibid, p. 1028
4 Ibid, p. 979
5 National Archives, PREM 4/71/1
6 H. V. Morton, *Atlantic Meeting*, London, 1943, p. 20
7 *The Diaries of Sir Alexander Cadogan, 1938–1945*, ed David Dilks, London, 1971, p. 395
8 *Atlantic Meeting*, p. 30
9 Ibid, p. 32

II. Voyage to Placentia, pages 29–50
1 *Atlantic Meeting*, pp. 39–40
2 Ibid, pp. 43–4
3 Howard Spring, *In the Meantime*, London, 1942, pp. 208–9
4 Ibid, pp. 212–13
5 *Atlantic Meeting*, pp. 54–5
6 Ibid, pp. 67–8
7 Ibid, pp. 69–71
8 Quoted in Karol Kulik, *Alexander Korda*, London, 1975, p. 251

III. Good Voyage, Churchill, pages 51–66
1 *Atlantic Meeting*, p. 123
2 Ibid, p. 127
3 *War Papers*, p. 1074
4 Ibid, pp. 1071–2
5 Ibid, p. 1078
6 W. S. Churchill, *The Second World War*, vol. III, *The Grand Alliance*, London, 1950, p. 394

IV. The Dull Pounding of the Great Seas, pages 67–88
1 W. Averell Harriman and Elie Abel, *Special Envoy to Churchill and Stalin, 1941–1946*, New York, 1975, pp. 111–12
2 *The Grand Alliance*, op cit, p. 539
3 Elizabeth Nel, *Mr Churchill's Secretary*, New York, 1958, p. 77
4 *War Papers*, p. 1609
5 Ibid, p. 1595
6 Sir Charles Richardson (ed.), *From Churchill's Secret Circle to the BBC*, London, 1991, p. 110
7 Ibid, p. 85
8 Lord Moran, *Winston Churchill, The Struggle for Survival*, London, 1966, p. 12
9 *Special Envoy to Churchill and Stalin, 1941–1946*, p. 113

V. A Flying Hotel in the Fog, pages 89–110
1 *The Grand Alliance*, p. 626
2 BA Archive: Captain Kelly Rogers, *Report of Prime Minister's Journey in 'Berwick'*, 16.1.42–18.1.42, p. 13
3 *The Grand Alliance*, p. 629
4 *Daily Telegraph*, 15 April 1950

VI. The Longest Flight, pages 111–120
1 National Archives, CAB 120/33

VII. Vanderkloot Brings It Off, pages 121–140
1 *Churchill, the Struggle for Survival*, p. 47
2 Bruce West, *The Man Who Flew Churchill*, Toronto, 1975, pp. 3–4
3 Ibid, pp. 6–7

4 Mitchell papers
5 W. Vanderkloot, *Handbook of Air Navigation*, New York and London, 1944, pp. 157–9
6 Charles T. Kimber, *Son of Halton*, 1977, pp 163, 178, 262
7 *The Man Who Flew Churchill*, p. 104
8 *Today's Officer*, October 2004, Verna Gates, *Churchill Was His Co-Pilot*, p. 5
9 *Speaking for Themselves, The Personal Letters of Winston and Clementine Churchill*, ed Mary Soames, London, 1998, p. 465
10 *The Man Who Flew Churchill*, p. 105
11 W. S. Churchill, *The Second World War*, vol IV, *The Hinge of Fate*, London, 1951, p. 411

VIII. To Moscow with an Atlas, pages 141–154
1 Lord Alanbrooke, *War Diaries 1939–1945*, London, 2001, p. 297
2 National Archives, CAB 120/67
3 Quoted in Cadogan, *Diaries*, p. 474
4 *The Hinge of Fate*, pp. 469–70
5 National Archives, CAB 120/67
6 *Son of Halton*, p. 263
7 National Archives, CAB 120/65
8 *The Man Who Flew Churchill*, p. 107

IX. Agreement in Casablanca, pages 155–172
1 *War Diaries*, p. 355
2 *Churchill, the Struggle for Survival*, p. 78
3 Gerald Pawle, *The War and Colonel Warden*, London, 1963, p. 223
4 *Speaking for Themselves*, pp. 471–3
5 *From Churchill's Secret Circle to the BBC*, p.164
6 Ibid, p. 164
7 Ibid, p. 165
8 James McGregor Burns, *Roosevelt, the Soldier of Freedom, 1940–1945*, London, 1971, p. 323
9 *From Churchill's Secret Circle to the BBC*, op cit, p. 165
10 National Archives, WO 204/64
11 *War Diaries*, p. 369
12 Ibid, pp. 369–70

X. Wild Dreams in Turkey, pages 173–186
1 Quoted in *The Diaries of Sir Alexander Cadogan*, ed David Dilks, London, 1971, p. 509

2 *Churchill, the Struggle for Survival*, pp. 79–80
3 Alanbrooke, *War Diaries*, p. 412
4 *From Churchill's Secret Circle to the BBC*, p. 186
5 Cunningham of Hyndhope, *A Sailor's Odyssey*, London, 1951, pp. 503–4
6 *From Churchill's Secret Circle to the BBC*, p. 186
7 *The Diaries of Sir Alexander Cadogan*, p. 513

XI. The Queen of the Ocean, pages 187–210
1 *Churchill, the Struggle for Survival*, p. 93
2 Joan Bright Astley, *The Inner Circle, A View of War at the Top*, Boston and Toronto, 1971, p. 90
3 Alanbrooke, *War Diaries*, p. 397
4 *The Inner Circle*, pp. 91–2
5 Lord Ismay, *Memoirs*, p. 294
6 Quoted in Martin Gilbert, *Winston S. Churchill*, vol. VII, *The Road to Victory*, London, 1986, p. 397
7 Alanbrooke, *War Diaries*, p. 400
8 National Archives, CAB 120/85
9 Alanbrooke, *War Diaries*, p. 401
10 Pim Papers, Public Record Office of Northern Ireland
11 Alanbrooke, *War Diaries*, p. 405
12 Ibid, p. 410

XII. Poetry in the North Atlantic, pages 211–232
1 National Archives, CAB 120/89
2 Ibid
3 Robert Copeland, *Warrior without Weapons*, Indianapolis, 1989, pp. 39–40
4 National Archives, ADM 202/424
5 *From Churchill's Secret Circle to the BBC*, p. 189
6 Pim Papers, Public Record Office of Northern Ireland
7 *Mr Churchill's Secretary*, p. 111
8 *Churchill, The Struggle for Survival*, p. 110
9 Richard Lovell, *Churchill's Doctor, a Biography of Lord Moran*, London, 1992, p. 206
10 *The War and Colonel Warden*, p. 247
11 Peter C. Smith, *Hit First, Hit Hard, The Story of HMS* Renown, London, 1979, p. 251

12 *The War and Colonel Warden*, pp 252–3
13 *Mr Churchill's Secretary*, p. 115
14 Churchill College, MART 5

XIII. The Big Three at Tehran, pages
233–254
1 *Stalin's Correspondence with Churchill,
Attlee, Roosevelt and Truman, 1941–45*,
London, 1958, pp. 92–3
2 Sarah Churchill, *A Thread in the
Tapestry*, London, 1967, p. 59
3 Lord Ismay, *Memoirs*, London, 1960, p.
333
4 *A Thread in the Tapestry*, p. 59
5 National Archives, CAB 104/171
6 Wellcome Insitute, Moran papers,
PP/CMW/Q1/3
7 Sarah Churchill, *Keep on Dancing*,
London, 1981, p. 70
8 W. Averell Harriman and Elie Abel,
Special Envoy ..., p. 265
9 Alanbrooke, *War Diaries*,
p. 483
10 Evelyn Waugh, *Unconditional Surrender*,
London, 1964, p. 22
11 Alanbrooke, *War Diaries*, p. 485

XIV. Convalescing at Marrakech, pages
255–266
1 *Churchill, The Struggle for Survival*,
p. 150
2 *Speaking for Themselves*, p. 492
3 Ibid, p. 495
4 Quoted in Gilbert, *The Road to Victory*,
p. 627
5 John Colville, *The Fringes of Power,
Downing Street Diaries, 1939–1955*,
London, 1985, p. 459
6 Harold Nicolson, *Letters and Diaries,
1939–1945*, pp. 344–5

XV. 'Just a Little Bit of Wishful
Thinking ...', pages 267–282
1 Pim Papers, Public Record Office of
Northern Ireland
2 *Speaking for Themselves*, p. 504
3 *Fringes of Power*, p. 510
4 Joanna Moody, *From Churchill's War
Rooms, Letters of a Secretary, 1943–45*,
p. 122
5 *The Inner Circle*, p. 151
6 Quoted in Gilbert, *Road to Victory*,
p. 968

7 *From Churchill's War Rooms*, p. 153

XVI. Percentages in Moscow, pages
283–298
1 Quoted in Gilbert, *Road to Victory*,
p. 983
2 *Stalin's Correspondence with Churchill,
Attlee, Roosevelt and Truman*, p. 259
3 *Mr Churchill's Secretary*, p.142
4 *Speaking for Themselves*, p. 505
5 National Archives, CAB 120/158
6 Alanbrooke, *War Diaries*, p. 610
7 *Mr Churchill's Secretary*, p. 150

XVII. Christmas in the Skymaster, pages
299–314
1 National Archives, AIR 8/708
2 Mitchell papers
3 National Archives, AIR 4/67/2
4 Mary Soames, *Clementine Churchill*,
London, 1979, pp. 363–4
5 Mitchell papers, p. 86
6 *Mr Churchill's Secretary*, p. 156
7 *The Fringes of Power*, p. 540
8 *The War and Colonel Warden*, p. 339
9 Mitchell papers, p. 89
10 *Fringes of Power*, p. 546
11 National Archives, AIR 4/67/2

XVIII. The Ways to Yalta, pages 315–332
1 Warren F. Kimball, ed, *Churchill and
Roosevelt, The Complete Correspondence*,
vol. III, *Alliance Declining*, Princeton,
1984, p. 368
2 *Stalin's Correspondence*, p. 170
3 *Churchill and Roosevelt*, vol III, p. 469
4 Ibid, p. 494
5 Ibid, p. 496
6 *The War and Colonel Warden*, op cit, p. 349
7 Pim Papers, Public Record Office of
Northern Ireland
8 Harry Grattridge, *Captain of the Queens*,
London, 1956, p. 183
9 Ibid, p. 184
10 National Archives, AIR 29/475
11 Ibid
12 Ibid

XIX. 'We Could Not Have Found a Worse
Place', pages 333–350
1 CAB 120/171
2 *Churchill, The Struggle for Survival*,
p. 220

3 Cadogan *Diaries*, p. 706

4 National Archives, AIR 29/475

5 *Churchill, The Struggle for Survival*, p. 226

6 National Archives, PREM 4/77/1b

7 *A Thread in the Tapestry*, pp. 81–2

8 Winston S. Churchill, *The Second World War,* vol. VI, *Triumph and Tragedy,* London, 1954, p. 346

9 Mitchell papers, p. 95

10 Ibid, p. 96

11 National Archives, AIR 29/475

12 Lovell, *Churchill's Doctor,* p. 368

13 Navy Records Society, vol. 146, *The Naval Miscellany,* ed Michael Duffy, 2003, *On Royal Duty ...,* ed C.H. H. Owen, p. 429

xx. Amid the Ruins, pages 351–368

1 National Archives, PREM 4/97/2

2 *The Inner Circle,* p. 211

3 National Archives, PREM 4/79/1

4 *Churchill, The Struggle for Survival,* p. 285

5 Alanbrooke, *War Diaries,* p. 709

6 Pim Papers, Public Record Office of Northern Ireland

7 Ibid

8 Alanbrooke, *War Diaries,* p. 712

Bibliography

CHURCHILL BIOGRAPHIES AND PAPERS

Winston S. Churchill, *The Second World War*, 6 vols, London, 1948–54. An invaluable but biased account, partly corrected by David Reynolds' *In Command of History* (London, 2004) which explains the circumstances in which it was written

Martin Gilbert, *Winston S. Churchill*, Vol. VI, *Their Finest Hour, 1939–1941*, London, 1983, Volume VII, *Road to Victory, 1941–1945*, London, 1986

Martin Gilbert, ed, *The Churchill War Papers*, Vol. 3, 1941, *The Ever Widening War*, London, 2000. One of the richest sources, but the series has so far only got to the end of 1941

Roy Jenkins, *Churchill*, London, 2002

Mary Soames, ed, *Speaking for Themselves, The Personal Letters of Winston and Clementine Churchill*, London, 1998

MAJOR POLITICAL AND MILITARY FIGURES

Lord Alanbrooke, *War Diaries, 1939–1945*, London, 2001. Perhaps the best diary of the war years, with many interesting comments on Churchill's leadership and other matters

A. J. P. Taylor, *Beaverbrook*, London, 1972

David Dilks, ed, *The Diaries of Sir Alexander Cadogan* , 1938–1945, London, 1971

Andrew Cunningham of Hyndhope, *A Sailor's Odyssey*, London, 1951

Anthony Eden, Lord Avon, *Facing the Dictators*, London, 1962

W. Averell Harriman and Elie Abel, *Special Envoy to Churchill and Stalin*, New York, 1975

Harold Macmillan, *War Diaries, Politics and War in the Mediterranean, 1943–1945*, London, 1984

Robin Brodhurst, *Churchill's Anchor, Admiral of the Fleet Sir Dudley Pound*, Barnsley, 2000

Phillip Ziegler, *Mountbatten*, Glasgow, 1985

Denis Richards, *Portal of Hungerford*, London, c. 1977

CHURCHILL'S ENTOURAGE

Joan Bright Astley, *The Inner Circle, A View of War at the Top*, Boston, 1971

Mary Soames, *Clementine Churchill*, London, 1979. Includes many letters between her and her daughters

Sarah Churchill, *A Thread in the Tapestry*, London, 1967

Sarah Churchill, *Keep on Dancing*, London, 1981

Sir John Colville, *The Fringes of Power, Downing Street Diaries, 1939–1955*, London, 1985. Perhaps the best diary account apart from Brooke's, though it does not begin to deal with the voyages until the second Quebec trip

Joanna Moody, ed, *From Churchill's War Rooms, Letters of a Secretary, 1943–45*, Stroud, 2007. The letters of Olive Christopher, later Margerison

Alex Danchev, *Establishing the Anglo-American Alliance, The Second World War diaries of Brigadier Vivian Dykes*, London, 1980

Leslie Hollis, *One Marine's Tale*, London, 1956. Ghost-written and apparently unreliable in places

Lord Ismay, *The Memoirs of General the Lord Ismay*, London, 1960

Sir Charles Richardson, ed, *From Churchill's Secret Circle to the BBC*, London, 1991. A selection from Sir Ian Jacob's papers, though not all of them by any means

John Martin, *Downing Street, The War Years*, London, 1991. Rather pedestrian compared with Colville's work

Lord Moran, *Winston Churchill, The Struggle for Survival, 1940–1965*, London, 1966. Despite questions of the authenticity of a 'diary' which was largely written up afterwards, it provides a detailed and intimate portrait of Churchill

Richard Lovell, *Churchill's Doctor, A biography of Lord Moran*, London, 1992

Elizabeth Nel, *Mr Churchill's Secretary*, New York, 1958

Gerald Pawle, *The War and Colonel Warden*, London, 1963. Based on the papers of Commander Thompson

Tom Hickman, *Churchill's Bodyguard, The Authorised Biography of Walter H. Thompson*, London, 2005. Far less speculative than the television series which accompanied it

SEAMEN AND AIRCREW

Sir James Bissett, *Commodore, War, Peace and Big Ships*, London, 1961

John Mitchell, *Diary of a Navigator*. Copies of this document are deposited in the Imperial War Museum, Churchill College and RAF Museum Hendon. Most of it is also available on the internet, in the 24 Squadron Association website

Bruce West, *The Man Who Flew Churchill*, Toronto, 1977. Not always reliable on matters away from Vanderkloot's own account

OTHERS

Harold Nicolson, *Diaries and Letters, 1939–45*, London, 1967

GENERAL BACKGROUND

F. H. Hinsley, *British Intelligence in the Second World War*, five vols, 1979–90

Warren F Kimball, ed, *Churchill and Roosevelt, The Complete Correspondence*, Vol. III, *Alliance Declining*, Princeton, 1984

Stalin's Correspondence with Churchill, Attlee, Roosevelt and Truman, 1941–45, London, 1958

A. J. P. Taylor, *English History, 1939–1945*, Oxford, 1975

SPECIFIC VOYAGES

To Placentia (Chapters I–III)

H. V. Morton, *Atlantic Meeting*, London, 1943. Can be corrected by reference to the comments in PREM 4/71/1

Howard Spring, *In the Meantime*, London, 1942

Richard Woodman, *The Real Cruel Sea*, London, 2004. Describes the meeting with convoy HX 143

National Archives:

ADM 53/114891, Log of the *Prince of Wales*, August 1941

ADM 199/393, 396, Home Fleet War Diaries

ADM 199/1145, convoy papers, including HX 143

CAB 120/21, Operation Riviera, correspondence with officers on board HMS *Prince of Wales*

CAB 120/20, includes administrative arrangements for travel and attending the conference

CAB 120/23, 'Sloane' telegrams, on position of convoy HX 143

PREM 4/71/1, includes comments on Morton's book, report by navigation officer of the *Prince of Wales*, details of members of the party, etc

Churchill College:

Jacob's diary, JACB 1/9

First Washington (Chapters IV–V)

The Aeroplane Directory, Who's Who in British Aviation, contains short biographies of Kelly Rogers and some of his crew

Air Ministry, *Merchant Airmen,* London, 1946, contains an illustrated account
  of the Clipper flight
BA News, 6 February 1981, obituary of Kelly-Rogers
National Archives:
ADM 53/14155, log of the *Duke of York*
AIR 2/4793, history of Atlantic meteorological operations
AIR 16/1085, order of battle of Fighter Command
AIR 22/28, War Room Daily summary
AIR 24/385, operations record book, contains the account of the Hudson
  bomber turning back over Brest
Air 25/182, No 10 Group operations record book
AIR 27/599, 712, 907, 922, 1439, 1488, 1551, 1661, 1673, 1681, 1692, 1707,
  1818, 1951, 2001, 2083, 2123, operation record books of various fighter
  squadrons
AIR 28/575, station record book, RAF Mountbatten
CAB 120/26, includes 'Beaverbrook's tour', the cover story for the conference
CAB 120/27, Operation Arcadia, travel and security arrangements
PREM 4/71/2, papers on the Arcadia conference
Churchill College:
CHU 4/29, contains correspondence on Churchill's published account of the
  Clipper flight
Jacob papers, JACB 1/12
Martin papers, MART 4
Imperial War Museum:
RA Bennet-Levy papers, 87/55/1, account by the *Prince of Wales*'s
  meteorological officer
British Airways archives:
Press cuttings on the Clipper flight
*Report by Captain Kelly Rogers of Prime Minister's Journey in 'Berwick', 16.1.42
  – 18.1.42*

Second Washington (Chapter VI)
National Archives:
CAB 120/33, administrative papers for the Argonaut conference
CAB 122/586, Visit of the Prime Minister to Washington
CAB 120/35, 'Stalky' telegrams
PREM 3/459, includes paper on the circulation of Argonaut telegrams

First Moscow (Chapters VII–VIII)

Charles T. Kimber, *Son of Halton,* np, 1977. Invaluable detail on the first Moscow trip

National Archives:

AIR 38/75, includes reports on the Liberator routes to Russia

CAB 120/65, Operation Bracelet, arrangements, meetings, papers

CAB 120/66, 67, 68, 69, 'Reflex' and 'Tulip' telegrams

PREM 4/71/4, Bracelet (Cairo and Moscow) conferences

Churchill College:

Jacob papers, JACB 1/16

Charles Kimber's log, WCHL 6/29

Casablanca (Chapter IX–X)

National Archives:

ADM 53/117091, log of the *Bulolo*

CAB 21/847, general arrangements and administrative papers

PREM 4/72/1, contains passenger lists, administrative arrangements, cover plan

WO 204/64, conference arrangements in Casablanca

Churchill College:

Jacob papers, JACB 1/21

Third Washington (Chapter XI)

National Archives:

ADM 53/117669, log of the *Indomitable*

ADM 117199, log of the *Charybdis*

ADM 53/118640, log of the *Uganda*

ADM 199/2263, Admiralty war diary

CAB 120/84, travelling and administrative arrangements

CAB 120/86, 'Pencil' telegrams

First Quebec (Chapter XII)

National Archives:

ADM 53/118434, log of *Renown*

ADM 101/644, medical officer's journal, HMS *Renown*

ADM 223/8, German naval dispositions in the Bight, Channel and Biscay areas

ADM 202/424, report on the Royal Marine detachment in operation Quadrant

CAB 104/179, administrative arrangements
CAB 120/89, preparations and travel arrangements
CAB 120/91, administrative arrangements
DEFE 2/525, operation Quadrant
Imperial War Museum:
86/61/1a, R. S. C. Langford, papers from the notice board of HMS *Renown*
92/4/1. J. Mowlem, memoirs, including report on the *Renown*'s voyage

Tehran (Chapter XIII–XIV)

National Archives:
ADM 53/118436, log of the *Renown*
ADM 101/644, medical officer's journal, HMS *Renown*
ADM 202/427, Report of the Royal Marine detachment with operation Sextant
CAB 104/171, administrative arrangements, Cairo
CAB 120/113, preparations, travelling arrangements and records of meetings
CAB 120/116, administrative arrangements, instructions to staff
CAB 120/117, security arrangements, including Thompson's report on the problems in Tehran
CAB 120/118, 'Frozen' telegrams
CAB 120/125, 'Grand' telegrams
CAB 120/129, 'Grand' telegrams
PREM 4/74/2, Eureka and Sextant conferences
Imperial War Museum:
02/53/1, Boyle papers

Second Quebec (Chapter 15)
ADM 53/119001, log of HMS *Berwick*
ADM 53/119254, log of HMS *Devonshire*
ADM 53/119638, log of HMS *Kent*
CAB 120/145, administrative arrangements
CAB 120/146, administrative arrangements, instructions to staff
CAB 120/147, communication arrangements
PREM 4/75/2, Octagon conference
PREM 10/3, diary of the visit to Quebec

Second Moscow (Chapter XVI)

National Archives:
AIR 20/2318, planning the flight to Moscow
AIR 20, 2316, includes details of flight arrangements

AIR 20/8060, military mission to Moscow

CAB 120/158, preparations, conclusion of meeting

CAB 120/164, 'Hearty' telegrams

PREM 4/76/1, Tolstoy (Moscow) conference, including a diary of the visit to Moscow

Yalta (Chapters XVIII–XIX)

National Archives:

AIR 8/841, Accident to the York aircraft off Lampedusa

AIR 20/2313, operation Argonaut, including report on co-operation with the Soviets and conditions at Saki

AIR 20/3116, history of air traffic control

AIR 29/475, airfield at Saki

CAB 104/178, correspondence and administrative arrangements, including report of party stranded at Istres

CAB 120/171, administrative arrangements

CAB 122/611, cover plan

FO 954/28b, correspondence with the Turkish authorities

PREM 4/77/1b, Yalta conference, various

Imperial War Museum:

94/42/1, Ilene Hutchison papers, including notes on the Crimea

Potsdam (Chapter XX)

National Archives:

AIR 29/461, operations of No 19 Staging Post, including setting up the Gatow airfield

AIR 55/33, air arrangements, Bordeaux to Berlin

CAB 120/187, administrative arrangements

CAB 120/188, administrative arrangements and instructions to staff

CAB 120/190, communications arrangements

FO 800/426, telegrams

PREM 4/79/2, various papers including the controversy over Attlee's position and a note on the luncheon with Truman on 18 July 1945

WO 219/1070, arrangements

WO 252/1434, Berlin, economic survey

Means of Transport

Ships

Neil Potter and Jack Frost, *The Queen Mary, Her Inception and History,* London, 1971

Leslie Reade, ed, *The Cunard White Star Quadruple-Screw North Atlantic Liner Queen Mary,* reprinted New York, 1979. Based on an original report in a trade magazine, with detailed desk plans etc

Peter C. Smith, *Hit First, Hit Hard, The Story of HMS* Renown, London, 1979

David Syrett, ed, *The Battle of the Atlantic and Signals Intelligence: U-Boat Situations and Trends, 1941–1945,* Navy Records Society, vol. 139, 1998

David Syrett, ed, *The Battle of the Atlantic and Signals Intelligence: U-Boat Tracking Papers, 1941–1947,* Navy Records Society, vol. 144, 2002

V. E. Tarrant, King George V *Class Battleships,* London, 1981

Aircraft

Air Ministry, *Air Navigation,* vol. I, London, 1944

L. F. E Coombs, *Control in the Sky, The Evolution and History of the Aircraft Cockpit,* Barnsley, 2005

M. D. Klaas, *The Last of the Flying Clippers, The Boeing 314 Story,* Altglen, Pennsylvania, 1997. Badly written, but full of information and illustrations

Jerrard Tickell, *Ascalon, The Story of Sir Winston Churchill's War-Time Flights,* London, 1964. Based on Mitchell's records. Includes biographies of the crew of *Ascalon*

National Archives:

AIR 8/708, York aircraft for the use of the Prime Minister

AIR 8/806, Skymaster for the Prime Minister

AIR 28/601, operations record book, Northolt Aerodrome

AVIA 18/1116, Skymaster, performance and landing trials

Index